OXFORD MONOGRAPHS IN
INTERNATIONAL LAW

General Editor: Professor Ian Brownlie QC, DCL, FBA
*Chichele Professor of Public International Law in the University of
Oxford and Fellow of All Souls College, Oxford.*

THE LEGALITY OF
NON-FORCIBLE COUNTER-MEASURES
IN INTERNATIONAL LAW

OXFORD MONOGRAPHS IN
INTERNATIONAL LAW

This new series of monographs will publish important and original pieces of research on all aspects of public international law. Topics which will be given particular prominence are those which, while of interest to the academic lawyer, also have important bearing on issues which touch the actual conduct of international relations. None the less the series is intended to be wide in scope and thus will include the history and philosophical foundations of international law.

ALSO IN THE SERIES

The Exclusive Economic Zone in International Law
DAVID ATTARD

The Juridical Bay
GAYL WESTERMAN

Judicial Remedies in International Law
CHRISTINE GRAY

Occupation, Resistance and Law
ADAM ROBERTS

The Shatt-Al-Arab Boundary Question:
A Legal Reappraisal
KAIYAN KAIKOBAD

THE
LEGALITY OF NON-FORCIBLE COUNTER-MEASURES IN INTERNATIONAL LAW

DR OMER YOUSIF ELAGAB,
BA (Hons.), LL M (London),
D.Phil. (Oxon.),
Advocate, Senior Lecturer in
Law at Ealing College of Higher Education,
London

CLARENDON PRESS · OXFORD
1988

Oxford University Press, Walton Street, Oxford OX2 6DP
Oxford New York Toronto
Delhi Bombay Calcutta Madras Karachi
Petaling Jaya Singapore Hong Kong Tokyo
Nairobi Dar es Salaam Cape Town
Melbourne Auckland
and associated companies in
Beirut Berlin Ibadan Nicosia

Oxford is a trade mark of Oxford University Press

Published in the United States
by Oxford University Press, New York

British Library Cataloguing in Publication Data
Elagab, Omer Yousif
The legality of non-forcible counter-measures in international law.—
(Oxford monographs in international law)
1. Sanctions (International law)
I. Title
341.7'5   JX1246
ISBN 0–19–825590–X

Library of Congress Cataloguing in Publication Data
Elagab, Omer Yousif.
The legality of non-forcible counter-measures in
international law/Omer Yousif Elagab
p.   cm.—(Oxford monographs in international law)
Bibliography: p. Includes index
1. Reprisals.   2. Economic sanctions.
I. Title.   II. Series
JX4486.E4 1988
341.5'8—dc19   87–22913 CIP
ISBN 0–19–825590–X

Set by Butler & Tanner Ltd,
Frome and London
Printed and bound in
Great Britain by Biddles Ltd
Guildford and Kings Lynn

This book is dedicated to my daughter Sakeena,
and to the memory of my parents
Yousif Elagab and Sakeena Mohamed Ahmed (née),
who both encouraged me continually to pursue my academic studies

Editor's Preface

The subject of Dr Elagab's study has been generally neglected by the literature, in spite of its evident significance in international relations, and thus the inclusion of this substantial work among the early titles to appear in the *Oxford Monographs* is a source of particular satisfaction to the editor of the series. There can be no doubt that it will become recognized as an essential element in any international law collection.

On a more personal note, I would pay tribute to the qualities of hard work, persistence, and toughness of mind, which Dr Elagab showed in bringing his work to a successful conclusion, and I would pay tribute also to his wife, Tineke, whose support was invaluable.

All Souls College,   IAN BROWNLIE.
  OXFORD.
21 July 1987.

Preface

M Y interest in the present topic was stimulated by the legal controversies arising from two episodes in recent international history: first, the Air Services Agreement dispute in 1978 between the United States and France, and, secondly, the freezing of Iranian assets by the United States in 1979. It is noteworthy that the whole question of non-forcible counter-measures has been curiously neglected by writers on public international law. Indeed, so far as the author is aware, there is only one monograph in existence which deals at any length with counter-measures, E. Zoller's *Peacetime Unilateral Remedies: An Analysis of Countermeasures,* 1984.

The present book, based on a considerable period of research, assembles in one place numerous instances of State practice from the seventeenth century up to the present time. Its main objective is to fill in gaps in the existing literature by offering a detailed examination of the criteria by which the legality of counter-measures may be determined.

This work makes clear that the topic of counter-measures is of practical significance in contemporary international relations. All States, whether weak or strong, may face situations in which they become objects of, or feel obliged to resort to, counter-measures. I hope that this book will provide guidance to States in such situations.

As far as possible I have attempted to state the law up to the end of June 1987.

O.Y.E

Wadham College, Oxford
June 1987

Acknowledgements

ALL the research for, and the bulk of the writing of, this book were completed while I was attached to Wadham College, Oxford, as a graduate student reading for the degree of Doctor of Philosophy. This was made possible by the award of a fellowship from the University of Khartoum. I wish therefore to express my gratitude to the University of Khartoum for that award. I am also grateful to my brother *Ustaz* Mamoun Yousif Elagab, who provided additional financial assistance.

I owe my greatest debt to Professor Ian Brownlie, QC, DCL, FBA, Chichele Professor of Public International Law in the University of Oxford, and Fellow of All Souls College, Oxford, who supervised my research at Oxford. His unfailing encouragement and constant advice concerning the content and presentation of my doctoral thesis have proved invaluable for the completion of the present work.

I should also like to record my thanks to Sir Ian Sinclair, KCMG, CMG, QC, Member of the International Law Commission, for useful advice and for sending research material; to Professor Michael Zander, BA, LL B, LL M, Solicitor, Professor of Law in the London School of Economics, for providing research material; to Dr Christine Gray, MA, Ph.D., Fellow of St Hilda's College, Oxford, for encouraging remarks; to Professor Derek Bowett, CBE, QC, FBA, Whewell Professor of International Law in the University of Cambridge, and Fellow of Queen's College, Cambridge, for his comments on Chapter 10; to my two examiners, Professor Sir James Fawcett, DSC, QC, Professor Emeritus of International Law in the University of London King's College and a former President of the European Commission of Human Rights, and Mr Derrick Wyatt, LL B, MA, JD, Fellow of St Edmund Hall, Oxford, for conducting the *viva* examination of my doctoral thesis; to my brother Dr Mansour Yousif Elagab, BA, MA, Ph.D., Member of Parliament (Sudan), for his constant encouragement; to Nigel Knight, MA, Andrew R. Turesky, BA, JD, M.Phil., and Stephen Vasciannie, B.Sc., BA, LL M, for undertaking proof-reading; to Serge Krebs, Maîtrise de droit (Panthéon Sorbonne), M.Litt., for translating texts from the French language; to Tineke Elagab, BA, for typing all the drafts of the manuscript; to the librarians and staff of the Bodleian (especially to Nikola Djurisic, who sadly died shortly before this book was published) and the Codrington Libraries, Oxford, for their prompt service; and to the staff of the Clarendon Press for their help and courtesy.

It hardly needs stating that none of the persons named above is to blame for any shortcomings that might appear in this work. The responsibility for the final text, therefore, is entirely mine.

Finally, I should like to express my deepest gratitude for the sacrifices made by my wife Tineke, and children Sakeena, Jeehaan, and Yousif, without whose love, patience, and support this book might never have been completed.

O. Y. E.

Contents

Abbreviations

AJIL	*American Journal of International Law*, 1907–
Annuaire	*Annuaire de l'Institut de Droit International*, 1875–
Annual Digest	*Annual Digest of Public International Law Cases* 1919–49
BFSP	*British and Foreign State Papers*, 1812–
BL ref.	British Library reference
Bownlie, 1963	*International Law and the Use of Force by States*, 1963
Brownlie, 1979	*Principles of Public International Law*, 3rd edn., 1979
Brownlie, 1983	*System of the Law of Nations; State Responsibility*, Part I, 1983
BYIL	*British Yearbook of International Law*, 1920–
Bynkershoek	*Quaestionum Juris Publici Libri Duo*, 1737, ed. Scott, 1930 (The Classics of International Law, 2)
CFR	*Code of Federal Regulations*
Cheng, 1953	*General Principles of Law as Applied by International Tribunals*, 1953
Conference for the Codification	League of Nations, *Conference for the Codification of International Law; Bases of Discussion*, vol. iii, 1929
Digest USPIL	*Digest of United States Practice in International Law*, 1973–
DSB	*United States Department of State Bulletin*, 1939–
ECR	*European Court Reports*, 1954–
Fed. Reg.	*Federal Register*
FRUS	*Foreign Relations of the United States*, 1870–
Gentili	*De Jure Belli Libri Tres*, 1612, ed. Scott, 1933 (The Classics of International Law, 2)
Grotius	*De Jure Belli Ac Pacis Libri Tres*, 1646, ed. Scott, 1925 (The Classics of International Law, 2)
GYIL	*German Yearbook of International Law*, 1976–
Hall	*A Treatise of International Law*, 2nd edn., 1884
Halleck	*International Law, Or, Rules Regulating the Intercourse of States*, 1861
Hatscheck	*An Outline of International Law*, 1930
Hansard, HC Debs.	*Parliamentary Debates* (*Hansard*) *House of Commons*

	Official Reports (originally published privately from 1066), 1909–
Hansard, HL Debs.	*Parliamentary Debates (Hansard) House of Lords Official Reports*, 1909–
HCR	*The Hague Court Reports*, 1st Series, ed. Scott, 1916; 2nd Series, ed. Scott, 1932
Hyde	*International Law Chiefly as Interpreted and Applied by the United States*, vol. ii, 2nd edn., 1947
ICJ Pleadings	*International Court of Justice Pleadings*, 1948–
ICJ Reports	*International Court of Justice Reports*, 1949–
ILM	*International Legal Materials*, 1962–
ILR	*International Law Reports*, 1950–
KCA	*Keesing's Contemporary Archives*, 1931–
Keith	*Wheaton's International Law*, vol. ii, *War*, 7th edn., 1944
Lawrence	*The Principles of International Law*, 1895
LNTS	*League of Nations Treaty Series*, 1920–33
McNair, *Opinions*	*International Law Opinions, Selected and Annotated*, 3 vols., 1956
McNair, 1961	*Law of Treaties*, 1961
Malloy	*Treaties, Conventions, International Acts, Protocol and Agreements between the United States of America and Other Powers*, 1776–1901, vols. i and ii, 1910
Marsden ii	*Documents Relating to Law and Custom of the Sea, 1649–1769*, vol. ii, 1916
Maule and Selwyn	*The English Reports*, vol. 105, 1910
Moore, *Arbitrations*	*History and Digest of the International Arbitrations to which the United States has been a Party*, vol i, 1898
Moore, *Digest*	*A Digest of International Law*, 8 vols., 1906
Ned. Tijd	*Nederlands Tijdschrift voor International Recht*, 1953–
NLYIL	*Netherlands Yearbook of International Law*, 1970–
Oppenheim, vol. i	*International Law, A Treatise*, vol. i, *Peace, 1905; 8th edn. by Lauterpacht, 1955*
Oppenheim, vol. ii	*International Law, A Treatise*, vol. ii, *War and Neutrality*, 1906; 6th edn. by Lauterpacht, 1940; 7th edn. by Lauterpacht, 1952
Parry	*Law Officers' Opinions to the Foreign Office 1793–1860*, vol. 80, 1970
PCIJ	*Publications of the Permanent Court of International Justice*, 1923–30
Phillimore iii	*Commentaries upon International Law*, vol. iii, 1885
R.d.C.	*Recueil des Cours de l'Académè de Droit International de La Haye*, 1923–

Répertoire Suisse, Vol. iii	*Répertoire suisse de droit international public; Documentation concernent la pratique de la Confédération en matière de droit international public* 1914–1939, vol. iii, 1975
RIAA	*United Nations, Reports of International Arbitral Awards,* 1948–
RIIA, *Documents*	Royal Institute of International Affairs, *Documents on International Affairs,* 1928–
Scott, *Conferences*	*The Reports to the Hague Conferences of 1899 and 1907,* 1917
Scott, *Conventions*	*The Hague Conventions and Declarations of 1899 and 1907,* ed. Scott, 2nd edn., 1915
Sinha	*Unilateral Renunciation of Treaty Because of Prior Violation of Obligations by the Other Party,* 1966
Sørensen, 1968	*Manual of Public International Law,* 1968
Stat.	*United States Statutes at Large*
Stat. Inst.	*Statutory Instruments*
Strupp	*Eléments du droit international public,* vol. i, 1930
Twiss	*The Law of Nations on the Rights and Duties of Nations in Time of War,* 1875
UNCIO Doc.	United Nations Information Organizations, *Documents of the United Nations Conference on International Organization, San Francisco,* 1945, 15 vols.
UNCLT Doc.	*United Nations Conference on the Law of Treaties, First and Second Session, Official Records, Documents of the Conference,* 1971
UNGAOR	*United Nations General Assembly Official Records*
UNTS	*United Nations Treaty Series,* 1946–
USC	*United States Code, Congressional and Administrative News*
Vattel	*The Law of Nations,* 1797, ed. Chitty, 1834
Wharton iii	*A Digest of the International Law of the United States,* vol. iii, 1887
Wheaton	*Elements of International Law,* 8th edn., 1866
Wildman	*Institute of International Law, International Rights in Time of Peace,* vol. i, 1849
YILC	*United Nations, Yearbook of the International Law Commission,* 1949–
Zoller	*Peacetime Unilateral Remedies: An Analysis of Countermeasures,* 1984

Tables of Cases

INTERNATIONAL ARBITRATION

Table of Treaties

and Fundamental Freedoms. Text: Council of Europe, *European Conventions and Agreements*, vol. i, 1949–61 (1971), p. 39.

1954 Agreement regarding the Suez Canal Base, between Egypt and the United Kingdom. Text: *BFSP*, vol. 161, 1954, p. 75.

1954 The Paris Agreements:

(1) Protocol to the North Atlantic Treaty on the Accession of the Federal Republic of Germany, signed by the Parties to the North Atlantic Treaty of 1949;

(2) Protocol on the Termination of the Occupation Régime in the Federal Republic of Germany, signed by United States of America, United Kingdom of Great Britain and Northern Ireland, France, and the Federal Republic of Germany;

(3) Convention on the Presence of Foreign Forces in Germany, signed by United States of America, United Kingdom of Great Britain and Northern Ireland, France, and the Federal Republic of Germany; and

(4) Tripartite Agreement on the Exercise of Retained Rights in Germany, signed by United States of America, United Kingdom of Great Britain and Northern Ireland, and France. Text: *RIIA, Documents*, 1954, pp. 102–7.

1955 Treaty of Amity, Economic Relations, and Consular Rights, between Iran and United States of America. Text: 284 *UNTS*, 4132.

1957 Treaty of Rome Establishing the European Economic Community. Text: 298 *UNTS*, 4300.

1958 Convention on the Territorial Sea and the Contiguous Zone. Text: UN Doc A/CONF. 13/L.52–L.55, Brownlie, *Basic Documents in International Law*, 1983, p. 87.

1961 Vienna Convention on Diplomatic Relations. Text: 500 *UNTS*, 7310.

1961 Vienna Convention on Diplomatic Relations, Optional Protocol Concerning the Compulsory Settlement of Disputes. Text: 500 *UNTS*, 7312.

1963 Vienna Convention on Consular Relations. Text: 596 *UNTS*, 8636.

1963 Vienna Convention on Consular Relations, Optional Protocol concerning the Compulsory Settlement of Disputes. Text: 596 *UNTS*, 8640.

1963 Treaty Banning Nuclear Weapon Tests in the Atmosphere, in Outer Space and Under Water, between the United States of America, the United Kingdom of Great Britain and Northern Ireland, and the Union of Soviet Socialist Republics. Text: *BFSP*, vol. 167, 1963–4, p. 178.

1964 Convention Relating to a Uniform Law on the International Sale of Goods. Text: 834 *UNTS*, 11929.

1966 International Covenant on Economic, Social, and Cultural Rights. Text: General Assembly Resolution 2200(XXI), Annex, 16 December 1966, *UNGAOR*, 21st Sess., suppl. 16(A/6316), 1966, p. 49.

1966 International Covenant on Civil and Political Rights. Text: General Assembly Resolution 2200(XXI), Annex, 16 December 1966, *UNGAOR*, 21st Sess., suppl. 16(A/6316), 1966 p. 53.

Introduction

A. SCOPE

THIS book is concerned with the legality of non-forcible counter-measures. The analysis to be undertaken will be confined to counter-measures taken in the context of bilateral relations. Accordingly, it is not the intended purpose of the book to examine the legality of sanctions applied on the basis of a decision taken by an international institution following a breach of an international obligation. It must be realized that international institutions are different from one another, and the jurisdiction of any one institution is derived from a constituent document peculiar to that body. In view of this, it is contended that any attempt at composing a generalized theory of counter-measures taken by international institutions may not be suited to every kind of international institution.

The major questions which will be addressed in this book are as follows: (*a*) do counter-measures constitute an autonomous category of justification for wrongful conduct? (*b*) if so, what are the conditions of the legality of that category? (*c*) what are the most important collateral constraints on the right to resort to counter-measures? and (*d*) given that the law respecting counter-measures is in a state of evolution, is it true that policy considerations become more important here than in other fields where the rules are clearly defined?

B. APPROACH

Although the principal aim of this work is to examine the *lex lata*, suggestions will frequently be made as to how the legal categories involved may be best applied to achieve clear rules. It must be stated that the present study is not directly concerned with any assessment of the effectiveness of counter-measures as an instrument of redress in international relations.

In studying the *lex lata*, it has been essential to analyse in depth the pertinent State practice, doctrinal views, and jurisprudence. In view of this, it has been deemed necessary to dedicate the first two chapters of the book to a study of the historical development of the law of reprisals. It should be noted that the conditions of the legality of non-forcible counter-measures have been developed well before the concept in question has come to be known by its present title.

C. THE OUTLINE OF THE BOOK

The book is composed of ten chapters. Chapters 1 and 2, as has just been mentioned, deal with the historical development of the doctrine of reprisals. Chapter 1 covers the period from the beginning of the seventeenth century to the end of the eighteenth century. The second chapter, which covers the period from the beginning of the nineteenth century to 1945, lays particular emphasis on non-forcible reprisals; at the end some conclusions will be made with respect to what might be regarded as the standard procedure for resort to non-forcible reprisals on the basis of customary law as it had evolved by 1945. In Chapter 3 it will be demonstrated by examples from modern State practice that the right of resort to non-forcible reprisals has not fallen into desuetude.

Chapters 4, 5, and 6 are devoted to examining the constituent conditions of the legality of non-forcible counter-measures, namely (*a*) breach; (*b*) prior demand for reparation; and (*c*) proportionality.

Chapter 7 focuses on the important question of collateral constraints on counter-measures. It will be shown that counter-measures which are otherwise lawful may be regarded as unlawful due to the presence of some collateral constraints. Chapter 8 considers the circumstances under which a treaty may be terminated or suspended as a counter-measure. A comparison will be made between the category of counter-measures and the legal regime established by the Vienna convention on the Law of Treaties of 1969.

Chapter 9 contains a discussion of the legality of counter-measures in the presence of a commitment to peaceful settlement. Chapter 10 is concerned with examining the legality of economic coercion under general international law. The object of this exercise is to ascertain whether any knowledge respecting the legality of counter-measures may be gleaned from a study of economic coercion. Finally, a concluding chapter will summarize the major characteristics of the existing legal regime in the light of the analysis that has been undertaken in this work.

D. USE OF TERMS

In the interest of lucidity, it is proposed to conclude this introduction by devoting this section to a clarification of the use of terms, and to set certain distinctions. In the first place, whereas the concept of counter-measures is in itself far from being a novelty in international law, the term as such is of comparatively recent usage. It was first coined by British lawyers in 1916.[1]

---

[1] See *British and Foreign State Papers* (hereinafter cited as *BFSP*), 105, Cv, 1916, p. 534, para. 14. Clearly therefore the term is not coined by Swiss lawyers in 1928 as suggested by Zoller; see Zoller, *Peacetime Unilateral Remedies: An Analysis of Countermeasures*, 1984 (hereinafter cited as Zoller), p. xvi n. 8. For recent illustrations of the use of the term see: Owen and Damrosch, 'The International Legal Status of Foreign Government Deposits in Overseas Branches of US

In its widest and non-technical connotation the term embraces a considerable range of responses open to States in the face of any reprehensible conduct. In this broad sense it can be used to define any reaction, whether legal or diplomatic, to a rupture in 'normal' inter-State relationships. However, this is not how the term is perceived in the present study. Rather it is employed here to define a category of justification, called legitimate counter-measures, which may be invoked as a ground to preclude responsibility for what would otherwise be wrongful conduct towards another State. In order that this category of justification may be successfully invoked, it would be imperative to establish that the conditions of legality had been complied with when the measures concerned were taken.

It is noteworthy that the United States Government used this term in its pleadings in the *Air Services Agreement Dispute* when it asserted that '[t]he proposed United States counter-measures were appropriate and in accordance with international law.'[2] The Arbitral Tribunal in that dispute employed the term in question when it indicated that an aggrieved State could 'affirm its rights through "counter-measures" '.[3] It may also be added that the International Court of Justice had itself accepted the term 'counter-measures' in its legal vocabulary.[4]

The issue of employing the term 'counter-measure' in legal vocabulary was faced squarely by the International Law Commission during the debates on Article 30 concerning legitimate counter-measures.[5] When that Article was first introduced by the Special Rapporteur, Professor Ago, under the title of 'Legitimate application of a sanction',[6] several Members of the Commission objected to the use of the word 'sanction'. Mr Yankov, for example, stated that the trend in contemporary international law was to regard the term 'sanction' as referring to measures adopted within an institutional framework.[7] Such apprehensions were finally conceded by Ago, who accordingly recommended the term 'counter-measures' in place of 'sanctions'.[8]

Banks', *University of Illinois Law Review*, 1982, p. 305, at pp. 309–10; Malanczuk, 'Countermeasures and Self-defence as Circumstances Precluding Wrongfulness in the International Law Commission's Draft Articles on State Responsibility', *Zeitschrift für ausländisches öffentliches Recht und Völkerrecht*, 1983, p. 705; Zoller, p. xvi n. 8; The American Law Institute, *Restatement of the Law: Foreign Relations Law of the United States (Revised)*, Tentative Draft 5, 1984, s. 905, p. 204, at p. 213, para 5.

[2] *Digest of United States Practice in International Law* (hereinafter cited as *Digest USPIL*), 1978, p. 769.

[3] *International Law Reports* (hereinafter cited as *ILR*), vol. 54, 1979, p. 337, para. 77.

[4] *International Court of Justice Reports* (hereinafter cited as *ICJ Reports*) 1980, p. 3, at p. 27, para. 53.

[5] *Yearbook of the International Law Commission* (hereinafter cited as *YILC*), vol. I, 1979, pp. 55 ff.

[6] Ibid., p. 8.

[7] Ibid., p. 57, paras. 29–30; for similar views see: Mr Ushakov, ibid., para. 28; Mr Njenga, ibid., p. 58, para. 35; Mr Jagota, ibid., p. 61, para. 15.

[8] Ibid., p. 63, para. 31.

These views were reflected in the Commission's report which provided that an aggrieved State could take 'legitimate counter-measures' in respect of an internationally wrongful act.[9] At this juncture it may be stated that the use of the term 'sanctions' in this book is intended to be synonymous with unilateral actions taken by way of counter-measures.

In assessing whether counter-measures are synonymous with reprisals, it should be noted at the outset that reprisals as a doctrine have undergone major changes as a result of the prohibition on the use of force as laid down in the Charter of the United Nations. Furthermore, the Declaration of Principles of International Law Concerning Friendly Relations and Co-operation among States in accordance with the Charter provides: 'States have a duty to refrain from acts involving the use of force.'[10] An inference which may be drawn from this legal development is that non-forcible reprisals still retain their validity as a category of justification for wrongful conduct. It would follow, therefore, that counter-measures may be regarded as synonymous with non-forcible reprisals.

As regards distinctions between counter-measures and retortive measures, it is sufficient to indicate that since the latter do not involve an infringement of international obligations, they can never be given the status of counter-measures. However, it is conceivable that the use of retortive measures may be restricted by treaty. In such a case the taking of the restricted retortive measures may have to be justified as a counter-measure.

Next it is proposed to ascertain the characteristics which differentiate between counter-measures and a 'state of necessity'.[11] First to be noted is that prior breach, which justifies the application of lawful counter-measures, is not applicable to a case in which a 'state of necessity' is involved. A second characteristic which serves to distinguish between these two categories relates to their respective rationales. Thus, the *raison d'être* of counter-measures, as will be shown,[12] may be self-protection, reciprocity, an inducement to settle, or a combination of these motivations. By contrast, the only motivation for invoking a 'state of necessity' as a ground for precluding wrongfulness of conduct is 'safeguarding an essential interest of the State against a grave and imminent peril'.[13]

[9] *YILC*, vol. 2, 1979, p. 115, para. 2; see also draft Articles 8 and 9(1) and Commentaries thereon, Riphagen, *Sixth Report on (1) The Content, Forms and Degrees of State Responsibility, and (2) The 'Implementation' (Mise en Œuvre) of International Responsibility and the Settlement of Disputes*, Doc. A/CN.4/389, 2 Apr. 1985, p. 18, para. 2, and p. 19, para. 1.

[10] General Assembly Resolution 2625 (XXV), Annex, *United Nations General Assembly Official Records* (hereinafter cited as *UNGAOR*), 25th Sess., suppl. 28(A/8028), 1970, p. 121.

[11] See Art. 33 concerning state of necessity and commentary thereon, *Report of the International Law Commission on the work of its thirty-second session*, 15 May–25 July 1980, *UNGAOR*, 35th Sess., suppl. 10(A/35/10), p. 69.

[12] Cf. *infra*, ch. 4, s. C.

[13] Art. 33(1)(*a*) (concerning state of necessity), *Report of the International Law Commission on the work of its thirty-second session*, 5 May–25 July, 1980, *UNGAOR*, 35th Sess., suppl. 10(A/35/10), p. 69.

Finally, a distinction must be made between counter-measures and the right of self-defence.[14] There is inevitably a certain overlap between the two in that both can be applied in response to breach. More importantly, however, one aspect of counter-measures is concerned with self-protection which is an analogue of self-defence. None the less, it needs to be remembered that counter-measures may be motivated by purposes other than self-protection. Thus, it will not be appropriate to regard the term self-defence as synonymous with the category of counter-measures, for the reason that the latter often involves objectives other than self-protection.

To sum up, the term counter-measures refers to a precise legal concept. Its usefulness for contemporary international law lies in the fact that it defines a particular category of justification, the bases of which are spread over wide-ranging fields.

---

[14] See Art. 34 (concerning self-defence) and commentary thereon, ibid., p. 111.

I

The Development of the Doctrine of Reprisals in the Seventeenth and Eighteenth Centuries

A. THE PURPOSE

THE purpose of this chapter is to examine the historical development of the practice of reprisals[1] in the seventeenth and eighteenth centuries. Since modern States began to emerge only in the seventeenth century, a study of the earlier periods would be of little benefit. It is to be noted at the outset that two types of reprisals were practised during the period under review: private reprisals and public reprisals. An attempt will be made to ascertain the conditions for the exercise of each type of reprisal.

B. PRIVATE REPRISALS

When an individual suffered an injury at the hands of a foreign State or any of her nationals, he could petition his sovereign for letters of marque authorizing him to take private reprisals.[2] The issuance of such letters represented the limit of the assistance that the sovereign was prepared to grant. This limited response on the part of the sovereign was mainly due to the lack of effective means of redress at his disposal.[3] What is more, even where such means were available to him, he might not be inclined to assume responsibility for his subjects' interests in foreign territories.[4]

The objective behind the practice of taking private reprisals was to provide redress for grievances suffered by private individuals in time of peace. Thus, in recognition of the necessity to preserve peace with foreign States, a sovereign

[1] The term reprisal is derived from the French *représailles* which itself originated from the Italian *ripresaglie*. The terms *repressaliae, pigneratio* (pledging), and *clarigatio* (a demand for redress) were used by lawyers who wrote in Latin.

[2] Grotius, *De Jure Belli Ac Pacis Libri Tres,* 1646, ed. Scott, 1925, (The Classics of International Law, 2) (hereinafter cited as Grotius), Book III, ch. 2, pp. 626–7; Bynkershoek, *Quaestionum Juris Publici Libri Duo,* 1737, ed. Scott, 1930 (The Classics of International Law, 2) (hereinafter cited as Bynkershoek), Book I, ch. 24 s. 173, p. 134; Vattel, *The Law of Nations,* 1797, ed. Chitty, 1834 (hereinafter cited as Vattel), Book II, ch. 18 s. 346, p. 284.

[3] Hindmarsh, 'Self-Help in Time of Peace', *American Journal of International Law* (hereinafter cited as *AJIL*), vol. 26, 1932, p. 315, at p. 317.

[4] Maccoby, 'Reprisals as a Measure of Redress short of War', *The Cambridge Law Journal,* vol. 2, 1924–6, p. 60 at p. 65.

would only grant letters of marque after the individual concerned had produced proof of manifest denial of justice.[5] Pertinent to this, Vattel stated as follows:

[such a party] should be able to show that he has ineffectually demanded justice, or at least that he has every reason to think it would be in vain for him to demand it [...] It would be too inconsistent with the peace [...] and safety of nations [...] that each one should be authorized to have immediate recourse to violent measures, without knowing whether there exist on the other side a disposition to do her justice, or to refuse it.[6]

As regards what constituted objects of reprisals, anything that belonged to the offending State or her citizens could be seized.[7] In addition to that, when occasion demanded, the citizens of that State themselves could be apprehended.[8] However, the licence to engage in such reprisals was subject to certain restrictions. First, the value of the movable property that was seized had to have some equivalence with the injury for which the initial claim was made.[9] Secondly, property entrusted to the public faith should not be seized.[10] Thirdly, when individuals were apprehended, their lives were not to be taken.[11]

At this point it becomes relevant to consider the propriety rights over the objects that had been seized. According to Grotius, 'ownership is acquired over seized goods by the mere act of seizure'.[12] As to individuals, they could only be detained 'as a security, or pledge, in order to oblige a nation to do justice'.[13]

Throughout the period under review attempts were made by States to regulate the practice of private reprisals. It was stipulated in several treaties

[5] For illustrations of refusal to issue letters of marque see the case of David Robertson who was asked to seek justice first in Hamburg, *Calendar of State Papers*, Domestic, ch. 1, 1629–31, p. 277; 'The Reply of the English Council of State to the Muscovy Company', ibid., 1651, p. 46; the refusal of the States-General to issue letters of reprisal to the traders of Middleburg against the people of Bremen, Bynkershoek, Book I, ch. 24 s. 177, pp. 136–7; the Opinion delivered by Sir Leoline Jenkins to the English Crown on 23 Feb. 1667 concerning the meaning of denial of justice as mentioned in the Treaty of 1667 between England and Spain, McNair, *International Law Opinions* (hereinafter cited as McNair, *Opinions*), 1956, vol. 2, pp. 298–300; for the text of the Treaty of 1667 see British Library reference (hereinafter cited as BL ref.) no. 6915.b.29(4).

[6] Vattel, Book II, ch. 18, s. 343; see also Gentili, *De Jure Belli Libri Tres*, 1612, ed. Scott, 1933 (The Classics of International Law, 2) (hereinafter cited as Gentili), Book II, Ch. 1 s. 216, p. 134; Grotius, Book III, ch. 2 svi, p. 627; Bynkershoek, Book I, ch. 24 s. 173, pp. 133–4.

[7] Vattel, Book II, ch. 18 s. 343; Grotius, Book III, ch. 2 s. v. 1, p. 627; Bynkershoek, Book I, ch. 24 s. 173, pp. 133–4.

[8] Ibid.

[9] Grotius, Book III, ch. 2 s. vii.3, p. 629; see also the Opinion delivered by Sir Leoline Jenkins, McNair, *Opinions*, vol. 2, p. 299.

[10] Vattel, Book II, ch. 18 s. 344, p. 284.

[11] Grotius, Book III, ch. 2 s. vi, p. 628; Vattel, Book II, ch. 18 s. 351, p. 287.

[12] Grotius, Book III, ch. 2 s. vii.3, p. 629.

[13] Vattel, Book II, ch. 18 s. 351, p. 287.

that specified periods should elapse between the time when redress was sought and the time when permission for reprisals was granted.[14] In some other treaties private reprisals were abolished altogether.[15] In the process of time, the seizures of private goods which lay within the territory of the other party came to be prohibited by treaty except for the purpose of settling a debt owed by the owner.[16] For a variety of reasons the practice of private reprisals had become virtually obsolete by the end of the eighteenth century.[17]

C. PUBLIC REPRISALS

Public reprisals were applied by one State against another in order to obtain redress for alleged injuries.[18] This type of reprisal was originally confined to the vindication of injuries sustained by the State herself. From the middle of the seventeenth century States came increasingly to regard grievances suffered by their nationals as instances of direct injury. Thus, following the seizure in French waters of a vessel belonging to an English Quaker, Cromwell made an immediate demand for redress. When this demand went unheeded, Cromwell dispatched English warships with orders to seize French vessels and goods.[19]

Similarly, in 1664 Charles II commanded the English fleet to take public reprisals against the Dutch on account of 'injuries affronts and spoyles done by the United Provinces unto and upon the shipps goods and persons of his subjects'.[20]

C.1. OBJECTS OF PUBLIC REPRISALS

The objects of public reprisals were the same as those of private reprisals. The following remarks were made by Vattel concerning the effects upon which reprisals could be imposed: 'in reprisals we seize on the *property* of the subject just as we would on that of the state or sovereign. Everything that

---

[14] e.g. Treaty between England and Holland, 1654, text: BL ref. no. 8122.ee.6(22); Treaty of Utrecht between France and England, 1713, text: BL ref. no. 8122.ff.2(1), cited by Phillimore, *Commentaries Upon International Law*, vol. iii, 1885 (hereinafter cited as Phillimore, iii), p. 24.

[15] Treaty between England and Denmark, 1660, text: De Bernhardt, *Handbook of Commercial Treaties, &c., Between Great Britain and Foreign Powers 1912*, p. 241; see Twiss, *The Law of Nations on the Rights and Duties of Nations in Time of War*, 1875 (hereinafter cited as Twiss), p. 41.

[16] e.g. Treaty between Sweden and the United States, 1783, text: Malloy, *Treaties, Conventions, International Acts, Protocol and Agreements between the United States of America and Other Powers 1776–1901*, 1910 (hereinafter cited as Malloy), vol. ii, p. 1724; Treaty between England and France, 1786, text: BL ref. no. 1484.9.4.

[17] See Butler and Maccoby, *The Development of International Law*, 1928, p. 177.

[18] Vattel, Book II, ch. 18 s. 342, p. 283.

[19] Phillimore, iii, p. 33.

[20] See Marsden, *Documents Relating to Law and Custom of the Sea, 1649–1767*, vol. ii, 1916 (hereinafter cited as Marsden ii), p. 48; for further illustrations on the use of power by the State to provide redress for private grievances see ibid., p. 8; Birch, *A Collection of the State Papers of John Thurloe*, vol. vi, 1742, pp. 268 ff.

belongs to the nation is subject to reprisals, whenever it can be seized, provided it be not a deposit intrusted to the public faith.'[21] Thus, in the case of the reprisals taken by Charles II against the Dutch, the fleet was ordered to 'seize and take all shipps, vessels, and goods belonging to the States of the United Provinces, or anie their subjects or inhabitants within anie the territories of the State of the United Provinces'.[22] The action taken by Prussia in 1752 against Great Britain provides a further illustration of the range of objects that could be seized by way of reprisals. Frederick II withheld payments of the Silesian Loan to English creditors and used the seized funds to compensate Prussian merchants for losses they had incurred in England.[23]

The seizure of individuals by way of public reprisals is recognized in the writings of Grotius, Bynkershoek, and Vattel.[24] Two instances from State practice may be cited. First, in 1665 the English imprisoned a secretary of the Dutch Ambassador, whereupon in retaliation his counterpart in the States-General was arrested by the Dutch.[25] The second instance was concerned with the response of Prussia to the arrest of one of her barons by the Empress of Russia in 1740. On that occasion the King of Prussia detained two Russians until the baron was released.[26]

There were certain categories of persons and property which were exempt from the operation of public reprisals. Thus, the persons and property of ambassadors and aliens temporarily resident or in transit could not be objects of public reprisals.[27] In addition, property entrusted to the public faith was considered outside the scope of public reprisals.[28] Limitations were also set on the treatment of individuals taken in reprisal. In the words of Vattel:

The persons, however, who are thus arrested, being detained only as a security, or pledge, in order to oblige a nation to do justice,—if their sovereign obstinately persists in refusing it, we can not take away their lives, or inflict any corporal punishment upon them, for a refusal, of which they are not guilty.[29]

C.2. PRIOR BREACH AND DENIAL OF JUSTICE AS CONDITIONS OF RECOURSE TO PUBLIC REPRISALS

The right to resort to public reprisals in the seventeenth century and the

---

[21] Vattel, Book II, ch. 18 s. 344, p. 284.
[22] Marsden ii, p. 48.
[23] See Phillimore, iii, pp. 33–4; Satow, *The Silesian Loan and Frederick the Great*, 1915, p. 82; McNair *Opinions*, vol. ii, p. 303.
[24] Grotius, Book III, ch. 2 s. v.2, p. 627; Bynkershoek, Book II, ch. 24 s. 178, p. 137; Vattel, Book II, ch. 18 s. 351, p. 287.
[25] Bynkershoek, Book II, ch. 24 s. 178, p. 137.
[26] Twiss, p. 37.
[27] Grotius, Book III, ch. 2 s. v.ii.2, pp. 628–9.
[28] Vattel, Book II, ch. 18 s. 344, p. 284.
[29] Vattel, Book II, ch. 18 s. 351, p. 287.

eighteenth century rested on the ground of injustice occasioned by an unredressed breach. Pertinent to this, Vattel stated that:

It is only upon evidently just grounds or for a well-ascertained and undeniable debt, that the law of nations allows us to make reprisals. For he who advances a doubtful pretension, cannot in the first instance demand anything more than an equitable examination of his right.[30]

Vattel further observed that resort to reprisals by one State against another could not be justified by a denial of justice against which a third State was protesting.[31] Thus, the reprisals taken in 1662 by England against the United Provinces in support of the Knights of Malta were objected to by France and Holland for the reason that England was not a party to the dispute in question. In recognition of the validity of those objections, the King of England ordered the release of the Dutch vessels that had been seized.[32] This clearly indicates that reprisals could only be intitiated by the particular State that had suffered injury.

Attention may now turn to an examination of the pertinent State practice with a view to confirming whether the occurrence of breach and the making of prior demand were considered as prerequisites of public reprisals. Thus, the reprisals taken in 1650 by Great Britain against France were justified by the injuries suffered as a result of the seizure of British ships and goods. Moreover, they were ordered after 'all faire courses have been taken and observed [. . .] in seeking and demanding redresse and reparation, yet none could be obteyned'.[33] The point may further be illustrated by the reprisals which Great Britain ordered against the Dutch in 1664. On that occasion the King took into consideration the injuries suffered by his subjects at the hands of the Dutch. A second factor to weigh with the King was '[the] many and frequent demands made by his Majestie unto the States Generall of the said United Provinces for redress and repairation, yet none could ever be obtained from them'.[34]

The two factors of prior breach and denial of justice continued to be regarded as prerequisites of resort to reprisals in the eighteenth century. Thus, the grounds on which Great Britain based her reprisals against Sweden in 1715 were the wrongful seizure of British ships with their cargo, and also the repeated representations made by British ministers which went unheeded.[35] The same grounds were advanced by Prussia as justification for withholding payments concerning the Silesian Loan.[36] Significantly, the Prussian Govern-

---

[30] Vattel, Book II, ch. 18 s. 343, p. 283.
[31] Vattel, Book II, ch. 18 s. 286, p. 285.
[32] See remarks by De Witt, cited by Vattel, ibid.
[33] Marsden ii, pp. 7–8.
[34] Ibid., p. 48.
[35] Chance, *British Diplomatic Instructions, 1689–1789*, vol. i, *Sweden, 1689–1727*, 1922, p. 75.
[36] See *supra*, p. 9.

ment resorted to this action only after it had made repeated and unsuccessful demands to Great Britain over a number of years. It is noteworthy that although the British Government disputed the allegation on grounds of fact, it nevertheless fully accepted the validity of the concepts of prior breach and denial of justice. This acceptance was reflected in the following excerpt from the Report of the Law Officers of the Crown dated 1753: 'The Law of nations [. . .] does not allow of reprisals, except in the case of violent injuries directed and supported by the state, and justice absolutely denied in *re minime dubiâ* by all the Tribunals, and afterwards by the prince.'[37]

Even where reprisals were concerned exclusively with abrogation of treaties, prior breach and denial of justice were advanced as justifications. For instance, the Act of 7 July 1798, by virtue of which the United States annulled her treaties with France, contained the following justifications for her action:

Whereas the treaties concluded between the United States and France have been repeatedly violated on the part of the French government; and the just claims of the United States for reparation of the injuries so committed have been refused, and their attempts to negotiate an amicable adjustment of all complaints between the two nations have been repelled with indignity.[38]

C.3. PROPORTIONALITY

The discussion in the preceding subsections has omitted all reference to the subsequent treatment of property seized by way of reprisals. The reason for introducing this issue at this point is that a close link existed between the disposal of the seized property and the concept of proportionality. In the view of Grotius, ownership over the seized property would be acquired by the very fact of seizure. He emphasized at the same time that it should not be extended beyond the 'limit of the debt and expenditure, in such a way that the residue shall be restored'.[39] According to Vattel, the seized property could be applied by the State taking the reprisals for her own benefit 'till she obtains payment of what is due to her together with interest and damages'.[40] Another alternative for that State would be to retain the seized property as a pledge until adequate satisfaction was received. In the latter case, such property should be preserved until all hope for redress had disappeared. Only then could it be confiscated, at which point the reprisals were regarded as accomplished.[41]

The principle of proportionality which was recognized by publicists of the

---

[37] Marsden ii, p. 348, at p. 355. The Report was received by eminent publicists of that time as an authoritative text.

[38] Moore, *A Digest of International Law* (hereinafter cited as Moore, *Digest*), vol. v, 1906, p. 356.

[39] Grotius, Book III, ch. 2 s. vii.3, p. 629.

[40] Vattel, Book II, ch. 18 s. 342, p. 283.

[41] Ibid.

seventeenth and eighteenth centuries was likewise demonstrated in the State practice of that period. Thus, in the case of the Silesian Loan,[42] the committee appointed by Frederick II reduced the claims of the Prussian merchants by one-third, while at the same time it levied an appropriate interest.[43] A further example of adherence to proportionality is to be seen in the reprisals taken by Cromwell against France.[44] In that instance the effects seized were sold, and the Quaker was compensated out of the proceeds to the extent of his losses. It is significant that what remained from the proceeds was handed over to the French ambassador.[45]

Although the above illustrations show that proportionality was recognized as a basic factor in the operation of reprisals, instances could be cited in which that factor was manifestly absent. Thus, when Charles II ordered the seizure in 1664 of all ships and goods belonging to the Dutch,[46] he was acting in a manner clearly disproportionate to his unvindicated grievance. On a similarly disproportionate scale were the retaliatory measures on the part of the Dutch. A further instance would be the disproportionate reprisals taken by England against France in 1755, involving the seizure of 300 of her ships valued at $6,000,000 and the detention of 6,000 French seamen.[47] It is to be noted in these two illustrations that despite the obvious disregard for proportionality shown by the parties concerned, none of them went so far as to challenge the very existence of the principle of proportionality. The fact that in each example war broke out within a year of the taking of the aforesaid reprisals would suggest that the parties were engaged in hostile conduct without making a declaration of war. Such conduct could fall within the category of 'pretended reprisals'.[48]

C.4. CONCLUSIONS

In the light of the prevailing doctrine and State practice, the following conclusions concerning the conditions of resort to public and private reprisals in the seventeenth and eighteenth centuries are offered:

1. Public reprisals were carried out by the State herself, while private reprisals were taken by individuals upon authority being granted by the State.

2. The property of the State and of her nationals, and her nationals themselves constituted objects of both public and private reprisals.

3. The occurrence of breach was held to be a prerequisite of both types of reprisals.

---

[42] See *supra*, p. 9.

[43] Martens, *Causes célèbres du droit des gens*, vol. ii, 1843, p. 167.

[44] See *supra*, p. 8.

[45] Phillimore, iii, p. 33.

[46] See *supra*, p. 9.

[47] Mahan, *The Influence of Sea Power Upon History 1660–1783*, 1889, pp. 284–5.

[48] Vattel, Book II, ch. 18 s. 354, p. 289.

4. In the case of private reprisals, the aggrieved individual was required to establish that he had been denied justice by the courts and by the Prince of the foreign State.

5. Resort to public reprisals was subject to the condition that the aggrieved State should have made an unsuccessful attempt at settlement.

6. In the application of both types of reprisals, there had to be a degree of proportionality between the injury sustained and the retaliatory measures taken. In assessing proportionality allowance was made for interest lost and expenses incurred.

7. Individuals seized as objects of reprisals were entitled to receive humane treatment.

8. The persons and property of ambassadors, and aliens in temporary residence or in transit, were exempt from the operation of reprisals. The same exemption applied to property entrusted to the public faith.

2

The Development of the Doctrine of Reprisals in the Nineteenth Century, and the Twentieth Century up to 1945, with particular reference to Non-forcible Reprisals

A. INTRODUCTION

The right of States to resort to war as a means of settling disputes continued to be recognized throughout the nineteenth century. In spite of this, there was a general reluctance among States to describe instances of forcible intervention as acts of war. The reasons for such an attitude were that reprisals, as an alternative to war, were more convenient to all parties concerned and appeared relatively more compatible with the prevailing pacific sentiment. In consequence, reprisals lost none of their earlier significance as a mode of redress. Furthermore, the fact that they were employed within the group of the European States indicates that they were not simply used as instruments of coercion by the Great Powers.

The period under review was marked by a range of legal developments which affected the general approach to all measures of self-help. By the end of the nineteenth century, war had come to be regarded as a means of last resort. In the twentieth century several constraints were placed on the use of force as a mode of redress. These, however, were not paralleled by the imposition of any compulsory procedure for judicial settlement. All these factors taken together had the effect of enhancing non-forcible reprisals as a means of redress.

In spite of the increasing importance set on non-forcible reprisals, the conditions governing their application were developed when both forcible and non-forcible reprisals were considered a single category. Nevertheless, a divorce between the two types of reprisals has been rendered necessary by the prohibition on the use of force by the Charter of the United Nations. The present chapter comprises a study of the development of the doctrine of reprisals with particular reference to non-forcible reprisals. This will involve an examination of the views of the publicists, State practice, and jurisprudence in the period 1800–1945.

B. DOCTRINAL VIEWS ON REPRISALS

It is proposed in this section to trace the development of the doctrine of reprisals as reflected in the literature of the period under review. Attention will first be given to the views of publicists of the nineteenth-century. This will be followed by an examination of the literature in the present century up to 1945, in order to discern any further development in doctrinal attitudes.

As regards the nineteenth-century writers, although they distinguished between war and other means of redress short of war, they made no such distinction between forcible and non-forcible reprisals.[1] Halleck, for example, defined reprisals as follows:

They consist in the forcible taking of things belonging to the offending State, or of its subjects, and holding them until a satisfactory reparation is made for the alleged injury. If the dispute is afterward arranged, the things thus taken by way of reprisals are restored, or if confiscated and sold, are paid for with interest and damages; but if war should result, they are condemned and disposed of in the same manner as other captured property, taken as prize of war.[2]

The above passage implies that what was considered as grounds for reprisals could equally be regarded as grounds for war. Hence, resort to reprisals represented a form of voluntary restriction on the right of a State to have recourse to war.

In the case of reprisals, however, certain conditions had to be complied with. In the first place, they could only be exercised by a State which had suffered injury to herself or to her nationals. Thus, in the words of Manning 'no nation has a right to exercise reprisals for the benefit of any but its own subjects'.[3] Some writers adopt the position that only where there was a denial of justice could an aggrieved State resort to reprisals.[4] The better view seems to be that any form of wrongful act, including a denial of justice, would constitute a legitimate ground for taking reprisals.[5]

The second condition of resort to reprisals recognized in the literature of the nineteenth century is the making of a prior demand for reparation. This requirement was emphasized by Halleck as follows:

---

[1] Wildman, *Institutes of International Law*, vol. ii, 1849 (hereinafter cited as Wildman), pp. 186–98; Halleck, *International Law, Or, Rules Regulating the Intercourse of States*, 1861 (hereinafter cited as Halleck), pp. 297 ff.; Wheaton, *Elements of International Law*, 8th edn., 1866 (hereinafter cited as Wheaton), pp. 368 ff.; Twiss, p. 31; Woolsey, *Introduction to the Study of International Law*, 5th edn., 1879, pp. 186–9; Hall, *A Treatise on International Law*, 2nd edn., 1884 (hereinafter cited as Hall), p. 338; Phillimore, iii, pp. 18, 77 ff.; Lawrence, *The Principles of International Law*, 1895 (hereinafter cited as Lawrence), pp. 293 ff.

[2] Halleck, p. 297.

[3] Manning, *Commentaries on the Law of Nations*, 1839, p. 110.

[4] Twiss, p. 36; Holland, *Studies in International Law*, 1898, p. 335; Halleck, p. 297.

[5] See Wheaton, p. 368; Hall, p. 335; Phillimore, iii, p. 22.

[I]f the claim be a national one, it must be properly demanded, and the demand refused. If it be of an individual, the claimant must first exhaust the legal remedies in the tribunals of the state from which the claim is due, and after an absolute denial of justice by such tribunals, his own government must make the demand of the sovereign authorities of the offending nations.[6]

Observance of proportionality features as a third condition of recourse to reprisals. In this respect Hall pointed out that '[t]o make reprisals either disproportioned to the provocation, or in excess of what is needed to obtain redress, is to commit a wrong'.[7] A similar position was taken by Phillimore when he noted that ownership over the seized property would be acquired to the extent of satisfying the original debt and expenses incurred in the reprisal. He then added that 'the residue is to be returned to the Government of the subjects against whom Reprisals have been put in force'.[8]

As regards objects of reprisals, it was recognized in the nineteenth-century literature that both property and individuals could be taken. In the case of individuals, however, some writers expressed certain reservations.[9] For instance, Halleck observed that when ships and their crews were seized, it was the practice to release the crews as soon as the ships had been brought into port.[10] Twiss, for his part, stated that the persons and property of political envoys, travellers, or those who were only temporarily resident in the country were exempt from reprisals.[11] The position adopted by Wheaton was that 'the practice of modern times discountenances the arrest and detention of innocent persons, strictly in the way of reprisals'.[12] Finally, Phillimore, while noting that the persons and goods of ambassadors and travellers were not liable for reprisals, expressed the hope that reprisals against any individual had fallen into desuetude.[13]

The views expressed by the various publicists of the nineteenth-century may be summarized as follows: reprisals were recognized as a legitimate form of redress in a response to breach. Such reprisals had to be preceded by a prior demand, and should be within the bounds of proportionality. As regards the seizure of individuals by way of reprisals, opinions were divided. Some accepted the practice unconditionally, while others accepted it subject to certain exceptions. There was a further school of thought which assumed that the seizure of individuals was becoming obsolete.

The above paragraph represents the doctrinal views on reprisals which prevailed at the turn of the century. It is proposed now to ascertain whether

---

[6] Halleck, p. 297; see also Wildman, p. 194; Lawrence, p. 299.
[7] Hall, p. 338.
[8] Phillimore, iii, p. 32.
[9] See Halleck, p. 301; Twiss, p. 37; Wheaton, p. 370 n. 151; Hall, p. 335.
[10] Halleck, p. 301.
[11] Twiss, p. 38.
[12] Wheaton, p. 370 n.151.
[13] Phillimore, iii, p. 32.

the attitudes of the publicists of the present century were in any way inconsistent with those earlier views. Oppenheim, writing in 1905, described reprisals as 'otherwise illegal acts performed by a State for the purpose of obtaining justice for an international delinquency by taking the law into its own hands'.[14] In his view, the conditions for exercising the right of reprisals were threefold: first, the existence of an internationally wrongful conduct;[15] secondly, failure to reach an amicable settlement through negotiations;[16] and thirdly, that reprisals should be in some proportion to the breach and should not exceed what would be necessary for securing reparation.[17] As concerns objects of reprisals, Oppenheim noted that anything which belonged to the offending State or to her nationals could be seized in reprisal; moreover, treaties concluded with that State might be suspended.[18] He further added that although nationals of the offending State could be apprehended, they should not be subjected to any form of punishment.[19] Finally, in Oppenheim's opinion reprisals could not be applied against diplomatic envoys or public debts, notwithstanding that both categories had been made objects of reprisals in the past.[20]

The views of the publicists who succeeded Oppenheim are found preponderantly to accord with his position regarding the conditions for, and the objects of, reprisals.[21] However, on the question of proportionality, Strupp and Hatschek pointed out that there was no necessity for reprisals to be proportionate to the injury suffered.[22] In similar vein Keith observed that 'any strict rule of proportion is out of the question'.[23] None the less he explicitly acknowledged the rule laid down in the *Naulilaa Case* that 'the means adopted should be proportional to the wrong'.[24]

Two further elements concerning the legality of reprisals are referred to in the literature. Strupp stated that reprisals were only limited by principles of

[14] Oppenheim, *International Law, A Treatise*, vol. ii, *War and Neutrality*, 1906 (hereinafter cited as Oppenheim, vol. ii), p. 34.

[15] Ibid., p. 35.

[16] Ibid., p. 41.

[17] Ibid., p. 39.

[18] Ibid., p. 38.

[19] Ibid.

[20] Ibid., p. 39.

[21] Butler, 'Reprisals as a Measure of Redress short of War', *Cambridge Law Journal*, vol. 2, 1924, p. 60, at pp. 67–8 s. 3; Butler and Maccoby, *The Development of International Law*, 1928, pp. 180–1; Hall, 8th edn. by Higgins, 1924, pp. 433, 436; Strupp, *Éléments du droit international public*, vol. i, 1930 (hereinafter cited as Strupp), p. 345; Stowell, *International Law: A Restatement Of Principles In Conformity With Actual Practice*, 1931, pp. 477, 480–2; Hatschek, *An Outline of International Law*, 1930 (hereinafter cited as Hatschek), pp. 290–2; Oppenheim, vol. ii, 6th edn. by Lauterpacht, 1940, pp. 111, 113, 115, 116; Rousseau, *Principes généraux du droit international public*, vol. i, 1944, p. 371 s. 240; Wheaton, *International Law*, vol. ii, *War*, 7th edn. by Keith, 1944 (hereinafter cited as Keith), pp. 90, 94.

[22] Strupp, pp. 345–6; Hatschek, pp. 290–1.

[23] Keith, p. 90.

[24] Ibid.

humanity, and good faith.[25] He also mentioned that third States, even if they were allies of the offending State, should not be made objects of reprisals.[26]

C. SOME INSTANCES OF STATE PRACTICE

C.1. THE DANISH REPRISALS AGAINST GREAT BRITAIN, 1807[27]

Prior to the outbreak of war between Great Britain and Denmark in 1807, Great Britain had seized Danish ships and property. By way of retaliation the Danish Government issued an ordinance for the sequestration of all ships, goods, and money belonging to English subjects. A suit then pending in a Danish Court for the recovery of a debt owed by a Dane to a Briton was quashed upon evidence that the former had, in compliance with the ordinance, paid the debt into the Danish Treasury.

An action for the recovery of that debt was heard before the English Court of King's Bench in *Wolff* v. *Oxholm*.[28] The defendant submitted that the Danish ordinance was consistent with the rules of international law concerning reprisals. In support of his submission, he cited Vattel to demonstrate that 'the *private property* of the members is considered as belonging to the body, and is answerable for the debts of that body [...] provided it be not a deposit intrusted to the public faith'.[29] The Court held that a debt owed to an individual in the course of trade should not be utilized for the settlement of a public debt.[30] In effect this meant that the Court was putting private debts on the same level as a deposit entrusted to the public faith. Wheaton noted this flaw in the reasoning of the Court when he remarked thus:

It has been justly observed, that between debts contracted under the faith of the law, and the property acquired on the faith of the same laws, reason draws no distinction; and the right of the sovereign to confiscate debts is precisely the same with the right to confiscate other property found within the country in the outbreak of the war.[31]

The present writer inclines to the stance taken by Wheaton for the reason that a debt, constituting as it does a form of property, could be seized by way of reprisals. Needless to say, such a debt should not be owed to aliens in transit or temporary residence or to ambassadors.

---

[25] Strupp, p. 345.

[26] Ibid.

[27] Wheaton, p. 391.

[28] 1813, *The English Reports*, vol. 105, ed. Maule and Selwyn, 1910 (hereinafter cited as Maule and Selwyn), p. 1177.

[29] Vattel, Book II, chapter 18, s. 344, p. 284.

[30] Maule and Selwyn, p. 1180.

[31] Wheaton, p. 391.

C.2. REPRISALS TAKEN BY THE UNITED STATES AGAINST
FRANCE, 1834[32]

The Treaty of 4 July 1831 between France and the United States specified
the spoliation debt owed by the former to the latter. It was further agreed
that the debt should be paid in six annual instalments. The French Chamber
of Deputies refused to appropriate the funds necessary to cover the first of
such instalments. The refusal provoked President Jackson into recommending
reprisals against French commerce. In his Sixth Annual Message in 1834 the
President stated that the failure by France to execute the terms of the Treaty
afforded sufficient grounds for the United States 'to take redress into their
own hands.'[33] In his opinion such conduct could be justified by the principle
of international law which provided that 'where one nation owes another a
liquidated debt, which it refuses or neglects to pay, the aggrieved party may
seize on the property belonging to the other, its citizens or subjects, sufficient
to pay the debt, without giving just cause of war'.[34] However, the Congressional Committee on Foreign Relations ruled that it would be inexpedient
to adopt the recommendation made by the President.[35]

When France continued to withhold payment even though the necessary
funds had been appropriated, the American President recommended reprisals
on two further occasions.[36] In due course the British Government offered to
mediate between the two States, whereupon President Jackson suggested
that all proceedings concerning his recommendations for reprisals should be
suspended. He justified his change of attitude on the following ground: 'It will
be obviously improper to resort even to the mildest measures of compulsory
character, until it is ascertained whether France has declined or accepted the
mediation.'[37]

There are three observations to be made on the above series of events. First,
full recognition was given to reprisals as a means for redressing grievances.
Secondly, although the United States was legally entitled to resort to reprisals,
policy considerations dissuaded her from exercising that right. The third
observation is that when a possibility of third party settlement arose, the
United States demonstrated her willingness to refrain from reprisals until it
became clear whether or not France was accepting responsibility for that
procedure.

---

[32] Wharton, *A Digest of the International Law of the United States*, vol. iii, 1887 (hereinafter
cited as Wharton iii), pp. 88 ff.

[33] Ibid., p. 90.

[34] Ibid., pp. 90–1.

[35] Ibid., p. 91.

[36] See President Jackson, Seventh Annual Message 1835, ibid., p. 92; President Jackson's
'French' Message of 15 Jan. 1836, ibid., p. 95.

[37] See President Jackson, special message of 8 Feb. 1836, ibid., pp. 95–6.

C.3. REPRISALS TAKEN BY GREAT BRITAIN AGAINST THE TWO
SICILIES, 1840[38]

Great Britain alleged that Sicily had violated the treaty of 1816 between the
two States by granting monopoly of the sulphur trade of Sicily to a French
company. Consequently, the British Government made several requests to
Sicily asking her to rescind that grant, and to compensate British subjects for
losses incurred as a result of the monopoly.[39] These requests were followed
by a warning to Sicily that reprisals would be taken against her within a week
if the British demands were not met. Sicily failed to meet these demands
whereupon the British Government ordered the detention of all Neapolitan
and Sicilian ships 'until such time [. . .] that the just demands of Her Majesty's
Government have been complied with'.[40]

The dispute was finally settled by third party mediation. As a result of this,
the Neapolitan Government abolished the grant of monopoly to the French
company, and Great Britain immediately restored the seized ships to their
Neapolitan owners.[41]

C.4. THE QUESTION OF THE SPANISH BONDHOLDERS' DEBT, 1847[42]

Lord Bentinck presented to the House of Commons a petition on behalf of
the British holders of Spanish bonds. The petitioners were seeking the assistance of the House in recovering substantial interest which had fallen into
arrears. Lord Bentinck informed the House of the fact that successive Spanish
Governments had acknowledged the debt in question. In view of this he
urged that reprisals be taken by the British Government to recover that
debt.[43]

Speaking on behalf of the British Government, Viscount Palmerston
acknowledged the right of a State to take reprisals where she had been denied
redress.[44] Nevertheless, he made the following qualification about the actual
application of reprisals: 'there may be a difference and distinction drawn in
point of expediency and in point of established practice, as to the application
of an indisputable principle to particular and different cases'.[45] The Viscount
stated that it would be the duty of the British Government to enforce redress

---

[38] For correspondence between Great Britain and Sicily relative to the sulphur monopoly in
Sicily see *BFSP*, vol. 29, 1840–1, p. 175.

[39] Letter dated 25 Mar. 1840 from the British Minister at Naples to Prince Scilla of Sicily,
ibid., p. 197.

[40] Orders from the British Government to the Admiral of the British Fleet in the Mediterranean
Sea, letter dated 3 Apr. 1840 from Admiral Stopford to Mr Temple, ibid., p. 204.

[41] *Annual Register*, 1840, p. 210.

[42] *Parliamentary Debates (Hansard) House of Commons Official Reports* (hereinafter cited as
Hansard, HC Debs.), vol. 93, cols. 1285–306, 6 July 1847.

[43] Ibid., col. 1289.

[44] Ibid., cols. 1298 and 1300.

[45] Ibid.

where property of its subjects had been violently seized by another State in breach of a treaty of amity. Similarly, redress would be insisted upon where the violated transaction was either based on a previous compact with another Government, or had been sanctioned by the British Government. A further ground for intervention by the Government of Great Britain would be an injustice suffered by one of her subjects in the prosecution of trade in a foreign State. In such a situation, however, the aggrieved individual should first seek redress according to the laws of the country concerned. Only where justice was denied to that individual, would the British Government step in and demand that 'either the laws shall be properly dealt out, or that redress shall be given by the Government of that State'.[46]

The illustration indicates that an individual who suffered injury in the course of trade with nationals of a foreign State, had to exhaust local remedies before seeking the help of his Government. However, for policy considerations, compliance with such procedure was not required where the injury related to a transaction which was either approved by the Government or performed within a treaty framework.

C.5. REPRISALS TAKEN BY GREAT BRITAIN AGAINST GREECE, 1850

The British Government made repeated demands for compensation from the Greek Government in respect of injuries suffered by British subjects in Greece.[47] When these demands were not met, the British Government issued a warning that unless satisfaction was made within twenty-four hours, it would resort to reprisals.[48] Upon receiving no positive reaction within the stipulated time Great Britain seized a number of Greek ships.[49] It is noteworthy that non-Greek merchants were permitted to remove such goods as belonged to them from the seized ships.[50] When it became apparent that the ships in question were of little value, the British Minister in Athens stated that the reprisals would be continued until 'the sum demanded for compensation [...] shall be liquidated'.[51]

A new element was introduced into this dispute when the contending parties accepted the mediation of France. Notwithstanding this opportunity for peaceful settlement, the British Government reiterated that the seized ships would be detained until full satisfaction had been given.[52] This attitude was justified by the assertion that little reliance could be placed on promises made by the Government of Greece.[53]

---

[46] Ibid., cols. 1298–9.
[47] *BFSP*, vol. 39, 1849–50, inclosure 2, p. 482, and No. 2, p. 483.
[48] Inclosure 1, ibid., pp. 509–10.
[49] Inclosure 9, ibid., p. 515.
[50] Inclosure 2, ibid., pp. 573–4.
[51] No. 15, ibid., p. 508.
[52] No. 27, ibid., p. 577.
[53] Ibid.

The above series of events shows that resort to reprisals must be in response to a manifest breach. As regards the making of prior demand, although Great Britain resorted to reprisals only after issuing a twenty-four-hour warning, one question needs to be asked: how far was she legally obliged to issue the aforesaid warning before resorting to those reprisals? In view of the fact that the British Government had already made repeated demands for reparation, the issuing of the warning should be considered as superfluous. With respect to the element of proportionality, it is clear that Great Britain was not content with seizing property which was not commensurate with the injury suffered by her nationals. At the same time, however, her threat to continue reprisals until compensation was made would suggest that she was prepared, if necessary, to engage in actions that went beyond the bounds of proportionality. Finally, the maintenance of reprisals by Great Britain during the process of third party settlement was clearly grounded on her distrust of the Greek Government.

C.6. THE REPRISALS TAKEN BY THE UNITED STATES AGAINST CHINA, 1855[54]

The United States demanded on several occasions that the Chinese Government should settle a claim for injury suffered by one of her citizens. Although the Chinese Government admitted that the claim was due, it nevertheless failed to comply with the aforesaid demands. Consequently, the United States instructed her minister to China to withhold duties equal to the amount involved in the claim.[55]

The above facts serve to show that when the United Stated failed to settle her claim amicably, she retaliated with measures proportionate to that claim.

C.7. THE CHINESE REACTION TO THE VIOLATION BY THE UNITED STATES OF THE SINO-AMERICAN TREATY OF 1880

Between 1844 and 1880 the United States concluded six treaties with China,[56] the last of which concerned residence of Chinese nationals in the United States. In 1888 the United States violated the last of these treaties by passing the Chinese Exclusion Act.[57] The reaction of the Chinese Government was

---

[54] Moore, *Digest*, vol. ii, p. 106.

[55] Ibid.

[56] Treaty of Peace, Amity, and Commerce, 1844, text: Malloy, vol. i, p. 196; Treaty of Peace, Amity and Commerce, 1858, ibid., p. 211; Treaty Establishing Trade Regulations and Tariff, 1858, ibid., p. 222; Claims Convention, 1858, ibid., p. 232; Treaty of Trade, Consuls, and Emigration, 1868, ibid., p. 234; Immigration Treaty, 1880, ibid., p. 237.

[57] Text: Ch. 1064, *United States Statutes at Large* (hereinafter cited as *Stat.*), vol. 25, 1887–9, p. 504.

communicated to the American Secretary of State in two letters delivered by successive Chinese ambassadors. It was indicated in the first letter that the violation of the treaty by the United States could not be justified by any wrongful conduct on the part of the Chinese Government.[58] In view of this, the United States' action was considered as no less than a denunciation of all existing treaties between the two countries.[59] Finally, the Chinese ambassador stated that it was hardly necessary to point out that 'the abrogation [...] of an important treaty stipulation, releases China from the observance of all its treaties with the United States'.[60]

The stance taken by the Chinese Government was amplified in the following excerpt from the second letter sent by its ambassador:

The Public Law of all nations recognises the right of China to resort to retaliation for these violated treaty guarantees, and such a course applied to the American missionaries and merchants has been recommended to the Imperial Government by many of its statesmen; but its long-maintained friendship for the United States, and its desire to observe a more humane and elevated standard of intercourse with the nations of the world, point to a better method of adjustment.[61]

The right of resort to reprisals as claimed by China was recognized by the chairman of the United States Senate Committee on Foreign Relations. In his view, the refusal of his Government to observe existing treaties would entitle China to terminate all her treaties with the United States.[62]

There are several interesting points to be noted here. In the first place, China adopted the position that resort to reprisals could be had only after the occurrence of breach. Secondly, an abrogation of an important treaty provision could justify the termination, by way of reprisals, of all existing and interrelated treaties between the two States in question. Although the reprisals threatened by China were quantitatively disproportionate to the breach, she obviously did not regard such measures as disproportionate for the reason that the breach in question related to an important treaty provision. Finally, while the Chinese government maintained that reprisals could be taken against nationals of the offending State, it nevertheless refrained from such actions on grounds of humanity, as well as of friendship for the United States.

---

[58] Letter of 8 July 1889. For text see *Foreign Relations of the United States* (hereinafter cited as *FRUS*), 1889, p. 132.

[59] Ibid., p. 135, para. 3.

[60] Ibid.

[61] Ibid., 1890, p. 217.

[62] Ibid., 1889, p. 135, para. 3.

C.8. THE DETENTION BY SWEDEN OF THE BRITISH TRANSIT MAIL TO
RUSSIA AS A REPRISAL FOR THE SEIZURE OF SWEDISH PARCELS MAIL
BY THE BRITISH GOVERNMENT, 1915[63]

During the month of December 1915 several bags of parcels mail belonging
to Sweden were removed for inspection by British authorities from vessels
which had arrived at Kirkwall.[64] By way of reprisal Sweden ordered the
detention of British transit mail to Russia.[65] Great Britain pointed out to
Sweden that she was exercising a belligerent right, and accordingly she had
not violated any rule of international law.[66] It was also maintained by Great
Britain that a friendly state should proceed to reprisals only after seeking an
explanation for the alleged breach.[67] When Sweden failed to lift the embargo
on British mail, the British Government intimated to her that it would be
obliged 'to place a similar embargo on all Swedish mails'.[68]

As regards the question whether an aggrieved party should refrain from
taking reprisals when there exists a specific means for settling disputes, the
British Government stated as follows:

It would be more consonant with the Principles governing the intercourse between
two Friendly Governments if, before resorting to an open violation of British rights
as a counter-measure to a supposed grievance, the correctness of the assumption on
which the neutral based his complaint were brought to the test in the manner and by
the machinery prescribed for this purpose by the consensus of all authorities of
international law.[69]

D. CERTAIN DEVELOPMENTS IN THE PERIOD BEFORE THE FIRST WORLD WAR

D.1. THE HAGUE CONVENTIONS OF 1899 AND 1907 FOR THE PACIFIC
SETTLEMENT OF INTERNATIONAL DISPUTES[70]

The growing desire among nations to establish procedures for settling international disputes by amicable means was reflected in the two Hague Conventions of 1899 and 1907.[71] The means envisaged in the Conventions for
attaining the goal were as follows: good offices or mediation, international
commissions of inquiry, and international arbitration.

---

[63] *BFSP*, vol. 110, 1916, pp. 531 ff.
[64] Ibid., No. 1, p. 531; and No. 4, p. 533.
[65] Ibid., No. 5, p. 534.
[66] Ibid.
[67] Ibid.
[68] Ibid., No. 6, p. 535.
[69] Ibid., No. 8, p. 534, para. 14.
[70] Text: *The Hague Conventions and Declarations of 1899 and 1907*, ed. Scott, 2nd edn., 1915
(hereinafter cited as Scott, *Conventions*).
[71] Art. 1 of both Conventions, ibid., pp. 42–3.

As regards recourse of good offices or mediation, Article 2 provided that the Contracting Powers should utilize these procedures wherever possible before resorting to force.[72] Although the purpose of this Article was to obviate recourse to armed force, Article 7 nevertheless stipulated that the acceptance of mediation could not impede mobilization for war, nor could it interrupt actual hostilities. At the same time, however, the provisions of Article 6, which permitted good offices and mediation to be undertaken by Powers, strangers to the dispute, proved their usefulness in the Dogger Bank incident in 1904.[73]

As has been mentioned, the procedure for good offices and mediation was intended to cater primarily for serious disputes such as might lead to the employment of force. It follows, therefore, that resort to non-forcible reprisals remained a viable means of settling disputes of a relatively less serious character.

We may now turn to international commissions of inquiry. This method of peaceful settlement suffered from certain inherent defects. Article 9[74] of the two Conventions excluded from the ambit of such inquiries international disputes involving honour or vital interests. Further, by referring specifically to disputes concerning points of fact, that article implicitly ruled out disputes relating to points of law. In addition, Article 9 laid no compulsion on the disputing parties to institute an international commission of inquiry. Finally, it may be observed that both Conventions stipulated that the reports of such commissions were limited to stating facts only; and hence, they did not have the character of arbitral awards.[75] In spite of all these defects, however, in three naval incidents international commissions conducted inquiries which laid the foundation for friendly settlement.[76] The general conclusion to be drawn from this analysis is that, as with the case of 'good offices and mediation', international commissions of inquiry did not reduce the significance of non-forcible reprisals.

The third means of settling disputes, as envisaged in the two Conventions, is the Permanent Court of Arbitration.[77] A major defect of this machinery is the lack of any provision for compulsory arbitration. The Final Act of the Second Peace Conference confirms unequivocally that it had not been found

[72] Ibid., p. 43.

[73] In that dispute the initiative taken by France led to an amicable settlement between Great Britain and Russia; see *The Hague Court Reports*, 1st Ser., ed. Scott, 1916 (hereinafter cited as *HCR*), p. 403.

[74] Scott, *Conventions*, pp. 45–6.

[75] Art. 14 of the 1899 Convention, and Art. 35 of the 1907 Convention, ibid., pp. 54–5.

[76] Dogger Bank incident 1905, between Great Britain and Russia, *HCR*, p. 403; the Tarignano, Camouna, and Gaulois Cases between France and Italy, 1912 and 1913, ibid., pp. 413, 616; the Loss of SS *Tubantia* Case 1922, between the Netherlands and Germany, ibid., 2nd Ser., 1932, p. 135.

[77] Art. 20 of the 1899 Convention, and Art. 41 of the 1907 Convention, Scott, *Conventions*, p. 57.

possible to conclude a convention which could provide for obligatory arbitration.[78] Moreover, even where a dispute is covered by a general treaty of arbitration, a contending party could claim that it was not within the category of disputes which were subject to compulsory arbitration.[79]

In spite of the above-mentioned deficiencies which surround the machinery of the Permanent Court, the Great Powers resorted on numerous occasions to arbitration under its auspices. Nevertheless, the absence of any provision for compulsory arbitration, and the increasing reluctance of States to avail themselves of this machinery, prove that the Court has had no influence on the legality of non-forcible reprisals.

D.2. THE CONVENTION RESPECTING THE LIMITATION ON THE EMPLOYMENT OF FORCE FOR THE RECOVERY OF CONTRACT DEBTS, 1907[80]

Article 1 of this Convention expressly prohibited recourse to armed force as a means for the recovery of contract debts owed to nationals of one State by the Government of another State.[81] An examination of this provision, however, reveals the existence of several gaps in the Convention as concerns the prohibition on resort to armed force for the aforesaid purpose. First, a State could employ force for the recovery of contract debts owed to herself by another State. Secondly, no restriction was put on the use of force in cases of non-contractual debts. Thirdly, the distinction between contractual and tortious liability could in some cases be blurred; hence it was possible for a State to take forcible reprisals on the pretext that her claim was tortious rather than contractual.

As regards the relevance of this Convention to the Law of reprisals, Williams observed that it might be concluded that 'resort to reprisals of any kind in a case covered by the Hague Convention is not in accordance with the spirit of that instrument'.[82] *Pace* Professor Williams, these remarks find no support either in the text of the Convention, or in its *travaux préparatoires*.[83] The better view seems to be that the Convention set a restriction on resort to forcible reprisals only. Accordingly, one must assume that freedom

---

[78] *The Reports of the Hague Conferences of 1899 and 1907*, 1917, ed. Scott (hereinafter cited as Scott, *Conferences*), pp. 215–16, see also Art., 19 of the 1899 Convention, and Art. 40 of the 1907 Convention, Scott, *Conventions*, p. 56.

[79] See Art 53(1) of the 1907 Convention, Scott, *Conventions*, p. 65.

[80] Ibid., p. 89.

[81] The following proviso is attached to Art. 1: 'This undertaking is, however, not applicable when the debtor State refuses or neglects to reply to an offer of arbitration, or, after accepting the offer, renders the settlement of the compromise impossible, or, after the arbitration, fails to submit to the award'. Ibid.

[82] Williams, *Chapters on Current International Law and the League of Nations*, 1929, p. 315.

[83] See Scott, *Conferences*, pp. 491–9.

to employ non-forcible reprisals was not impaired. Finally, it is apparent that the failure to back the constraint laid on forcible reprisals with an effective arbitration machinery served to put a premium on non-forcible reprisals.

E. THE COMPATIBILITY OF NON-FORCIBLE REPRISALS WITH THE COVENANT OF THE LEAGUE OF NATIONS

It should be noted at the outset that the Covenant of the League of Nations merely provided for procedural constraints on the right of States to have recourse to war.[84] In essence, therefore, war remained a valid instrument of redress. The question to be addressed here concerns the extent to which the provisions of the Covenant regulated resort to non-forcible reprisals.

Although the term 'reprisals' was nowhere mentioned in the Covenant, it is important nevertheless to ascertain whether any of its provisions in effect set a restriction on resort to reprisals. It was declared in Article 11 that a 'threat of war' in itself was 'a matter of concern to the whole League, and the League shall take any action that may be deemed wise and effectual to safeguard the peace of nations'. This provision could hardly be interpreted as a prohibition on reprisals as such, still less on the specific category of non-forcible reprisals. In Article 12, the Members undertook to submit either to arbitration or to inquiry by the Council any dispute between them that was 'likely to lead to a rupture'. It is clear that the objective of this provision was to restrain conduct that might develop into war. By implication, therefore, the provision was not intended to restrict the use of non-forcible reprisals which did not present a danger to peace. However, where this type of reprisal threatened to cause a rupture, the parties concerned were obliged to submit the matter to arbitration or investigation by the Council. The question is begged as to whether the parties who had submitted the dispute in the aforesaid manner were precluded from taking non-forcible reprisals during the period of arbitration or investigation.

The compatibility of reprisals with the Covenant was discussed by some writers in the light of the report of the Committee of Jurists on the Corfu incident of 1923.[85] The majority view was that Member States were entitled to resort to reprisals prior to the consideration of their dispute by the League.[86] Professor de Visscher, for his part, laid the emphasis on whether the measures adopted might cause a rupture, rather than on the relative strength of the contending parties. Thus, in his opinion 'les représailles d'ordre économique ou financières' would be compatible with the Covenant, whereas

---

[84] See Art. 12, 13, 15, and 16 of the Covenant.

[85] Between Greece and Italy. For a summarized account of the facts see *British Yearbook of International Law* (hereinafter cited as *BYIL*), vol. 5, 1925, pp. 251 ff.

[86] Wright, 'Opinion of Commission of Jurists on Janina–Corfu Affair', *AJIL.*, vol. 18, 1924, p. 536 at p. 541; McNair, 'The Legal Meaning of War, and Relation of War to Reprisals', *Transactions of the Grotius Society*, vol. 11, 1926, p. 29, at p. 43; Oppenheim, vol. ii, 1944, p. 127.

'les représailles armées' would be incompatible with it.[87] The present writer inclines to the view that the reply given by the Committee of Jurists to the question submitted by the League could not, on account of its vagueness, lend itself to any precise interpretation.[88]

F. THE COMPATIBILITY OF NON-FORCIBLE REPRISALS WITH CERTAIN LEGAL DEVELOPMENTS IN THE INTER-WAR PERIOD

The first notable development in this period was that the Permanent Court of International Justice began to function in 1921. The contentious jurisdiction of the court was hindered by two basic limitations: (*a*) that a party to a dispute could declare that a given treaty laid no obligation on it to have recourse to arbitration; (*b*) under the 'Optional Clause' of Article 36 of the Statute of the Court, the parties were allowed scope to make reservations concerning the competence of the court. Hence, the establishment of this Court cannot be said to have had any direct impact on the legality of non-forcible reprisals.

The conclusion of a large number of treaties for pacific settlement of disputes represents the second development to be noted in the inter-war period.[89] Two specific illustrations may be examined. The Treaty of Mutual Guarantee between Germany, Belgium, France, Great Britain, and Italy was concluded in 1925 as one of the Locarno Treaties.[90] By virtue of Article 2 of that Treaty, Germany, Belgium, and France undertook not to attack each other.[91] Under Article 3, the same parties assumed obligations in respect of peaceful settlement of disputes. The effect of these two provisions was to prevent any of the three States which gave the aforesaid undertaking from applying any kind of reprisals against each other. Such consequences, however, were shortlived on account of the fact that Germany withdrew from the Treaty of 1936.[92]

The second illustration to be examined is the General Treaty for the Renunciation of War of 1928.[93] The combined effect of the recitals in the preamble, and of Articles I and II of that Treaty has been to renounce war as an instrument of national policy among the Contracting Parties. Opinions differ, nevertheless, as to the extent to which the Treaty curtailed the right of

---

[87] De Visscher, 'L'Interpretation du pacte au lendemain du différend italo-grec', *Revue de droit international et de législation comparée*, vol. 5, 1924, p. 377, at p. 385.

[88] See Brownlie, *International Law and the Use of Force by States*, 1963 (hereinafter cited as Brownlie, 1963), p. 222.

[89] See United Nations, *Systematic Survey of Treaties for the Pacific Settlement of International Disputes, 1928–1948*, 1948, p. 1179.

[90] Text: *AJIL*, supp. 20, 1926, p. 21.

[91] Subject to certain exceptions.

[92] *Royal Institute of International Affairs, Documents* (hereinafter cited as *RIIA, Documents*), vol. 1, 1935, p. 41.

[93] Text: 94 *League of Nations Treaty Series* (hereinafter cited as *LNTS*), p. 57.

States to take measures of force short of war.[94] The present writer takes the view that the absence of any provision in the Treaty for compulsory adjudication, together with the subsequent practice of the parties, indicates that the Treaty has had virtually no impact on the legality of resort to non-forcible reprisals.

G. STATE PRACTICE PERTINENT TO THE LEGALITY OF NON-FORCIBLE REPRISALS IN THE INTER-WAR PERIOD

G.1. REPRISALS TAKEN BY FRANCE AGAINST GERMANY, 1922[95]

Under the Treaty of Versailles Germany was obliged to make monthly payments of £2,000,000 to the Allied Clearing Office. Owing to difficulties in the German Exchange, Germany sought the consent of the allied Governments for a reduction in her July payment to the level of £500,000. France, who was a principal beneficiary of these payments, withheld her consent, and threatened to take reprisals unless Germany continued to make the payments to which she was committed.[96]

The reprisals contemplated by France were threefold: expulsion of 500 Germans from Alsace and Lorraine; refusal to give recognition to German clearing claims; and confiscation of the assets of German companies in Alsace. Although the French Government commenced these reprisals, it soon countermanded them, following strong protests from business circles in the district concerned.

The above facts indicate clearly that France resorted to non-forcible reprisals in order to induce compliance with a demand for redress which had already been made. There remains, on the other hand, an obscurity in the evidence as to how far France observed the principle of proportionality.

G.2. OPINION OF THE SWISS MINISTER OF THE DEPARTMENT OF POLICY, 1928

The Department of Policy was asked for an opinion as to whether Switzerland could impose reciprocal taxes upon aliens whose Governments had levied inequitable taxes on Swiss nationals resident in their jurisdictions.[97] The Department replied that retaliatory measures could be in the form of reprisals

---

[94] See Oppenheim, vol. ii, 7th edn., by Lauterpacht, 1952, p. 196; Bowett, *Self-Defence in International Law*, 1958, p. 136; Brownlie, 1963, p. 87.

[95] *Annual Register*, 1922, pp. 165–6.

[96] Ibid., p. 166.

[97] Request made by the Federal Administration of Taxes on 17 Nov., 20, and 30 Dec. 1927; the reply was given on 14 June 1928, see *Répertoire suisse de droit international public: Documentation concernant la pratique de la Confédération en matière de droit international public 1914–1939*, vol. iii, 1975 (hereinafter cited as *Répertoire Suisse*, vol. iii), pp. 1785–96.

or retorsion, depending on whether or not the measures in question were permitted under international law. Reprisals, the Department explained, would entail conduct otherwise wrongful but for its justification as response to breach, whereas retorsion would not involve any breach of international obligations. Furthermore, retorsion would not have to be analogous with the breach, nor lie within the same field as that breach. However, where that was the case, the retortive measures taken would be referred to as measures of reciprocity. The present writer argues that two possible interpretations may be drawn from the foregoing remarks. First, it was acknowledged by implication that reprisals had to be analogous with the breach and lie within the same field as that breach. Secondly, the absence of any explicit reference to reprisals makes it doubtful whether the above implication merits serious consideration.

Notwithstanding the uncertainty surrounding the issue treated in the preceding paragraph, the Opinion spoke with a measure of clarity on various other aspects concerning legitimate reprisals. It was emphasized that each instance of reprisals should be examined individually in order to determine whether the particular measures taken could be justified in the circumstances. The sole criterion for making such a determination was held to be the existence of a state of necessity.[98] The Opinion explained that a true state of necessity could only arise after all available means of amicable redress had been exhausted.[99] It was particularly noted that in the case of a commitment to a third party settlement, reprisals would be unlawful since by virtue of that commitment a state of necessity could not be envisaged.[100] On a different line, the Opinion stated that certain measures of retorsion could be categorized as unlawful reprisals if they were shown to be in breach of the specific treaty obligation. Breach of a treaty provision respecting quality of treatment was offered as an illustration of this particular point.[101]

G.3. ACTS OF THE CONFERENCE FOR THE CODIFICATION OF INTERNATIONAL LAW OF 1930[102]

The Preparatory Committee drew up Basis of Discussion No. 25 for the Codification Conference in these terms: 'A State is not responsible for damage caused to a foreigner if it proves that it acted in circumstances justifying the exercise of reprisals against the State to which the foreigner belongs.'[103] In

---

[98] Ibid., p. 1786, para. I.

[99] Ibid., p. 1787, para II.

[100] Ibid., p. 1788, para. II(*b*), cf. *infra*, ch. 9.

[101] Ibid, pp. 1791–2, para. III(*a*).

[102] League of Nations, *Conference for the Codification of International Law: Bases of Discussion*, vol. iii ('Responsibility of States for damage caused in their territory to the person or property of foreigners'), 1929 (hereinafter cited as *Conference for the Codification*), p. 128.

[103] Ibid., p. 130.

formulating this Basis the Committee was guided by the replies of States to the request for information which it had addressed to them. The request was concerned with the following question: 'What are the conditions which must be fulfilled when the State claims to have acted in circumstances which justified a policy of reprisals?'[104]

The replies received from Governments in response to the above question reveal a unanimity among those Governments that reprisals could only be justified by the occurrence of an internationally wrongful conduct.[105] With regard to the consequences of a refusal by a State to make reparation, five Governments took the view that reprisals could lawfully be taken against that State;[106] and with regard to the right of resort to reprisals where means of pacific settlement existed, three States indicated that such a right could be exercised only after a failure to obtain satisfaction through those means.[107] Belgium was the only State to express any view on the question of proportionality. She stated that reprisals should be 'proportionate to the gravity of the violation'.[108]

H. THE OPINION OF THE INSTITUTE OF INTERNATIONAL LAW

The Institute of International Law adopted a resolution in its 1934 session concerning reprisals taken in time of peace.[109] Article 5 of the resolution made recourse to non-forcible reprisals conditional on compliance with any existing commitment to peaceful settlement.[110] The conditions for resort to reprisals (forcible or non-forcible) in time of peace were set out in Article 6 as follows:

Dans l'exercice des représailles, l'Etat doit se conformer aux règles suivantes:

1. Mettre au préalable l'Etat auteur de l'acte illicite en demeure de le faire cesser et d'accorder éventuellement les réparations requises;
2. Proportionner la contrainte employée à la gravité de l'acte dénoncé comme illicite et à l'importance du dommage subi;
3. Limiter les effets des représailles à l'Etat contre qui elles sont dirigées, en respectant, dans toute la mesure du possible, tant les droits des particuliers que ceux des Etats tiers;
4. S'abstenir de toute mesure de rigueur qui serait contraire aux lois de l'humanité et aux exigences de la conscience publique;
5. Ne pas détourner les représailles du but qui en a déterminé initialement l'usage; et

---

[104] Point XI (*b*), ibid., p. 128.
[105] Ibid., pp. 128–30.
[106] South Africa, Australia, Great Britain, New Zealand, India, ibid., pp. 128–9.
[107] Belgium, Denmark, ibid., p. 128; Switzerland, ibid., p. 130.
[108] Ibid., p. 128.
[109] *Annuaire de l'institut de Droit International* (hereinafter cited as *Annuaire*), 1934, pp. 692, 708–11.
[110] Ibid., pp. 709–10; cf. *infra*, ch. 9.

6. Cesser les représailles aussitôt qu'il aura été obtenu une satisfaction raisonnable.[111]

An observation to be made is that the Institute recognized the necessity of resorting to reprisals as measures of self-help.[112] As to the legal significance of the provisions contained in Article 6, the *travaux préparatoires* do not clarify whether they represented customary law, or merely denoted *ius constituendum*.[113] In spite of the obscurity of this particular point, considerable weight should be attached to the views of this learned body.

I. THE DEVELOPMENT OF THE DOCTRINE OF REPRISALS THROUGH THE CASES

I.1 *THE NORTH ATLANTIC FISHERIES ARBITRATION,* 1910[114]

In this dispute the United States contended that Great Britain was not entitled to regulate the activities of American fishermen in waters governed by treaty without her consent.[115] The Tribunal did not uphold this contention for the reason that there was no such implied right in favour of the United States. By way of elaboration the Tribunal stated that

every State has to execute the obligations incurred by treaty *bona fide,* and is urged thereto by the ordinary sanctions of international law in regard to observance of treaty obligations. Such sanctions are, for instance, appeal to public opinion, publication of correspondence, censure by parliamentary vote, demand for arbitration with the odium attendant on a refusal to arbitrate, rupture of relations, reprisals, etc.[116]

The above extract denotes that the term 'sanction' was held to embrace various modes of pressure which could be applied against an offending State, irrespective of the legal significance of each particular mode. In this connection, it hardly needs to be stated that a distinction exists, for example, between resort to arbitration, and the taking of reprisals. For present purposes, however, what is significant is that the Tribunal included reprisals within the category of non-forcible means of settlement of disputes. This clearly indicates that the right to resort to non-forcible reprisals had been affirmed judicially in 1910.

[111] *Annuaire*, 1934, p. 710.
[112] Ibid, p. 29.
[113] Ibid., p. 5.
[114] *Great Britain* v. *the United States* 1910, *HCR*, p. 141.
[115] Ibid., p. 143, 167, para. 10.
[116] Ibid., p. 167.

I.2. *THE NATIONAL NAVIGATION COMPANY OF EGYPT V. TAVOULARIDIS,* 1927[117]

The plaintiffs requested the Court to seize two Soviet vessels anchored in the port of Alexandria, as security for an action concerning the confiscation of their vessel by Soviet authorities.[118] They submitted that such a seizure would be justified on the following ground: 'that a State which has been injured by the abusive exercise of the sovereign powers of another State may act in a similar way against that State by way of reprisals or retorsion'.[119] The Court did not accede to the plaintiffs' request as, in its opinion, measures of reprisals could only be implemented by the Egyptian Government.[120] The conclusion to be drawn from this case is that non-forcible reprisals may only be performed by the aggrieved State herself.

I.3. *THE NAULILAA CASE,* 1928[121]

In this dispute, Portugal claimed that certain forcible reprisals taken by Germany against her were unjustified. She therefore submitted that Germany should be held responsible for making reparation. The decision of the Tribunal in this case has particular importance for the present work in that it lays down the conditions of resort to reprisals in general. Some of these conditions were alluded to in the following definition of reprisals given by the Tribunal:

Reprisals are an act of taking the law into its own hands (*Selbsthilfehandlung*) by the injured State, an act carried out—after an unfulfilled demand—in response to an act contrary to the law of nations by the offending State. Their effect is to suspend temporarily, in the relations between the two States, the observance of a particular rule of the law of nations. They are limited by the experience of mankind and the rules of good faith, applicable in the relations between States. They would be illegal if an earlier act, contrary to the law of nations, had not furnished the motive.[122]

After an examination of the attendant circumstances of this dispute, the Tribunal held that Germany was responsible. The grounds on which it based its decision were as follows: (*a*) The existence of breach as a necessary condition of legitimate reprisals was not established.[123] (*b*) The reprisals were not 'preceded by a request to remedy the alleged wrong'.[124] Hence, the

---

[117] Decision of the Mixed Court of Alexandria, Case No. 110, 1927, *Annual Digest of Public International Law Cases* (hereinafter cited as *Annual Digest*), vol. 4, 1927–8, p. 173.

[118] Ibid.

[119] Ibid., p. 174, para. 4.

[120] Ibid.

[121] *Reports of International Arbitral Awards* (hereinafter cited as *RIAA*), vol. ii, p. 1013.

[122] Ibid., pp. 1025–6 (trans. from French by author).

[123] *The Naulilaa Case*, No. 360 1928, *Annual Digest*, vol. 4, 1927–8, p. 526, at p. 527, para (*a*).

[124] Ibid., p. 527, para (*b*).

contention by Germany that the Portuguese authorities could not have remained in ignorance of her intention could not be upheld.[125] The reprisals taken were disproportionate to the breach allegedly committed by Portugal. In this respect the Tribunal noted thus:

Reprisals which are altogether out of proportion with the act which prompted them, are excessive and therefore illegal. This is so even if it is not admitted that international law requires that reprisals should be approximately of the same degree as the injury to which they are meant as an answer.[126]

1.4. THE CYSNE CASE, 1930[127]

This arbitral decision arose from a dispute concerning the sinking of the Portuguese vessel, the *Cysne*, by a German submarine as an act of reprisal. The Tribunal reaffirmed that 'an act contrary to international law may be justified, by way of reprisals, if motivated by a like act'.[128] However, in this particular instance it ruled against Germany on the ground that Portugal, being then a neutral State, had committed no wrongful conduct. It was added by the Tribunal that:

Only reprisals taken against the provoking State are permissible. Admittedly, it can happen that legitimate reprisals taken against an offending State may affect the nationals of an innocent State. But that would be an indirect, an unintentional, consequence which, in practice, the injured State will always endeavour to avoid or to limit as far as possible.[129]

Although this decision was concerned with forcible reprisals, it may be regarded as a judicial pronouncement on the legality of reprisals in general. The Tribunal made it clear that reprisals should, in principle, be taken only against the State perpetrating the breach. As regards the legality of reprisals which affect innocent third States, the Tribunal appears to have determined that injury to such States would not vitiate the legality of the measures taken by the aggrieved State against the delinquent State.

1.5. THE RAILWAY TRAFFIC BETWEEN LITHUANIA AND POLAND, 1931[130]

The Council of the League of Nations requested the Permanent Court for an Advisory Opinion on the following question: 'Do the international engage-

---

[125] Ibid.
[126] Ibid., para. (*c*).
[127] *RIAA*, vol. ii, p. 1035.
[128] Ibid., p. 1056.
[129] Ibid., p. 1057.
[130] *Publications of the Permanent Court of International Justice* (hereinafter cited as *PCIJ*), Ser. A/B, no. 39, p. 108.

ments in force oblige Lithuania, in the present circumstances, to open for traffic the Landwarów–Kaisiadorys railway sector?'[131] The Lithuanian representatives declared in Court that their Government would not restore for traffic the Landwarów–Kaisiadorys railway sector, 'as a form of pacific reprisals' against Poland.[132] They further stated that the reprisals would be maintained until a certain territorial dispute between Lithuania and Poland had been settled by judicial procedure.[133]

As regards the question of whether Lithuania was entitled to exercise reprisals, the Court stated that such a question would only arise if Lithuania was shown to be under an obligation to open the aforesaid railway sector for traffic.[134] The Court held that no such obligation existed,[135] and hence the argument concerning the exercise of pacific reprisals had ceased to be of any significance.[136]

Some brief observations on this case are called for. As far as the Lithuanian Government was concerned, resort to non-forcible reprisals was a right recognized under international law. Further, in its opinion such reprisals could be of a negative character, and could be employed during the process of adjudication. Although the Court did not adopt a position on the question of the legality of non-forcible reprisals, it did not rule them out as a means of redress.

J. CONCLUSIONS

From an examination of the pertinent doctrinal views, State practice, and jurisprudence in the period 1800–1945, certain conclusions concerning resort to non-forcible reprisals may be drawn. It must be stated at the outset that the conditions governing the exercise of reprisals were developed when forcible and non-forcible reprisals were regarded as a single category. However, the gradual restriction placed on resort to force, and the establishing of various vehicles for peaceful settlement without compulsion on States to use those vehicles, served to put a premium on non-forcible reprisals.

The salient features and conditions of resort to non-forcible reprisals are as follows:

1. It is recognized by international law that only an aggrieved State has the right to take non-forcible reprisals. The measures involved can be of a positive or a negative character.

2. The reprisals taken must be in response to a breach of an international obligation.

[131] Ibid., p. 111.
[132] Ibid., p. 113.
[133] Ibid., pp. 113–14.
[134] Ibid., p. 114.
[135] Ibid., p. 122.
[136] Ibid., p. 114.

3. Resort to such reprisals must be preceded by a demand for reparation.

4. The preponderant view is that reprisals must be proportionate to the injury suffered. Where the particular circumstances render impossible the application of equivalent measures, the reprisals taken must not be disproportionate to the breach.

5. As concerns the objects of reprisals, only the property of the offending State, her nationals, and their property may be seized.

6. Where individuals are apprehended by way of reprisals, they must be treated in a humane manner.

7. The following categories of individuals are exempt from reprisals: diplomatic envoys, travellers, and those who are temporarily resident in the territory of the offending State.

8. Where the breach entails injury to an individual, he must first exhaust local remedies before the State of his nationality may resort to reprisals on his behalf.

9. Reprisals are precluded in cases where there exists a commitment to peaceful settlement.

10. Policy considerations have been a factor in persuading States to initiate, or refrain from non-forcible reprisals.

3

The Status of Non-forcible Counter-measures in Customary International Law since 1945: A Preliminary Sketch

A. INTRODUCTION

THE conclusions reached in the preceding chapter represent what might be regarded as the standard procedure for resort to non-forcible counter-measures on the basis of customary law as it had evolved by 1945. From those conclusions it is possible to delineate what appear to be the prima-facie conditions of legitimate non-forcible counter-measures. These are: (*a*) existence of breach; (*b*) the making of an unfulfilled demand for redress; and (*c*) observance of the principle of proportionality. The definitive character of these conditions and the particular aspects of their application will be analysed in the ensuing chapters of the present study. While the nuances of these conditions present questions, it will be shown that unequivocal recognition has been accorded in post-war State practice to the right of resort to counter-measures.

B. THE POSITION AFTER 1945

The Charter of the United Nations has prohibited the use of force as a means for the settlement of disputes except in clearly defined cases. Consequently, it is due to this restraint that the concept of non-forcible counter-measures has steadily gained prominence. An examination of the Charter provisions reveals no contradiction between the concept of non-forcible counter-measures and the principles embodied in the Charter. It could even be said that the conditions of the legality of counter-measures as existed prior to 1945 are fully compatible with the Charter. The debates of the San Francisco Conference leave no doubt that the use of the word 'force' in Article 2(4) was not intended to include economic coercion. One should not, however, assume from this that economic reprisals can be taken in violation of the conditions of legality of counter-measures.[1] At the institutional level, the Charter explicitly

---

[1] Cf. *infra* ch. 10.

provides that the Security Council may decide what non-forcible measures are 'to be employed to give effect to its decisions, and it may call upon the Members of the United Nations to apply such measures'.[2]

The period immediately following the adoption of the Charter witnessed several instances where claims were made with respect to the right to adopt non-forcible counter-measures. Regardless of whether the conditions of legality had been complied with in each case, the crucial feature was the very fact of such claims being staked at all. This provides a presumption of continuity of counter-measures as a viable mode of redress. Such an argument may be illustrated by the United States' freezing of assets belonging to China, Romania, Bulgaria, and Hungary. As regards the Chinese assets, following the outbreak of hostilities in Korea, President Truman proclaimed a state of emergency in the United States. He also declared an economic embargo against Communist China, and ordered the freezing of all assets belonging to that country within the jurisdiction of the United States.[3] The justification offered ran thus:

This action has been forced upon us by the intervention of Chinese Communist military forces in Korea [...] In view of the commitment of Chinese resources in this unprovoked aggressive activity, this Government cannot permit the Chinese Communists to have access to [...] assets in the United States, the use of which under present circumstances clearly runs counter to the interests and objectives of the United Nations in the Far Eastern crisis.[4]

As a matter of interpretation, the above passage scarcely reveals any claim for the application of the laws of war; hence the actions taken could only be characterized as an exercise of the right of non-forcible reprisals. Although the evidence itself is not without obscurity, the aforementioned measures were undoubtedly motivated by political animosity on the part of the United States. In view of such factors, it would be inaccurate to ascribe the title of legitimate counter-measures to the steps that had been taken.

In the wake of the freezing of Chinese assets by the United States, China imposed a retaliatory freeze on all American assets including diplomatic, missionary, and commercial properties.[5] These actions could be construed as a recognition on the part of the Chinese Government that the seizure of her assets in the United States constituted a breach justifying its decision to retaliate. However, on the basis of the evidence drawn from the settlement Agreement[6] between the two States, it would appear that China could not

[2] Art. 41 of the UN Charter.
[3] *FRUS*, vol. vi, 1950(vi), pp. 682–3.
[4] *Department of State Bulletin* (hereinafter cited as *DSB*), vol. 23, no. 599, 1950, p. 1004.
[5] *FRUS*, vol. vi, 1950, pp. 270ff.
[6] Agreement Between the Government of the United States of America and the Government of the People's Republic of China Concerning the Settlement of Claims. Text: *International Legal Materials* (hereinafter cited as *ILM*), vol. 18, 1979, pp. 551–2.

have adhered to the principle of proportionality. Accordingly, the course adopted by her could in no sense qualify as legitimate counter-measures.

With respect to the Romanian, Bulgarian, and Hungarian assets, these were originally blocked under Executive Order 8389 of 10 April 1940, during the Second World War. In the Peace Treaties of 15 September 1947,[7] the Governments of Romania, Bulgaria, and Hungary had severally undertaken to pay a certain level of compensation for the war damage suffered by American-owned property in their respective countries. The Treaties further provided that any property which was blocked in accordance with Executive Order 8389 could be utilized to satisfy the American claims.[8] The aforesaid undertakings were never honoured. This state of affairs provoked the American Government into passing an Act which authorized 'vesting and liquidation of Bulgarian, Hungarian, and Rumanian property'.[9] The legislative history of this Act indicates that authorization for 'vesting and liquidation' was based on the provisions of the Peace Treaties as well as on customary law.[10] As concerns the exercise of rights under customary law, a report of the Senate Committee on Foreign Relations offered the following justification:

Because there is at present no other way for American owners to obtain recompense for their losses except against the assets made available in this bill, the administration has decided that the claims of American citizens should be met by utilization of the funds referred to.[11]

In this case, however, there was no apparent violation of the principle of proportionality for the reason that the assets disposed of under the Act amounted to $27,000,000 as against the $100,000,000 or more claimed by the Americans.

The imposition of counter-measures has remained a familiar instrument of redress throughout the post-war period. In addition to the State practice cited above, there had also been repeated instances of resort to non-forcible counter-measures by the United States.[12] Examples of similar claims made by other States during this period include the reaction of France and Great Britain to the appropriation of the Suez Canal.[13]

---

[7] e.g. Art. 23(4)(a), Treaty of Peace with Bulgaria, 1947, 41 *United Nations Treaties Series* (hereinafter cited as *UNTS*), 643; Art. 26(4)(a), Treaty of Peace with Hungary, 1947, ibid., 644; Art. 24(4)(a), Treaty of Peace with Roumania, 1947, 42 *UNTS*, 645.

[8] Art. 25, Treaty of Peace with Bulgaria, 1947, 41 *UNTS*, 643; Art. 29. Treaty of Peace with Hungary, 1947, ibid., 644; Art. 27, Treaty of Peace with Roumania, 1947, 42 *UNTS*, 645.

[9] Public Law No. 25, *Stat.*, vol. 69, 1955, p. 562, at p. 570.

[10] *United States Code, Congressional and Administrative News* (hereinafter cited as *USC*), 84th Congress 1st Sess., vol. 2, *Legislative History*, 1955, p. 2745, at p. 2746.

[11] Ibid., p. 2747.

[12] Against: (1) Yugoslavia, *DSB*, 25 Jan. 1948, p. 118; (2) Egypt, Whiteman, *Digest of International Law*, vol. 12, 1971, p. 320; (3) France, *Digest USPIL*, 1978, p. 768; (4) Iran, *DSB*, vol. 80, 1980, pp. 42–3.

[13] Whiteman, *Digest of International Law*; for a further example see *ICAO Case, International Court of Justice Pleadings* (hereinafter cited as *ICJ Pleadings*), 1973, pp. 3ff.

To examine at this particular juncture the full range of evidence supporting a claim for the legitimacy of counter-measures might anticipate the substance of the remaining chapters. Suffice it to confine our reference to the views of the Netherlands Government on non-forcible reprisals. Thus, in the course of a debate on the subject of the 'Principles of International Law Concerning Friendly Relations and Co-operation among States in Accordance with the Charter' the Dutch representative stated:

I would like to stress, that any State, no matter to what region of the world it belongs, may find itself in a position of suffering damage from illegal acts on the part of another State, and for that reason, would be justified in taking measures of nonviolent reprisals.[14]

He professed scepticism, moreover, about the propriety of abolishing non-forcible reprisals, deeming it unrealistic to expect a wronged State to continue discharge of obligations towards the offending State as though oblivious of the occurrence of breach. Indeed, for him, the mere possibility of abusing non-forcible counter-measures could not in itself constitute a justification for discarding them. Hence, their abolition should be attendant on a substantial improvement in the system of judicial remedies. Meanwhile abuse of resort to counter-measures could be minimized by underlining the conditions of their application. In this connection he stated the following prerequisites of lawful counter-measures:[15]

(1) Such reprisals are admissible solely in cases where the State against which they were directed had committed acts which constituted violations of international law in respect of the State engaging in the reprisals;
(2) They were admissible only if negotiations for the purpose of obtaining reparation had been conducted in vain;
(3) They must be proportionate to the wrong done and to the amount of compulsion necessary to obtain reparation;
(4) [T]he obligations arising from treaties must also be taken into account, especially those establishing international organisations with regard to settlement of disputes.

More recently, the concept of non-forcible counter-measures had been the subject of a careful examination by the International Law Commission which, by unanimous vote, affirmed its validity in contemporary international law.[16] Consequently, the Commission adopted Article 30 concerning counter-measures as a ground precluding wrongfulness in the following terms:

---

[14] *UNGAOR*, 23rd Sess., 6th Com. 1045th mtg., 13 Dec. 1963, p. 3; reprinted in the *Netherlands Yearbook of International Law* (hereinafter cited as *NLYIL*), vol. 1, 1970, p. 171, para. 13.12.
[15] Ibid.
[16] See debates on draft Art. 30 concerning 'Legitimate application of a Sanction', *YILC*, vol. i, 1979, pp. 55–63.

The wrongfulness of an act of a State not in conformity with an obligation of that State towards another State is precluded if the act constitutes a measure legitimate under international law against that other State, in consequence of an internationally wrongful act of that other State.[17]

Although the above provision affirms the essential legality of counter-measures, it nevertheless omits to delineate the legitimate scope of their application. However, the Commission indicated in its report that such questions would be examined in Part Two of the Draft Articles dealing with 'the content, forms and degrees of international responsibility'.[18]

The concept of counter-measures had latterly been reaffirmed by a distinguished Tribunal in the *Case concerning the Air Services Agreement of 27 March 1946*.[19] In the course of examining the legality of the counter-measures that had been taken there, the Tribunal delivered the following opinion:

If a situation arises which, in one State's view, results in the violation of an international obligation by another State, the first State is entitled, within the limits set by the general rules of international law pertaining to the use of armed force, to affirm its rights through counter-measures.[20]

To conclude, it is evident from the material reviewed in this chapter that non-forcible counter-measures have continued to be a viable mode of redress even after the adoption of the Charter of the United Nations.

[17] Ibid., vol. ii, part 2, 1979, p. 115.
[18] Ibid., p. 121; see Riphagen, *Fifth Report on the Content, Forms, and Degrees of State Responsibility*, Doc. A/CN.4/380, 4 Apr. 1984, Riphagen; *Sixth Report*, A/CN.4/389, 2 Apr. 1985.
[19] *ILR*, vol. 54, 1979, pp. 304ff.
[20] Ibid., p. 337, para. 81.

4

Prior Breach as a Condition of the Legality of Non-forcible Counter-measures

A. THE PURPOSE

THE role of breach as a condition of the legality of non-forcible counter-measures might at first sight appear so obvious as to barely merit any examination. In fact, the issues involved call for careful study and the subject has generated some interesting debates. This chapter begins with an explanatory note on the correlation between breach and State responsibility. Then follows a consideration of the relation between the purposes of legitimate counter-measures and the occurrence of breach. The need for such an enquiry arises from the continuing absence of clearly defined rules for the emerging doctrine of legitimate counter-measures. It will be shown that the different motives for taking counter-measures will give rise to different questions for State responsibility.

Section D of this chapter will dwell on the subject of prior breach as a condition of counter-measures. This will entail a study of contemporary State practice, jurisprudence, and doctrine. An important issue which will be faced in section E concerns the legality of anticipatory non-forcible counter-measures. Finally, after some observations on the question of identifying the injured party, issues pertaining to the standard of proof necessary to establish breach will be reviewed.

B. THE CORRELATION BETWEEN BREACH AND STATE RESPONSIBILITY

There is a definite correlation between breach and responsibility. Thus, conduct which results in breach of an international obligation will give rise to responsibility, regardless of whether the obligation in question is based on custom or treaty.[1] However, different forms of obligation have different bases

---

[1] See *The Wimbledon Case*, PCIJ, Ser. A., no. 1, 1923, p. 11, at pp. 30 and 33; *The Spanish Zone of Morocco Claims*, 1925, RIAA, vol. ii, p. 615, at p. 641; *The Chorzow Factory (Indemnity) case*, PCIJ, Ser. A., no. 17, 1928, p. 3, at p. 29; League of Nations, *Bases for Discussion*, vol. v, 1929, p. 20; Art. 36(2)(d) of the Statute of the ICJ; *The Reparation for Injuries Case, ICJ Reports*, 1949, p. 174, at p. 184; *The Corfu Channel Case, ICJ Reports*, 1949, p. 4, at p. 23; Art. I of the

for determining the precise conditions under which breach may be said to have occurred in each case. This is because international obligations have varying structures as to the manner in which such obligations are to be implemented. Therefore, it may be useful to resort to the distinction between 'obligations of result' and 'obligations of conduct' with a view to determining whether a particular obligation has been breached.[2] Once the occurrence of breach has been established responsibility will attach to it, and the offending State must then make reparation.

It should not, however, be assumed that reparation is the sole remedy for internationally wrongful conduct. An aggrieved State has a right to apply counter-measures to a State perpetrating wrongful conduct. Pertinently, Judge Ago remarked:

[A]lthough international jurisprudence and State practice undoubtedly justify the conclusion that in general international law an internationally wrongful act imposes on the offending State an obligation to make reparation, it would be reading too much into this jurisprudence and State practice to try to draw the further conclusion that the creation of such an obligation is necessarily the only consequence which general international law attaches to an internationally wrongful act.[3]

Thus, it should evoke no surprise that Professor Riphagen drafted Article 9(1) of Part Two of the Draft Articles on State responsibility as follows:

[T]he injured State is entitled, by way of reprisals, to suspend the performance of its other obligations towards the State which has committed the internationally wrongful act.[4]

International Law Commission's Draft Articles on State Responsibility, *YILC*, vol. ii, 1973, p. 173. But see Brownlie's criticism of the latter Article, Brownlie, *System of The Law of Nations, State Responsibility*, Part I, 1983 (hereinafter cited as Brownlie, 1983), pp. 26 and 29–30; see also Art. 17 which explicitly states that 'An act of a State which constitutes a breach of an international obligation is an internationally wrongful act regardless of the origin, whether customary, conventional or other, of that obligation.' Adopted in the Commission's Report to the General Assembly on its 28th Sess., Doc. A/31/10, 3 May–23 July 1976, *YILC*, vol. ii, part 2, 1976, p. 1, at p. 79.

[2] See Arts. 20 and 21 on 'obligations of conduct' and 'obligations of result', and Commentaries thereto adopted in the Commission's *Report to the General Assembly on the twenty-ninth session*, 9 May–29 July 1977, Doc. A/32/10, p. 1, at pp. 11–30; cf. *infra*, ch. 7.

[3] Ago, *Second Report on State Responsibility*, Doc. A/CN. 4/233, 20 Apr. 1970, *YILC*, vol. ii, p. 177, at p. 181 n. 17; see also Ago, *Fifth Report on State Responsibility*, Doc. A/CN. 4/29 and Add. 1–2, 22 Mar., 14 Apr., and 4 May 1976, *YILC*, vol. ii, part 1, 1976, p. 3, at pp. 27–8, paras. 82–7; Brownlie, 1983, pp. 33–4.

[4] Riphagen, *Sixth Report on (1) The Content, Forms and Degrees of State Responsibility, and (2) The 'Implementation' (Mise en Œuvre) of International Responsibility and the Settlement of Disputes*, Doc. A/CN. 4/389, 2 Apr. 1985, p. 19; see also Art. 8, ibid., p. 18.

C. A CONSIDERATION OF THE PURPOSES OF COUNTER-MEASURES

C.I. INTRODUCTION

As has been noted, the term non-forcible counter-measure *as such* embraces a range of actions which an aggrieved State may take in retaliation for objectionable behaviour on the part of another State.[5] According to this, it may involve the imposition of retortive measures such as the introduction of stringent entry visa requirements. However, a retaliatory measure which assumes that form will not constitute breach of international law, and consequently will not fall within the ambit of this enquiry. By contrast, the category of counter-measures addressed here entails resort to conduct which is internationally wrongful but for its justification as a legitimate counter-measure. It may, for example, take the form of a violation of a commercial treaty.

As mentioned, the renunciation of the right to use force as a means of redress has not been superseded by an obligatory judicial system. As a corollary to this, a heavy premium has been put on non-forcible counter-measures as means of redress.[6] Probably it will not be an exaggeration to suggest that the fear of resort to non-forcible counter-measures is the main factor which prompts States to perform their international obligations voluntarily. Foreign Ministries know of this only too well, as was recently evidenced by the events leading to the severance of diplomatic relations between Libya and the United Kingdom.[7]

The right to resort to counter-measures is built on a paradox: States are permitted as a form of redress to take measures that are in themselves a threat to order. It is due to this that an aggrieved State is entitled to invoke counter-measures as a justification for retaliatory measures taken against another State which has committed a breach of international law previously. This rule is defensible in view of the fact that remedies for breaches of international law are still not highly organized. However, the deficiency in the system of remedies is not the sole factor which induces States to resort to counter-measures. It is a well-known fact that States are generally reluctant to appear as parties to international litigation due to the belief that such litigation is expensive and time-consuming. Furthermore, they put scant trust in third parties, particularly where embarrassing reaction is likely to occur on the domestic front.[8] As a matter of observation, however, counter-measures are usually motivated by self-protection, reciprocity, or the desire to

---

[5] Cf. *supra*, Introduction s. D.

[6] Cf. *supra*, ch. 2 s. A.

[7] See 'Major World Events', *Keesing's Contemporary Archives* (hereinafter cited as *KCA*), vol. 30, Apr. 1984; cf. *infra*, ch. 7 s. C.5.3.

[8] Compare the attitude of the United States in the *Case Concerning United States Diplomatic and Consular Staff in Tehran, ICJ Pleadings*, 1982, pp. 1 ff., with her attitude in the *Case Concerning the Military and Paramilitary Activities in and against Nicaragua, ICJ Reports*, 1986, p. 14; see United States Department of State letter and statement concerning termination of

induce expeditious settlement of the dispute in question. It should be emphasized that these motivations are by no means exhaustive or mutually exclusive. A brief descriptive account may now be given about each of them. The legal significance of the differences between the various motivations will be particularly highlighted in the chapter dealing with proportionality.[9]

C.2. SELF-PROTECTION

There are some situations in which a State is entitled to resort to counter-measures on grounds of self-protection. This may be explained by several examples. First, the case in which the character of the violated obligation does not allow for a reciprocal treatment.[10] Secondly, the application of reciprocity may not produce a realistic solution to the problem. Thirdly, it should be noted that counter-measures are not confined to cases of dire emergency but also extend to wrongful acts lasting over a period of time. Thus, with regard to the latter category, the aggrieved party could resort to counter-measures in order to achieve redress for the wrong suffered, as well as to compel the offending party to observe the law. Finally, the State perpetrating the breach may refuse to admit responsibility, or to comply with third party settlement. In all such circumstances, an aggrieved State would be justified in taking counter-measures on the basis of self-protection. This motivation, as we shall see, allows for a wide scope of action.[11]

Where the incentives for taking counter-measures are self-protection and inducement to settle a dispute, it is tenable that the former incentive will predominate and hence the rules appertaining to it will apply to the case in question. Similar reasoning would, *mutatis mutandis*, govern situations in which self-protection together with reciprocity are the pertinent motives.

C.3. RECIPROCITY

The motive of reciprocity may be invoked by an aggrieved State as a justification for taking counter-measures particularly, though not exclusively, within a treaty context. This proposition is based on the notion that the existence of a quid pro quo relationship is a prerequisite of resort to reciprocal counter-measures.[12] Accordingly, as a matter of proportionality, where reciprocity seems to be the exclusive motive behind counter-measures, the prin-

acceptance of the ICJ compulsory jurisdiction, 7 Oct. 1985, texts: *ILM*, vol. 24, 1985, pp. 1742–5.

[9] Cf. *infra*, ch. 6 s. C.2.
[10] e.g. violations of *jus cogens*, cf. *infra*, ch. 7 s. B.2.
[11] Cf. *infra*, ch. 6 s. C.2.2.
[12] See Art. 8 and Commentary thereto, Riphagen, *Sixth Report on (1) The Content, Forms and Degrees of State Responsibility, and (2) The 'Implementation' (Mise en Œuvre) of International Responsibility and the Settlement of Disputes*, Doc. A/CN. 4/389, 2 Apr. 1985, p. 18, para. 4.

ciple of 'an eye for an eye' should be applied. On the other hand, where that motive is allied to a wish to induce settlement, the aggrieved State may exert pressure beyond what is strictly reciprocal. In such a situation, therefore, despite the resulting tilt in the balance between the counter-measure taken and the precipitating breach, the principle of proportionality will not have been violated.

C.4. PRESSURE TO INDUCE EXPEDITIOUS SETTLEMENT OF DISPUTES

Where the purpose of counter-measures is to induce an expeditious settlement an aggrieved State may, with justification, take counter-measures to nudge a recalcitrant State towards accepting a procedure of third party settlement. The measures involved in such a case should go beyond reciprocity so as to bring enough pressure to bear on the defaulting State to induce her to reach a peaceful solution. Albeit, measures adopted to this end, being essentially of a provisional character, must terminate as soon as there is an acceptance of an amicable procedure.[13] When the stimuli of self-protection and inducement are harnessed together, the former would usurp any function that the latter may serve.

C.5. COUNTER-MEASURES AS REVENGE

Sometimes States take retaliatory steps in the absence of any legitimate grievance, but purely as a means of expressing revenge for some extraneous conduct. It is submitted that such steps cannot be regarded as lawful counter-measures since they are not based on any legally acceptable motivation.[14] If this exclusion is not made, the way would be open for States to use counter-measures as a cloak to justify actions that are contrary to international legal policy. In short, counter-measures must always be grounded on some legitimate motivation.

C.6. THE RELEVANCE OF AN EXISTING PROCEDURE FOR PEACEFUL SETTLEMENT

The significance of the availability of a peaceful settlement procedure on the legality of counter-measures will receive comprehensive treatment in another chapter.[15] For the moment the general rule may be stated to the effect that: where the purpose is to induce settlement, then the machinery must be given the chance to function. Notwithstanding this proposition, where either self-

---

[13] Cf. *infra*, ch. 6 s. C.2.4; see also Zoller, p. 51.
[14] See Zoller, p. 62.
[15] Cf. *infra*, ch. 9.

protection or reciprocity is the paramount motive, counter-measures may be resorted to under certain circumstances.[16]

D. PRIOR BREACH AS A PREDICATE TO COUNTER-MEASURES

International law holds that counter-measures may only be applied by an aggrieved State in response to breach which has in fact been consummated.[17] This assertion is widely supported by State practice, doctrine, and juris-prudence. Thus it will be recalled that when the Principles of Friendly Relations were being debated in the Sixth Committee of the General Assembly, the representative of the Netherlands, Jonkheer Van Panhuys, asserted the legitimacy of counter-measures.[18] Among the conditions instanced by him for the exercise of this right was that '[s]uch reprisals were admissible solely in cases where the State against which they were directed had committed acts which constituted violation of international law in respect of the State engaging in the reprisals.'[19] Although these remarks are safe from contradiction, unfortunately they overlook any underlying relationship between breach and the purposes of counter-measures.

When a dispute concerning the Shatt-al-Arab arose between Iraq and Iran in 1969,[20] the latter denounced a boundary treaty between the two countries,[21] on the ground that it had been persistently violated by the former. Iraq described this abrogation of the treaty as a contravention of the principles of international law, and in apparent retaliation expelled about 10,000 Iran-ians from her territory.[22] In this illustration each opposing party had cited the other's breach as ground for its own action.

In the *Air Services Award*, France argued that her disapproval of Pan American's plan for a change of gauge in the territory of a third State 'did not run counter to the 1946 Agreement,[23] and hence could not justify reprisals'.[24] In fact, she claimed that only the flouting of an arbitral decision could justify resort to counter-measures.[25] The United States Government replied that '[w]hile disregard of the judgment of an arbitral tribunal would certainly be one type of conduct justifying the application of sanctions, it is not the only one'.[26] It may be inferred from these remarks that there are

---

[16] Ibid., ss. E.3 and E.4.

[17] In order to avoid repetition, the question of characterizing a particular conduct as a breach of international obligation of 'result' or of 'conduct' will be pursued in ch. 7 ss. F.2 and F.3.

[18] *NLYIL*, vol. i, 1970, p. 171, para. 13.12; see *supra*, ch. 3 s. B.

[19] *UNGAOR*, 23rd Sess., 6th Com., 1095th mtg., 13 Dec. 1968, p. 3, para. 9.

[20] *KCA*, 1969, p. 23544.

[21] Treaty concluded between Iraq and Iran on 4 July 1937, 190 *LNTS*, 4423.

[22] *KCA*, 1969, p. 23544.

[23] Text: 139 *UNTS*, 1879.

[24] *ILR*, vol. 54, 1979, p. 319, para. 17.

[25] French Memorial, *Digest USPIL*, 1978, p. 771.

[26] Ibid.

several types of breach which could justify recourse to counter-measures. In fact, the United States emphasized that the particular conduct itself displayed by France constituted the breach which led her to take 'steps toward a limited withdrawal of certain rights of the French carrier corresponding to the rights denied the U.S. carriers'.[27]

The decision of the International Court of Justice in the *Hostages Case* lends support to the view that a prior violation is a prerequisite of resort to lawful counter-measures. The following remarks made by the Court may pertinently be cited here: '[The measures taken by the United States] were measures taken in response to what the United States believed to be grave and manifest violations of international law by Iran.'[28] The inference to be drawn from these remarks is that the counter-measures would not have been justifiable in the absence of the wrongful conduct which provoked them.

The Resolution adopted by the Institut de Droit International in 1934,[29] concerning the conditions of lawful reprisals, implicitly recognized that prior breach was to be considered as one of such conditions. Support for this assumption is to be found in the fact that Article 6(1) stipulates that the State taking the reprisals must first ask the State responsible for the *illicit act* to desist from it. Moreover, paragraph (2) of that Article provides that there should be proportionality between the reprisals and the *act denounced as illicit*.

The predominant opinion among writers holds that reprisals constitute legitimate response to *internationally wrongful conduct*. Professor Oppenheim, for example, writing in 1905 stated as follows:

Reprisal is the term applied to such injurious and otherwise internationally illegal acts of one State against another as are exceptionally permitted for the purpose of compelling the latter to consent to a satisfactory settlement of a difference created *by its own international delinquency*.[30]

He added that reprisals may be resorted to in 'all the cases of an international delinquency [...] be it non-compliance with treaty obligations [...] or any other internationally illegal act'.[31] For Colbert, peacetime retaliations feature as measures to extract from the delinquent State 'a recognition of the illegality

---

[27] Ibid., p. 772.

[28] *ICJ Reports*, 1980, p. 28, para. 53.

[29] For the text see *supra*, ch. 2 s. H.

[30] Oppenheim, vol. ii, 1906, p. 34, emphasis added; see also Kelsen, *Principles of International Law*, 1952, pp. 23–5; Cheng, *General Principles of Law as Applied by International Courts and Tribunals*, 1953 (hereinafter cited as Cheng, 1953), p. 97; Fenwick, *International Law*, 4th edn., 1965, pp. 636–7; Akehurst, *A Modern Introduction to International Law*, 5th edn., 1984, p. 6; Green, *International Law of Peace*, 2nd edn., 1982, p. 218.

[31] Oppenheim, vol. ii, 1906, p. 35; see also Hall, 8th edn. by Higgins, 1924, p. 433; Hyde, *International Law Chiefly as Interpreted and Applied by the United States*, vol. ii, 2nd edn., 1947 (hereinafter cited as Hyde), pp. 1658–9; Waldock, 'The Regulation of the Use of Force by Individual States in International Law', *Recueil des Cours de l'Académie de Droit International de la Haye* (hereinafter cited as *R.d.C.*), vol. 81(2), 1952, p. 455, at pp. 458–9.

of its actions through the compensation of those injured and the cessation by the State concerned of its objectionable policies'.[32] Professor Jiménez de Aréchaga stated that reprisals are measures taken exceptionally 'when one state violates the right of another state'.[33]

Mrs Damrosch, who was Deputy Agent for the United States in the Arbitration concerning the *Air Services Agreement Dispute* with France, used the Award as the basis of a case study for analysing the relationship between counter-measures and procedures for peaceful settlement. Of interest for the present purposes is her questioning of the long-held assumption that only an underlying breach could justify resort to counter-measures.[34] She explained:

It seems preferable to adopt a ruling allowing a State to implement counter-measures without risk of later liability when it acts upon a good faith belief that it is the victim of a breach, even though that belief later turns out to be erroneous in the light of the result of the arbitration.[35]

Damrosch indicated that she based the above opinion, first, on the repeated references made by the Tribunal to the 'alleged' violation; and, secondly, on the views expressed by the French arbitrator to the effect that the United States possessed the right to apply the counter-measures notwithstanding that France had not violated the terms of the Agreement.

The present writer finds the above views respecting bona fide belief in the occurrence of breach to be highly controversial. This is because the rules governing State responsibility allow no scope for the plea of mistake which is recognized in the municipal law of some States. That said, it is proposed to examine the views expressed by the Tribunal in order to ascertain whether the conclusions reached by Damrosch were in fact justified.

As regards the use of the adjective 'alleged' to qualify the word breach, this could imply that counter-measures may be resorted to with impunity on the basis of a bona fide, though erroneous, belief respecting the occurrence of breach. However, such an interpretation is unrealistic in view of the fact that the French word *allégué* means 'referred to'.[36] It is submitted, therefore, that the significance attached by Damrosch to the word 'alleged' is much greater than the evidence could bear. However, it is certain that the Tribunal held that the legality of the measures taken by the United States could be determined 'regardless of the answer to the question of substance concerning the alleged violation of the 1946 Agreement by the French Government'.[37] These remarks seem to imply that counter-measures would be lawful regard-

---

[32] Colbert, *Retaliation in International Law*, 1948, pp. 1–2.

[33] Jiménez de Aréchaga, 'International Responsibility', *Manual of Public International Law*, ed. Sørensen, 1968 (hereinafter cited as Sørensen, 1968, p. 753).

[34] Damrosch, 'Retaliation or Arbitration or Both? The 1978 United States–France Aviation Dispute', *AJIL*, vol. 74, 1980, p. 785, at p. 793.

[35] Ibid., p. 795.

[36] For a similar view see Zoller, pp. 95–6.

[37] *ILR*, vol. 54, p. 336, para. 74.

less of whether the breach provoking them was subsequently established or not.

The present writer argues that serious objection must be raised here since there was no justification for overriding the conditions of resort to reprisals set by the Tribunal in the *Naulilaa Case*. It will be recalled that the Tribunal stated there that 'the first requirement—the *sine qua non*—of the right to take reprisals is a motive furnished by an earlier act contrary to the law of nations'.[38] It is submitted that if the condition of prior breach has not been complied with the likely effect of that would be to cause a rapid escalation of the dispute.

It is noteworthy that Professor Wengler has criticized the decision of the Tribunal in the *Air Services Award* on the point concerning good faith. He states:

If this would mean that a government which believes in good faith, but objectively, without reason, that there has been a violation of an international obligation by another State, is entitled not to perform one of its own obligations under international law, that would be absolutely wrong.[39]

He reiterated further by saying that reprisals 'are allowed only against activities of other people who are objectively violators of international law. Reprisals resorted to in error, and even in excusable error, are not lawful.'[40]

The present writer is inclined to suggest that a half-way compromise may be countenanced as a solution to the dogmatic complexities arising from a mistaken but bona fide belief. To borrow the phrase employed by the European commission of Human Rights in the *Belgian Linguistics Case*,[41] the allegedly aggrieved State should be allowed 'a margin of discretion' when assessing the extent of the counter-measures required by the exigencies of the situation. This would mean that the State in question should enjoy a 'margin of appreciation' in assessing breach as a precipitating factor. Thus, when a Government weighs the extent of counter-measures dictated by an immediate crisis, a reasonable discretion should not be denied.

Attention may now turn to the views expressed by the International Law Commission on the question of prior breach as a condition of lawful resort to counter-measures. The Commission emphasized that counter-measures could only be justified by 'an internationally wrongful act committed previously'.[42] It reiterated further that '[o]nly where conduct of this nature is a reaction to an international offence by another party can it have the effect

---

[38] *RIAA*, vol. ii, p. 1027.

[39] Wengler, 'Public International Law. Paradoxes of a Legal Order', *R.d.C.*, vol. 158(5), 1977, p. 16, at p. 20.

[40] Ibid.

[41] 1968, *ILR*, vol. 45, 1972, p. 136, at p. 172, para. 6.

[42] Commentary on Art. 30 concerning legitimate counter-measures, *YILC*, vol. ii, part 2, 1979, p. 115, para. 2.

of nullifying its otherwise undeniably wrongful character'.[43] Moreover, the Commission cited with approval the principle set by the Tribunal in the *Naulilaa Award* that lawful reprisals had to be preceded by breach.[44]

At a different level, the Commission stated that

[...] there is a whole series of internationally wrongful acts which, under international law, do not justify resort—or at any rate, immediate resort—to punitive measures or enforcement, but merely create the right to demand reparation for injuries. What is more, the conditions governing the various forms of reaction permissible under international law are not necessarily the same in all cases.[45]

An important question of principle is raised in the above passage, namely, that not every internationally wrongful conduct justifies immediate resort to counter-measures. Thus, for example, where the wrongfulness of conduct is precluded by state of necessity, *force majeure*, fortuitous event, or distress, resort to counter-measures will not be justified so long as the particular precluding circumstance prevails.[46] However, once the grounds for invoking such a circumstance have disappeared, the aggrieved party may resort to counter-measures in the absence of redress being made. From a different angle, where the breach affects a self-contained regime,[47] or an obligation of a fundamental character, the aggrieved party's liberty to resort to counter-measures will be severely restricted. In this respect it is worth citing, in part, Article 2 of Part Two of the Draft Articles adopted provisionally by the Commission in its Thirty-fifth Session:

[T]he provisions of this Part govern the legal consequences of any internationally wrongful act of a State, except where and to the extent that those legal consequences have been determined by other rules of international law relating specifically to the internationally wrongful act in question.[48]

E. THE GRAVITY OF BREACH

The purpose of this section is to ascertain whether counter-measures may be taken in response to minor breaches. It may be stated at the outset that neither the text of Draft Article 30 concerning legitimate counter-measures nor its *travaux préparatoires* make any distinction between minor and serious

---

[43] Ibid., p. 116, para. 3.

[44] Ibid., p. 117, para. 7.

[45] Ibid., p. 121, para. 22.

[46] For list of circumstances precluding wrongfulness see ch. 5 of the Draft Articles on State Responsibility: *Report of the Commission on the work of its thirty-first Session*, 14 May–3 Aug. 1979, *UNGAOR*, 34th Sess., suppl. 10(A/34/10), pp. 284–369; *Report of the Commission on the work of its thirty-second session*, 5 May–25 July 1980, *UNGAOR*, 35th Sess., suppl. 10(A/35/10), pp. 69–131.

[47] e.g. the special regime governing the breach of diplomatic immunities, cf. *infra*, ch. 7 s. C.5.

[48] *Report of the Commission on the work of its thirty-fifth session*, 22 May–22 July 1983, *UNGAOR*, 38th Sess., suppl. 10(A/38/10), p. 91.

breaches. Similarly, the six Reports so far submitted by the Special Rapporteur for Parts Two and Three of the Draft Articles do not exclude the possibility of minor breaches justifying resort to counter-measures.[49]

If one examines the views expressed by the parties in the *Air Services Agreement Dispute*, France is found to argue that 'reprisals may be resorted to only in case of necessity, i.e. in the absence of other legal channels to settle the dispute'.[50] It may be deduced from this view that resort to counter-measures is dependent on the element of necessity irrespective of whether the breach was material or not. However, when France viewed the problem from the perspective of the law of treaties, she stated that the breach should be material.[51] It is arguable that this limitation is confined to treaty violations only and is subject to the element of necessity.

Although the United States accused France of a material breach, she asserted that her reaction was justified 'under the theory of reprisals and the law of treaties, for both require a prior breach of an international obligation'.[52] This implies that in the view of the United States counter-measures could be taken regardless of the seriousness of the breach. The fact that she accused France of a *material* breach had no bearing on her right to take counter-measures as such.

Finally, it is submitted that subject to compliance with the conditions of legality and in the absence of collateral constraints, minor breaches could be responded to by proportionate counter-measures. Although the occurrence of breach *as such* is a prerequisite of counter-measures, it is probably the seriousness of the breach in question which persuades an aggrieved State to resort to counter-measures.

F. THE RIGHT TO TAKE ANTICIPATORY NON-FORCIBLE COUNTER-MEASURES

This question has received no treatment in the literature, in marked contrast to the voluminous attention devoted to the anticipatory use of force. It was, however, alluded to by the International Law Commission in its commentary on Draft Article 30 concerning counter-measures as follows: 'The circumstances precluding wrongfulness with which this article is concerned is thus one of those "counter-measures" which international law regards as legitimate following an internationally wrongful act *committed previously*.'[53] It is beyond doubt that these remarks rule out anticipatory counter-measures from the scope of Article 30.

Similarly, the question was taken up indirectly in the *United States–France*

---

[49] For citations see *infra*, ch. 6 n. 35.
[50] *ILR*, vol. 54, 1979, p. 319, para. 17.
[51] Ibid., pp. 319–20, para. 17.
[52] Ibid., p. 320, para. 18.
[53] *YILC*, vol. ii, part 2, 1979, p. 115, para. 2, emphasis added.

Air Services Agreement Dispute. The Tribunal declared that where one State interpreted a particular action by another State as a breach of an international obligation, she could resort to counter-measures within the limits pertaining to the use of force.[54] There is little room for dispute that the Tribunal had recognized the right to resort to counter-measures but only *after* the occurrence of breach.[55]

As regards the Tribunal's reference to the parallel application of the rules governing the use of force to counter-measures, Article 51 of the United Nations Charter confines the use of force in self-defence to situations in which an armed attack has already taken place. The preponderant view of publicists, to which the present writer subscribes, considers Article 51 as having removed from States the right to take anticipatory self-defence.[56]

There is a body of opinion, however, which holds that this Article neither circumscribes the use of force in dangerous situations, nor prejudices the right to take anticipatory self-defence under customary law.[57] Professor Bowett, an advocate of the latter interpretation of that Article, might have attached undue significance to a statement emanating from such a subsidiary source as the United Nations Atomic Energy Commission. In its 1946 first report this Commission stated:

In consideration of the problem of violation of the terms of the treaty or convention, it should also be borne in mind that a *violation* might be so grave a character as to give rise to the inherent right of self-defence recognised in Art. 51.[58]

Bowett deduced from the above passage that 'it cannot be supposed that a treaty violation falls within the definition of an armed attack, so that the Commission clearly understood Art. 51 as permitting "anticipatory" self-defence'.[59] One notes in passing that both Bowett[60] and Brownlie[61] objected to the inference drawn by Waldock that in the *Corfu Channel Case*[62] the Court had recognized the right of anticipatory self-defence in the event of 'a strong probability of armed attack—an imminent threat of

---

[54] *ILR*, vol. 54, 1979, p. 337, para. 81.

[55] For a discussion of the controversial view which holds that counter-measures are permissible as long as there is a bona fide belief in the existence of a prior breach, see *infra* s. D.

[56] Brownlie, 1963, p. 278. This view has recently been affirmed judicially by the ICJ in the *Nicaragua Case* where it was held that the exercise of the right of self-defence 'is subject to the State concerned having been the victim of an armed attack'. *ICJ Reports*, 1986, p. 14, at p. 103, para. 195.

[57] Wright, 'The Strengthening of International Law', *R.d.C.*, vol. 98(3), 1959, p. 5, at p. 167; Stone, *Legal Controls of International Conflict*, 1959, p. 244; Waldock, 'The Regulation of the Use of Force by Individual States', 1952, pp. 498–9; Fawcett, 'Intervention in International Law', *R.d.C.*, vol. 103(2), 1961, p. 347, at pp. 361–3.

[58] UN Doc. AEC/18/Rev. I, p. 24, emphasis added.

[59] Bowett, *Self-Defence in International Law*, 1958, p. 189.

[60] Ibid., p. 190.

[61] Brownlie, 1963, p. 277.

[62] *ICJ Reports*, 1949, p. 4.

armed attack'.[63] However, in spite of any apparent differences with regard to the occurrence of a prior breach in cases involving the use of force, Waldock took an unambiguous stand as concerns non-forcible reprisals. Thus, he stated explicitly that their legality 'would depend on whether there had been any international delinquency on the part of the other State and on the other principles in the Naulilaa Case'.[64] In short, it may be stated that the occurrence of breach, which is a condition for the use of force, is likewise a condition of legitimate non-forcible counter-measures.

The conditions undergirding legitimate counter-measures may be ascertained by scrutinizing State practice pertinent to non-forcible reprisals, thus avoiding exclusive recourse to the mirror image of the use of force. As has already been pointed out,[65] it was not always consistently possible to distinguish between forcible and non-forcible reprisals; yet, in several of the instances which bore a non-forcible character, breach had in each case clearly preceded the reprisals.

Such clarity concerning the occurrence of breach prior to counter-measures was evident in the steps taken by the United States against Iran in the hostages crisis. President Carter, as will be recalled, announced that he was freezing Iranian assets due to 'an unusual and extraordinary threat to the national security, foreign policy, and economy of the United States'.[66] The Statement accompanying the Presidential Order proclaimed that the assets were frozen as a 'response to reports that the Government of Iran is about to withdraw its funds'. The Statement added that the measure would 'ensure that claims on Iran by the United States and its citizens are provided for in an orderly manner'.[67] For one reason or another, the American Government had never categorized the freeze order as a legitimate counter-measure in response to the seizure of the hostages. In contrast, the Presidential Order prohibiting certain transactions with Iran was explicitly tied with the detention of the hostages.[68] However, there can be little doubt that breach had occurred before the assets were frozen. In fact, as has been mentioned,[69] the International Court seemed to have accepted that position in the *Hostages Case*.[70]

From a slightly different angle, the United Kingdom had justified the freeze of Argentinian assets by the belief that action detrimental to her own economy

---

[63] Waldock, 'The Regulation of the Use of Force by Individual States', p. 500.

[64] Ibid., p. 494.

[65] Cf. *supra*, chs. 1 and 2.

[66] Executive Order No. 12170, of 14 Nov. 1979, 44 *Federal Register* (hereinafter cited as *Fed. Reg.*), 65729, 1979; *DSB*, Dec. 1979, p. 50.

[67] *DSB*, Dec. 1979, p. 50.

[68] Executive Order No. 12205 of 7 Apr. 1980, 45 *Fed. Reg.*, 24099–100, 1980; *DSB*, May 1980, pp. 1–2.

[69] See *supra*, s. D.

[70] *ICJ Reports*, 1980, p. 28, para. 53.

was being or was 'likely to be taken' by the Government of the Argentine.[71] Despite the impression given here of anticipatory counter-measures, the British Prime Minister stated explicitly that the assets were frozen 'in connection with the operation to recover the Falkland Islands'.[72]

A more recent instance which could be cited here concerns the freezing by the United States of all Libyan Government assets in United States banks and their overseas branches. President Reagan indicated that this measure was taken 'to help assure the orderly management of the dissolution of the United States economic ties with Libya and to protect against the possibility of unlawful Libyan actions which adversely affect American interests'.[73] It is submitted that the attitude adopted by the United States in this case can in no way be reconciled with her attitude in the freezing of the Iranian assets. This view is based on the fact that the freezing of the Libyan assets was not in response to an actual breach that had been committed by Libya. Thus, since the sanction imposed by the United States in this instance appears to be of an anticipatory character, it cannot be regarded as a lawful counter-measure.

G. THE QUESTION OF IDENTIFYING THE INJURED PARTY

G.1. THE PURPOSE

The right of any State to take counter-measures depends to a large extent on whether the State in question could be looked upon as an aggrieved party. Thus, for example, Utopia may take counter-measures against Ruritania where the latter has violated a treaty between the two States. However, situations may sometimes arise in which the aggrieved party cannot be readily identified. The purpose of this section is to determine the legal position where a State suffers injury to interests which she has through another State, or injury to interests derived from a treaty. Attention will also be given to the question of whether a breach of universally recognized rules of international law entitles any State to take counter-measures as an aggrieved party.

G.2. WRONGFUL CONDUCT WHICH INJURES TWO OR MORE STATES SEPARATELY

There are two categories of injury which call for distinction: (*a*) injury to an interest which two or more States have in common; and (*b*) injury to interests

---

[71] Statutory Instrument, No. 512, *Statutory Instruments*, (hereinafter cited as *Stat. Inst.*), part i s. 2, 1982, p. 1296.

[72] Hansard, *HC Debs.*, vol. 29, cols. 258–9, 25 Oct. 1982.

[73] Letter of 9 Jan. 1986, to the speaker of the House of Representatives and the President of the Senate, *ILM*, vol. 25, 1986, p. 181, at p. 182. For the text of Executive Order No. 12544 which authorized the blocking of Libyan assets see ibid., p. 181.

which a State has 'through' another State. The former embraces instances in which international law recognizes parallel rights of protection such as relate to persons working in international organizations,[74] or cases where concurrent claims are made on behalf of persons having dual nationality.[75] In such situations the State of the effective nationality of the individuals concerned will be deemed to have a direct interest which, in the absence of other constraints, entitles her to impose counter-measures to redress injury suffered by such individuals.

Relevant to this discussion, Professor Riphagen stated: 'if a particular coastal State denies a vessel of a particular flag State innocent passage through its territorial sea this is an internationally wrongful act which creates a new legal relationship as between that coastal and that flag State only'.[76] In other words, although the interests of other States may be affected by this infringement, such States will not be regarded as injured States since the freedom of navigation is currently a right peculiar to the flag State only.[77]

As regards the second category of injury, the principle involved appears to have underlain the Court's decision in the *Barcelona Traction Case*. The Court rejected the Belgian Government's claim on behalf of her nationals who were holding 88 per cent of the shares in a Canadian Company. This was because the nationality of the Company was Canadian. None the less, the Court did not rule out the possibility that the secondary right of the national State of the shareholders could come 'into existence at the time when the original right ceases to exist'.[78] The conclusion to be drawn is that until such a time when a secondary right clearly crystallizes, the State claiming violation of such a right cannot be categorized as an aggrieved party.

G.3. BREACH OF A SPECIAL INTEREST RECOGNIZED IN A MULTILATERAL TREATY

A multilateral treaty may embody a special interest provision which confers certain rights on some or all the contracting parties.[79] As a specific example it may be recalled that the various instruments establishing mandate contained two distinct obligations: 'conduct provisions' relating to the carrying out of the mandates as mandates, and 'special interest provisions' conferring

---

[74] *The Reparation for Injuries Case, ICJ Reports*, 1949, p. 185; *The Barcelona Traction Case* (Judgment), *ICJ Reports*, 1970, p. 3, at p. 50, para. 98.

[75] *Nottebohm Case* (Judgment), *ICJ Reports*, 1955, p. 4.

[76] Riphagen, *Fourth Report on the Content, Forms and Degrees of Responsibility* (Part 2 of the Draft Articles), Doc. A/CN. 4/366/Add. I, 15 Apr. 1983, p. 12, para. 33.

[77] Cf. *infra*, ch. 7 s. C.4.2.

[78] *Barcelona Traction Case* (Judgment), *ICJ Reports*, 1970, p. 3, at p. 49, para. 96.

[79] See Art. 60(2)(*b*) of the Vienna Convention on the Law of Treaties; *infra*, ch. 8 s. C.4.2; Art. 5(*d*)(i), Riphagen, *Sixth Report on (1) The Content, Forms and Degrees of State Responsibility, and (2) the 'Implementation' (Mise en Œuvre) of International Responsibility and the Settlement of Disputes* (Parts 2 and 3 of the Draft Articles), Doc. A/CN. 4/389, 2 Apr. 1985, p. 6.

certain rights relative to the mandated territory directly upon members of the League as individual States. In the *South West Africa Cases* (Judgement),[80] the Court ruled that Ethiopia and Liberia, which were previously held to have *locus standi*,[81] were not entitled to insist that South Africa should carry out obligations arising from 'conduct provisions' of the mandate. It was here that the Court distinguished between the consequences of breach respectively of 'conduct provisions' and 'special provisions'.[82] Thus, apparently only in the latter case could a party to an instrument establishing a mandate claim the right of unilateral action. If an analogy is made with the category of counter-measures, the position would appear to be as follows: where a multilateral treaty embodies a special interest provision in favour of a particular party, the latter may claim to be an aggrieved party where the tenor of that provision is violated. In such a situation it would have the right to take counter-measures against the defaulting party.

G.4. BREACH OF A RIGHT ARISING FROM A TREATY PROVISION FOR A THIRD STATE

As a general rule a treaty can impose neither obligations nor rights for a third State without her consent.[83] However, a right can properly arise from a treaty in favour of a third State. In such a case any violation of that right will constitute an infringement of the rights of the third State concerned.[84]

A recent illustration of the point under review is Article 24(1)(*b*) of the United Nations Convention on the Law of the Sea. It lays down that a coastal State shall not 'discriminate in form or in fact against the ships of any State or against ships carrying cargoes to, from or on behalf of any State'. According to this provision, if a coastal State unlawfully denies innocent passage to a ship carrying cargo belonging to a third State, then the interests of both the flag State and the third State are affected. It is submitted that in a case covered by that provision, the third State which owns the cargo may, in her own right, take counter-measures against the coastal State. It must,

---

[80] *ICJ Reports*, 1966, pp. 4ff.

[81] *South West Africa Cases*, Preliminary Objections, *ICJ Reports*, 1962, p. 319.

[82] *ICJ Reports*, 1966, pp. 28–9, para. 33, p. 46, para. 86, p. 61, para. 99; this distinction was reaffirmed in the *Namibia Case*, ibid., 1971, p. 16, at p. 49, paras. 102–3; see also Riphagen, *Preliminary Report on the Content, Forms and Degrees of State Responsibility* (Part 2 of the Draft Articles), A/CN. 4/330, 1 Apr. 1980, p. 17, para. 41.

[83] See *Island of Palmas Case*, 1928, *RIAA*, vol. ii, p. 831, at pp. 842 and 870; *Free Zones of Upper Savoy and the District of Gex Case*, *PCIJ*, ser. A/B, no. 46, 1932, p. 96, at p. 141; *Clipperton Island Case 1931*, *RIAA*, vol. ii, p. 1105; Commentary on Draft Articles 30–2 on the Law of Treaties, *YILC*, vol. ii, 1966, p. 177, at pp. 226–9; Arts. 34–8 of the Vienna Convention on the Law of Treaties.

[84] See Article 5(*a*), Riphagen, *Sixth Report on (1) the Content, Forms and Degrees of State Responsibility, and (2) the 'Implementation' (Mise en Œuvre) of International Responsibility and the Settlement of Disputes* (Parts 2 and 3 of the Draft Articles), Doc. A/CN. 4/389, 2 Apr. 1985, p. 6, and commentary on p. 7, para. 4.

however, be emphasized that such measures should not be of a reciprocal character as might impede the right of innocent passage.[85]

To conclude, a third State which resorts to counter-measures on the basis of a right arising from a treaty provision must be able to establish that that provision in fact assigns to her those interests which she is seeking to protect by counter-measures.

G.5. BREACH OF UNIVERSALLY RECOGNIZED RULES OF INTERNATIONAL LAW

There is a long line of doctrinal opinion which maintains that third States may respond to serious breaches of international law pertaining to matters of great importance.[86] Pertinent to this, the British Government argued before the International Court that Albania's refusal to pay the damages which had been awarded against her in the *Corfu Channel Case*[87] entitled all States 'to take all such reasonable and legitimate steps as may be open to them to prevent such an occurrence, and either individually or by common action to do what they can to ensure that judgments [...] are duly implemented and carried out'.[88] These remarks are a clear assertion of the right of third States to take reprisals. Although, for want of jurisdiction as to the merits of the case, the Court had not expressed an opinion on the validity of that assertion, its contents have nevertheless been approved by a number of publicists.[89]

In 1970 the International Court distinguished between a State's obligations towards the international community as a whole, and her duties with respect to diplomatic protection. In its view the importance of the former lies in the fact that they constitute obligations *erga omnes*; hence all States are deemed to have 'a legal interest in their protection'.[90] The inference to be drawn from this view as far as counter-measures are concerned is that where such measures are imposed by an aggrieved State in response to a breach of an *erga omnes* obligation all other States have a right to support such measures.[91]

With parallel intent, Article 19(2) of the Draft Articles on State responsibility provides that the breach of an international obligation so essential

---

[85] Cf. *infra*, ch. 7 ss. C.4.2. and C.4.4.

[86] See Grotius, Book II, ch. 20 s. xl, pp. 504–6; Vattel, Book II, ch. 5 s. 70, p. 160; Stowell, *Intervention in International Law*, 1921, pp. 46–7; Hall, 8th edn. by Higgins, 1924, pp. 65–6; Oppenheim, vol. i, 8th edn. by Lauterpacht, 1955, p. 308; Akehurst, 'Reprisals by Third States', *BYIL*, vol. 44, 1970, p. 1, at p. 18; Schachter, 'International Law in Theory and Practice: General Course in Public International Law', *R.d.C.*, vol. 176(5), 1985, p. 167, at p. 183; *contra:* Root, 'The Outlook for International Law', *Proceedings of American Society of International Law*, 1915, p. 2, at pp. 8–9; Jessup, *A Modern Law of Nations*, 1948, pp. 10–12.

[87] *ICJ Reports*, 1949, p. 4, at p. 36.

[88] *Case of the Monetary Gold Removed from Rome in 1943, ICJ Pleadings*, 1954, p. 8, at p. 126.

[89] e.g. Jenks, *The Prospects of International Adjudication*, 1964, pp. 703–6; Rosenne, *The International Court of Justice*, 1957, pp. 97–102.

[90] *Barcelona Traction Case* (Judgement), *ICJ Reports*, 1970, p. 3, at p. 32, para. 33.

[91] Cf. *infra*, ch. 7 s. C.7.2.

for the protection of fundamental interests of the international community constitutes an international crime. Some examples of such international crimes are listed in Article 19(3). It is evident from this Article that not only the State directly affected by the international crime committed, but all States may be taken to have an interest in remedying the harm caused.

Draft Article 5(*c*) of Parts Two and Three of the Draft Articles submitted by Professor Riphagen provides that '[i]f the internationally wrongful act constitutes an international crime, all other States [are regarded as injured States]'.[92] Furthermore, Article 14(1) of his Report stipulates that '[a]n international crime entails all the legal consequences of an internationally wrongful act and, in addition, such rights and obligations as are determined by the applicable rules accepted by the international community as a whole'.[93] The text of these two paragraphs can mean that any *state* will be entitled to take unilateral counter-measures against the perpetrator of an international crime. The illusion is removed, however, by the Commentary on Article 14 which reserves that right for regional or international organizations.[94]

To conclude, the long doctrinal view which advocates the right of any State to retaliate against an international crime has no support in State practice. None the less, the *erga omnes* principle may be applied to widen the category of 'an aggrieved party' so as to include all States where the violated obligation has an *erga omnes* character. Accordingly, all States, including those which have not been injured directly, will be deemed to have the right to impose counter-measures against the perpetrator of the breach. That said, it needs, however, to be recognized that measures taken in such circumstances might exceed the limits of proportionality. It follows, therefore, that difficulties would arise when the legality of such measures is being considered.

H. THE QUESTION OF THE STANDARD OF PROOF PERTAINING TO ISSUES OF FACT AND RELEVANT LEGAL PRINCIPLES

H.I. GENERAL CONSIDERATIONS

There is no hard and fast rule governing the standard of proof in international litigation.[95] The State which bears the burden of proof must, in order to

---

[92] Riphagen, *Sixth Report on (1) The Content, Forms and Degrees of State Responsibility, and (2) the 'Implementation' (Mise en Œuvre) of International Responsibility and the Settlement of Disputes*, Doc. A/CN. 4/389, 2 Apr. 1985, p. 6; see commentary on para. (*c*), p. 12, para. 25.

[93] Ibid., p. 24.

[94] Ibid., p. 26, paras. 9–10.

[95] See Sandifer, *Evidence before International Tribunals*, rev. edn., 1975, pp. 15–16 s. 4; Lauterpacht, 'The So-called Anglo-American and Continental Schools of Thought in International Law', *BYIL*, vol. 12, 1931, p. 31, at pp. 41–2; Aufricht, 'Extrinsic Evidence in International Law', *Cornell Law Quarterly*, vol. 35, 1949–50, p. 327, at pp. 335 and 348; Art. 21(1) of the ILC Model Draft on Arbitral Procedure, which provides that '[t]he tribunal shall be the judge of the admissibility and the weight of the evidence presented to it', *YILC*, vol. 2, 1958, p. 14; Evensen,

succeed, adduce evidence of fact which outweighs that offered by her opponent. With respect to the jurisprudence of the International Court, Rosenne observed that

The Court's function in establishing the facts consists in its assessing the weight of the evidence produced in so far as is necessary for the determination of the concrete issue which it finds to be the one on which it has to be decided. For this reason there is little to be found in the way of rules of evidence.[96]

So far from there being any set standard of proof in international jurisprudence, the required evidence may indeed vary in degrees of cogency according to the circumstances of each case. Hence, with regard to the nationality of the claimant where proof of a particular fact presented an exceptional hardship, the Tribunal was content to accept prima-facie evidence in the absence of a rebutting evidence.[97] Similarly, with reference to the exclusive control exercised by Albania over her territory, the International Court stated in the *Corfu Channel Case* that '[b]y reason of this exclusive control, the other State, the victim of a breach of international law, is often unable to furnish direct proof of facts giving rise to responsibility. Such a State should be allowed a more liberal recourse to inferences of fact and circumstantial evidence.'[98] The Court made it clear that such indirect evidence 'must be regarded as of a special weight when it is based on a series of facts linked together and leading logically to a single conclusion'.[99] *A fortiori*, where a series of facts could point to two different conclusions, then the circumstantial evidence would stand as inadequate. In another part of the judgment the Court stated succinctly that the 'proof may be drawn from inferences of fact, provided that they leave *no room* for reasonable doubt'.[100]

On the other hand, there are cases in which international tribunals have insisted on a high standard of proof as a prerequisite for sustaining claims that involved grave allegations. Thus, for example, where bad faith had been imputed, a higher degree of persuasion was required. In the words of the arbitrator in the *Tacna-Arica Arbitration*:

Undoubtedly, the required proof may be supplied by circumstantial evidence, but the *onus probandi* of such a charge should not be lighter where the honour of a Nation is involved than in a case where the reputation of a private individual is concerned.

'Evidence before International Courts', *Nordisk Tidsskrift For International Ret Og Ius Gentium: Acta Scandinavica Juris Gentium*, vol. 25, 1955, p. 44, at pp. 45–6.

[96] Rosenne, *The Law and Practice of the International Court*, vol. ii, 1965, p. 580.

[97] *The Lynch Case*, decision of the British–Mexican Claims Commission, 1929, *RIAA*, vol. ii, p. 17, at p. 19, paras. 3 and 4; see Cheng, 1953, p. 324.

[98] *ICJ Reports*, 1949, p. 18.

[99] Ibid.

[100] Ibid.; see also Diss. Op. Judge Badawi Pasha, ibid., pp. 59–60; Diss. Op. Judge Azevedo, ibid., pp. 90–1.

A finding of the existence of bad faith should be supported not by disputable inferences but by clear and convincing evidence which compels such a conclusion.[101]

In the *Corfu Channel Case* the Court rejected hearsay evidence of the assertion that minefields had been laid by Yugoslavian ships with the connivance of the Albanian Government, 'as allegations falling short of conclusive evidence'.[102] The Court added: 'A charge of such exceptional gravity against a State would require a degree of certainty that has not been reached.'[103]

A high standard of proof is similarly called for where a State is accused of carrying out her international obligation negligently. The British–Mexican Commission rejected, for lack of sufficient proof, affidavits declaring the amount of loss suffered by each claimant involved. In the words of the Commission:

[T]he Mexican Government, in the absence of clear evidence, cannot be obliged to pay more to each claimant than the amount representing the value of such objects as may be *safely* supposed to constitute the average portable property of young, unmarried men of the social class for which the Hostels of the Y.M.C.A. are particularly destined.[104]

In a like manner, the occurrence of unlawful acts in the territory of a particular State does not *per se* render that State liable if she is unaware of it. In this connection the International Court stated in reference to the laying of minefields in Albanian territory that

it cannot be concluded from the mere fact of the control exercised by a State over its territory and waters that that State necessarily knew, or ought to have known, the authors. This fact, by itself and apart from other circumstances, neither involves *prima facie* responsibility nor shifts the burden of proof.[105]

H.2. THE STANDARD OF PROOF AND THE INVOCATION OF COUNTER-MEASURES AS A DEFENCE

When the legality of a particular counter-measure is put in issue before a tribunal, the standard of proof becomes germane to the question of determining issues of fact and relevant legal principles. For instance, in order to establish proportionality, issues of fact pertaining to breach will have to be weighed against the actions taken by way of counter-measures. In order to

---

[101] 1925, *RIAA*, vol. ii, p. 921, at p. 930; see also dissenting opinion of Mexico's Commissioner in the *Mexico City Bombardment Claims, James Kelly Claim*, 1930, ibid., vol. v., p. 76, at p. 89, para. ii.

[102] *ICJ Reports*, 1949, p. 4, at p. 17.

[103] Ibid.

[104] *The Claims of Messrs Baker, Webb, Woodfin, and Poxon*, 1930, *RIAA*, vol. v, p. 77, at p. 81, para. 7.

[105] *The Corfu Channel Case* (Merits), *ICJ Reports*, 1949, p. 4, at p. 18.

achieve this, consideration must be given to the pertinent legal criteria proposed for determining proportionality.[106]

With respect to the standard of proof in ordinary international litigation, it has been demonstrated that tribunals allow scope for varying degrees of cogency.[107] The question which remains to be answered is whether the same flexibility applies to proceedings in which a contending party asserts that the breach which had been committed by its opponent provided a justification for its own wrongdoing. For one reason or another this issue has not hitherto been treated in the literature. However, the invocation of counter-measures as a category of justification presents a paradoxical situation because of the necessity for establishing the breach which is allegedly committed by the other party. This paradox inevitably has a direct bearing on the standard of proof which is required for establishing the breach in question. To begin with, a Respondent State does not usually bear a persuasive burden of proof except where she makes a particular claim. In the latter case she will be required to afford proof with such cogency as befits the question at issue. Accordingly, if that State invokes *lawful counter-measures* as a defence, she will bear the burden of establishing the breach committed by the Applicant State. In some cases this may prove to be a difficult task. To ease this difficulty, different degrees of cogency of evidence should be permitted. Thus, an allegation of breach involving a serious accusation such as inhibition of the movement of persons will require a higher standard of proof than, for example, an allegation of a relatively minor wrongful conduct.

I. CONCLUSIONS

In the light of the foregoing analysis the following may be offered as conclusions:

1. The right to take counter-measures, as distinct from the right merely to seek reparation, is recognized as a legitimate response to the occurrence of breach of international obligations.

2. There are three legally acceptable purposes for taking counter-measures, namely self-protection, reciprocity, and inducement towards a speedy settlement of disputes.

3. There is a legal significance underlying the distinction between each purpose. In the case of self-protection a wide range of action is permissible, whereas in the case of reciprocity that notion itself necessarily restricts the scope of the action to be taken. As to the case in which the motive is inducement to settle, the action taken can go beyond the limits of reciprocity. Where the motives are mixed, then the counter-measures should be based as far as possible on the motive which offers the widest scope for action.

[106] Cf. *infra*, ch. 6 s. C. 2
[107] See *supra*, s. H.1.

4. Whether a particular conduct constitutes a breach which justifies resort to counter-measures is a question to be decided on the basis of the content of obligations breached, and also by considering whether that conduct can be justified on other grounds.

5. Preclusion of wrongfulness of conduct on the basis of counter-measures is restricted to actions taken only against the State perpetrating the breach.

6. State responsibility would arise in respect of counter-measures where the existence of a prior breach could not be established.

7. Where counter-measures are motivated by a bona fide belief, albeit not subsequently substantiated, a margin of appreciation should be allowed within the context of State responsibility.

8. Counter-measures may be taken only by an injured party. In particular cases, however, a State can resort to counter-measures where her rights which are derived through other States, or through a treaty, have been violated. Furthermore, in cases of breach of *erga omnes* obligations, all States can assume the right to take counter-measures.

9. Anticipatory non-forcible counter-measures are unlawful since by definition they precede actual occurrence of breach.

10. Where a State invokes the right to take *lawful counter-measures* against another State, it will be incumbent on her to establish the breach committed by that other State with such a degree of cogency as is commensurate with the seriousness of the allegation.

5

Prior Demand for Redress as a Condition of Lawful Counter-measures

A. THE PURPOSE

THE preceding chapter was concerned with the establishment of breach as a prerequisite of counter-measures. This chapter will deal with the question of submitting prior demand as a condition of resort to counter-measures in the face of wrongful conduct. The conclusions that will be reached are based on analyses of doctrine (including the views of the International Law Commission), jurisprudence, and State practice, as pertain to the issue under review. For purposes of comparison, the procedure stipulated in Article 65 of the Vienna Convention on the Law of Treaties will be examined in section E of this chapter.

B. DOCTRINE

B.I. THE LITERATURE

The striking feature to be observed in doctrinal views concerning 'prior demand' as a condition of the legality of counter-measures is that none of them reflects an analytical approach. Such views as have been expressed are limited for the most part to a mere recognition of the existence of the concept. For example, the Institute of International Law prescribed in Article 6(1) of its resolution of 1934 that the State perpetrating the breach should first be given the opportunity to terminate the breach and offer reparation.[1] This approach is also adopted by Oppenheim, who conceded the admissibility of reprisals when 'the injured State cannot get reparation through negotiation or other amicable means'.[2] In another passage he reiterated that '[i]f the delinquent State refuses reparation for the wrong done, the wronged State can, consistently with any existing obligation of pacific settlement, exercise such means as are necessary to enforce adequate reparation'.[3] Although the above illustrations establish no specific acceptance of the necessity of prior

---

[1] *Annuaire*, 1934, p. 710.
[2] Oppenheim, vol. ii, 7th edn. by Lauterpacht, 1952, p. 136.
[3] vol i, 8th edn., 1955, p. 354; see also Cheng, 1953, p. 99; Gould, *An Introduction to International Law*, 1956, p. 590; Schwarzenberger and Brown, *A Manual of International Law*, 6th edn., 1976, p. 150; Green, *International Law*, 1982, p. 218.

demand as a condition of lawful reprisals, they implicitly indicate that such a demand would be required.

For an explicit comment on the question at issue, reference may be made to the views expressed by Skubiszewski. He stated: 'In order to be lawful, recourse may be had to reprisals only after a demand for redress has been made, followed by a failure to comply with the demand.'[4] A recent affirmation of this position is to be found in Articles 9 and 10 of the draft Convention prepared by Grafrath and Steiniger on 'Kodifikation der völkerrechtlichen Verantwortlichkeit'.[5] These provisions require a prior notification (*Ankündigung*) to the State perpetrating the breach of the intention to take counter-measures. In similar vein, the American Law Institute's Restatement provides that resort to counter-measures is justified only 'when the accused state wholly [...] rejects or ignores requests to terminate the violation or pay compensation'.[6] Further support to this position is given by Schachter who states: 'Although authority on the point is sparse, it is reasonable to consider that prior notification of a reprisal should be a condition of the legality of the reprisal.'[7] Zoller, on the other hand, argues that resort to counter-measures is 'free of any procedural conditions'.[8] None the less, she accepts that in the case of counter-measures not based on reciprocity, the duty to negotiate requires that such steps should be preceded by some form of request.[9]

B.2. THE VIEWS OF THE INTERNATIONAL LAW COMMISSION

Although Draft Article 30, concerning legitimate counter-measures,[10] contains no specific reference to 'prior demand' as a condition of legality, the Commission's acceptance of the necessity of such a demand can be gleaned from a study of the various statements that are on record. In the course of a debate held by the Commission on that draft Article, Mr Yankov stated that for a counter-measure to be legitimate 'a prior claim must have been made for reparation. Moreover the concept of a 'prior claim' should be taken to signify that the application procedure has been exhausted, particularly in the case of coercive action'.[11]

---

[4] Skubiszewski, 'Use of Force by States. Collective Security. Law of War and Neutrality', Sørensen, 1968, p. 753.

[5] See *Neue Justiz: Zeitschrift für Recht und Rechtswissenshaft*, (Berlin), No. 8, 1973 (hereinafter cited as *Neue Justiz*), p. 227; at p. 228.

[6] American Law Institute, *Restatement of the Law: Foreign Relations Law of the United States (Revised)* Tentative Draft 5, 1984, s. 905, p. 204, at p. 206, para *c*.

[7] Schachter, 'International Law in Theory and Practice: General Course in Public International Law', *R.d.C.*, vol. 178(5), 1982, p. 167, at p. 170.

[8] Zoller, p. 119.

[9] Ibid.

[10] For text see *YILC*, vol. II, part 2, 1979, p. 115.

[11] Ibid., vol. i, 1979, pp. 57–8, para 31.

Speaking in the same debate, Mr Francis concurred that in order to be able to take counter-measures in accordance with Article 30 the aggrieved party 'would be required to make a prior demand for reparation'.[12] These views were reflected in the Commission's Commentary on draft Article 30. Thus it was pointed out that even where a counter-measure was not in principle precluded, international law required an aggrieved State 'not to resort to such actions until it had first sought adequate reparation'.[13] The Commission also noted that in situations where international law permitted only the right to seek reparation, the aggrieved State should not take counter-measures unless reparation was unduly denied. To employ such measures without first exhausting all means to secure reparation would, in the opinion of the Commission, amount to unlawful conduct.[14]

Furthermore, the Commission accepted that if the necessary conditions were fulfilled 'there is nothing to prevent a State which has suffered an internationally wrongful act from reacting against the State which committed the act by a measure consisting of unarmed reprisals'.[15] It then listed four conditions in a footnote; two of which are as follows:

[T]hat the offence to which the reprisals are intended to be a response must not be such as to entail any consequence other than to give rise to the right of the injured party to obtain reparation; and that, if such is the case, the injured party must have made a prior attempt to obtain reparation.[16]

The inference drawn by Zoller from the above-mentioned two conditions is that, whereas measures equivalent to the breach committed are 'not subject to prior request',[17] measures which go beyond equivalence are 'subject to that condition'.[18] With respect, the present writer interprets the Commission's remarks somewhat differently. In his view, by using the phrase 'must not be such as to entail any consequence other than to give rise to the right of the injured party to obtain reparation', the Commission intended to distinguish merely between delictual and criminal responsibility.[19] Thus, where counter-measures relate exclusively to the delictual responsibility of a given State, there will always be a need for such measures to be preceded by a request for redress.

With regard to the views evidenced in Part Two of the Draft Articles, the Special Rapporteur conceded in his Fourth Report that a prior demand for

---

[12] Ibid., p. 60, para 7.
[13] Ibid., vol. ii, part 2, 1979, p. 116, para 4.
[14] Ibid., p. 121, para 22.
[15] Ibid., p. 118, para 11.
[16] Ibid., p. 118 n. 595.
[17] Zoller, p. 126.
[18] Ibid.
[19] On the distinction between delictual and criminal responsibility see Brownlie, 1983, p. 32.

reparation was one of the requirements for the admissibility of reprisals.[20] Such a stance was also maintained by him in his Sixth Report. Thus, he proposed the following condition:

[I]f a State, considering itself to be an 'injured State', wishes to invoke Article 8 ('reciprocity') or Article 9 ('reprisals') as a justification for the suspension of the *performance* of its obligations, it should notify the (alleged) author State of its reasons for doing so.[21]

It is noteworthy that Mr Ushakov stated in the course of a debate on Draft Articles 4 and 5 that '[c]ounter-measures could be taken as soon as an internationally wrongful act had been committed and in advance of any request for *restitutio in integrum* or for reparation.'[22]

C. JURISPRUDENCE

C.1. *THE NAULILAA CASE*, 1928

As has been noted,[23] the Tribunal in the *Naulilaa Case* stated that '[r]eprisals are illegal if they are not preceded by a request to remedy the alleged wrong'.[24] It may also be recalled that the Tribunal considered the relationship between indirect methods of communicating an intention to take reprisals and the legality of the retaliatory measures involved. It ruled that reliance on the possibility of the target State being indirectly informed of such an intention did not in itself constitute an acceptable mode of seeking redress. Significantly, although the International Law Commission took no cognizance of the aforesaid relationship, it approved, in the context of non-forcible counter-measures, the principle of prior demand as featured in the *Naulilaa Award*.[25]

C.2. *THE UNITED STATES–FRANCE AIR SERVICES AWARD*, 1978[26]

The Tribunal examined several different aspects of the legal intricacies involved in this dispute but, surprisingly, made no explicit reference to the question of whether prior demand is a prerequisite of lawful counter-measures. It nevertheless indicated that resort to counter-measures should be subject to the limits prescribed by international law on the use of armed

[20] Riphagen, '*Fourth Report on the Content, Forms and Degrees of State Responsibility*', (Part 2 of the Draft Articles), Doc. A/CN.4/366/Add. 1, 15 Apr. 1983, p. 21, para 57.
[21] Riphagen, *Sixth Report on (1) the Content, Forms and Degrees of State Responsibility, and (2) the 'Implementation' (Mise en œuvre) of International Responsibility and the Settlement of Disputes* (Parts 2 and 3 of the Draft Articles), Doc. A/CN.4/389, 2 Apr. 1985.
[22] Ushakov, *YILC*, vol. i, 1981, p. 213, para 15.
[23] Cf. *supra*, ch. 2, s. 1.3.
[24] *Annual Digest*, vol. 4, 1927–8, p. 526, at p. 527.
[25] *YILC*, 1979, vol. ii, part 2, p. 117, para 7.
[26] *ILR*, vol. 54, 1979, p. 304.

force.[27] Following this assertion, the question needs to be asked as to whether prior demand is viewed as a prerequisite of the use of force. According to customary international law the answer appears to be in the affirmative. It has already been emphasized that the conditions governing the right of resort to forcible and non-forcible reprisals were basically the same. Thus, although forcible reprisals have been outlawed, the same conditions of legality that hitherto existed will continue to apply with equal validity to non-forcible reprisals. The relevance of these conditions as criteria for determining the legality of economic reprisals has been emphasized in the writings of Professor Bowett. He explicitly states that such reprisals must comply with the traditional conditions governing recourse to armed reprisals. In his view, one of these conditions is that 'redress by other means must be either exhausted or unavailable'.[28]

On a different, though no less relevant line, the Tribunal asserted that it was impossible 'in the present state of international relations, to lay down a rule prohibiting the use of counter-measures during negotiations'.[29] These remarks beg the question as to whether the making of prior demand is a prerequisite of lawful counter-measures. It would seem to the present writer that the fact of commencing negotiations implies that unfulfilled demand has already been made. Were that not the case, international relations would inevitably be brought to a standstill as a consequence of denying States the opportunity to redeem themselves.

C.3. *CASE CONCERNING UNITED STATES DIPLOMATIC AND CONSULAR STAFF IN TEHRAN*, 1980[30]

The Court took due note of the various counter-measures that had been instituted by the United States against Iran during the hostage crisis.[31] Although the legality of these measures was not in issue, the Court expressed itself in terms that would leave room for an interpretation that such measures were lawful.[32] Such an indication was undoubtedly guided by what the Court described as '[t]he total inaction of the Iranian authorities [...] in the face of urgent and repeated requests for help'.[33] These requests, together with the nature of the Iranian attitude, were recounted in detail as follows:

---

[27] Ibid., p. 337, para. 81.
[28] Bowett, 'Economic Coercion and Reprisals by States', *Virginia Journal of International Law*, vol. 13, (1) 1972, p. 1, at p. 10; also by the same author, 'The Legality of Economic Coercion', *Virginia Journal of International Law*, vol. 16 (2), 1976, p. 245, at p. 252.
[29] *ILR*, 1979, p. 390, para 91.
[30] *ICJ Reports*, 1980, p. 3.
[31] Ibid., pp. 16–17, paras, 30–31.
[32] Ibid., pp. 27–8, para 53.
[33] Ibid., p. 31, para. 64.

The occupation of the United States Embassy by militants on 4 November 1979 and the detention of its personnel as hostages was an event of a kind to provoke an immediate protest from any government, as it did from the United States Government, which despatched a special emissary to Iran to deliver a formal protest. Although the special emissary was denied all contact with Iranian officials, never entered Iran, the Iranian Government was left in no doubt as to the reaction of the United States to the taking over of its Embassy and the detention of its diplomatic and consular staff as hostages. Indeed, the Court was informed that the United States was meanwhile making its views known to the Iranian Government through its Chargé d'Affaires, who was kept since 4 November 1979 in the Iranian Foreign Ministry itself [...] In any event, by a letter of 9 November 1979, the United States brought the situation in regard to its Embassy before the Security Council. The Iranian Government did not take part in the debates on the matter in the Council, and it was still refusing to enter into any discussions on the subject when, on 29 November 1979, the United States filed the present Application submitting its claim to the Court.[34]

A notable aspect of the above passage is the allusion made to what may be categorized as a concept of 'constructive demand'. This is evident from the fact of the acceptance by the Court that Iran was deemed to be fully aware of the United States' demands, notwithstanding that these demands had never been formally communicated to Iran. The deduction to be drawn here is that the condition of a prior demand will be considered as being fulfilled where appropriate alternative means of intimation have been utilized.

D. SOME INSTANCES OF STATE PRACTICE

D.1. THE DEMANDS MADE BY THE UNITED STATES IN 1946, FOR THE RELEASE OF AMERICAN PLANES, THEIR CREW, AND PASSENGERS FROM YUGOSLAVIA, AND THE DEMANDS MADE BY YUGOSLAVIA IN 1948, FOR THE RELEASE OF HER GOLD AND DOLLAR RESERVES FROM THE UNITED STATES[35]

Following the shooting down by Yugoslavia of two American aircraft, the United States delivered a protest Note to Yugoslavia detailing the injuries suffered by herself and her nationals as a result of the incident, and seeking satisfaction.[36] A second Note, referred to in the media as the strongest Note issued from Washington since Pearl Harbor, was presented to the Yugoslav Government on 21 August 1946.[37] It demanded the release of the passengers and crew of the first aircraft to be shot down, and permission for United States personnel to investigate the loss of the second.[38] A warning was added

[34] Ibid., p. 25, para 47.
[35] *FRUS*, vol. vi, 1946, pp. 920 ff.; *DSB*, vol. 15, no. 374, 1 Sept. 1946, p. 415; ibid., 25 Jan. 1948, pp. 117–19.
[36] *FRUS*, vol. vi, 1946, p. 921.
[37] *KCA*, 1946–8, p. 8086.
[38] *DSB*, vol. 15, no. 374, 1 Sept. 1946, p. 417.

that if these demands were not complied with within forty-eight hours 'the United States Government will determine its course in the light of the evidence then secured and the efforts of the Yugoslav Government to right the wrong done'.[39] Yugoslavia duly acceded to both demands, and made reparation for injuries sustained by the United States nationals. In addition she made several offers in 1947 to compensate for, *inter alia*, the loss of the two aircraft, but all these were rejected by the United States.[40]

It is against this background that one must view the refusal by the United States in 1948 to release to Yugoslavia her gold and dollar reserves which had been deposited in the Federal Reserve Bank.[41] Among the various reasons that were stated for this refusal one in particular is pertinent here, namely, 'the United States claims compensation for two United States airplanes shot down by Yugoslav forces in August 1946'.[42] The above remarks, if considered in isolation, might denote that the fact of freezing the Yugoslav assets was performed prior to the making of a demand for compensation. But when viewed in conjunction with the initial demand made by the United States in 1946, the remarks would then appear to be a reiteration of that same demand.

The decision by the United States to block the Yugoslav assets from which she was expecting to be compensated, raises the question of compatibility between the necessity of prior demand and the competence to make the required compensation. It is submitted that if a State demands reparation, and then blocks the very funds from which reparation is to be effected, that State cannot be said to have made a valid prior demand.

D.2. BRITISH, FRENCH, AND AMERICAN FINANCIAL MEASURES AGAINST EGYPT FOLLOWING THE EGYPTIAN NATIONALIZATION OF THE SUEZ CANAL, 1956[43]

D.2.1. The reaction of the British Government[44]

On 26 July 1956 President Nasser of Egypt announced the nationalization of the Suez Canal. The reaction of the British Government, like that of the French Government, was immediate. Sir Anthony Eden, the British Prime Minister at the time, condemned the Egyptian measure as a unilateral decision, taken 'without notice and in breach of the Concession Agreements'.[45] Within twenty-four hours of the nationalization the British Government presented a Note to Egypt affirming that 'H.M. Government

---

[39] Ibid., p. 418.
[40] *DSB*, vol. 18, no. 447, 25 Jan. 1948, p. 119.
[41] For text of the Yugoslav Note dated 25 Jan. 1948, see ibid., pp. 118–19.
[42] For the full text of the Note sent by the Secretary of State to the Yugoslav Government see ibid., p. 117.
[43] *RIIA Documents*, 1956, ed. Frankland, 1959, pp. 72–240.
[44] Ibid., p. 73, at pp. 115–17, para 3.
[45] *Hansard, HC Debs.*, vol. 557, 1955–6, col. 777.

reserve all their rights, and those of the U.K. nationals as sanctioned by the agreements'.[46] On 28 July Eden announced that the British Government had imposed restrictions in relation to Egypt's sterling balances and the assets of the Suez Canal Company.[47] Some three days later, the Egyptian Government indirectly replied to the British Note through a circular sent to all diplomatic missions in Cairo, declaring its intention to honour all her international obligations.[48]

Three deductions may be drawn from the above series of events. First, the conduct of the British Government indicates that it recognized the necessity of making a demand as a prerequisite for an apparent counter-measure. Secondly, in presenting a demand, a State is not required to give more than a broad indication of the injury to her interests, nor to disclose the nature of the counter-measure she is contemplating. Thirdly, where a demand for reparation is submitted and it becomes apparent that this demand is not likely to be met, then counter-measures may be immediately imposed.

D.2.2. *The reaction of the French Government*[49]

The French Government announced, on 29 July 1956, financial restrictions against Egypt similar to those imposed by Great Britain. Prior to that action it had been intimated in an official Communiqué to the Egyptian authorities that France would take 'all measures to ensure the protection of French subjects and interests in Egypt'. On 27 July the French Foreign Minister presented to the Egyptian Ambassador in Paris an *aide-mémoire* defining his Government's position. The Ambassador, however, declined to receive that document.[50] Nevertheless, the Minister was able to make a verbal representation of the content of the *aide-mémoire*.

There are four deductions to be made here: (*a*) there is ample evidence that France accepted the making of a demand for redress as a prerequisite of retaliatory action; (*b*) such a demand may be conveyed either in written form, or by verbal communication; (*c*) where the State perpetrating the alleged breach refuses to receive a written demand, yet takes cognizance of a verbal representation of its content, then the inference may reasonably be drawn that that State will not act on it; and (*d*) consequently, the aggrieved State may have immediate recourse to counter-measures.

D.2.3. *The reaction of the United States Government*[51]

The Department of State announced on 27 July 1956 that the nationalization

---

[46] *KCA*, 1956, p. 1500.
[47] *Hansard, HC Debs.*, vol. 557, 1955–6, col. 918.
[48] *KCA*, 1956, p. 1500.
[49] *RIIA, Documents*, 1956, pp. 118–19, para 7; pp. 137–8, para. 13.
[50] See statement by the Egyptian Embassy in Paris, ibid., p. 119, para. 8.
[51] Ibid., pp. 117–18, paras 4, 5, and 6; p. 122, para. 10; *DSB*, vol 35, no. 894, 13 Aug. 1956, pp. 259–63.

of the Suez Canal Company 'affects the nations whose economies depend upon the products which move through this international waterway and the maritime countries as well as the owners of the Company itself'.[52] Further, it was added that the United States was holding urgent consultations with other Governments whose interests were affected by the nationalization. On 31 July the United States Government issued a temporary order freezing all assets of the Egyptian Government and the Suez Canal Company in the United States.[53]

The above facts may now be analysed legally. One must observe at the start that the United States was not a party to the Concession Agreements concerning the Suez Canal. It was perhaps for that reason that she referred to the Egyptian conduct in terms of unlawful economic coercion. Such an approach would be plausible only if passage of American ships through the Canal were threatened. Even if it is accepted that the United States had some basis for retaliating against Egypt, one cannot ignore the fact that she acted without giving prior notice.

D.3. THE VIEWS OF THE PARTIES IN THE *APPEAL RELATING TO THE JURISDICTION OF THE ICAO COUNCIL*, 1972[54]

The action arose out of the hijacking of an Indian aircraft and its subsequent destruction in Lahore airport on 2 February 1971. India accused Pakistan of complicity in that incident, and in retaliation denied her aircraft the right to overfly Indian territory.[55] In a strongly worded protest, India claimed damages for the destruction of her aircraft and for the loss of baggage, cargo, and mail therein.[56] India pleaded in her application that since 'no positive and satisfactory response was made by the Respondent' she had felt obliged on 4 February to suspend forthwith the overflights of Pakistani aircraft.[57] She pleaded further in her Memorial that the right of unilateral denunciation of a treaty by an innocent party existed independently of any provision made in that treaty concerning withdrawal.[58] Pertinent to this, she construed Article 95 of the Convention of Civil Aviation, 1944, as dealing exclusively with withdrawal from that Convention.[59] Pakistan, for her part, stated that the prohibition respecting overflight was imposed by India '[a]lmost simultaneously with the demand for compensation'.[60] Pakistan stated further

---

[52] *RIAA Documents*, 1956, p. 117, para 4; *DSB*, vol. 35, no. 893, 6 Aug. 1956, pp. 221–2.

[53] *KCA*, 1956, p. 1500; this Freeze Order was not reported in *DSB*, vol. 35, 1956, and the last published edition of *FRUS* covers events up to 1954.

[54] *ICJ Pleadings*, 1973, p. 3.

[55] Ibid., p. 7, para, II; cf. ch. 9 s. C.4.2.

[56] *ICJ Pleadings*, 1973, p. 5.

[57] Ibid.

[58] Ibid., p. 43, para. 47.

[59] Ibid., p. 44, para. 50.

[60] *Aide-mémoire* by Pakistan to India, ibid., p. 72, at p. 73, para. 12.

that, instead of attempting to settle this dispute through diplomatic channels, India had sought to pressurize her into submitting to 'unilateral and unreasonable demands for compensation'.[61] As to the relevance of Article 95, Pakistan submitted in her Counter-memorial that since the Article contained the necessary procedure for denunciation, India was obliged to comply with the provisions.[62]

The conclusions to be drawn from the views expressed by the contending parties are as follows: (*a*) Both India and Pakistan appear to have accepted the necessity for prior demand. (*b*) From the point of view of the Indian Government, counter-measures could be applied within two days of making an unfulfilled demand. To Pakistan, on the other hand, such precipitate measures did not allow enough scope for the diplomatic process. Although there is merit in the argument of Pakistan regarding the interval between the making of the demand and the taking of unilateral action, less plausibility attaches to her assertion that prior demand must be followed by a lengthy diplomatic procedure. (*c*) With respect to the application of Article 95, it has been noted that the parties adopted different positions. In order to make an objective interpretation, the pertinent provisions of that Article need to be cited:

(*a*) Any contracting State may give notice of denunciation of this Convention [. . .] by notification.

(*b*) Denunciation shall take effect one year from the date of the receipt of the notification.[63]

The present writer submits that India was correct in taking the above provision as applying solely to a denunciation of the Convention by one party as against the remaining contracting parties. Hence, it had no bearing on the legality of the Indian conduct so far as the giving of notice was concerned.

D.4. THE VIEWS OF THE PARTIES IN THE *CASE CONCERNING THE AIR SERVICES AGREEMENT OF 27 MARCH 1946*, 1978[64]

In this aviation dispute, France cited the *Naulilaa Case* as authority for the view that the making of an unfulfilled demand constituted a prerequisite of lawful reprisals.[65] Hence she argued that the retaliatory procedure by the United States 'should have been preceded by an unsuccessful formal request, as required by international law'.[66]

From the point of view of the United States, the principles of the *Naulilaa*

---

[61] Ibid.
[62] Ibid., p. 384, para. 39.
[63] 15 *UNTS*, p. 296, at p. 360.
[64] *ILR*, vol. 54, 1979, p. 304.
[65] *Digest USPIL*, 1978, p. 773.
[66] *ILR*, vol. 54, 1979, p. 319, para. 17.

Case were of relevance only to armed reprisals; thus *a fortiori* they could not be applied to this particular incident.[67] In spite of the limited context in which she perceived the *Naulilaa Case*, the United States saw fit none the less to recount her repeated demands for amicable settlement in her dispute with France. The following statement appeared in her Memorial:

[T]he United States formally requested that France acknowledge the U.S. Carrier's change of gauge right on March 22, April 18, May 4, and on each occasion that U.S. and French officials met to consult up to date of signature of the *compromis*. On May 18 the U.S. specifically warned, by diplomatic note, that counter-measures would be taken if France did not end the violation.[68]

The above passage leaves unclarified the question whether the United States considered herself legally bound to make a demand prior to the taking of counter-measures. Nevertheless, the United States recognized in the same Memorial a duty under general international law to participate in bona fide consultations with a view to reaching a settlement.[69] This duty she claimed to have fulfilled by taking part in consultations, and by exchanging written communications, with the French authorities.[70] It is possible to conclude that the United States had expressed a qualified recognition of the necessity of making a prior demand, as is seen in the following remarks: 'All [the] demands remained unsatisfied to the present day. There is no merit to the French argument that the C.A.B.'s action preceded a demand, and France certainly does not admit that if such a demand were renewed it would be satisfied.'[71] This would suggest that where the defaulting party receives an initial demand, but shows no inclination to make satisfaction, the aggrieved party may then take counter-measures without further procrastination.

D.5. EXAMINATION OF THE EVIDENCE OF PRIOR DEMAND DURING THE HOSTAGES CRISIS IN TEHRAN

D.5.1. The chronology of events

In some disputes it is difficult to determine which of the parties involved has committed the initial breach. Consequently, in such cases confusion will undoubtedly surround the question as to which party should make a prior demand. In view of this, it becomes all the more necessary to establish the correct chronology of events. This approach will be adhered to for the purpose of ascertaining whether it was on Iran or on the United States that the onus lay for making prior demand. An analysis will also be undertaken with respect to the manner in which such a condition was fulfilled.

[67] *Digest USPIL*, 1978, p. 773.
[68] Ibid.
[69] Ibid., pp. 773–4.
[70] Ibid., p. 774.
[71] Ibid., p. 773.

It will be recalled that in October 1979 the United States Government decided to admit the former Shah of Iran into her domain for medical treatment. This decision was duly communicated to the Government of Iran, which in turn gave assurances as to the safety of the United States Embassy.[72] However, on 4 November a group of militants seized the premises of the United States Embassy in Tehran, and kept its personnel together with two other American citizens as hostages. The American chargé d'affaires and two further diplomats who were present at the Iranian Foreign Ministry at the time of the seizure of the Embassy were also regarded by the militants as hostages.[73] The militants made it known that this situation would prevail until certain demands were met. These demands, which included the return of the Shah, were ratified by the 'new' Iranian Government on 6 November.[74]

The above actions taken against the diplomatic personnel and premises evoked an immediate response from the United States Government. The chargé d'affaires protested against the failure of the Iranian Government to prevent the assault, and demanded full protection for the Embassy and its personnel.[75] On 7 November a Special Emissary of the United States was sent to Tehran to negotiate the release of the hostages.[76] Although the Ayatollah prohibited all Iranian officials from making any contact with the Special Emissary, the latter was able, prior to that prohibition, to hold several telephone conversations with senior Iranian officials. In the course of these conversations he managed to convey his Government's protests over the seizure of the hostages and the diplomatic premises.[77] In addition to this, the United States Government asked other Governments to make *démarches* to the Iranian authorities to release the hostages.[78]

It was against this background that the United States on 12 November commenced what proved to be a series of wide-ranging non-forcible counter-measures. These measures were maintained until January 1981 when, through Algerian mediation, the hostages were released.

D.5.2. *Conclusions concerning the demands made by the United States and Iran*

Although the refusal of the United States Government to extradite the Shah without due process had inevitable political repercussions, it did not constitute a violation of any rule of international law. Consequently, the request made by Iran cannot be considered as a prior demand to redress an internationally

---

[72] *Digest USPIL*, 1979, pp. 612–13.
[73] Ibid., p. 579.
[74] Ibid., pp. 577–8.
[75] *ICJ Pleadings*, 1982, p. 260.
[76] Ibid.
[77] Ibid., p. 261.
[78] Ibid.

wrongful conduct. It could only be seen as an attempt on her part to secure her own political objectives.[79]

As regards the stance taken by the United States, there is clear evidence that she recognized the need to make prior demand as a requisite for counter-measures. This recognition was evidenced in the several attempts which she made to communicate her grievance to the Iranian authorities. Although direct demands were in fact never delivered, the United States availed herself of other means to convey her protest. Granted that the chargé d'affaires was unaware of the precise intentions of his Government, his demands for rectifying the situation nevertheless represented the position of that Government.

E. THE QUESTION OF PRIOR DEMAND AS FEATURED IN THE VIENNA CONVENTION ON THE LAW OF TREATIES, 1969

By way of comparison, reference may be made to the procedure laid down by the Vienna Convention on the Law of Treaties with respect to termination or suspension of the operation of a treaty.[80] Article 65 of the Convention pertinently provides:

1. A party which, under the provisions of the present Convention invoked [breach as] a ground for [. . .] terminating [a treaty] or suspending its operation, must notify the other parties of its claim. The notification shall indicate the measure proposed to be taken with respect to the treaty and the reasons therefor.
2. If, after the expiry of a period which, except in cases of special urgency, shall not be less than three months after the receipt of the notification, no party has raised an objection, the party making the notification may carry out [. . .] the measures which it has proposed.

Certain differences immediately present themselves between demand as a prerequisite of counter-measures and notification under Article 65. For instance, in the latter case an aggrieved party must define the reasons for and the nature of the measures which it is contemplating. No such detailed formulation is required for a demand which is made prior to the imposition of counter-measures. A further difference concerns the time permitted in each case between the lodging of the demand and the taking of action. As a matter of observation, counter-measures are often resorted to after only a minimal waiting period. By contrast, Article 65 provides that, in non-urgent situations, an aggrieved party must wait for at least three months before terminating or suspending its obligation. On the question of urgency, there is no clear

---

[79] For the legality of the detention of the diplomats as a form of counter-measures, see *infra*, ch. 7 s. C.5.2.

[80] Text: UN Doc. A/CONF.39/27 (1969), *United Nations Conference on the Law of Treaties First and Second Session, Official Records, Documents of the Conference,* 1971 (hereinafter cited as *UNCLT Doc.*), pp. 289–301.

indication either in the text, or in the *travaux préparatoires* as to how this may be determined. For example, Sir Humphrey Waldock merely stated that 'it is possible to imagine some cases, such as a case of a grave breach of the treaty, where there might be special reasons for a shorter period of notice'.[81] However, this flexibility in the length of the waiting period brings the regime of Article 65 to the level of counter-measures as pertaining to the interval which usually elapses following an unfulfilled demand.

Paragraph 5 of Article 65 has specific significance for the notification of claim to be made to the offending party. It reads as follows: 'the fact that a State has not previously made the notification prescribed in paragraph I shall not prevent it from making such notification in answer to another party claiming performance of the treaty or alleging its violations'. The International Law Commission accepted in its Commentary on this provision that a party which failed to make a prior notification could nevertheless make it 'in answer to a demand for performance of the treaty or to a complaint alleging its violation'.[82] From all this it can be inferred that failure to present a prior notification does not vitiate the legality of the termination or suspension of a treaty under the Vienna Convention. Such a conclusion is hard to reconcile with the explicit terms of paragraph I of Article 65. The contradiction could be resolved only by considering the content of paragraph 5 to be applicable merely to cases of special urgency.

F. CONCLUSIONS

F.I. THE SUBSTANTIVE ASPECT OF PRIOR DEMAND

On the basis of the material that has been examined, the following conclusions are reached as to the substance of the making of prior demand:

1. In principle, counter-measures must always be preceded by an unfulfilled demand. The rationale behind the taking of counter-measures is to bring about an effective remedy. If this result can be achieved by simply presenting a demand, then the need for implementing such counter-measures will not arise.

2. Although there is no hard and fast rule respecting the content of demand, it should be so decisively expressed as to impress upon a delinquent State the seriousness of the legal implications involved.

3. In making a decisive demand there is no obligation for the aggrieved party to specify the form of counter-measures which it is contemplating.

4. When a party submits a demand for reparation, it must not demonstrate

---

[81] Waldock, *Second Report on the Law of Treaties*, Doc. A/CN.4/156 and Add. 1–3, 20 Mar., 10 Apr., 30 Apr. and 5 June 1963, *YILC*, vol. ii, 1963, p. 36, at p. 89, para. 11.

[82] *Report of the Commission to the General Assembly on the work of its eighteenth session*, Doc. A/6309/Rev.1, 4 May, 19 July 1966, *YILC*, vol. ii, 1966, p. 172, at p. 263, para. 8.

conduct which is prejudicial to the fulfilment of that demand. On the basis of logical reasoning, any claim by that party to have fulfilled the condition of making a prior demand would be invalidated by conduct of that kind. By the same reasoning, if a defaulting party wilfully blocks standard channels of communication, it will be deemed to have waived its right to receive a prior demand.

5. On the question of the interval which elapses between the making of demand and resort to counter-measures, there is no precise rule which prescribes the length of the period to be observed.[83] However, where the indications suggest that the demand is unlikely to be met, the aggrieved party may, on grounds of reciprocity or self-protection, have recourse to counter-measures without delay. Again, where the motive is to induce a speedy settlement, counter-measures may follow shortly after the lodging of the demand. By contrast, where there exists a commitment to peaceful settlement, a defaulting party should, as a general rule, be allowed sufficient opportunity to make redress. In such a case, therefore, no hasty action should follow the submission of a demand.

6. When a demand remains unfulfilled, there is no necessity for the aggrieved party to renew its demand in the course of imposing cumulative counter-measures.

7. A demand which precedes counter-measures has to be distinguished from a treaty provision which specifies that a minimum period must elapse prior to the denunciation of such a treaty.

F.2. THE MODALITY OF PRIOR DEMAND

The following conclusions pertaining to the mode of presenting a demand can be drawn from the material reviewed in this chapter:

1. There is no rule which requires compliance with a particular procedural form when a demand is being submitted as a prerequisite of counter-measures. Prior demand may accordingly be conveyed, *inter alia*, in written form, by direct verbal expression, or by telephone.

2. Where the communication of a demand through any of the aforesaid methods is impeded either by the conduct of the defaulting State, or by other circumstances, it is arguable that the use of alternative means such as a radio message will be considered as adequate. By analogy with the dictum in the *Nuclear Tests Case*[84], there will be a presumption that such a message is transmitted not *in vacuo*, but in relation to a particular dispute between the parties.

---

[83] For an interesting account of the preliminary formal procedure respecting measures of self-help as developed by the Romans, see Phillipson, *The International Law and Custom of Ancient Greece and Rome*, vol. ii, 1911, pp. 333–6.

[84] *Nuclear Tests Case* (Judgment), *ICJ Reports*, 1974, p. 253, at p. 269, para. 50.

3. The prior authorization by an official of the aggrieved State is necessary for a valid communication of a prior demand. Such an official must be of a status which permits him to issue statements that are held in international relations as acts of his Government.

6

Proportionality as a Condition of the Legality of Non-forcible Counter-measures

A. THE PURPOSE

THE purpose of this chapter is to examine the role of proportionality as a condition of the legality of non-forcible counter-measures. At the same time, it is thought pertinent to make a brief reference to other contexts in which proportionality has been a significant factor. This will be followed by an assessment of the main criteria by which proportionality may be appraised, namely the purposes of counter-measures (self-protection, speedy settlement, and reciprocity), and the 'questions of principle'. Finally, it is proposed to examine whether the factor of dependence or reliance figures as one of these criteria.

B. THE ROLE OF PROPORTIONALITY IN CONTEXTS NOT INVOLVING NON-FORCIBLE COUNTER-MEASURES

The concept of proportionality is relevant to international law in two respects. First, as a general principle of law which is used in any sphere of relationship.[1] According to this, therefore, any act or statement must bear some relation to its purpose. Hence, where such an act or statement exceeds its purpose, it will be regarded in a general way as disproportionate. Secondly, in some particular context proportionality becomes a refined and structured concept which determines the relationship between two elements. For example, the right of self-defence under customary law presupposes that the force employed must be proportionate to the danger which led to its employment.[2] This view is not inconsistent with the provisions of the Charter of the United Nations.

Proportionality has been discussed in international jurisprudence in numerous contexts, including reprisals.[3] Thus reference may be made to the decision of the European Court of Human Rights in the *Belgian Linguistics Case* (Merits)[4]. Section 7 of the Act of 2 August 1963 imposed a 'residence'

[1] See Cheng, 1953, p. 133.
[2] Ibid.; Brownlie, 1963, p. 261.
[3] For a discussion of the *Naulilaa Case*, see *supra*, ch. 2 s. 1.3.
[4] 1968, *ILR*, vol. 45, 1972, p. 114.

condition for establishing schools for the benefit of children whose maternal or usual language was French. This condition had been imposed in the interest of schools, for administrative and financial considerations. The task of the Court was to ascertain whether an administrative measure governing access to French-language education was compatible with Article 14 of the Convention, read in conjunction with Article 2 of the Protocol, or with Article 8 of the Convention.[5] The Court held that the measure in question was incompatible with Article 2 of the Protocol, read in conjunction with Article 14 of the Convention.[6] This decision was justified on the following ground: 'the measure in issue does not fully respect, in the case of the majority of the Applicants and their children, the relationship of proportionality between the means employed and the aim sought'.[7] Accordingly, the administrative measure was held not to be compatible with the enjoyment of the right of education by everyone without discrimination on the ground of language.

The role of proportionality in the delimitation of the areas of the continental shelf was first raised by the International Court of Justice in the *North Sea Continental Shelf Cases*.[8] In the course of making reference to the factors that should be taken into account, the Court stated that 'A final factor [. . .] is the element of a reasonable degree of proportionality which a delimitation effected according to equitable principles ought to bring about between the extent of the continental shelf appertaining to the States concerned and the length of their respective coastlines.[9] Thus, in the opinion of the Court, proportionality did not in itself serve as the criterion for effecting delimitation; rather, it was a principle which could be invoked to achieve an equitable solution in a particular geographical situation. This view on proportionality was underlined by the Tribunal in the *Anglo-French Continental Shelf Case*.[10] In that case France invoked the principle of proportionality as a specific rule of customary international law applicable in the delimitation of the continental shelf.[11] In rejecting this contention, the Tribunal maintained that the adoption of proportionality in the *North Sea Continental Shelf Case* did not mean it could be applied in every case.[12] The Tribunal amplified that

In the present case, the rôle of proportionality in the delimitation of the continental shelf is [. . .] a broader one, not linked to any specific geographical feature. It is rather

---

[5] Ibid., p. 200, para. 32.
[6] Ibid., p. 201.
[7] Ibid., p. 200.
[8] *ICJ Reports*, 1969, p. 4.
[9] Ibid., p. 52, para. 98; see also p. 54, para. 101(D)(3).
[10] *Case Concerning the Delimitation of the Continental Shelf between the United Kingdom of Great Britain and Northern Ireland, and the French Republic*, Judgment of 30 June 1977, *RIAA*, vol. xviii, p. 3.
[11] Ibid., p. 57, para. 98.
[12] Ibid., paras. 98–99.

a factor to be taken into account in appreciating the effects of geographical features on the equitable or inequitable character of a delimitation, and in particular of a delimitation by the application of the equidistance method.[13]

Furthermore, the Tribunal emphasized that 'it is disproportion rather than any general principle of proportionality which is the relevant criterion or factor'.[14] Similarly, in the *Tunisia–Libya Continental Shelf Case*,[15] the International Court used the concept of proportionality as a means of testing whether its method of delimitation had produced an equitable solution. The Court maintained that the element of proportionality was 'indeed required by the fundamental principle of ensuring an equitable delimitation between the States concerned'.[16] Therefore, the stance taken by the Court in this case is clearly consistent with the approach adopted by the Tribunal in the *Anglo–French Continental Shelf Case*.

In a more recent case *Concerning the Delimitation of the Continental Shelf* between Malta and Libya, the Court stated that: 'Proportionality is certainly intimately related both to the governing principle of equity, and to the importance of coasts in the generation of continental shelf rights.'[17] In view of this, the Court rejected Libya's submission that the ratio of coastal lengths as of itself should determine the area of the continental shelf pertaining to each party. The Court explained that such a proposition would 'go far beyond the use of proportionality as a test of equity, and as a corrective of the unjustifiable difference of treatment resulting from some method of drawing the boundary line'.[18]

Proportionality also plays a role in determining the property rights of a predecessor State and a successor State in the event of a succession occurring. This was clearly indicated in the Report of the International Law Commission on Succession of States in respect of matters other than treaties.[19]

It is noteworthy that in the course of a debate on the first three Draft Articles of Part Two of the Draft Articles Professor Riphagen made the following statement of principle: 'the rule of proportionality—or rather the "rule against disproportionality"—was, in a broad sense, an *existing rule of international law* which played a part in respect of the new obligations of the State that had committed a wrongful act'.[20] In marked contrast, Mr Ushakov took the view that 'the so-called "rule of proportionality" *did not exist as a rule of international law*, the role of which was, on the contrary, to establish

---

[13] Ibid., para. 99.
[14] Ibid., p. 58, para. 101.
[15] *ICJ Reports*, 1982, p. 18.
[16] Ibid., p. 75, para. 103.
[17] *ICJ Reports*, 1985, p. 4, at p. 43, para. 55; see generally, pp. 43–6, paras. 55–9.
[18] Ibid., p. 45, para 58.
[19] *Report of the Commission on the work of its thirty-first session* (14 May–3 Aug. 1979), Doc. A/34/10, *YILC*, vol. ii, part 2, 1979, p. 1, at pp. 21–24.
[20] *YILC*, vol. i, 1981, p. 130, para. 9, emphasis added.

the consequences of every wrongful act precisely'.[21] Although it is not disputed that proportionality could not determine the legal consequences of every wrongful act precisely, it is undoubtedly one of the factors which determine the legality of counter-measures. Thus, it is submitted that the hesitation on the part of Mr Ushakov to accept proportionality as a condition could not be justified.

It emerges from this review that the wide acceptance of proportionality in various areas of international law suggests that proportionality could in fact be characterized as a principle of international law. Indeed, in certain cases it has become accepted as one of the essential considerations for measuring relationships. A further observation to be made is that in all the illustrations offered proportionality has called for no more than relative equality. In the remaining parts of this chapter it will be shown how proportionality looms as a special problem in the context of non-forcible counter-measures.

C. THE RELATION OF PROPORTIONALITY TO COUNTER-MEASURES

C.1. RECOGNITION OF THE RULE

As a general rule, if a State violates an international obligation that is owed to another State, the latter may respond by taking proportionate counter-measures. This rule is widely accepted in jurisprudence, State practice, and doctrine. Thus, as has been noted,[22] the Tribunal in the *Naulilaa Arbitration*[23] stated quite clearly that reprisals which were manifestly disproportionate to the breach would be unlawful. It is also worth recalling the view expressed by the Belgian and the Finnish Governments in their respective replies to the question concerning the conditions of legitimate reprisals against foreigners, during the Codification Conference in 1930.[24] Both Governments had explicitly recognized that reprisals should be proportionate to the breach; the latter adding that '[t]he only case in which action in the form of reprisals might be taken against the rights of the foreigners is when these reprisals are provoked by an offence of the same kind committed by the other party and of essentially the same character as the subsequent reprisals'.[25] In a recent purposive statement, the Netherlands Government had asserted that non-forcible reprisals 'must be proportionate to the wrong done and to the amount of compulsion necessary to obtain reparation'.[26]

The draft convention 'Kodifikation der völkerrechtlichen Ver-

---

[21] Ibid., p. 134, para. 26, emphasis added.
[22] See *supra*, ch. 2 s. 1.3.
[23] *Annual Digest*, vol. 4, 1927–8, p. 526, at p. 527, para (C).
[24] *Conference for the Codification*, p. 128.
[25] Ibid., p. 129.
[26] *UNGAOR*, 23rd Sess., 6th Com., 1095th mtg, 13 Dec. 1963, p. 3.

antwortlichkeit' prepared by Graefrath and Steiniger dealt, *inter alia*, with the legal consequences of internationally wrongful acts which did not constitute 'military aggression' or 'forceful maintenance of a racist or a colonial regime'. One of its provisions stipulated that reprisals should 'sie sind nach Art und Umfang auf das Erforderliche zu beschränken', meaning that the character and scope of such reprisals must be restricted to what is necessary.[27]

The relationship of proportionality to non-forcible reprisals was considered by Sir Gerald Fitzmaurice in his Draft Article 18 concerning non-performance by way of legitimate reprisals.[28] He stated in the Commentary on that Draft Article that 'the action taken must have some appropriate relationship to the act or omission provoking it, and must be proportionate or commensurate in its effects—or at any rate not manifestly the contrary—and also must be limited to what is necessary in order to obtain redress'.[29]

More recently, however, the International Law Commission had considered the relevance of proportionality to counter-measures during the debates on Draft Article 30 on legitimate counter-measures. There was no reference to proportionality in the text but the issue appeared in the Commentary thus:

[R]eprisals [. . .] would cease to be a legitimate form of counter-measures if they were no longer commensurate with the injury suffered as a result of the offence in question. Here too, the justification pleaded by the State that it was applying a sanction would cease to be a justification.[30]

In addition, a footnote in the Commentary emphasized that 'in any event, the reaction must not have been disproportionate to the offence'.[31] The requirement of proportionality as a condition of legitimate counter-measures was sufficiently attested by members of the Commission. Mr Yankov, for example, remarked that 'it was only common sense that there should be proportionality between the internationally wrongful act and the corresponding responsive action or sanction'.[32] Similarly, Mr Njenga stated that 'the sanction must be commensurate with the internationally wrongful act'.[33]

---

[27] See Art. 9, Graefrath and Steiniger, 'Kodifikation der völkerrecthlichen Verantwortlichkeit', *Neue Justiz*, No. 8, 1973, p. 227, at p. 228; see also Sect. 905 (*b*) and Comment thereon, American Law Institute, *Restatement of the Law: Foreign Relations Law of the United States (Revised), Tentative Draft 5, 1984, s. 905, p. 204, and p. 206, para. d*; Zoller, pp. 136–7.

[28] Fitzmaurice, *Fourth Report on the Law of Treaties*, Doc. A/CN.4/120, *YILC*, vol. ii, 1959, p. 37, at p. 46; for similar remarks by the same authority see 'The General Principles of International Law Considered from the Standpoint of the Rule of Law', *RdC*, vol. 92(2), 1957, p. 5, at pp. 119–20.

[29] *Fourth Report on the Law of Treaties*, p. 67, para. 85; for a more recent affirmation of this view see Schachter, 'International Law in Theory and Practice: General Course in Public International Law', *RdC*, vol. 178(5), 1982, p. 167, at pp. 178–9.

[30] *YILC*, vol. ii, part 2, 1979, p. 116, para 5.

[31] Ibid., p. 118 fn. 595.

[32] *YILC*, vol. i, 1979, p. 58, para. 32.

[33] Ibid., p. 58, para. 35.

Mr Tabibi acquiesced, adding further, '[i]f the sanction failed to remain commensurate with the wrongful act, the sanction itself becomes a violation of the obligation of the State applying the sanction'.[34] This view indicates that an initially proportionate counter-measure may become unlawful where it subsequently becomes incommensurate with the wrongful act which provoked it.

The International Law Commission is currently undertaking a study of Parts Two and Three of the Draft Articles on State responsibility.[35] Professor Riphagen alluded in his Fourth Report to proportionality as setting a limitation to the admissibility of non-forcible reprisals. He distinguished between quantitative proportionality and qualitative proportionality in the following manner:

[T]he requirement of *quantitative* proportionality, obliging the State which takes reprisals 'to make the coercion applied proportional to the gravity of the act denounced as wrongful and to the extent of the damage suffered'. Nevertheless there are instances of *qualitative* proportionality, even outside the case of peremptory norms of general international law'.[36]

Article 9(2) of the Sixth Report submitted by Riphagen read as follows: 'The exercise of this right [reprisal] by the injured State shall not, in its effects, be manifestly disproportional to the seriousness of the internationally wrongful act committed.'[37] The distinction made by Riphagen in his Fourth Report makes clear that there should be a 'quantitative' proportionality between the counter-measures taken and the breach which provoked them. He admitted at the same time that in some cases proportionality imposes a constraint on the quality of the measures to be taken.[38] However, as can be seen from the text of Draft Article 9(2) cited above, the Special Rapporteur has simply reaffirmed the quantitative aspect of proportionality with regard to the relation between counter-measures and breach.

The question of proportionality of counter-measures was dealt with in a substantial way by the Tribunal in the *Air Services Award*. The following passage will reveal the stance taken by the Tribunal:

[34] Ibid., p. 60, para. 12.

[35] See Riphagen, *Preliminary Report on the Content, Form and Degrees of State Responsibility* (Part 2 of the Articles), Doc. A/CN.4/330, 1 Apr. 1980; *Second Report*, Doc. CN.4/344, 1 May 1981; *Third Report*, Doc. A/CN.4/354, 30 Mar. 1982; *Third Report*, Doc. A/CN.4/354/Add. 1, 12 Mar. 1982; *Third Report*, Doc. A/CN.4/354/Add. 2, 5 May 1982; *Fourth Report*, Doc. A/CN.4/366, 14 Apr. 1983; *Fourth Report*, Doc. A/CN.4/366, Add. 1, 15 Apr. 1983; *Fifth Report*, Doc. A/CN.4/380, 4 Apr. 1984; *Sixth Report on* (*1*) *The Content, Forms and Degrees of State Reponsibility, and* (*2*) *The 'Implementation'* (*Mise en Œuvre*) *of International Responsibility and the Settlement of Disputes*, Doc. A/CN.4/389, 2 Apr. 1985.

[36] *Fourth Report*, p. 15, para. 41.

[37] *Sixth Report*, Doc. A/CN.4/389, 2 Apr. 1985, p. 19; see Commentary on Article 9, ibid., p. 20, para. 2.

[38] See *infra*, ch. 7 on collateral constraints on counter-measures.

It is generally agreed that all counter-measues must, in the first instance, have some degree of equivalence with the alleged breach, this is a well-known rule. In the course of the present proceedings, both parties have recognized that the rule applies to this case, and they both have invoked it. It has been observed, generally, that judging the 'proportionality' of counter-measures is not an easy task and can at best be accomplished by approximation.[39]

To conclude, the various views that have been cited here confirm that resort to counter-measures must be subject to the rule of proportionality. The important question of the criteria by which proportionality should be gauged will be addressed in the remaining parts of this section.

C.2. THE CRITERIA FOR DETERMINING PROPORTIONALITY

C.2.1. Introduction

In order for proportionality to play a meaningful role in determining the legality of a recourse to counter-measures, there must be clearly defined criteria by which it can be appraised. The following excerpt of the *Air Services Award* may provide assistance in the quest for such criteria:

The scope of the United States action could be assessed in very different ways according to the object pursued; does it bear on a simple principle of reciprocity measured in economic terms? Was it pressure aiming at achieving a quicker procedure of settlement? Did such action have, beyond the French case, an exemplary character directed at other countries and, if so, did it have to some degree the character of a sanction?[40]

What emerges from these remarks is that the proportionality of counter-measures may be assessed by reference to their motivations, such as reciprocity, or a desire for a speedy settlement of disputes. In another part of the Award, the Tribunal referred also to the 'positions of principle'[41] as a yardstick by which proportionality could be determined. In the opinion of the present writer, the important motivation of self-protection should also be regarded as one of such criteria. Finally, it is intended to examine whether the factor of dependence or reliance could be taken into consideration in assessing what may be regarded as proportionate.

C.2.2. The motivation of self-protection as a criterion for determining proportionality

In principle, the objective of any counter-measure is to protect the interests of the aggrieved State. However, as has been noted elsewhere in the present work,[42] there are some instances in which resort to counter-measures could

---

[39] *ILR*, vol. 54, 1979, p. 338, para. 83.
[40] Ibid., p. 337, para. 78.
[41] Ibid., p. 338, para. 83.
[42] Cf. *supra*, ch. 4, s. C.2.

be justified on ground of self-protection. The legal import of claiming self-protection as the rationale for counter-measures lies in the wide scope of the actions that may be adopted. For example, if the breach touches on a particular provision of a demilitarization treaty, the wronged State may take counter-measures involving the non-performance of obligations under a treaty other than the treaty violated. As a further example, reference may be made to the measures taken by the United States during the hostage crisis. It is submitted that these measures were not disproportionate, since the seriousness of the hostages' detention warranted the employment of counter-measures on a scale sufficient to compel their release. In fact, even more drastic actions could have been taken.

Zoller argues that the effects of counter-measures are always temporary.[43] The present writer submits that although such an assertion deserves the greatest sympathy, it cannot apply to every situation. The exigencies of a particular situation may dictate the necessity for imposing irreversible counter-measures. This may be illustrated by the case in which a defaulting State ignores requests for third party settlement, or refuses to comply with a judgment of a competent tribunal. In such cases it is submitted that the wronged State can impose decisive measures by way of self-protection. Thus, for example, frozen assets which belong to the defaulting State can be appropriated by the wronged State to such an extent as would compensate for her injuries.

C.2.3. The motivation of reciprocity as a criterion for determining proportionality

(i) *The significance of reciprocity*

As has been stated,[44] the notion of reciprocity hinges on the presence of a quid pro quo relationship between two States. Thus, if two States undertake by a treaty to grant the nationals of each other the right of establishment in their territory, and one State violates that undertaking, the other State may resort to non-performance by way of reciprocity. Some writers trace the right to react in this manner to the theory which implies a condition of international customary law whereby an aggrieved party is released from its commitments to a defaulting party.[45] Lord McNair, in reference to the practice of suspending the operation of a provision corresponding to or analogous with that broken, observed that

[T]he practice referred to illustrated one of the most important, though little noticed, sanctions behind international law—namely reciprocity; Governments learn by experience that they cannot expect certain treatment for their nationals abroad, their

---

[43] Zoller, pp. 54–5.
[44] See *supra*, ch. 4, s. c.3.
[45] e.g. Hall, 8th edn. by Higgins, 1924, p. 408; Fitzmaurice, *Fourth Report on the Law of Treaties*, Doc. A/CN.4/120, 17 Mar. 1959, *YILC*, vol. ii, 1959, p. 37, at p. 66, para. 82.

ships in foreign waters and on the high seas, their fisheries, etc., unless they give the same treatment to foreign governments and their nationals. No State can claim from other States as a matter of binding obligation, conduct which it is not prepared to regard as binding upon itself.[46]

A particular example cited by McNair concerns a consular convention providing for freedom of travel by all consular staff except in defence areas, with one of the parties imposing a limit of ten miles from the consular premises. He concluded that the other party to that convention would be entitled to impose similar restrictions during the same period.[47] In other words, the legal significance of invoking reciprocity is that the measures taken do not affect the validity of the treaty involved. In short, reciprocity can never be invoked with a view to attaining an irreversible result.

The notion of reciprocity plays two major roles within the category of counter-measures. In one sense it is synonymous with counter-measures.[48] Thus, Professor Riphagen states in Draft Article 8 of his Sixth Report on Parts Two and Three of the Draft Articles that

[T]he injured State is entitled, by way of reciprocity, to suspend the performance of its obligations towards the state which has committed an internationally wrongful act, if such obligations correspond to, or are directly connected with, the obligation breached.[49]

Furthermore, he indicated in the Commentary on that draft Article that the element of proportionality is also 'relevant for the *qualification* of the measures taken *as* counter-measures by way of reciprocity'.[50] Hence, where reciprocity is the sole motive for implementing counter-measures, steps equivalent or analogous to the breach may be taken by the aggrieved party in order to maintain the symmetry of the situation until reparation is made. Where a neat calculation of what is regarded as equivalent can be made, then a strict balance between the breach and the reciprocal measures must be maintained. By contrast, where such calculation is not possible it would be sufficient to show that the measures taken do not appear to be manifestly disproportionate to the breach.

Attention may now turn to the second role of reciprocity for the category of counter-measures. It may be used as a criterion for determining the proportionality of counter-measures which involve, *inter alia*, a parallel suspension of obligation. Hence, where the underlying motivation is self-protection, reciprocity should be applied to evaluate the proportionality of those

---

[46] McNair, *Law of Treaties*, 1961 (hereinafter cited as McNair, 1961), p. 573 fn. 11.

[47] Ibid.

[48] This position was assumed by the United States in the *Air Services Award*, see *Digest USPIL*, 1978, p. 722.

[49] Riphagen, *Sixth Report on (1) The Content, Forms and Degrees of State Responsibility, and (1) the 'Implementation' (Mise en Œuvre) of International Responsibility and the Settlement of Disputes*, Doc. A/CN.4/389, 2 Apr. 1985, p. 18.

[50] Ibid., paras. 2–3.

segments of the counter-measures which can be appraised by reciprocal standards. It is also submitted that the same reasoning would, *mutatis mutandis*, apply to the case in which the purposes of the counter-measures are the imposition of reciprocity and the making of an inducement to settle the dispute.[51]

(ii) *The limitations of the notion of reciprocity*

There are several limitations on the usefulness of the notion of reciprocity for the category of counter-measures. An obvious one relates to the nature of the breach. For example, were Ethiopia to divert the course of the Blue Nile thereby denying the Sudan her share of the waters of that river, the Sudan would obviously not be able to apply reciprocal measures. A similar dilemma is likely to arise where one State defaults in settling her indebtedness to another State, or where foreign property is expropriated without adequate compensation.

Another limitation on the usefulness of reciprocity arises from the content of the rules involved. For instance, a violation of a *jus cogens* rule cannot be responded to by a reciprocal treatment. Indeed, as Professor Reuter pointed out, reciprocity would have no application if, for example, 'a State decided to cut off the hands of its prisoners of war'.[52] There are other categories of rules which are extremely important but do not constitute part of *jus cogens*. For an illustration, in the field of diplomatic and consular relations, an aggrieved State would never be entitled to apply reciprocal counter-measures.[53]

There are situations in which a group of States may be said to have waived or modified significantly the right of resort to reciprocal measures. For example, the jurisprudence of the Court of Justice of the European Communities unequivocally precludes reciprocal reprisals as responses to violations of the law of the Communities.[54] By the same token, States may accept a temporary limitation on their freedom to take reciprocal retaliatory measures. Pertinent to this point, Sir Joseph Gold argues that the Articles of the International Monetary Fund Agreement do not accommodate a notion of reciprocity 'by which the failure of one member to observe an obligation releases another member or members from their obligations to the delinquent member'.[55] Consequently, where a member introduces discriminatory currency arrangements without the approval of the Fund, 'other members are

---

[51] See also *infra*, ch. 9 s. E. 5.

[52] *YILC*, vol. i, 1981, p. 139, para. 28; cf. *infra*, ch. 7 s. B.2.

[53] Cf. *infra*, ch. 7 s. C.5.

[54] Cf. *infra*, ch. 9, s. B.1.

[55] Gold, 'Reciprocity and Legal Order', *The International Monetary Fund, 1945–1965*, vol. ii: *Analysis*, ed. Horsefield *et al.*, 1969, p. 591, at p. 592.

not entitled to adopt countermeasures without the Fund's approval if they are measures that require the Fund's approval'.[56]

C.2.4. The motivation of an expedited settlement as a criterion for determining proportionality

As has been noted elsewhere[57] in this work, when the underlying motivation for counter-measures is to induce a defaulting party to reach an expedited settlement, the measures involved can be maintained in an asymmetrical ratio to the breach. Such a position is justified by the need to nudge the defaulting party to perform its obligation or to agree to third party settlement procedure. As regards the scope of the permissible measures, when the motivation is a speedy settlement, it is clear from what has been said so far that the action taken may go beyond reciprocity. It needs to be emphasized, however, that the aggrieved party is not entitled to take rigorous action as though it was seeking self-protection. Consequently, when choosing between two objects of reprisals, the one which is likely to suffer less irreparable damage should be chosen. Thus, for example, if the choice is between impounding a consignment of essential medical provisions or the freezing of assets, the latter option should be preferred.

It stands to reason that where a desire for an expedited settlement is one of the purposes for taking counter-measures, the measures taken must be accompanied by an offer for third party settlement. Pertinent to this, the Tribunal in the *Air Services Award* was of the opinion that 'a State resorting to such measures, however, must do everything in its power to expedite the arbitration'.[58] It may also be recalled that, during the hostage crisis in Tehran, the United States had begun imposing counter-measures against Iran in about the middle of November 1979. Towards the end of that same month, she instituted legal proceedings against Iran.[59] The immediacy of these proceedings is indicative of the willingness of the United States to give every opportunity to Iran to challenge the legality of the counter-measures taken.

Finally, where the motivation is to achieve a speedy settlement, the counter-measures imposed must be vacated as soon as the parties have agreed on interim arrangements that will restore a balance between their respective positions. Similarly, where the offending party has agreed to restore the status quo, for example by offering to pay compensation, the counter-measures taken must cease forthwith.

---

[56] Ibid.
[57] *Supra*, ch. 4, s. C.4.
[58] *ILR*, vol. 54, 1979, p. 341, para. 98.
[59] *ICJ Pleadings*, 1982, p. 3.

C.2.5. The 'questions of principle' as a criterion for determining proportionality

An attempt has been made in the preceding three subsections to assess the significance of using three of the more important motivations for counter-measures as criteria for determining proportionality. However, in the *Air Services Award*, the Tribunal adopted a different approach in its endeavour to ascertain whether the counter-measures in that particular dispute would have been proportionate. It stated that not only the losses suffered by the companies concerned should be taken into consideration but also 'the importance of the questions of principle arising from the alleged breach'.[60] It is noteworthy that the views expressed by the French Arbitrator, Reuter, on this point were consistent with those expressed by the Tribunal. He stated:

I accept the Tribunal's legal analysis, in particular the idea that, in order to accept the proportionality of the counter-measures, it is necessary to take into account, not only the actual facts, but also the questions of principle raised by them. Those questions should however be considered in the light of their probable effects.[61]

Although the reference to 'questions of principle' was nowhere defined, its meaning may be gleaned from the following extract from the *Air Services Award*:

If the [issue of proportionality] is viewed within the framework of the general air transport policy adopted by the United States Government and implemented by the conclusion of a large number of international agreements with countries other than France, the measures taken by the United States do not appear to be clearly disproportionate to those taken by France.[62]

It appears, therefore, that the use of the term 'questions of principle' implies that a balance should be established between the effects of the United States counter-measures on France and the effects of the French interdiction on the United States. Thus, the factor of proportionality was applicable not so much to the losses which would have been incurred by the two airlines, but rather to the eventual losses that might have been suffered by the two Governments concerned.[63]

In assessing the proportionality of the United States' measures, the Tribunal laid emphasis on a factor which might be regarded as extraneous to the dispute. In its view, cognizance should be taken of the serious losses which the United States might have suffered if France's example had been followed by other States with which the United States had similar agreements.[64] This raises the issue of how much significance should be

[60] *ILR*, vol. 54, 1979, p. 338, para. 83.
[61] Ibid., pp. 343-4.
[62] Ibid., p. 338, para. 83.
[63] See Zoller, p. 134.
[64] See Greenwood, 'The U.S.–French Air Services Arbitration', *The Cambridge Law Journal*, vol. 38, 1979, p. 233, at p. 238.

attached to the deterrent effect of counter-measures when assessing pro-portionality. Two possible approaches may be suggested here. First, where the effects of the breach are likely to be serious, the counter-measures taken need not be limited to the short-term effects of that breach. In such a case, therefore, proportionality can be determined by taking into consideration not only the immediate injury caused by the breach, but also the potential effects arising from it. The difficulty inherent in such an approach is that it is not always possible to distinguish between actual and remote damage. As regards the second approach, it may be argued that deterrence should never be taken into account for the reason that it entails action which is incom-mensurate with the breach committed by the particular delinquent State. The present writer is inclined to favour the first of these two approaches. However, it needs to be emphasized that restraint must be exercised in any assessment of the potential effects of the breach, otherwise the dispute could escalate beyond control.

C.2.6. The factor of dependence or reliance

It is proposed to examine whether the factor of dependence or reliance may be regarded as one of the criteria for assessing proportionality. Such an examination is thought to be necessary for the reason that counter-measures may have as their objects commodities or services that are vital to the well-being of the target State.

It may be recalled that, by amending the Sugar Act of 1948, the United States Congress reduced the sugar quota for Cuba 'in the national interest'.[65] Pursuant to this amendment, the President of the United States issued a Proclamation reducing the Cuban sugar quota by 700,000 tons from the original level of 3,119,655 tons.[66] In spite of the pretext offered for this conduct, there were clear indications that it was intended as a form of retaliation.[67] However, in the *Sabbatino Case*[68] the Court rejected the con-tention that the United States in reducing the sugar quota had acted unlaw-fully by exerting undue pressure on Cuba.

On the assumption that the action taken by the United States constituted prima facie a counter-measure, the question would still remain as to what criteria should be used for assessing proportionality in such a case. For instance, should allowance have been made for the heavy dependence of the Cuban economy on the revenue derived from the sale of the sugar to the United States?[69] The present writer submits that the answer should be in the

---

[65] Text of the 1960 Amendment: *Stat.*, vol. 74, 1961, pp. 330–1.

[66] Proclamation No. 3355, *USC*, 86th Congress, 2nd Sess., vol. 1, 1960, pp. 1612–13.

[67] Ibid., pp. 12311, 12534, and 12624.

[68] *Federal Reporter*, 2nd Ser., vol. 307, 1963, p. 845, at p. 866, para. 27.

[69] But see remarks by Schrieber who argues that there was no such dependence, 'Economic Coercion as an Instrument of Foreign Policy: U.S. Economic Measures against Cuba and the Dominican Republic', *World Politics*, vol. 25(3), Apr. 1973, p. 387, at p. 395.

affirmative. However, it may be argued that in the absence of other avenues of redress, the factor of dependence or reliance might not be an appropriate criterion for assessing proportionality.

Support for the view that the factor of dependence or reliance may be a possible criterion for assessing proportionality of counter-measures was expressed in some quarters during the 1973 Arab oil boycott. In this line Mr Paust and Mr Blaustein argued that a sudden disruption of constant supplies of a vital commodity to regular customers would be disproportionate to the objective sought.[70] While agreeing in principle with this view, the present writer argues that it could not be applied to the 1973 Arab oil boycott. This position is based on two grounds: first, the boycott was imposed by belligerent States against other States which had compromised their neutrality. In the words of Mr Shihata: 'Such measures of reprisal or retorsion are not merely punitive retaliatory acts, but must be considered as instruments for discouraging the offending nonbelligerent from committing further violations of international law with regard to the injured party'.[71] It is contended that where the pertinent international institutions are shown to be ineffective, an aggrieved State may resort to counter-measures in order to preserve her rights as a belligerent. It is here that one sees how neutrality may still play a useful role in international relations. As to the second ground, the factor of reliance or dependence might not be relevant to the 1973 oil embargo, arguably because there were no other means of redress available to the Arab States.

A further example to demonstrate that the factor under review is not in all cases an apt criterion for determining proportionality is the counter-measures taken by the United States against Iran during the hostage crisis.[72] In the opinion of the present writer, the proportionality of these measures could not be challenged on the ground that they involved an abrupt disruption of banking services vital to Iran. The fact that the motivation behind the actions taken was to save the hostages clearly outweighed all other considerations.[73]

D. CONCLUSIONS

Looking back over the substance of this chapter it becomes evident that proportionality is recognized as a general principle of international law. In certain fields, however, it has assumed a particular importance through its

---

[70] Paust and Blaustein, 'The Arab Oil Weapon—A Threat to International Peace', *AJIL*, vol. 68, 1974, p. 410, at pp. 420 and 435.

[71] Shihata, 'Destination Embargo of Arab oil: Its legality under International Law', *AJIL*, vol. 68, 1974, p. 591, at pp. 614–15; see also Shihata, 'Arab Oil Policies and the New International Economic Order', *Virginia Journal of International Law*, vol. 16(2), 1976, p. 261, at p. 267.

[72] See remarks by Higgins concerning 'Legal Responses to the Afghan–Iranian Crises', *Proceedings of American Society of International Law*, vol. 74, 1980, p. 250, at p. 255.

[73] See remarks by Mr Hinton, Assistant Secretary, US Department of State, ibid., p. 248, at p. 249.

acceptance as a criterion by which a relation may be established between two given factors.

In the field of non-forcible counter-measures, the weight of opinion is that proportionality is one of the conditions by which legality may be determined. In other words, the measures taken must be commensurate with the breach. This rule, however, will take on a fuller significance when the criteria for measuring proportionality have been identified. The principal criteria are as follows: the purposes for resorting to counter-measures; the probable effects of the breach and of the counter-measures; and the factor of dependence and reliance.

As regards the proportionality of counter-measures when the purpose is self-protection, an aggrieved State is not obliged to restrict her response to any one particular field. Furthermore, the measures taken by that State may be intensifed to such a degree as is necessary to compel the offending State to put an end to her wrongful conduct. Should all these endeavours prove ineffective, an aggrieved State may go so far as to impose irreversible counter-measures.

In cases where reciprocity is the purpose for resorting to counter-measures, the action taken must correspond to the breach which provoked it. For instance, if a treaty between two States provides for preferential treatment for the nationals of each other in their respective territories, a breach of this stipulation by one State entitles the other to impose reciprocal measures. It needs to be said, however, that measures taken in these circumstances must be vacated as soon as the breach of that stipulation is rectified. Finally, one notes that the element of reciprocity cannot be employed for the purpose of assessing proportionality in all cases. In the first place, by the very nature of things it may not be possible to impose a reciprocal measure. In the second place, the possibility of resort to reciprocal measures may be precluded by a rule of international law.

Where the purpose for imposing counter-measures is to achieve a speedy settlement, the measures taken should be in an asymmetrical ratio to the breach in order to induce the other party to respond. Such imbalance must not go beyond what is required to achieve that purpose, and must not involve the infliction of irreparable damage. Moreover, since the motive is to achieve a speedy settlement, the measures taken need to be accompanied by an offer to submit the dispute to third party settlement. Finally, the counter-measures in question must be vacated as soon as the parties have reached an interim agreement, or where the offending party has made satisfaction.

The Tribunal in the *Air Services Award* laid stress on the relation between the effects of the breach and the effects of counter-measures. This approach sets in a new perspective the role of proportionality as a criterion for determining the legality of counter-measures. However, one particular aspect of this approach appears to be somewhat controversial. This can be seen in the

Tribunal's legal analysis concerning the likely effects of breach. In giving a special weight to the factor of deterrence, the Tribunal allowed a wide discretion to the aggrieved State in determining what was proportionate. Finally, the present writer submits that the 'effects' approach propounded by the Tribunal does not eliminate the need to examine the purposes of counter-measures when assessing proportionality.

There is room for the view that counter-measures applied without deference to the factor of dependence or reliance may be regarded as disproportionate. None the less, where an aggrieved State finds herself with no other avenues for obtaining redress, she may take counter-measures notwithstanding the existence of that factor. In such an instance, therefore, the factor of dependence or reliance should not stand as a criterion for assessing the proportionality of the measures taken.

7

Certain Collateral Constraints: The Relation between Legitimate Counter-measures and Other Rules of International Law

A. THE PURPOSE

IT has been shown in the preceding three chapters that for a retaliatory action to be categorized as a lawful counter-measure, it must comply with the constituent conditions of legality. Thus the action in question should be in response to, and commensurate with, a particular breach, and be taken only after an unsuccessful demand for reparation has been made. As an addition to these conditions, international law recognizes further collateral constraints on the legality of counter-measures. The number of collateral constraints which can be covered may prove to be quite considerable. For this reason, however, it is thought that only the more significant collateral constraints should be discussed. Hence, the next section of this chapter will deal with the important question of *jus cogens* as a collateral constraint on counter-measures. The other legal principles that are thought to constitute collateral constraints on the legality of counter-measures will be examined in section C.

B. OBLIGATIONS IMPOSED BY THE RULES OF *JUS COGENS* AS A COLLATERAL CONSTRAINT ON COUNTER-MEASURES

B.I. SOME INTRODUCTORY REMARKS

The purpose of this section is to examine the effect which the violation of rules of *jus cogens* may have on the legality of counter-measures.[1] The

---

[1] For the recognition of the principles of *jus cogens* generally see: Lauterpacht, 'Sovereignty over Submarine Areas', *BYIL*, vol. 27, 1950, p. 376, at pp. 397–8; *First Report on the Law of Treaties,* Doc. A/CN.4/63, *YILC*, vol. ii, 1953, p. 90, at p. 155, para. 4; Fitzmaurice, *Third Report on the Law of Treaties*, Doc. A/CN.4/115), *YILC*, 1958, p. 20, at p. 27 (Art. 17 conflict with international law); 'The General Principles of International Law Considered from the Standpoint of the Rule of Law', *R.d.C.*, vol. 92(2), 1957, p. 5, at p. 120 s. 70, p. 122 s. 73, p.

difficulty to be faced at the outset stems from the lack of clear authority pertaining to the actual content of the category of *jus cogens*. This uncertainty is reflected, for instance, in Article 53 of the Vienna Convention on the Law of Treaties, 1969,[2] which refers to a *jus cogens* rule in the following terms:

[A] peremptory norm of general international law is a norm accepted and recognised by the international community of States as a whole as a norm from which no derogation is permitted and which can be modified only by a subsequent norm of general international law having the same character.

The lack of substance evident in the above provision is matched by the circular reasoning respecting the manner in which the norm in question may be modified. In practice, however, the difficulty may prove more apparent than real, as is seen from the readiness with which municipal courts apply *jus cogens* rules.[3] A comment on the position of principle which is acceptable to the present writer is offered by Hersch Lauterpacht as follows:

These principles would not necessarily have crystallized in a clearly accepted rule of law such as prohibition of piracy or of aggressive war. They may be expressive of rules of international morality so cogent that an international tribunal would consider them as forming part of those principles of law generally recognised by civilised nations[.][4]

B.2. THE RELATION BETWEEN *JUS COGENS* RULES AND THE LEGALITY OF COUNTER-MEASURES

There is a dearth of analysis in both doctrine and jurisprudence concerning the effect of violation of a *jus cogens* rule on the legality of non-forcible counter-measures. The International Law Commission considered the circumstances precluding wrongfulness, and concluded that neither a plea of 'consent'[5] nor one of 'necessity'[6] could justify breach of an obligation which arose out of a peremptory norm of general international law. In marked contrast, the Commission omitted all reference to *jus cogens* rules in the text

125 s. 73(ii); McNair, 1961, pp. 214–15; *The Barcelona Traction Case* (Second Phase), *ICJ Reports*, 1970, p. 3, at p. 32, paras. 33–4; for commentary on earlier drafts of Art. 53 of the Vienna Convention on the Law of Treaties, see *ILC Report on the Law of Treaties* (Doc. A/6309/Rev. I), *YILC*, vol. ii, 1966, p. 170, at pp. 247–9, paras. 1–6.

[2] Text: UN Doc. A/Conf.39/27 (1969), *UNCLT* Doc, p. 289.

[3] See Riesenfeld, 'Jus Dispositivum and Jus Cogens in International Law in the light of a recent decision of the German Supreme Constitutional Court', *AJIL*, vol. 60, 1966, pp. 511–15; Schwelb, 'Some Aspects of International *Jus Cogens* as formulated by the International Law Commission, *AJIL*, vol. 61, 1967, p. 946, at pp. 950–1; Crawford, *The Creation of States in International Law*, 1979, p. 81; Zoller, pp. 82–4.

[4] Lauterpacht, *First Report on the Law of Treaties*, Doc. A/CN.4/63, 24 Mar. 1953, *YILC*, vol. ii, 1953, p. 90, at p. 155, para. 4.

[5] Text of 'Article 29(2) Consent': *YILC*, vol. ii, part 2, 1979, p. 87, at p. 109, and Commentary at pp. 114–15, paras. 21, 22, and 25.

[6] Text of 'Article 33(2)(a) State of necessity'; *YILC*, 1980, p. 26, at p. 34, and Commentary at p. 43, para. 22, and p. 51, para. 41.

of Draft Article 30 respecting legitimate counter-measures. What is more, the question had, surprisingly, never figured in the Commission's discussion,[7] nor in its report to the General Assembly.[8]

Subsequently, the Special Rapporteur for Part Two of the Draft Articles on State responsibility proposed Article 4 in these terms:

An internationally wrongful act of a State does not entail an obligation for that State or a right for another State to the extent that the performance of that obligation or the exercise of that right would be incompatible with a peremptory norm of general international law unless the same or another peremptory norm of general international law permits such performance or exercise in that case.[9]

Although the above provision brings a solution to the problem of the content of *jus cogens* no nearer, it has a bearing on the relation between the rules of *jus cogens* and the category of counter-measures. Professor Riphagen, the Special Rapporteur, stated that Draft Article 4 prohibited any derogation from peremptory rules even if the reaction involved was 'a legal consequence of an internationally wrongful act'.[10] Hence, by deduction, where performance of an obligation appears to be inconsistent with a peremptory rule, the party to which that obligation is owed cannot employ counter-measures as a means of compelling such performance. It should be added, however, that compliance with the rules of *jus cogens* is not subject to the notion of reciprocity. This means that an aggrieved party is not permitted to take reciprocal counter-measures without deference to the prevalence of the principles of *jus cogens*.

The foregoing deductions are borne out by the new Draft Articles proposed by the Special Rapporteur as replacement for all earlier Articles submitted by him.[11] Thus, although Article 8 affirms the right to take reciprocal measures and Article 9 the right to make reprisals, Article 12 stipulates certain restrictions on the exercise of those rights.[12] The pertinent part of Article 12 reads as follows:

Articles 8 and 9 do not apply to the suspension of obligations: (*a*) of the receiving State regarding the immunities to be accorded to diplomatic and consular missions and staff; (*b*) of any State by virtue of a peremptory norm of general international law.[13]

---

[7] *YILC*, vol. i, 1979, pp. 55–63, paras. 8–35.

[8] Ibid., vol. ii, part 2, p. 87, at pp. 115–22, paras. 1–24.

[9] Riphagen, *Third Report on the Content, Forms and Degrees of State Responsibility*, Doc. A/CN.4/354/Add. 2, May 1982, p. 11, para. 139; see also Draft Article 18(2) on State Responsibility, *YILC*, vol. ii, part 2, 1976, p. 69, at p. 87, and Commentary at p. 88, para. 4.

[10] Riphagen, *Third Report*, p. 11, para. 139(2).

[11] Riphagen, *Fifth Report on the Content, Forms and Degrees of State Responsibility* (Part 2 of the Draft Articles), Doc. A/CN.4/380, 4 Apr. 1984, p. 2, para. 4.

[12] Ibid., p. 6.

[13] Ibid., p. 8.

B.3. SOME MATTERS OF PRINCIPLE

The present writer accepts the position taken by Professor Riphagen for two reasons. First, the existence of the rules of *jus cogens* should be regarded as axiomatic. Secondly, it seems clear that derogation is not possible from rules which have the character of *jus cogens*. Accordingly, there is no justification for exempting the category of counter-measures from the operation of this general rule. In this way counter-measures are brought into line with the regime of the Vienna Convention on the Law of Treaties which provides that '[a] treaty is void if, at the time of its conclusion, it conflicts with a peremptory norm of general international law'.[14]

If the problem is viewed from the perspective of the *raison d'être* for counter-measures, the answer will still be the same. This is because, as has been noted, the fulfilment of obligations which have the character of a *jus cogens* is not dependent on reciprocity. Furthermore, neither the motivation of self-protection, nor that of speedy settlement can justify a violation of basic rules of *jus cogens*. In short, counter-measures can never be employed to frustrate basic values. Finally, it is submitted that violations of *jus cogens* rules may be responded to by suspending the performance of some *other* obligations owed by the injured State to the State author of the breach. A good example, as we shall see, is the counter-measures taken by the United States against Iran during the hostage crisis in 1980.[15]

C. COLLATERAL CONSTRAINTS OTHER THAN *JUS COGENS*

C.1. THE EFFECT OF VIOLATION OF HUMAN RIGHTS ON THE LEGALITY OF COUNTER-MEASURES

C.1.1. *The purpose*

Although this subsection deals specifically with human rights, it has to be recognized from the outset that there is a certain overlap between the spheres of human rights and of *jus cogens* in general. The intention here is to examine whether human rights, regardless of their *jus cogens* character, constitute a constraint on counter-measures.

C.1.2. *A review of the relevant material*

The issue of the detention of aliens by way of reprisals was alluded to by the Danish Government in its reply to point XI(*b*) of the Basis of Discussion of the 1930 Codification Conference. The position taken was that 'reprisals involve [...] the imprisonment of foreigners'.[16] It should be noted in passing that none of the replies received from other States made any reference

---

[14] Art. 53.
[15] Cf. *infra*, s. C.5.3.
[16] *Conference for the Codification*, p. 128.

to the question of whether aliens could be seized as part of a reprisals scheme.

The Institute of International Law adopted a resolution in 1934 which outlined the rules applicable to all forms of peacetime reprisals. The pertinent paragraphs of Article 6 of that Resolution read as follows:

> 3 Limiter les effets des représailles à l'Etat contre qui elles sont dirigées, en respectant, dans toute la mesure du possible, tant les droits des particuliers que ceux des Etats tiers;
>
> 4 S'abstenir de toute mesure de rigueur qui serait contraire aux lois de l'humanité et aux exigences de la conscience publique.[17]

As can be seen, the above two provisions have a definite bearing on the question of reprisals against individuals. Paragraph 3 stipulates that a State taking reprisals should, to the extent possible, respect the rights of private persons. The wording of this paragraph does not categorically rule out the possibility of reprisals against individuals. By allowing some discretion in the application of such reprisals, it presupposes good faith on the part of the sanctioning State. By contrast, paragraph 4 explicitly prohibits any harsh measures which violate the laws of humanity. However, the use of the adjective 'harsh' implies that counter-measures which involve less rigorous violations of humanitarian laws would not be unlawful.

The principles of human rights germinating from the Charter of the United Nations as developed by subsequent practice of the parties have evidently superseded the long-held rule according to which individuals could be taken as objects of reprisals. Although both the Charter of the United Nations and the Universal Declaration of Human Rights preceded the seventh edition of Oppenheim, they clearly had no influence on the views expressed by its editor on the legality of reprisals against individuals. In this respect it is stated in Oppenheim that '[t]he persons of officials, and even of private citizens, of the delinquent State are possible objects of reprisals'.[18]

With deference to Lauterpacht, the better view would seem to be stated by Fitzmaurice, a former legal adviser to the British Foreign and Commonwealth Office and a Judge of the International Court. He remarked that

[T]here are certain forms of illegal action that can never be justified by or put beyond the range of legitimate complaint by the prior illegal action of another State, even when intended as a reply to such action. These are acts which are not merely illegal, but *malum in se,* such as certain violations of human rights, certain breaches of the laws of war, and other rules in the nature of *jus cogens*—that is to say obligations of an absolute character, compliance with which is not dependent on corresponding

---

[17] *Annuaire,* 1934, p. 710; cf. *supra*, ch. 2 s. H.

[18] Oppenheim, vol. ii, 7th edn. by Lauterpacht, 1952, p. 139.

compliance by others, but is requisite in all circumstances, unless under stress of literal *vis major*.[19]

Pertinent to the question under review, Judge Tanaka stated in 1966 that 'the principle of the protection of human rights has received recognition as a legal norm under three main sources of international law, namely (1) international conventions, (2) international custom, and (3) the general principles of law'.[20] Thus it can be concluded that from about the middle of the 1960s respect for human rights crystallized into a recognized legal standard.[21] Obviously, this has the effect of weakening the case for seizing individual persons as objects of reprisals. The need to ensure the protection of individuals from acts of reprisals has received explicit recognition in the Vienna Convention on the Law of Treaties.[22] The first three paragraphs of Article 60 deal with the right to invoke material breach as a ground for the termination or suspension of a violated treaty. Paragraph 5 of that Article provides by way of exception that '[p]aragraphs 1 to 3 do not apply to provisions relating to the protection of the human person contained in treaties of humanitarian character, in particular to provisions prohibiting any form of reprisals against persons protected by such treaties'.

It should be noted that Article 60 is widely regarded as evidence of the existing law on the right of termination or suspension of treaties on ground of material breach.[23] Although paragraph 5 precludes the exercise of this right only *vis-à-vis* treaty provisions prohibiting reprisals, one could reasonably argue that the paragraph reflects modern development in the customary law concerning reprisals against individuals. According to this approach, reprisals against individuals should not be permitted in any circumstances.

The Court in the *Barcelona Traction Case* distinguished between 'the obligations of a State towards the international community as a whole, and those arising *vis-à-vis* another State in the field of diplomatic protection'.[24] The Court added that the former type of obligations were by their very nature obligations *erga omnes*. It explained further: 'Such obligations derive, for example, in contemporary international law, from the outlawing of acts of aggression, and of genocide, as also from the *principles and rules concerning the basic rights of the human person*, including protection from slavery and racial discrimination.'[25] The presumption to be drawn from the views expressed by the Court is that *erga omnes* obligations have an import

---

[19] Fitzmaurice, 'The General Principles of International Law considered from the Standpoint of the Rule of Law', *R.d.C.*, vol. 92(2), 1957, p. 5, at p. 120 s. 70.

[20] Diss. Op. Judge Tanaka, *South West Africa Cases, ICJ Reports,*1966, p. 248, at p. 300; see also remarks by the Court in the *Namibia Case, ICJ Reports*, 1971, p. 16, at p. 57, para. 131.

[21] See Brownlie, 1979, p. 596.

[22] Cf. *infra*, ch. 8 s. c.6.

[23] Cf. *infra*, ch. 8 s. c.1.

[24] *ICJ Reports*, 1970, p. 4, at p. 32, para. 34

[25] Ibid., emphasis added.

equivalent to that of *jus cogens* rules. The specific mention of human rights in the above passage presupposes the acceptance of a general principle of human rights in international law.

Article 19[26] of Part One of the Draft Articles on State responsibility provides that an international crime may result, *inter alia*, from '(c) a serious breach on a widespread scale of an international obligation of essential importance for safeguarding the human being, such as those prohibiting slavery, genocide and apartheid'. This provision indicates that serious breaches of human rights standards could be regarded as violations of the rules of *jus cogens*.

The International Law Commission had never considered the possibility of including respect for human rights as part of the text of Draft Article 30 concerning counter-measures. However, the view of the Commission on the underlying issue could be gleaned from its commentary on that Article. This provided that

[E]ven where the internationally wrongful act in question would justify a reaction involving the use of force, whatever the subject responsible for applying it, action taken in this guise certainly cannot include, for instance, a breach of obligations of international humanitarian law. Such a step could never be 'legitimate' and such conduct would remain wrongful.[27]

The question under review has been receiving a closer consideration in Part Two of the Draft Articles on State responsibility. Article 4 as proposed by Professor Riphagen in his third report addressed the issue of the inadmissibility of conduct which violated a peremptory norm of general international law.[28] Subsequently, Riphagen conceded in his fourth report that there existed rules of international law for the protection of human rights in armed conflicts which precluded reprisals.[29] To this he added, 'there are *other* objective regimes which impose on States the respect of human rights, whatever the nationality of the person affected, and whatever the circumstances. Reprisals in breach of such rules are obviously inadmissible, even if they do *not* amount to an international crime.'[30] Riphagen then proceeded to explain that this inadmissibility had already been included in Article 4 of his third report.[31]

To make the record more complete, it is necessary to refer to Article 11 as proposed by Professor Riphagen in his fifth report. Paragraph (1)(c) of that Article forbids an injured State to suspend her obligations *vis-à-vis* the State perpetrating the breach where 'such obligations are stipulated (in a multi-

---

[26] *YILC*, vol. ii, part 2, 1976, p. 95.
[27] *YILC*, vol. ii, part 2, 1979, p. 116, para. 5.
[28] UN Doc. A/CN.4/354/Add. 2, May 1982, p. 11, para. 139.
[29] UN Doc. CA/CN.4/366/Add. 1, 15 Apr. 1983, p. 17, para. 47.
[30] Ibid., para. 48.
[31] Ibid.

lateral treaty) for the protection of individual persons irrespective of their nationality'.[32]

As part of the review of the relevant material, attention may now be turned to the *Hostages Case*. In the course of the oral hearings, Mr Owen argued that the United States was entitled to measures of protection as a matter of law. He further submitted that 'humanitarian considerations require no less'.[33] In reference to the detention of the hostages as an instrument of pressure against the United States, the Court stated its view thus:

> Wrongfully to deprive human beings of their freedom and to subject them to physical constraint in conditions of hardship is in itself manifestly incompatible with the principles of the Charter of the United Nations, as well as with the fundamental principles enunciated in the Universal Declaration on Human Rights.[34]

This excerpt serves as an illustration of how the International Court interpreted and applied the human rights norms as enunciated in the Universal Declaration of Human Rights of 1948, in a concrete case before it.

C.1.3. *An opinion on the question of principle*

It must be accepted as indisputable that a relationship exists between the attitudes adopted towards aliens and the principles of human rights. As a corollary, where these principles are violated as part of a scheme of reprisals against the nationals of a particular State, such conduct will probably not be considered as a legitimate counter-measure. Indeed, there are certain violations of human rights that can in no case be regarded as lawful even if they form part of an otherwise lawful counter-measure. An example of these would be a counter-measure that involves a violation of human rights which is looked upon as part of *jus cogens*.

The law of the United Nations, that is to say, the Charter as developed by the subsequent practice of the parties, has set forth a new foundation for the observance of human rights. Thus, where a State orders a mass expulsion of aliens ostensibly on the basis of nationality while the underlying motive is racial discrimination, that State will be violating her obligations under the Charter. Further, there is little doubt that some of the provisions of the Universal Declaration of Human Rights constitute general principles of international law. In the light of these principles, acts such as the incarceration or torture of aliens would clearly be examples of impermissible counter-measures.

Although self-protection or reciprocity can in some cases justify a retaliatory expulsion of aliens, the manner in which that expulsion is carried out must conform with basic humanitarian standards, and remain within the

---

[32] UN Doc. A/CN.4/380, 4 Apr. 1984, p. 7.
[33] *ICJ Pleadings*, 1982, p. 31.
[34] *ICJ Reports*, 1980, p. 42, para. 91.

limits of proportionality. Thus, for instance, the dumping at some desert point of children and pregnant women could never be justified.

C.2. THE TAKING OF PROPERTY BELONGING TO ALIENS AS A COUNTER-MEASURE

C.2.1. The purpose

According to the traditional theory of reprisals, alien property could be seized and disposed of as an act of reprisal.[35] It is proposed to test the validity of this statement against the limits set by international law on the treatment of foreign nationals, and by international human rights standards. As a starting-point, some remarks will be made on the international minimum standard doctrine. This will be followed by an examination of the relationship between the international law norms as to lawful expropriation and the category of counter-measures. A distinction will be drawn between the confiscation and freezing of alien property. Finally, it will be shown whether human rights standards prohibit the taking of alien property as a counter-measure.

C.2.2. International law standards

Traditional international law provides a minimum standard of treatment for aliens.[36] In illustration it was stated in the *Neer Claim* that

([F]irst) propriety of government acts should be put to the test of international standards, and (second) that the treatment of an alien, in order to constitute an international delinquency should amount to an outrage, to bad faith, to wilful neglect of duty, or to an insufficiency of governmental action so far short of international standards that every reasonable and impartial man would readily recognize its insufficiency.[37]

Hence, failure on the part of a State to conform to that standard will give rise to State responsibility. The International Law Commission dealt with the topic of the treatment of aliens under the rubric of State responsibility. The Special Rapporteur, Dr Garcia-Amador, attempted to synthesize international minimum standards and the emerging norms of international human

---

[35] See Vattel, Book II, ch. 18 s. 342, p. 283; s. 344, p. 284; and s. 351, p. 287; the views expressed by President Jackson of the United States in 1834, Wharton iii, pp. 90–2; the confiscation by the French government of property belonging to German companies in 1922, *Annual Register*, 1922, p. 165; *Conference for the Codification*, pp. 124–30; Oppenheim, vol. ii, 7th edn. by Lauterpacht, 1952, p. 139.

[36] See Brownlie, 1979, and references cited by him, p. 524. For recognition of the international minimum standard by international tribunals see *British Claims in the Spanish Zone of Morocco* (1925), *RIAA*, vol. ii, p. 617, at p. 644, para. 4; separate opinion of Commissioner Nielsen, the *Neer Claim*, ibid., vol. iv, p. 60, at p. 65; the *Hopkins Claim*, 1926, ibid., p. 41, at p. 47, para. 16.

[37] *RIAA*, vol. ii, pp. 61–2.

rights.[38] In his view, international minimum standards had now been subsumed under the new human rights norms which protected nationals and foreigners alike. The present writer takes the view that such a proposition would apply only to the cases in which the human rights in question have become a part of customary international law.[39] Be that as it may, it is arguable that a counter-measure which involves a violation of the international minimum standard will be deemed unlawful.

C.2.3. *Expropriation of foreign property*

(i) *General considerations*

According to traditional international law any interference with alien property by a State will be regarded as a breach of acquired rights, and hence an international wrongful conduct. By contrast, contemporary international law admits that alien property may lawfully be expropriated. None the less, the traditional view held by the capital exporting countries is that adequate, effective, and prompt compensation must be paid for expropriated alien property. Furthermore, the taking should be in the public interest, and must not be discriminatory.[40] Against that, it must be pointed out that although there is a controversy as to the adequacy of compensation and the guiding principles by which it may be measured, it is beyond the scope of the present work to examine such issues.[41] What is significant for present purposes is that the condition concerning payment of compensation is not ruled out altogether. Pertinent to this point, reference may be made to the widespread practice since the Second World War of compensating expropriated alien property by 'lump-sum' agreements.[42] Although such practice represents a departure from the traditional approach to the question of compensation, it nevertheless embodies the basic idea that alien property may not be taken with impunity.

---

[38] See Art. 5 of ch. 3 'Violations of Fundamental Human Rights', Garcia-Amador, *Second Report on State Responsibility*, Doc. A/CN.4/106, 15 Feb. 1957, *YILC*, vol. ii, 1957, p. 104, at pp. 112–13.

[39] See Brownlie, 1979, p. 528.

[40] See Brownlie, 1979, and references cited by him, pp. 533–6; see also *BP* v. *Libya*, ILR, vol. 53, 1979, p. 296, at p. 329, para. 4.

[41] See General Assembly Resolution 1803, para. 4; *UNGAOR*, 17th Sess., suppl. 17(A/5217), p. 15; UK Note to Iraq, *British Practice in International Law*, 1967, p. 121; for US State practice see *Digest USPIL*, 1974, p. 490; see *Texaco Arbitration*, ILM, vol. 17, 1978, p. 1, at p. 30, para. 87; the Charter of Economic Rights and Duties of States, Art. 2, *UNGAOR*, 29th Sess., suppl. 31(A/9631), p. 50, at p. 52; see again *Texaco Arbitration*, pp. 30–1, paras. 88–9 and paras. 90–1; Dolzer, 'New foundations of the Law of Expropriation of Alien Property', *AJIL*, vol. 75, 1981, p. 553; American Law Institute, *Restatement of the Law: Foreign Relations Law of the United States (Revised) Tentative Draft 3, 1982, s. 712, pp. 193–209;* Higgins, 'The Taking of Property by the State: Recent Developments in International Law', *R.d.C.*, vol. 176(3), 1982, p. 259.

[42] For a list of the agreements made until 1960, see White, *Nationalisation of Foreign Property*, 1961, pp. xix–xxv.

Of particular relevance to the present work is the question of whether an expropriation that is otherwise unlawful can be deemed lawful when it is imposed as a counter-measure. In attempting to answer this question there is little enlightenment to be found in State practice. Such evidence as is available concerns reprisals which do not fall within the category of counter-measures. As an illustration, the Netherlands Government stated that the nationalization of Dutch-owned property by Indonesia in 1958 was based on considerations of political reprisals. Furthermore, in the opinion of the Dutch Government, the nationalization was unlawful in that it was not consistent with the rules of international law governing expropriation of alien property.[43] As regards the position adopted by the Indonesian Government, it is clear that that Government never sought to justify its conduct on the ground of being a counter-measure. An interesting question suggests itself here: Would such prima-facie unlawful expropriation have been justified, if the Indonesian Government had invoked the plea of counter-measures in defence of its conduct? To reiterate, there is no evidence from State practice that has a direct bearing on this question. Nevertheless, some guidance can be obtained from the attitudes of States whose property has been expropriated. These indicate that expropriation cannot in all circumstances be an acceptable counter-measure. For instance, if the steps taken purport to be confiscatory they cannot be justified as counter-measures. By implication, therefore, where such steps entail temporary dispossession there may be a case for arguing that they can be accepted as lawful counter-measures. Accordingly, it is submitted that the temporary freezing of alien assets can be differentiated as a method which does not involve permanent confiscation. This point will be elaborated on in the next subsection.

(ii) Freezing of alien assets as a counter-measure
In the substantial period since 1945, State practice provides several instances in which alien assets had been frozen as purported counter-measures. Reference may first be made to the views expressed by the United States Government in connection with the blocking of Yugoslav private assets:

[The Treasury] Department has no intention of using the private assets as a bargaining weapon in connection with the settlement of US claims against Yugoslavia. However, it has been the invariable policy of the Treasury Department to make general agreements or to unblock simultaneously all assets of specified foreign countries and

---

[43] Netherlands Note of 18 Dec. 1959, 'Regarding Nationalization of Dutch-owned Enterprises,' *AJIL*, vol. 54, 1960, p. 484, at p. 485; see McNair, 'The Seizure of Property and Enterprises in Indonesia', *Ned. Tijd.*, vol. 6, 1959, p. 218, at pp. 247 and 256; Rolin, 'Avis de Monsieur le Professeur H. Rolin', ibid., p. 260, at p. 277; Seidl-Hohenveldern, 'Title to Confiscated Foreign Property and Public International Law', *AJIL*, vol. 56, 1962, p. 507, at p. 510; see also Domke, who asserted that the concept of retaliation was exclusively reserved 'for actions against foreign governments and not at all applicable to the private property of its citizens', Domke, 'Foreign Nationalizations', *AJIL*, vol. 55, 1961, p. 585, at p. 601.

consequently the Yugoslav private assets have remained blocked pending the outcome of the negotiations with regard to US claims and the Yugoslav Government assets.[44]

This excerpt formed part of a document that was once *highly* confidential. It begins by stating that assets belonging to Yugoslav citizens would not be utilized as a lever of policy against Yugoslavia. By contrast, its second sentence indicates that Yugoslav private assets would remain frozen pending satisfactory settlement of American claims against Yugoslavia. However, what may be gleaned from this excerpt is that the United States was asserting a right to freeze private assets as a form of counter-measures.

A somewhat similar reflection of the attitude of the United States Government towards the blocking of private assets appears in the legislation concerning 'vesting and liquidation of Bulgarian, Hungarian, and Rumanian property'.[45] According to this Act, frozen public assets belonging to these States were utilized in satisfying American claims. Although private assets owned by individuals from the three States concerned were not vested, they nevertheless remained blocked.[46]

The attitude of the British Government with respect to the blocking of private assets is evidenced by her retaliatory measures against Egypt in the face of the Suez Canal crisis. The British Government issued a Statutory Instrument which prohibited transfers respecting Egyptian sterling accounts in the United Kingdom without Treasury permission.[47] This restriction was intended to apply to both private accounts and those held by the Egyptian government in London. Although the restriction on private accounts was lifted in a matter of days, the fact remains that private property was indeed temporarily frozen as a form of counter-measures.

Attention may now focus on two more recent instances of State practice. The first concerns the 'Carter Freeze Order' which authorized the blocking of 'all official Iranian assets' in order to put pressure on Iran to release the American hostages.[48] The undoubted implication of this Order was that no such action was to be taken against private property held by Iranian citizens. As an apparent shift from this policy, a subsequent Executive order was issued prohibiting trade with '[any] Iranian governmental entity in Iran, any other person or body in Iran or any other person or body for the purposes of any enterprise carried on in Iran'.[49] This was followed by yet another Executive Order which enlarged the scope of the sanctions to cover 'any

---

[44] *FRUS*, vol. iv, 1948, p. 1059.

[45] Public Law No. 25, *Stat.*, vol. 69, 1955, p. 562.

[46] *USC*, 84th Congress, 1st Sess., vol. 2, 1955, p. 247.

[47] Exchange Control (Payments) (Egyptian Monetary Area) Order No. 1163, *Statutory Instruments* (hereinafter cited as *Stat. Inst.*), 1956, part 1, 1957, p. 838.

[48] Executive Order No. 12170 of 14 Nov. 1979, 44 *Fed. Reg.*, 65729, 1979; *DSB*, Dec. 1979, p. 50.

[49] Executive Order No. 12205 of 7 Apr. 1980, 45 *Fed. Reg.*, 24099–100, 1980; *DSB*, May 1980, pp. 1–2.

payment, transfer of credit, or other transfer of funds or other property or interests therein [to any person in Iran], except for purposes of family remittance'. [50]

Although, as mentioned, Executive Order No. 12170 had implicitly excluded private assets from its ambit, such a lenient attitude was hardened by the two subsequent Executive Orders. Thus, Executive Order No. 12205 exposed private assets to the operation of the sanctions stipulated therein, while Executive Order No. 12211 effectively blocked all such assets.

The second recent instance of State practice concerns the freezing of Argentine assets, held in the United Kingdom, by the British Government during the armed conflict over the Falkland Islands. Article 2 of the Statutory Instrument containing the directions issued by the British Treasury provided:

[N]o order given by or on behalf of the Government or of any person resident in the Argentine Republic [. . .] shall be carried out in so far as the order—

(I) requires the person to whom the order is given to make any payment or to part with any gold or securities; or
(II) requires any change to be made in the persons to whose credit any sum is to stand or to whose order any gold or securities is to be held. [51]

A notice issued by the Bank of England defined a 'resident of the Argentine Republic' as 'any person, including any body corporate, resident in that country on 3 April 1982 or at any later time'. [52] It becomes apparent from this notice that the British Treasury had effectively blocked Argentine private assets.

The third instance of State practice is the subject of the Executive Order No. 12544 of 8 January 1986 which served to block all Libyan Government property in the United States or held by US persons. The President of the United States intimated that '[t]his Order does not apply to the property of Libyan citizens or entities not controlled by the Government of Libya'. [53] The President, however, did not explain why assets held privately by Libyan nationals were exempt from the operation of his Order. It is possible that he might either have believed that a rule of international law prohibited the blocking of such assets or that States had discretion in the matter. But this is speculation and only broad conclusions can be drawn from this episode.

To conclude, the majority of the instances of State practice cited above would suggest that alien property may be frozen as a counter-measure. It needs to be emphasized, however, that in general States have not expressed

---

[50] Executive Order No. 12211 of 17 Apr. 1980, 45 *Fed. Reg.*, 26685–6, 1980, reproduced in *AJIL*, vol. 74, 1980, pp. 671–3; for excerpts of the President's speech see *DSB*, May 1980, p. 8.

[51] Statutory Instrument 1982, No. 512, *Stat. Inst.*, part 1, s. 2, 1982, p. 1296.

[52] Notice issued on 3 Apr. 1982, *BYIL*, vol. 53, 1982, p. 509, at p. 510, para. 5.

[53] Extract from letter of 9 Jan. 1986, to the Speaker of the House of Representatives and the President of the Senate, *ILM*, vol. 25, 1986, p. 181, at p. 182. For the text of Executive Order No. 12544 see ibid., p. 181.

clearly defined views on this point. Such evidence as is available relates to mere episodes. Some doubt, therefore, still remains as to whether the freezing of alien property can be justified as a counter-measure.[54]

(iii) The taking of alien property and human rights

In our search for a line between the acceptable and the unacceptable modes of counter-measures, it is proposed to examine whether human rights standards preclude the expropriation or freezing of property belonging to aliens. The outcome of this enquiry will depend on whether the notion of property rights may be regarded as a form of human rights.[55]

Article 17 of the Universal Declaration on Human Rights[56] provides:

(1) Everyone has the right to own property alone as well as in association with others.
(2) No one shall be arbitrarily deprived of his property.

The tenor of this provision raises the question as to whether there is an obligation for States not to take alien property as an act of reprisal. However, one should not lose sight of the fact that the Declaration as such was never intended to be a legally binding instrument.[57]

Attention may now turn to the International Covenant on Economic, Social, and Cultural Rights,[58] and the International Covenant on Civil and Political Rights.[59] It is noteworthy that both instruments contain provisions which relate to aliens. In the case of the former, its provisions recognize 'the right of everyone' to enjoy benefits of various types. In the case of the latter, Article 2(1) provides that each contracting State undertakes to ensure 'to all individuals within its territory' the rights recognized in the Covenant. However, neither of the two covenants contains provisions concerning protection of private property.

As evidence of State practice reference may be made to the European Convention on Human Rights, 1950.[60] Article 1 of its First Protocol pertinently provides: 'No one shall be deprived of his possessions except in the public interest and subject to the conditions provided for by law and *by*

---

[54] But see McNair, 1961, p. 578, who instanced 'the blocking of the banking accounts of the nationals of the wrongdoing State', as a form of lawful non-forcible reprisals.

[55] See Higgins and references cited by her, 'The Taking of property by the State: Recent Developments in International Law', *R.d.C.*, vol. 176(2), 1982, p. 258, at p. 355.

[56] Adopted by General Assembly Resolution 217 A(iii) of 10 Dec. 1948, UN Doc. A/811, reprinted in Brownlie, *Basic Documents in International Law*, 3rd edn., 1983, p. 250.

[57] For the debates leading to its adoption in 1948 see *UNGAOR*, 3rd Sess., part 1, p. 934; see generally Lauterpacht, *International Law and Human Rights*, 1950, pp. 394 ff.; Waldock, 'General Course on Public International Law', *R.d.C.*, vol. 106(2), 1962, p. 5, at p. 199; Sieghart, *The International Law of Human Rights*, 1983, pp. 53–4; Lillich, *The Human Rights of Aliens in Contemporary International Law*, 1984, p. 44.

[58] General Assembly Resolution 2200 (1966), *UNGAOR*, 21st Sess., suppl. No. 16(A/6316), p. 49.

[59] Ibid., p. 53.

[60] Text: Council of Europe, *European Conventions and Agreements*, vol. i, (*1949–1961*), 1971, p. 21.

the general principles of international law.[61] This provision clearly prohibits permanent dispossession of private property except when the aforementioned conditions are complied with. As regards the meaning of the phrase 'the conditions provided for by general international law', there is a unanimous agreement among the parties to the Convention that a taking of alien property is subject to the requirement to pay compensation.[62] This provides a clear example of a synthesis of the international minimum standards and human rights standards. None the less, it must be stated that the provisions of the Convention and its Protocol are somewhat vague and have failed to give unqualified right of protection.

It is noteworthy that Professor Brownlie takes the view that there is now 'a legal principle of non-discrimination which at least applies in matters of race'.[63] In his opinion, such a principle is based, in part, upon the United Nations Charter, and the other instruments already referred to in this sub-section. He further points out that expropriation which is aimed at individuals belonging to a particular racial group is to be considered unlawful. The present writer inclines to agree with this exposition. In his opinion, therefore, the legality of any counter-measure which is directed at persons of a particular race must be put in question.

It is worth recalling the attitude of the United States Government when it ordered the freeze of Iranian assets, and that of the British Government when it froze Argentinian assets. As regards the former, although private Iranian property was not affected by the initial Executive Order,[64] it was effectively blocked by a subsequent Executive Order.[65] Despite this, some concession was made with respect to the making of payments in the form of family remittances. As regards the latter, Point No. 11 of the Notice issued by the Bank of England provided, *inter alia,* that

> The Bank of England will consider applications to debit Argentine Accounts for the following purposes:—
>
> (*a*) Living, medical, educational and similar expenses of residents of the Argentine Republic in the United Kingdom [...]. For all these purposes, reasonable amounts will normally be permitted.[66]

Although funds held in private accounts were frozen, nevertheless it was possible to draw from them for basic human needs. The present writer views the concession in each case as no more than a mere humanitarian gesture.

---

[61] Ibid., p. 22, emphasis added.

[62] See Resolution 52(1) of 20 Mar. 1952, passed by the Committee of Ministers prior to the signing of the approved text of Protocol I.

[63] Brownlie, 1979, pp. 596–7.

[64] Executive Order No. 12170 of 14 Nov. 1979, 44 *Fed. Reg.*, 65729, 1979; *DSB*, Dec. 1979, p. 50.

[65] Executive Order No. 12211 of 17 Apr. 1980, 45 *Fed. Reg.*, 26685–6, 1980, reproduced in *AJIL*, vol. 74, 1980, pp. 671–3.

[66] Notice issued on 3 Apr. 1982, *BYIL,* vol. 53, 1982, p. 511, para. 11.

C.2.4. Conclusions

On the basis of the material that has been examined the following deductions may be made:

1. It may reasonably be assumed that no form of confiscatory expropriation will be acceptable as counter-measures. This assumption is based on the following grounds: first, the old concept of the minimum standard may still serve to prohibit the taking of alien property as an act of reprisal; secondly, general international law as to lawful expropriation lays down that alien property may be taken provided that compensation is paid; and thirdly, although there is some controversy as to whether property rights are recognized as human rights, few would deny that expropriation based on racial discrimination is unlawful.

2. Since the freezing of alien assets does not entail irreversible effects, it is arguable that such conduct may be justified when it forms part of a counter-measure. Although this view is not supported by State practice, it may nevertheless be regarded as a compromise between two extremes: total inaction on the part of the aggrieved party on the one hand, and confiscation of alien property by it on the other.

3. Where private assets are frozen as part of a counter-measure, the available evidence indicates that allowance should be made on humanitarian grounds.

C.3. COUNTER-MEASURES WHICH INFRINGE THE RIGHTS OF A THIRD STATE

C.3.1. The problem stated

It is possible to envisage situations in which rights of third States, or that of their nationals, may be adversely affected by counter-measures taken by one State against another. This subsection will examine the question whether counter-measures which are otherwise lawful may cease to be so when they violate the rights of the aforementioned categories. Attention will also be paid to the rights which accrue to a third State in consequence of the occurrence of such a violation.

C.3.2. Review of the pertinent material

The principle of traditional international law is that objects of reprisals, where property is concerned, should be confined to assets belonging to the State perpetrating the breach, or to her nationals.[67] Thus, as a logical corollary, a State which initiates counter-measures must ensure that they do not infringe the property rights of a third State and her nationals. This statement of principle finds recognition even in the laws of war. The Tribunal

---

[67] Cf. *supra*, chs. I and 2.

stated in the *Cysne Case* that 'reprisals are not admitted against neutrals. There is no legal justification for reprisals except when they have been provoked by an act contrary to international law'.[68] While the Tribunal conceded that legitimate reprisals might indirectly cause injury to the nationals of a neutral State, it noted that the reprisals in the present case were mounted deliberately against such neutral subjects. The Court held that '[a]s Portugal had not violated, in relation to Germany, any rule of international law, acts of reprisals directed against her were contrary to international law'.[69]

The principles affirmed by the Tribunal in *The Cysne Case* have been reiterated by authoritative opinion. For example, The Institute of International Law proclaimed, in Article 6(3) of its resolution adopted in 1934, that the following rule applied to all peacetime reprisals: 'Limiter les effets des représailles à l'Etat contre qui elles sont dirigées, en respectant, dans toute la mesure du possible, tant les droits des particuliers que ceux des États tiers.'[70]

The International Law Commission Commentary on Article 30 concerning legitimate counter-measures omitted to pronounce on the question of whether the 'legality' would be vitiated as a result of injury caused to third States. The Commission merely concentrated on the wrongful conduct which constituted the breach, and on the conduct of the aggrieved State which constituted the counter-measure against the offending State.[71]

As regards the question of responsibility for injuries sustained by a third State, the Commission made its position much clearer by stating that 'the legitimate application of a sanction against a given State can in no event constitute *per se* a circumstance precluding the wrongfulness of an infringement of a subjective international right of a third State against which no sanction was justified'.[72] As to the range of responses open to an aggrieved third State, Professor Ago, Special Rapporteur, stated that 'any infringement of a substantive right of a third State remained wrongful and required reparation'.[73] Going further, Mr Tabibi expressed the view that, following an unfulfilled demand for reparation, a third State would be entitled to apply sanctions.[74]

---

[68] Case No. 287, *Portugal v Germany, Annual Digest*, vol. v, 1929–30, p. 487, at p. 490, para. (*d*).

[69] Ibid.

[70] *Annuaire*, vol. 38, 1934, p. 710; see also Hyde, vol. ii, p. 1662; Cheng, 1953, p. 98; Stone, *Legal Controls of International Conflict*, 1959, p. 290.

[71] *YILC*, 1979, vol. ii, part 2, p. 122, para. 24.

[72] Ibid., p. 120, para. 18.

[73] Ibid., vol. i, p. 56, para. 24.

[74] Ibid., p. 61, para. 13.

C.3.3. An opinion on questions of principle

As has already been stated in the opening sentence of this subsection, situations may conceivably arise where a third State suffers injury as a result of counter-measures aimed by one State against another. The present writer takes the view that the injury thus committed can in no way affect the legality of the initial counter-measures. That said, however, the party which takes counter-measures should strive to ensure that injury to a third State be kept to the minimum. To suggest otherwise would mean that the legally acceptable motivations for taking counter-measures become stretched to the limits of plausibility. This argument has particular cogency when there are different options open to the State taking counter-measures. Clearly, where one of the options involves inflicting injury on third States, that option should not be preferred.

As regards the question of providing remedy for the infringement of the rights of the third State by the initial counter-measure, the aggrieved State must first claim reparation. In the event that such a claim remains unfulfilled, that State becomes entitled to resort to counter-measures within the bounds of proportionality and other applicable collateral constraints.

C.3.4. Conclusions

A review of the material that has been presented leads to the following conclusions:

1. The legality of an initial counter-measure which is otherwise lawful will *not* be vitiated merely because it has infringed the rights of an innocent third State or those of her nationals.

2. On the other hand, where there exists an option that would allow the achievement of the aim of the counter-measures without causing injuries to third parties, that option should be taken.

3. An aggrieved third State will be entitled to seek reparation for her injuries. Failing satisfaction, such a State may resort to legitimate counter-measures.

C.4. COUNTER-MEASURES WHICH IMPEDE INNOCENT PASSAGE THROUGH TERRITORIAL SEA OR THROUGH STRAITS

C.4.1. The principle of innocent passage through territorial sea

The right of innocent passage through the territorial sea of a coastal State has long been recognized in customary international law.[75] This right has been codified in Article 14 of the 1958 Geneva Convention on the Territorial Sea and the Contiguous Zone. Paragraph (1) of that Article provides that

---

[75] See Commentary on Draft Article 15(1), 'ILC Report on the Law of the Sea', Doc. A/3159, *YILC*, vol. ii, 1956, p. 252, at p. 272; Brownlie, 1979, p. 203; O'Connell, *The International Law of the Sea*, vol. i, ed. Shearer, 1982, pp. 263, 270.

'ships of all States, whether coastal or not, shall enjoy the right of innocent passage through the territorial sea'.[76] The right in question has further been emphasized in Article 15(1) which stipulates that '[t]he coastal State must not hamper innocent passage through the territorial sea'. Nevertheless, the right in question is subject to the following qualifications envisaged in Article 16(3)[77]: '[T]he coastal State may, without discrimination among foreign ships, suspend temporarily in specified areas of its territorial sea the innocent passage of foreign ships if such suspension is essential for the protection of its security.' The inference to be drawn from the above provision is that the coastal State is precluded from hindering innocent passage of foreign ships in her territorial sea, except where a temporary suspension of such passage is considered essential for the protection of her security.

C.4.2. The suspension of innocent passage through territorial sea as a form of counter-measure

The analysis attempted in subsection C.4.1. above reveals that no specific reference has been made in the Territorial Sea Convention as to whether innocent passage may be suspended as a counter-measure. The problem may be illustrated by a hypothetical example. Suppose that a coastal State announces the suspension of innocent passage of ships of a particular State, for a period of one year as a purported counter-measure. In order to pronounce on the legality of this conduct analogies may be drawn between the principle of innocent passage and the principles governing diplomatic relations.[78] This is because the Law of the Sea is another example of a system which has its own peculiar features. Hence, it is not seen as appropriate to bring in the regime of counter-measures within that system.

A further understanding of the analogy with diplomatic law may be gained by reference to the deterrent effect of reciprocity on the conduct of States as regards maritime passage. It is perhaps due to that factor that there is no record of a single instance of State practice in which innocent passage has been suspended as a purported counter-measure. Finally, in order to remove any injustice which might occur as a result of the constraint imposed on the freedom of action of the coastal State, such a State would be entitled to take counter-measures against the delinquent 'State of the flag' in another sphere of relations where there are no collateral constraints.

C.4.3. The principle of innocent passage through straits

The right of innocent passage through straits is recognized in both customary and conventional law. In the *Corfu Channel Case* the Court stated that warships could enjoy the right of innocent passage 'through straits used for

---

[76] See Art. 17 of the United Nations Convention on the Law of the Sea, 1982.

[77] See ibid., Art. 24 and 25(3).

[78] Cf. *infra*, s. C.5.

international navigation between two parts of the high seas'.[79] Although the Court did not explicitly address the question of whether such a right existed for merchant vessels, it would be reasonable to assume that its existence is established *a fortiori*. Be that as it may, the right under review is explicitly recognized in Article 16 of the 1958 Convention on the Territorial Sea and the Contiguous Zone. Paragraph 4 of this Article provides: 'There shall be no suspension of the innocent passage of foreign ships through straits which are used for international navigation between one part of the high seas and another or the territorial sea of a foreign State.' As can be seen, this provision deals with the question of non-suspendability of innocent passage through straits in quite a wide scope. At any rate, much wider than was originally envisaged in the draft submitted by the International Law Commission.[80]

Although the 1982 United Nations Convention on the Law of the Sea has not yet come into force, reference may nevertheless be made to its provisions. It is pertinently provided in Article 45(1) of this Convention that the regime of innocent passage shall apply where straits used for international navigation are:

(*a*) excluded from the application of the regime of transit passage under article 38, paragraph 1; or

(*b*) between a part of the high seas or an exclusive economic zone and the territorial sea of a foreign State.

Further, Article 45(2) expressly forbids the suspension of innocent passage through these straits.

C.4.4. *The suspension of innocent passage through straits as a form of counter-measure*

It has been argued by the present writer[81] that suspension of innocent passage through the territorial sea as a purported counter-measure should be precluded on two grounds. First, that the Law of the Sea has its own features; and secondly, the deterrent effect of reciprocity. There is a stronger reason for this argument to apply, *mutatis mutandis*, to counter-measures which impede innocent passage through international straits. It is through such straits that the bulk of the world's shipping trade is transported. One can imagine the chaos that would result if that flow were to be interrupted. One may take as an example the Strait of Gibraltar, which decreases in width to $7\frac{1}{2}$ nautical miles between Tarifa and Punta Ciris. If at this narrow point the ships of a particular nation were denied passage as a counter-measure, the probable effect of such action would be to inflict serious damage on world trade as well as on safety of navigation. In this connection, it is a striking

---

[79] *ICJ Reports*, 1949, p. 4, at p. 28.

[80] See Art. 17(3), *Report of the ILC on Law of the Sea*, Doc. A/3159, *YILC*, vol. ii, 1956, p. 253, at p. 273.

[81] Cf. *supra*, s. C.4.2.

fact that there is no evidence in State practice of innocent passage through straits being suspended as a counter-measure. Finally, although the States bordering the straits are precluded from imposing counter-measures which effectively suspend innocent passage through the waters forming such straits, they would be entitled to take action in another sphere of relations where there are no collateral constraints.

C.5. THE RELATIONSHIP BETWEEN DIPLOMATIC IMMUNITIES AND PRIVILEGES AND THE CATEGORY OF COUNTER-MEASURES

C.5.1 Introduction

The purpose of this subsection is to examine the question whether diplomatic immunities and privileges can be violated as a form of legitimate counter-measures. As a preliminary approach to that question, it seems pertinent to mention in outline the salient issues dealt with in the 1961 Vienna Convention on Diplomatic Relations.[82] The rules governing diplomatic relations are founded upon centuries of State practice and doctrinal views.[83] The Convention has codified those parts of diplomatic law which were recognized in customary law. It has also progressively developed other parts of diplomatic law where there were not any clearly defined rules. The fact that the Convention has been ratified, or acceded to by an overwhelming majority of States, indicates that the Convention is now accepted as providing a contemporary standard of general international law in the field of diplomatic immunities and privileges.[84]

The most important diplomatic immunities and privileges embodied in the Convention may be summarized as follows: inviolability of the premises of the mission (Article 22); inviolability of archives and documents (Article 24); the accordance of full facilities for the performance of the function of the mission (Article 25); inviolability of communication, correspondence, and the diplomatic bag (Article 27); inviolability of the person of a diplomatic agent (Article 29); immunity from criminal jurisdiction, and also from the giving of evidence, together with substantial immunity from civil and administrative jurisdiction (Article 31).

---

[82] 500 *UNTS*, 7310 (hereinafter cited as the Convention). It is not intended to examine the provisions of the 1963 Vienna Convention on Consular Privileges and Immunities. However, some of its provisions will be cited when the *Hostages Case* is discussed, *infra*, s. C.5.2. For its text see 569 UNTS, 8638.

[83] See generally: Grotius, Book II, ch. 18 s. iii.1, p. 440, and s. viii, p. 447; ibid., Book III, ch. 2, para. vii(2), p. 629; Bynkershoek, Book I, ch. 24, para. 178, p. 137; Vattel, Book iv, ch. 7 s. 102, pp. 481–2; Twiss, p. 38; Phillimore, iii, p. 32; Oppenheim, vol. i, 1905, p. 440, where he argues the old cases in which ambassadors were temporarily detained but were eventually sent home safely; Hurst, *The Collected Papers of Sir Cecil Hurst*, 1950, p. 225; 'Diplomatic Intercourse and Immunities', UN Doc. A/CN. 498, 'Memorandum prepared by the Secretariat of the ILC, *YILC*, vol. ii, 1956, pp. 129–72; *Satow's Guide to Diplomatic Practice*, 5th edn. by Lord Gore-Booth, 1979, ch. 15, pp. 120–34.

[84] The only reservations that have been made related to Art. 27(3).

As a corollary to the above privileges and immunities, the Convention has specified certain obligations respecting the conduct of the diplomatic agents, and the proper use of diplomatic premises. Thus, paragraph 1 of Article 41 stipulates that '[w]ithout prejudice to their privileges and immunities, it is the duty of all persons enjoying such privileges and immunities to respect the laws and regulations of the receiving State'. The International Law Commission commented that the phrase 'without prejudice to their privileges and immunities' meant that '[f]ailure by a diplomatic agent to fulfil his obligations does not absolve the receiving State from its duty to respect the agent's immunity'.[85] As regards diplomatic premises, paragraph 3 of Article 41 provides that they must not be used for any purposes incompatible with the function of the mission as set out in the Convention and established by general international law. The International Law Commission emphasized in its Commentary on this Article that failure to fulfil the duty laid down in paragraph 3 'does not render Article (22) inoperative'.[86]

To guard against possible abuse of diplomatic immunities and privileges, Article 6 provides the following sanction:

1. The receiving State may at any time, and without having to explain its decisions, notify the sending State that the head of the mission or any member of the diplomatic staff of the mission is *persona non grata* or that any other member of the staff of the mission is not acceptable. In any such case, the sending State shall either recall the person concerned or terminate his functions with the mission. A person may be declared *non grata* or not acceptable before arriving in the territory of the receiving State.

2. If the sending State fails or refuses within a reasonable period to carry out its obligations under paragraph 1 of this Article, the receiving State may refuse to recognize the person concerned as a member of the mission.

The question of the limits set on discriminatory treatment between States is dealt with in Article 47. In principle the receiving State is precluded from applying such treatment. However, paragraph 2 of that Article provides that discrimination shall not be considered as being imposed '(*a*) where the receiving State applies any of the provisions of the present Convention restrictively because of the restrictive application of that provision to its mission in the sending State'. It is clear from the *travaux préparatoires* that this provision was not intended to permit reciprocal reprisals in response to a prior derogation from the terms of the Convention on the part of another State. In the words of Mr Sandstrom, Special Rapporteur, the Article was introduced in order 'to exclude the question of reprisals and to refer only to those rules in the application of which a certain latitude was possible'.[87]

---

[85] *YILC*, vol. ii, 1958, p. 104, para. 1.

[86] Ibid., para. 4.

[87] Ibid., vol. i, 1958, p. 197, para. 44; for views of similar inclination expressed by other members of the Commission see ibid., pp. 194–7, paras. 9, 22, 31, and 40; see also Commentary on Draft Art. 44, ibid., vol. ii, p. 105, para. 3.

C.5.2. The violation of diplomatic immunities and privileges as a form of counter-measure

The inference to be drawn from the material reviewed in subsection C.5.1 above is that there is no place for the general principle of reprisals within the framework of diplomatic relations. In the light of this, little weight should be accorded to the view expressed by the Netherlands Government that the draft Articles which subsequently formed the Convention did not 'interfere with the possibility of taking reprisals in virtue of the relevant rules of general international law'.[88] In the *Hostages Case* the International Court examined the question whether diplomatic immunities and privileges could be violated as a form of counter-measures.[89] The Court emphasized at the outset that the obligations of Iran relevant to that dispute were 'not merely contractual obligations established by the Vienna Conventions of 1961 and 1963, but also obligations under general international law'.[90] The Court then proceeded to determine which Articles of the two Conventions had been violated by the Iranian authorities. To that end it focused on the seizure of the diplomatic and consular personnel, and on the occupation of the embassy by the militants. The Court ruled that Iran had violated her obligations under Articles 22, 24, 25, 26, 27, and 29 of the 1961 Vienna Convention on Diplomatic Relations, and also Articles 5 and 36 of the 1963 Vienna Convention on Consular Relations.[91] With respect to the threats made by the Iranian authorities that the hostages would face prosecution or be forced to testify before a tribunal, the Court ruled that such conduct would violate Article 21(1) and (2) of the 1961 Vienna Convention.[92]

The Court then considered the crucial question of whether the conduct of the Iranian authorities constituted a legitimate response to the alleged violations on the part of the United States of diplomatic law. It held that, even if such allegations were to be established, they could not be a justification for that conduct since diplomatic law itself contained 'the necessary means of defence against, and sanctions for, illicit activities by members of diplomatic and consular missions'.[93] Elaborating further on the notion that diplomatic law represented a closed system, the Court stated as follows:

---

[88] See 'Comments by Governments on the draft Articles concerning diplomatic intercourse and immunities adopted by the International Law Commission at its ninth session in 1957', A/3623, para. 16, *YILC*, vol. ii, 1958, p. 111, at p. 124, para. 3.

[89] *ICJ Reports*, 1980, p. 3.

[90] Ibid., p. 31, para. 62.

[91] Ibid., p. 32, para. 67; as regards the attacks on the two American Consulates at Tabriz and Shiraz, it was held by the Court that the inaction by Iran amounted to a breach of several Articles of the 1963 Vienna Convention on Consular Relations.

[92] *ICJ Reports*, 1980, p. 37, para. 79.

[93] Ibid., p. 38, para. 83.

The rules of diplomatic law, in short, constitute a self-contained regime which, on the one hand, lays down the receiving State's obligations regarding the facilities, privileges and immunities to be accorded to the diplomatic missions and, on the other hand, foresees their possible abuse by members of the mission and specifies the means at the disposal of the receiving State to counter any such abuse.[94]

As pertains to 'the means' embodied in diplomatic law, the Court indicated that they were 'by their nature entirely efficacious'.[95] It explained further that failure on the part of the sending State to recall an erring envoy would immediately expose him to the loss of his privileges and immunities. The Court added that this would 'in practice compel that person, in his own interest to depart at once'.[96] The essence of these remarks is that in order for a body of rules to be characterized as 'a self-contained regime' it must carry within itself the means to counterbalance a violation of those rules.[97]

The special characteristics of diplomatic law were similarly delineated by Professor Riphagen, Special Rapporteur of Part Two of the Draft Articles on State responsibility.[98] In his view the fact that an aggrieved State was entitled to make a declaration of *persona non grata* and to sever diplomatic relations 'takes away the necessity for determining other legal consequences'.[99] The implications of this view were indicated in Article 12(*a*) of this Fifth and Sixth Report where he stated that reciprocity and reprisal would not apply to the suspension of obligations 'of the receiving State regarding the immunities to be accorded to diplomatic and consular missions and staff'.[100] Notwithstanding this provision, he proposed in Draft Article 10 that interim measures of protection might be taken by the injured State within her jurisdiction, and also that she could take counter-measures against a State which had failed to comply with interim measures of protection ordered by a competent tribunal.[101]

C.5.3. *Some matters of principle*

The obligations laid on a receiving State to maintain unqualified respect for diplomatic immunities and privileges are based on the representative character of diplomatic agents, and on the necessity for them to perform their diplomatic functions.[102] Furthermore, the principle of the inviolability of diplomatic immunities is manifestly to the advantage of all nations. In the

---

[94] Ibid., p. 40, para. 86.
[95] Ibid., p. 40, para. 86.
[96] Ibid.
[97] Cf. *infra*, ch. 9 s. E.6.
[98] Riphagen, *Fourth Report on the Content, Forms and Degrees of State Responsibility*, Doc. A/CN. 4/366/Add. I, 15 Apr. 1983, p. 29, para. 81.
[99] Ibid.
[100] Riphagen, *Fifth Report*, Doc. A/CN.4/380, 4 Apr. 1984, p. 8; *Sixth Report*, Soc. A/CN. 4/389, 2 Apr. 1985, p. 23.
[101] Ibid., p. 7.
[102] See the *Hostages Case*, *ICJ Reports*, 1979, p. 19, para. 38; ibid., 1980, p. 42, para. 91.

words of the international court, the institution of diplomacy proved to be 'an instrument essential for effective co-operation in the international community, and for enabling States [...] to achieve mutual understanding and to resolve their differences by peaceful means'.[103] It is precisely owing to these factors that the rules of diplomatic law have evolved into a self-contained system. Under this system, not only are diplomatic privileges and immunities set out, but also the means for countering their violation are clearly defined. Consequently, where a member of a diplomatic mission violates diplomatic law, the receiving State will be entitled to counter that breach by employing the means prescribed within the limits of that system. Thus, she may declare the offending diplomat to be *persona non grata* or, more drastically, terminate diplomatic relations with the sending State. The effect of these procedures is to preclude the receiving State from resorting to counter-measures such as would violate the immunities and privileges of the erring diplomatic envoy. It should, however, be emphasized that where a diplomatic envoy is caught *in flagrante delicto*, he may be temporarily detained by officials of the receiving State in order to prevent the commission of the offence in question.[104]

Although breach of diplomatic law can never justify resort to reciprocal counter-measures, obviously this does not mean that the sending State is absolved from responsibility for any consequential injuries sustained by the receiving State. In the *Hostages Case* the Court stated that if the alleged wrongful conduct on the part of the United States was duly established, that could 'have some relevance in determining the consequences of the responsibility incurred by the Iranian State'.[105] This implies that Iran, as a receiving State, could lodge a claim against the United States for damages to the extent of the injury suffered by her. To take a concrete example from State practice, the British Government has claimed compensation from Libya for the death of a police officer near the entrance of the Libyan Embassy in London on 17 April 1984.[106] It emerges from these illustrations that a sending State cannot under the cloak of diplomatic protection evade responsibility for harmful consequences which may arise from the mischievous conduct of her diplomatic envoys. Thus, it is submitted that if a receiving State fails to secure reparation for her injuries, she may resort to counter-measures against the sending State. This is because the issue of compensation is not regulated by the law governing diplomatic relations. It hardly needs pointing out that such counter-measures should not violate diplomatic immunities and privileges.

[103] Ibid., 1979, p. 19, para. 38.
[104] Ibid., 1980, p. 40, para. 86.
[105] Ibid., p. 41, para. 89.
[106] *The Times*, 7 Apr. 1985, p. 6. It must be made clear, however, that the Libyan Government has at no time admitted responsibility for that death, nor has the British Government been able to offer more than circumstantial evidence in support of its allegation against Libya.

Consideration may now be given to a second situation in which counter-measures may be taken in a collateral field in response to a violation of diplomatic privileges and immunities. Such a situation will occur when diplomatic law and other principles of international law are infringed side by side. For example, in the *Hostages Case* the United States pleaded that Iran had violated her international obligations towards the United States on several fronts: (*a*) diplomatic and consular relations; (*b*) the Treaty of Amity, Economic Relations, and Consular Rights between the two Countries; and (*c*) the Convention on the Prevention and Punishment of Crimes against Internationally Protected Persons, including Diplomatic Agents. It is submitted that the freeze of the Iranian assets would have had to be justified, not on the basis of the infringement of diplomatic law by Iran, but on the basis of the breach of her other international obligations. In that case the breach related to the non-observance of treaty obligations, and of human rights standards.

The question of the inviolability of diplomatic privileges and immunities must be viewed in the light of the underlying policy considerations, the foremost of which is the deterrent affect of reciprocity. Each State is essentially both a sending and a receiving State. The safety and welfare of her diplomatic agents in foreign countries will be seriously compromised if she violates the privileges and immunities of foreign diplomatic envoys in her own territory. The position assumed by the British and the Libyan Governments following the shooting incident outside the latter's embassy in London serve to indicate that reciprocity is the keynote of observing diplomatic immunities. It was stated in a Memorandum drawn up by the British Foreign and Commonwealth Office that diplomatic envoys abroad could be looked upon as 'hostages and even on minor matters their treatment will depend on what the sending State itself accords'.[107]

In the same Memorandum the question was addressed as to whether the receiving State could adapt particular provisions of the Convention to meet serious abuses of diplomatic law. It was stated that the Convention should be understood within the context of the rules of international law which permitted resort to 'counter-measures in response to a material breach'.[108] This view was amplified in the following comment:

[W]here considerations of reciprocity play in practice so central a role, the possibility of retaliatory action, however unlawful, by the other party would clearly have to be taken into account before any decision was taken to resort to counter-measures; and any such recourse would have to be undertaken with the greatest restraint and with full awareness of the wider implications.[109]

---

[107] House of Commons, First Report from the Foreign Affairs Committee, Sess. 1984–5, *The Abuse of Diplomatic Immunities and Privileges*, Minutes of Evidence taken on 20 June 1984, p. 1, para. 1.

[108] Ibid., p. 8, para. 44.

[109] Ibid.

C.5.4. Conclusions

The right to take counter-measures within the framework of diplomatic law is excluded by virtue of the fact that its rules constitute a self-contained system. This system, which is shaped to the benefit of all States, is predominantly maintained by the mutual fear of reciprocity. Despite this constraint, however, an aggrieved State may in two types of situations resort to counter-measures in a sphere of relations which is not within the ambit of diplomatic privileges and immunities. First, when reparation for injuries arising from abuse of diplomatic privileges has been denied; and secondly, where other rules of international law have been infringed as well.

C.6. THE RELATIONSHIP BETWEEN EXHAUSTION OF LOCAL REMEDIES AND THE CATEGORY OF COUNTER-MEASURES

C.6.1. The purpose

This subsection will assess whether the local remedies rule operates as a bar on the invocation of legitimate counter-measures taken in response to indirect injury.[110] The analysis will be undertaken within the context of breach of obligations of conduct, and of obligations of result. It must be stressed, however, that it is not the intention here to consider the significance of that rule for proceedings which relate to diplomatic interposition.[111]

C.6.2. Obligations of conduct

Where injury to an alien entails a breach of international law, the application of the local remedies rule is linked to the question of whether the obligation violated is one of conduct or one of result. This subsection will focus on breach of obligations of conduct.[112] When a State assumes an obligation of that kind, she is required to maintain a specific pattern of behaviour either in the form of an 'active conduct', or in the form of a 'conduct of omission'. The International Law Commission observed that failure to fulfil an obligation of conduct through means 'specially determined' by that obligation

---

[110] For a discussion of whether the rule of the exhaustion of local remedies is substantive or procedural see Waldock, 'The Plea of Domestic Jurisdiction Before International Legal Tribunals', *BYIL*, vol. 31, 1954, p. 96, at p. 101; Fawcett, 'The Exhaustion of Local Remedies: Substance or Procedure?', ibid., pp. 452–8; Commentary on Art. 22 of Part I of the Draft Article on State responsibility, *YILC*, vol. ii, part 2, 1977, pp. 34–5, paras. 13–14, and p. 42, para. 35.

[111] See Freeman, *The International Responsibility of States, for Denial of Justice*, 1938, pp. 404–5; *Interhandel Case* (Preliminary Objections, Judgment), *ICJ Reports*, 1959, p. 6, at p. 29; Meron, 'The Incidence of the Rule of Exhaustion of Local Remedies', *BYIL*, vol. 35, 1959, p. 83, at pp. 84–5; discussion of Draft Art. 22 ('Exhaustion of local remedies'), *YILC*, vol. i, 1977, p. 263; Ago, at pp. 264–5, paras. 9–17; Quentin-Baxter, at pp. 272–3, paras. 44–6; Pleadings of the United States in the *Dispute Concerning the Air Services Agreement of 27 March 1946, Digest USPIL*, 1978, pp. 1208–16; United States Pleadings in the *Hostages Case, ICJ Pleadings*, 1982, pp. 289–91.

[112] See Art. 20 of Draft Articles of State responsibility and the Commentary thereon, *YILC*, vol. ii, part 2, 1977, pp. 11–18; see *supra*, ch. 4 s. B.

would constitute 'a direct breach of the obligation in question, without any other condition being required for such a finding'.[113]

Obligations involving 'active conduct' may be illustrated by Article 1 of the Convention Relating to a Uniform law on the International Sale of Goods, 1964.[114] Paragraph 1 provides:

Each Contracting State undertakes to incorporate into its own legislation, in accordance with its constitutional procedure, not later than the date of the entry into force of the present Convention in respect of that State, the Uniform Law on the International Sale of Goods [...] forming the Annex to the present Convention.

Suppose that State X and State Y are parties to the aforementioned Convention. Suppose further that State X fails to legislate in line with paragraph 1, and as a consequence some financial losses have been incurred by traders who are nationals of State Y. In this example, the failure on the part of State X to enact the legislation required constitutes a direct breach of her obligation to State Y. It follows that the latter may resort to counter-measures irrespective of whether local remedies have been sought by those of her nationals who have incurred losses in State X.

As regards 'conduct of omission', some international obligations require that administrative governmental organs should refrain from certain modes of conduct. As an example, general international law imposes an obligation on all States not to violate the territorial sovereignty of one another. Thus, if Ruritanian security forces enter Utopian territory without consent, in order to make arrests there, the Utopian Government may resort to counter-measures without, for instance, seeking the release of the detainees through writs of habeas corpus.

C.6.3. *Obligations of result*

This subsection will examine the significance of the rule of local remedies for breach of obligations of result concerning the treatment of aliens.[115] Two categories of obligations must be distinguished. The first concerns obligations of result which allow a State an initial choice as to the means to be employed to achieve that result. This may be illustrated by reference to paragraph 3 of Article 189 of the Treaty Establishing the European Economic Community[116] which provides: 'Directives shall bind any Member State to which they are addressed, as to the result to be achieved, while leaving to domestic agencies a competence as to form and means.'

There are two aspects to be noted in the above provision. First, that a

---

[113] *YILC*, vol. ii, part 2, 1977, p. 16, para. 18.

[114] Text: 834 *UNTS* 11929.

[115] See Art. 21 of Draft Articles on State responsibility and the Commentary thereon, *YILC*, vol. ii, part 2, 1977, pp. 18–30.

[116] 298 *UNTS*, No. 4300. As to whether counter-measures may be imposed within the EEC system, see *infra*, ch. 9 s. E.6.

directive lays on the State to which it is addressed the responsibility of carrying out certain obligations; and secondly, in discharging those obligations the organs of the State concerned are allowed to choose the particular method to be employed. Once that choice has been made without however achieving the required result, breach will be deemed to have occurred. Accordingly, by the strictest interpretation of the aforementioned provision, the State of the nationality of an aggrieved individual may resort to counter-measures without waiting for him to exhaust local remedies. Nevertheless, this licence must be subordinated to the wider obligation concerning peaceful settlement embedded in the legal framework of the European Communities.[117]

Consideration may now be given to the second category of obligations of result. Here, breach will definitively occur only when a State has not availed herself of the opportunity to rectify an incompatible situation produced by her initial conduct. It is noteworthy that where the obligation in question is intended to guarantee a particular treatment to a class of aliens, it is usual to stipulate that an aggrieved member of that class should first seek redress at the municipal level.[118] The purpose for stipulating the aforementioned condition is to give the State bound by the obligation full opportunity to remedy any harm that may have been caused by her initial conduct. It follows logically that counter-measures cannot be taken prior to the exhaustion of local remedies by the individual concerned. On the other hand, the subsequent conduct of the State of the forum may constitute a denial of justice which gives rise to State responsibility. This will entitle the State of the nationality of the alien concerned to resort to counter-measures without the necessity for that individual to seek redress at the local level. In such a situation the non-observance of the local remedies rule will not operate against the invocation of legitimate counter-measures.[119]

C.6.4. Conclusions

1. The invocation of counter-measures that are taken in response to breach of obligations of conduct will not be barred by the rule of the exhaustion of local remedies.

2. As regards obligations of result which permit an initial choice as to the means to be employed to attain the required result, breach will occur when such a result has not been achieved. An aggrieved State may take counter-measures, notwithstanding that any of her nationals who may have sustained injury has not exhausted local remedies. Consequently, the local remedies rule does not bar the invocation of legitimate counter-measures.

---

[117] Cf. *infra*, ch. 9 s. E.6.

[118] See Commentary on Art. 22 of the Draft Articles on State responsibility, *YILC*, vol. ii, part 2, 1977, p. 30, at pp. 48–9, paras. 53–4.

[119] On the question of the 'availability' and 'effectiveness' of remedies see ibid., pp. 47–8, paras. 47–51.

3. Where an obligation of result is intended to ensure certain guarantees to individual aliens, and it is stipulated that local remedies should be exhausted, a failure to observe that condition will constitute a bar to the invocation of legitimate counter-measures. This principle does not, however, apply to a case in which the subsequent conduct of the State of the forum amounts to a denial of justice. In a case of this kind the non-exhaustion of local remedies will not preclude resort to counter-measures. *A fortiori*, such measures may be legitimately invoked.

C. 7. THE RELATIONSHIP BETWEEN EXTRATERRITORIAL EXERCISE OF JURISDICTION AND THE CATEGORY OF COUNTER-MEASURES

C.7.1. Introduction

It is proposed to examine whether the principles of jurisdiction may be invoked with a view to preventing counter-measures from being implemented in the territories of third States. The practical significance of this issue for our study of counter-measures can be evidenced from two recent instances, namely: (*a*) the Carter Freeze Order; and (*b*) the Siberian gas pipeline sanctions.

As regards the first instance mentioned, the steps taken purported to be lawful counter-measures involving, *inter alia*, the freezing of Iranian assets in France and the United Kingdom.[120] This action was followed by the initiation of legal proceedings in London and Paris by the Bank Markazi Iran with the aim of lifting the freeze on the aforementioned assets.[121] Although these proceedings were discontinued, there is little doubt that the courts would have been obliged to examine the effect of the principles of jurisdiction on the legality of the counter-measures in question. With that in mind it is our intention to ascertain whether these measures were in fact taken consistently with the principles of jurisdiction. One must consider further whether, in the event of such consistency not being apparent, these measures may nevertheless be justifiably enforced in the territories of third States.

With respect to the second instance cited above, it may be recalled that there were mixed motives for the imposition of the sanctions involved. They were imposed initially as a mark of disapproval of the Soviet military intervention in Afghanistan in December 1979,[122] but were maintained subsequently as a reaction to the imposition of martial law in Poland in December

---

[120] Executive Order No. 12170 dated 14 Nov. 1979, 44 *Fed. Reg.*, 65729, 1979; *DSB*, Dec. 1979, p. 50.

[121] Suits in London were commenced on 30 Nov. 1979 in the High Court of Justice. The docket numbers were 1979-B-No. 5873, 1979-B-No. 5903, 1979-B-No. 5907, 1979-B-No. 5908, 1979-B-No. 5955, and 1980-B-No. 549. The Paris suits were commenced on 5 Dec. 1979 in the Tribunal de Grande Instance, Paris.

[122] See Memorandum dated 29 Dec. 1979 prepared by Owen, Legal Adviser of the Department of State, *AJIL*, vol. 74, 1980, pp. 418–20.

1981.[123] Thus, as a form of intensified pressure, the ban imposed by the United States on the export of high technology to the Soviet Union, including equipment for the Siberian gas pipeline, was extended to foreign subsidiaries of American companies on 22 June 1982.[124] This step, however, aroused consternation among Western European Governments. Pertinent to this, two issues must be considered: (*a*) whether the sanctions in question were consistent with the principles of jurisdiction; and (*b*) if the sanctions are shown not to be thus consistent, can they nevertheless be given effect in the territories of third States?

This subsection will examine the aforementioned issues by focusing on four of the principles on which jurisdiction is commonly based, namely: (*a*) the territoriality principle; (*b*) the nationality principle; (*c*) the protective principle; and (*d*) the effects principle.

Article VIII(2) of the International Monetary Fund Agreement provides for a special type of unenforceability.[125] It is not, however, our purpose to penetrate the extensive case law and literature which this Article has given rise to.[126] This said, it is conceded that it may have a bearing on the issue of enforcing counter-measures involving exchange contracts which violate the exchange control regulations of an IMF Member. It must also be stated that it is not intended to address questions of conflict of laws.[127]

C.7.2 *The territoriality principle*

According to this principle a State is entitled to exercise jurisdiction over persons and property within her domain 'to the exclusion of the jurisdiction of the other States'.[128] As a corollary to this, the Permanent Court stated in the *Lotus Case* that territorial jurisdiction 'cannot be exercised by a State

---

[123] President's speech on 13 Nov. 1982 concerning East–West Trade Relations and the Soviet Pipeline Sanctions, *ILM*, vol. 22, 1983, p. 349.

[124] 15 *Code of Federal Regulations* (hereinafter cited as *CFR*), parts 376, 379, and 385, 'Amendment of Oil and Gas Controls to the U.S.S.R.', 1982; reprinted in *ILM*, vol. 21, 1982, p. 864.

[125] 'Exchange contracts which involve the currency of any member and which are contrary to the exchange control regulations of that member maintained or imposed consistently with this Agreement shall be unenforceable in the territories of any member.' For the text of the IMF Agreement as amended see International Monetary Fund, *Articles of Agreement*, 1978.

[126] See Mann, *The Legal Aspects of Money*, 4th edn., 1982, ch. 14, pp. 372–400; Gold, *The Fund Agreement in the Courts*, vol. ii, 1982, generally but particularly ch. 11, p. 331, at pp. 353–9 and pp. 360–427; Pardieu, 'The Carter Freeze Order: Specific Problems Relating to the International Monetary Fund', *International Business Lawyer*, vol. 9, 1981, p. 97; Schneider, 'Problems of Recognition of the Carter Freeze Order by the German Courts', ibid., p. 103; Westrick, 'The Legality of Freeze Orders and the Extra-Territorial Effect of Foreign Freeze Orders in Germany in the Light of the Iranian Events', ibid., p. 105; Edwards, 'Extraterritorial Application of the U.S. Iranian Assets Control Regulations', *AJIL*, vol. 75, 1981, p. 870, at pp. 881ff.

[127] See Mann, *The Legal Aspects of Money*, ch. 15, pp. 401–33; Lowe, 'Public International Law and the Conflict of Laws: The European Response to the United States Export Administration Regulations', *International and Comparative Law Quarterly*, vol. 33, 1984, p. 515, at p. 519.

[128] Brierly, *The Law of Nations*, 1963, p. 162.

outside its territory except by virtue of a permissive rule derived from international custom or from a convention'.[129] However, this distinct statement of principle has been blurred by the following passage from the same judgment:

Far from laying down a general prohibition to the effect that States may not extend the application of their laws and the jurisdiction of their courts to persons, property or acts outside their territory, it leaves them in this respect a wide measure of discretion which is only limited in certain cases by prohibitive rules; as regards other cases, every State remains free to adopt the principle which it regards as best and most suitable.[130]

This passage when taken at its face value will indicate that a State has a wide discretion with respect to the extraterritorial application of her jurisdiction. Such an interpretation, however, will be inconsistent with the clear remarks made by the Permanent Court which are cited above. The way in which this apparent inconsistency may be removed is to interpret the reference to 'wide measure of discretion' in the light of other remarks uttered by the Court. According to this reasoning such discretion will be confined to those measures which States 'have been able to adopt without objections or complaints on the part of other States'.[131] It is submitted that such an interpretation is consistent with the principles of sovereign equality and non-intervention in matters concerning domestic jurisdiction of other States as enshrined in the Charter of the United Nations.[132]

It is now proposed to apply this conclusion to the Carter Freeze Order with a view to ascertaining whether its implementation was consistent with the principle of territoriality. The Order in question had the effect of freezing Iranian assets in London and Paris. In view of this fact the United States acted swiftly to persuade both the French and British Governments that her Order 'was justified as a matter of international law and enforceable in foreign courts'.[133] The two named governments avoided expressing any views on the question publicly, and to that extent they might be seen to acquiesce in the action taken by the United States. It is arguable, therefore, that due to this apparent acquiescence of the Governments of France and Great Britain the Order was not inconsistent with the principle of territoriality. On the other hand, the fact of that acquiescence does not of itself determine the legality of the counter-measures involved. Such legality must be established by ref-

---

[129] *The Lotus Case, PCIJ*, Ser. A, no. 10, 1927, p. 4, at pp. 18–19.

[130] Ibid., p. 19; for a criticism of this passage see Brownlie, 1979, p. 302.

[131] *The Lotus Case, PCIJ*, Ser. A, no. 10, 1927, p. 19.

[132] See Bridge, 'The Law and Politics of United States Foreign Policy Export Controls', *Legal Studies*, vol. 4(1), Mar. 1984, p. 2, at p. 9.

[133] Owen and Damrosch, 'The International Legal Status of Foreign Government Deposits in Overseas Branches of U.S. Banks', *University of Illinois Law Review*, 1982, p. 305, at p. 308; but see remarks by Higgins, 'Legal Responses to the Afghan–Iranian Crisis', *Proceedings of American Society of International Law*, vol. 74, 1980, pp. 250–5; Rosenthal and Knighton, *National Laws and International Commerce*, 1982, p. 7; Zoller, p. 99.

erence to the reasons underlying these measures and by considering whether the conditions of legality have been complied with. Given the establishment of the required legality, and subject to compliance with any constitutional requirement, French and British Courts would have had to give effect to the Freeze Order by virtue of its being a lawful counter-measure. It should be emphasized that such effect should be given even where the Freeze Order is shown to be in breach of the territoriality principle. The basis for this conclusion is that one of the main reasons for resorting to that action was to preserve the lives of the hostages. Hence, it is submitted that, since a breach of basic human rights standards was at issue, the idea of *erga omnes* obligations should impel even third States to support the counter-measures taken.

Turning now to the Siberian gas pipeline sanctions,[134] one must first consider whether these sanctions were imposed consistently with the principle of territoriality. The effect of the regulations promulgated by the United States Government on 22 June 1982[135] was to prohibit persons subject to the jurisdiction of the United States[136] from exporting or re-exporting to the Soviet Union products manufactured abroad by use of United States technology.[137] Thus, the regulations purported to extend to companies not incorporated in the United States, and to non-US equipment relating to oil and gas machinery.

The European Communities presented the United States with a Note setting out detailed arguments against the legality of these regulations. It was stated in the Note that the territoriality principle 'is a fundamental notion of international law, in particular insofar as it concerns the regulation of the social and economic activity in a State'.[138] Accordingly, the regulations were viewed as unlawful 'since they purport to regulate the activities of companies in the E.C., not under the territorial competence of the U.S.'.[139] For its part, the United Kingdom presented a further Note in which she supported the representation made on behalf of the European Communities. The British Note stated explicitly that 'HMG will not accept actions against persons in

---

[134] See 15 *CFR*, parts 379, 385, 399, 'Control of Export of Petroleum Transmission and Refining Equipment to the U.S.S.R.', 1981, reprinted in *ILM*, vol. 21, 1982, p. 855; see generally Bockslaff, 'The Pipeline Affair 1981/82: A Case History', *German Yearbook of International Law* (hereinafter cited as *GYIL*), vol. 27, 1984, p. 28; Hein, 'Extraterritorial Application of U.S. Export Controls—The Siberian Pipeline', *Proceedings of American Society of International Law*, 1983, pp. 241–50.

[135] 15 *CFR*, parts 376, 379, and 385, 'Amendment of Oil and Gas Controls to the U.S.S.R.', 1982, reprinted in *ILM*, vol. 21, 1982, p. 864.

[136] This included companies incorporated outside the USA if owned or controlled by US citizens, residents, or corporations. See 15 *CFR*, part 385, 2(*c*), 1982, reprinted in *ILM*, vol. 21, 1982, p. 866.

[137] See 15 *CFR*, parts 376, 379, and 385, 1982, reprinted in *ILM*, vol. 21, 1982, pp. 864–6.

[138] European Communities, 'Comments on the U.S. Regulations Concerning Trade with U.S.S.R.', *ILM*, vol. 21, 1982, p. 891, at p. 893, para. 5; see also Kuyper, 'The European Community and the US Pipeline Embargo: Comments on Comments', *GYIL*, vol. 27, 1984, p. 72, at p. 78.

[139] European Communities Comments, p. 893, para. 5.

the United Kingdom by authorities of other countries whose jurisdiction does not extend to such persons'.[140] Furthermore, acting under Section I of the Protection of Trading Interests Act, 1980, the Secretary of State for Trade directed United Kingdom companies with contracts for the supply of oil and gas equipment to the Soviet Union, to perform these contracts notwithstanding the sanctions imposed by the United States.[141] It is noteworthy that similar ministerial pronouncements were made in the three other States most affected by the sanctions.[142]

From the evidence so far examined it would appear that the Siberian gas pipeline sanctions were in breach of the principle of territoriality. There remains the question of whether, in spite of the existence of that breach, the sanctions should nevertheless be supported by third States. In this respect one recalls that the sanctions were imposed in response to the situation prevailing first in Afghanistan, and secondly in Poland. It seems clear that the motives underlying them were purely political and were not connected with a wish to apply lawful counter-measures.[143] Hence, they could not be regarded as lawful counter-measures even if they happened to be consistent with the principle of territoriality.

C.7.3. The nationality principle

It has been shown in the preceding subsection that a State may not in general exercise jurisdiction over acts performed outside her borders. However, the so-called 'nationality principle' provides one of the exceptions to that general rule. Thus, according to this principle jurisdiction may be assumed by a State to regulate the conduct of her nationals wherever they happen to be.[144] It must, however, be noted at the outset that there are limits to the extraterritorial exercise of jurisdiction over nationals. In this respect, Oppenheim points out:

[A] State is prevented from requiring such acts from its citizens abroad as are forbidden to them by the Municipal Law of the Land in which they reside, and from ordering them not to commit such acts as they are bound to commit according to the Municipal Law of the Land in which they reside.[145]

---

[140] Note No. 177 dated 18 Oct. 1982, which was presented to the US Department of State by the British Embassy in Washington. Text: *BYIL*, vol. 53, 1982, p. 453, at p. 454.

[141] Ibid.; see generally Lowe, 'International Law Issues Arising in the "Pipeline" Dispute: The British Position', *GYIL*, vol. 27, 1984, p. 54.

[142] See Kuyper, 'The European Community and the US Pipeline Embargo', p. 73.

[143] Although it may be argued that the situation in Afghanistan constitutes a breach of international law, there is no evidence to suggest that the sanctions imposed were intended to have the effect of lawful counter-measures.

[144] See Brownlie, 1979, p. 303, and other references cited by him; the decision of the District Court of The Hague in *Compagnie Européene des Pétroles S.A.* v *Sensor Nederland B.V.*, 1982, *ILM*, vol. 22, 1983, p. 66.

[145] Oppenheim, vol. i, 8th edn. by Lauterpacht, 1955, p. 296.

The criterion for determining the nationality of an individual is that of a genuine connection between that individual and the State asserting the nationality.[146] As regards the nationality of a corporation, the International Court declared that it should be the nationality of the State where it has been incorporated and where it has its registered office.[147] The Court further alluded to the fact that corporate nationality based on criteria other than incorporation and registration would not be admitted unless they satisfy the test of a 'genuine connection'.[148] In this respect, the American Law Institute takes the view that links of ownership and control by nationals of the United States are analogous to links of nationality.[149] However, the Institute has noted in its draft that the United States should not exercise her jurisdiction over foreign subsidiaries and corporations 'to require conduct that is prohibited, or to prohibit conduct that is required, in the State where the [...] corporation is organized or is doing business'.[150] From this it may be gathered that the nationality principle will be considered as an exception to the territoriality principle provided that its application does not violate the laws of the foreign State.

It is now proposed to relate this principle to the Carter Freeze Order. The Order was designed to extend to any corporation 'wheresoever organized or doing business which is owned or controlled'[151] by persons subject to the jurisdiction of the United States. However, the United States banks in which Iranian assets were deposited operated abroad as unincorporated branches of American banks rather than subsidiaries organized under English or French Law. It was probably due to this fact that neither of the two Governments concerned objected to the application of the Freeze Order.[152] To that extent it may be said that the Freeze Order did not conflict with the nationality principle. At the same time, it must be observed that even supposing such a conflict had existed, that would not in itself have constituted a bar to the recognition of the Freeze Order in the United Kingdom or France since that Order was part of a lawful counter-measure.

The Siberian pipeline dispute furnishes a more striking example of the tension which can arise as a result of an extraterritorial exercise of jurisdiction

---

[146] See *Nottebohm Case, ICJ Reports*, 1955, p. 4.

[147] See *Barcelona Traction Co. Case, ICJ Reports*, 1970, p. 3, at p. 42, para. 70.

[148] Ibid.; for a contrary view see Vagts, 'The Pipeline Controversy: An American Viewpoint', *GYIL*, vol. 27, 1984, p. 39, at p. 50.

[149] See American Law Institute, *Restatement of the Law: Foreign Relations Law of the United States (Revised)*, Tentative Draft 2, 1981, s. 418(2), p. 147; and see Comment *b*, on pp. 148–9.

[150] Ibid., s. 418(4)(*a*), p. 148.

[151] 31 *CFR*, ss. 535, 329(*c*), 1984.

[152] See Owen and Damrosch, 'The International Legal Status of Foreign Government Deposits in Overseas Branches of U.S. Banks', p. 305, at p. 309.

[153] See Sinclair, 'Responses to Extraterritorial Exercise of Jurisdiction: The Diplomatic Response', p. 1, at p. 7, paper read to the International Law Association Conference on Extra-

on the basis of nationality.[153] As has been noted,[154] the United States purported to impose her corporate nationality on companies incorporated within
the territory of the Member States of the European Communities and on
goods produced abroad by the use of United States technology.

The European Communities objected to the purported extension of United
States jurisdiction on several grounds.[155] First, the regulations claimed an
extraterritorial application over companies which were incorporated and
had their registered offices in European States. Therefore, according to the
nationality principle, such companies could not be regarded as nationals of
the United States. Secondly, the United States government could not insist
on an irreversible national identity for goods or technology once sold from
its territory. It would, therefore, follow that goods or technology situated
abroad could not serve as a basis for establishing jurisdiction over companies
trading in them. Thirdly, the regulations were designed to force European
companies to carry out United States trade policy towards the Soviet Union.
Such an attitude was considered by the European Communities as an
encroachment upon their public policy. Finally, the use of private agreements
to secure compliance with the regulations could not circumvent the limitations
imposed by international law.[156] At this point it may be stated that the British
Government observed that the measures in question were tantamount to a
frustration of existing contracts.[157]

The District Court of The Hague had an occasion to rule on the extraterritorial application of the regulations controlling re-export to the Soviet
Union of equipment relating to gas and oil.[158] The defendant was a company
incorporated in the Netherlands and had its registered office in The Hague.
The defendant pleaded that since it was a subsidiary of an American corporation it could not fulfil its obligations towards the plaintiff because of the
export embargo of June 1982. The Court rejected this plea, holding that '[t]he
American jurisdiction rule would not appear to be justified by the nationality

territorial Application on Laws and Responses Thereto held in London on 11 and 12 May 1983.
Copy provided to the present writer by courtesy of Sir Ian Sinclair.

[154] See *supra*, s. C.7.2.

[155] European Communities, 'Comments', *ILM*, vol. 21, 1982, p. 891, at pp. 893–5, paras. 6–
10. For similar views expressed by the British Government on this question see speech by Lord
Cockfield, *Hansard, HL Debs.*, vol. 434, col. 544, 2 Aug. 1982; Note No. 177 dated 18 Oct. 1982
which was presented to the US Department of State by the British Embassy in Washington on
'West Siberian Pipeline: US Export Administration Regulations and Related US Department
of Commerce Proceedings'. Text reproduced in *BYIL*, vol. 53, 1982, pp. 453–8.

[156] See also American Law Institute, *Restatement of the Law: Foreign Relations Law of the
United States (Revised)*, Tentative Draft 2, 1981, s. 402, pp. 97–8; Bridge, 'The Law and Politics
of United States Foreign Policy Export Controls', p. 2, at p. 15; see also Lowe, 'International
Law Issues Arising in the "Pipeline" Dispute' (and references cited).

[157] See statement by the Minister for Trade, *Hansard, HC Debs.*, vol. 31, col. 293, 8 Nov. 1982.

[158] *Compagnie Européene des Pétroles S.A.* v *Sensor Nederland B.V.*, 1982, *ILM*, vol. 22, 1983,
p. 66.

principle in so far as that rule brings within its scope companies of other than U.S. nationality'.[159]

To conclude, the present writer finds himself in agreement with the views expressed in the Memorandum of the European Communities and in the *Sensor Case,* to the effect that the sanctions were not in conformity with the nationality principle. To relate this finding to our main theme: as has been mentioned,[160] since the sanctions could not have been justified on any legal grounds, they would have remained as unlawful counter-measures even if compliance with the nationality principle had not been in issue.

C.7.4. *The protective principle*

The protective principle provides that a State may assume jurisdiction to proscribe offences taking place outside her territory but threatening her own security.[161] The kind of acts which may be guarded against include espionage, counterfeiting of the State's currency, as well as the falsification of her official documents.[162] In modern times, it may also be necessary to assume jurisdiction to protect the economy of the State.[163] That said, any claim for the exercise of jurisdiction on the basis of the protective principle must not be inconsistent with the so-called balance-of-interest factor.[164]

The foregoing points may now be related to the freezing of the Iranian assets. The President of the United States based his Order on the following grounds: 'the situation in Iran constitutes an unusual and extraordinary threat to the national security, foreign policy and economy of the United States'.[165] It is evident from these remarks that the principal aim of the Order was to protect the national security and the economy of the United States from being destabilized by the action of Iran. The motive of protecting the economy was reiterated in the statement which accompanied the Order: 'This Order is in response to reports that the Government of Iran is about to withdraw its funds.'[166] Furthermore, the Freeze Order was apparently not inconsistent with the balance-of-interest factor in that the interests of the United States, France, and the United Kingdom were closely connected. Accordingly, it is arguable that the Freeze Order was in conformity with the protective principle. Finally, irrespective of whether or not such conformity

---

[159] Ibid., p. 72, para. 7.3.2.

[160] See *supra*, s. C.7.2.

[161] See Brownlie, 1979, and other authors cited by him. See also American Law Institute, *Restatement of the Law: Foreign Relations Law of the United States (Revised)*, Tentative Draft 2, 1981, s. 402(3), p. 98.

[162] See Comment *d.*, ibid., p. 99.

[163] See Bowett, 'Jurisdiction: Changing Patterns of Authority over Activities and Resources', *BYIL*, vol. 53, 1982, p. 1, at p. 11.

[164] See American Law Institute, *Restatement of the Law: Foreign Relations Law of the United States (Revised)*, Tentative Draft 2, 1981, s. 403, pp. 103–4.

[165] Executive Order No. 12170 of 14 Nov. 1979, 44 *Fed. Reg.*, 65729, 1979.

[166] *DSB*, vol. 79, Dec. 1979, p. 50.

existed, the Order in question would have had to be given extraterritorial effect since it constituted a legitimate counter-measure.

To consider now the relation of the protective principle to the gas pipeline sanctions, it must be noted at the outset that the United States herself had not sought to base these sanctions on that principle.[167] This is evident from the fact that she based her embargo on the foreign policy controls[168] and not on the national security controls. The following interesting remarks were pertinently made by the District Court of The Hague:

> Under the protection principle, it is permissible for a State to exercise jurisdiction over acts—wheresoever and by whomsoever performed—that jeopardise the security or creditworthiness of that State or other State interests. Such other State interests do not include the foreign policy interest that the U.S. measure seeks to protect. The protection principle cannot therefore be invoked in support of the validity of the jurisdiction rule here at issue.[169]

Furthermore, it is worth recalling the reasons which prompted the United States to impose a ban on the export of high technology to the Soviet Union. First, the military intervention by the Soviet Union in Afghanistan,[170] and secondly, the declaration of martial law in Poland.[171] It is submitted that in neither of these two instances was the security of the United States threatened. Furthermore, unlike the case of the freeze of the Iranian assets, there was no sense of common interest in these particular instances. Hence, it is difficult to see how the interests of the United States at stake could be regarded as being of equal importance to those of the European States involved.

On the basis of the foregoing considerations, the present writer concludes that the Siberian gas pipeline sanction could not be justified on the basis of the protective principle. Finally, to reiterate, the very nature of the motives behind these sanctions preclude them from being considered as legal counter-measures even if jurisdiction is not in issue.

C.7.5. The effects principle

This principle provides that acts carried out abroad which produce a direct and substantial harmful effect on a State's territory may be proscribed by that State.[172] However, it must be noted from the start that there is a considerable

---

[167] See European Communities Comments, p. 897, para. 13; Bridge, 'The Law and Politics of the United States Foreign Policy Export Controls', p. 10.

[168] 50 *USC*, Appendix, s. 2405. Unger, former General Counsel, US Department of Commerce, argued that furtherance of foreign policy objectives was connected to the protective principle; see his remarks on 'Extraterritorial Application of U.S. Export Controls—The Siberian Pipeline', *Proceedings of American Society of International Law*, 1983, p. 250, at p. 254.

[169] *Compagnie Européene des Pétroles S.A.* v *Sensor Nederland B. V.*, 1982, *ILM*, vol. 22, 1983, p. 66, at p. 72, para. 7.3-3.

[170] See *DSB*, vol. 80, 1980, pp. 45-6.

[171] See 'US Measures Against Polish Government and Soviet Union', *AJIL*, vol. 76, 1982, p. 379.

[172] See Brownlie, 1979, p. 307, and other references cited by him.

controversy surrounding the scope of this principle.[173] The American Law Institute, for example, has recently stated that

Jurisdiction on the basis of effect in the territory [. . .] may be more acceptable when it is applied to persons who have the nationality (or corporate affiliation) of the state exercising jurisdiction, than would be the same jurisdiction applied to nonresident aliens.[174]

Although these remarks are safe from contradiction, they do not take account of the possibility that conduct displayed abroad may produce widely different effects within the jurisdiction of a given State. It is therefore submitted that only in cases where the conduct involved produces harmful effects may the principle under review be invoked to justify breach of the territoriality principle. To conclude otherwise would imply that conduct involving purely minor breaches in one State would become automatically amenable to the jurisdiction of another State simply because it violates the laws of that State.

This may now be related to the Carter Freeze Order. To begin with, the claim made by the United States for an extraterritorial jurisdiction was not based on the effects principle. Rather, it was based on the nationality principle. None the less, it is worth considering whether the Freeze Order was in fact consistent with the effects principle. It is submitted that the establishment of such consistency would depend on whether the withdrawal of the Iranian assets from branches of American banks in London and Paris would have had direct and substantial effects in the United States. However, had the Freeze Order proved to be inconsistent with the effects principle, it could still have been enforced by virtue of its being a lawful counter-measure.

Turning to the Siberian gas pipeline embargo, the United States had at no time claimed that failure to enforce the embargo would adversely affect her national economy.[175] In this respect the European Communities argued that in all probability exports from their Member States to the Soviet Union could have 'no direct effect on U.S. trade'.[176] Similarly, the District Court of The Hague stated that 'it cannot, however, be seen how the export to Russia of goods not originating in the United States by a non-American exporter could have any direct and illicit effects within the United States'.[177]

---

[173] See *Aide-mémoire* delivered by the British Government to the Commission of the EEC on 20 Oct. 1969 in connection with measures taken by the Commission which affected ICI, *British Practice in International Law*, 1967, p. 58, at p. 59. Professor Jennings accepts the 'effects principle' provided that it is not relied upon for causing interference with the territorial jurisdiction of other States. 'Extraterritorial Jurisdiction and the United States Antitrust Laws', *BYIL*, vol. 33, 1957, p. 146, at p. 153; Bridge, 'The Law and Politics of United States Foreign Policy Export Controls', p. 9.

[174] American Law Institute, *Restatement of the Law: Foreign Relations Law of the United States (Revised)*, Tentative Draft 2, 1981, s. 402(1)(c), p. 98, and Comment *b*, p. 99.

[175] But see Vagts, 'The Pipeline Controversy', p. 52.

[176] European Communities Comments, p. 897, para. 13.

[177] *Compagnie Européene des Pétroles S.A.* v *Sensor Nederland B.V.*, *ILM*, vol. 22, 1983, p. 66, at p. 73, para. 7.3.4.

On the basis of the material examined in this subsection, therefore, it is difficult to reach a conclusion different from that which was arrived at by the European Communities, and by The Hague Court. As has been emphasized already, these sanctions could not have been justified as lawful counter-measures due to the lack of any legally acceptable motivation.

C.7.6. *Conclusions*

1. In order to give effect to any retaliatory action, it needs to be shown that the action in question constitutes a lawful counter-measure.

2. The foregoing requirement must be fulfilled irrespective of whether or not the action involved is compatible with principles of jurisdiction.

3. As to whether counter-measures should be given effect by the courts of third States particularly where such measures are in breach of the principles of jurisdiction, the state of the evidence is equivocal. However, it appears reasonable to argue in support of giving such effect in cases where the measures taken are proven to be lawful.

4. Where the breach justifying resort to counter-measures involves an obligation *erga omnes*, it is arguable that an extra incentive is given to third States to support the action taken.

D. A GENERAL CONCLUSION ON COLLATERAL CONSTRAINTS

This chapter has dealt with those collateral constraints which have been given substance both by practice and principle. No doubt both the identity and the content of collateral constraints are subjects which may be developed further in the future. It is hoped that those of contemporary relevance have been covered in this review.

8

The Legality of Non-forcible Counter-measures within the Law of Treaties

A. THE PURPOSE

According to general international law a violation of a treaty provision opens several avenues of redress for the injured party. One such avenue is the right to resort to non-forcible counter-measures. This chapter will initially examine the pertinent doctrine, jurisprudence, and State practice in order to determine the extent to which that right may be exercised in response to a treaty violation. Against such a background it is proposed to study how far there might be a relationship between the category of counter-measures and Article 60 of the 1969 Vienna Convention on the Law of Treaties.[1] It will be shown in the process whether these two forms of remedy are identical, or related but not identical.

B. THE POSITION ACCORDING TO CUSTOMARY LAW

B.1. THE WRITINGS OF PUBLICISTS

The majority of publicists recognize that the breach of a treaty entitles the aggrieved party to abrogate or suspend the treaty as between itself and the party perpetrating the breach.[2] Thus Oppenheim, writing in 1905, acknowledged that reprisals were admissible in the case of 'non-compliance with treaty obligations'.[3] Similarly, Hall noted that reprisals could consist in the 'suspension of the operation of treaties'.[4] In a like manner Rousseau admitted that reprisals would specifically apply to the case in which a treaty had been violated.[5] Fitzmaurice stated that 'effective self-redress must include the

---

[1] Text: *UNCLT Doc.*, pp. 289–301.

[2] See Sinha, *Unilateral Denunciation of Treaty Because of Prior Violations of Obligations by the Other Party*, 1966 (hereinafter cited as Sinha), pp. 83–4 and the authors cited by him, ibid., pp. 8–26. For different views see the *Harvard Draft Convention on the Law of Treaties*, Commentary on Art. 27 concerning 'Violation of Treaty Obligations', *AJIL*, vol. 29, suppl., 1935, p. 1077, at p. 1089; Briggs, 'Unilateral Denunciation of Treaties: The Vienna Convention and the International Court of Justice', *AJIL*, vol. 68, 1974, p. 51, at p. 55.

[3] Oppenheim, vol. ii, p. 35.

[4] Hall, 8th edn. by Higgins, 1924, p. 433.

[5] Rousseau, *Principes généraux du droit international public*, vol. i, 1944, p. 371.

possibility in certain cases of resorting to action that may involve [. . .] a non-performance or infraction [. . .] of a different treaty. This would have to be based on reprisals'.[6] Finally, this citation of the opinions of diverse authorities may be concluded by the following passage from McNair's treatise on the Law of Treaties:

[T]he right to resort to non-forcible reprisals or other non-forcible measures in order to stop or redress a breach of treaty remains. [. . .] We are aware of no reason why a State injured by the breach of a treaty by another party should not take non-forcible reprisals against it, that is, non-forcible measures (economic, financial, or other) which would, but for the fact that they are reprisals, be illegal; for instance, the partial non-observance of a commericial treaty [. . .] such as the prohibition of exports to or imports from the wrongdoing country.[7]

Attention may now be given to the limitations on the right of abrogation. Many of the classical jurists maintain that the violation of any one Article releases the aggrieved party from further performance of its obligations under the treaty.[8] However, relatively recent doctrinal views hold that the right of termination may only be exercised in the event of material breach. Hall, for example, states that

There can be no question that the breach of a stipulation which is material to the main object, or if there are several, to one of the main objects, liberates the party other than that committing the breach from the obligations of the contract; but it would be seldom that the infraction of an article which is either disconnected from the main object, or is unimportant [. . .] with respect to it, could in fairness absolve the other party from performance of his share of the rest of the agreement.[9]

The question which remains to be answered is whether a treaty may be violated in some minor respect with impunity. According to the Harvard research group, an aggrieved State 'may provisionally suspend performance of its obligations under the treaty *vis-à-vis* the State charged with failure'.[10] Similarly, the publicists who reserve the right of termination to cases involving

---

[6] Fitzmaurice, *Fourth Report on the Law of Treaties*, Doc. A/CN.4/120, 17 Mar. 1959, *YILC*, vol. ii, 1959, p. 37, at p. 67, para. 84.

[7] McNair, 1961, p. 579. For similar views see Simma, 'Reflections on Article 60 of the Vienna Convention on the Law of Treaties and its Background in General International Law', *Österreichische Zeitschrift für öffentliches Recht*, 1970, p. 5, at p. 22; David, *The Strategy of Treaty Termination, Lawful Breaches and Retaliations*, 1975, p. 258; Zoller, p. 43.

[8] e.g. Grotius, Book II, ch. 15, s. xv, p. 405; Vattel, Book II, ch. 13, s. 202, p. 215.

[9] Hall, 8th edn. by Higgins, 1924, p. 409. For a confirmation of this view see: Crandall, *Treaties, Their Making and Enforcement*, 1916, p. 456; Brierly, *The Law of Nations*, pp. 327–8; Oppenheim, vol. i, 8th edn. by Lauterpacht, 1955, p. 947 n. 4; McNair, 1961, p. 571; Fitzmaurice, *Second Report on the Law of Treaties*, Doc. A/CN.4/107, 15 Mar. 1957, p. 16, at p. 30; Parry, 'The Law of Treaties', in Sørensen, 1968, p. 239.

[10] Art. 27(*b*), *The Harvard Draft Convention on the Law of Treaties*, p. 1094. It should be noted, however, that this is the only permissible form of unilateral action envisaged in *The Harvard Draft Convention* irrespective of the seriousness of breach, ibid., p. 1089.

material breaches acknowledge the right of suspension in all other cases. McNair, for example, has this interesting comment to make:

In practice, at any rate in regard to minor breaches of treaty it is not uncommon for the injured State, by way of sanction, to suspend the operation of a provision broken. The precise juridical status of this practice is not clear, and little authority exists. The practice seems to fall into the category of non-forcible reprisals and does not evince an intention to abrogate either the whole treaty or the portion of it which has been broken.[11]

Furthermore, it has been noted that an aggrieved State may, for policy considerations, opt for a provisional suspension even in the case of a material breach.[12] In such a case the suspension will not assume an irreversible character.[13] In other words, the suspension will not have an impact on the legal existence of the treaty in question.

A second limitation on the right of termination is that such a right must be exercised within a reasonable time after the occurrence of the breach. Oppenheim states that 'if the State possessing such a right does not exercise it in due time, it must be taken for granted that such a right has been waived'.[14]

A third limitation on the exercise of the right of abrogation concerns proportionality. Thus, after instancing non-compliance with treaty obligations as a form of reprisals, Oppenheim has admitted that reprisals 'must be in proportion to the wrong done, and to the amount of compulsion necessary to get reparation'.[15] Fitzmaurice equally recognizes the right in question provided that the action taken is proportionate in its effects.[16] An aspect of proportionality that is specifically mentioned in the literature concerns the separability of treaty provisions. Thus, where it is possible to sever the particular provision which has been violated, the abrogation of the whole treaty in which it is embodied will not be permitted.[17] Nevertheless, it has also been mentioned by some publicists that a retaliatory measure may

[11] McNair, 1961, p. 571; see also Fitzmaurice, *Fourth Report on the Law of Treaties*, Doc. A/CN.120, 17 Mar. 1959, *YILC*, vol. ii, 1959, p. 37, at p. 69, para. 69; Sinha, pp. 206–7; Simma, 'Reflections on Article 60 of the Vienna Convention', p. 38.

[12] Ibid., pp. 37–8.

[13] Ibid., p. 14; see also Jiménez de Aréchaga, 'International Law in the Past Third of a Century', *R.d.C.*, vol. 159(1), 1978, p. 1, at p. 81; Sinclair, *The Vienna Convention on the Law of Treaties*, 2nd edn., 1984, p. 189.

[14] Oppenheim, vol. i, 8th edn. by Lauterpacht, 1955, p. 948; see also Draft Art. 19(3) (iii), Fitzmaurice, *Second Report on the Law of Treaties*, Doc. A/CN.4/107, 15 Mar. 1957, *YILC*, vol. ii, 1957, p. 16, at p. 31; McNair, 1961, p. 571, note *c*; American Law Institute, *Restatement of the Law: Second, Foreign Relations Law of the United States*, 1965, s.158(1)(*a*), p. 484; Simma, 'Reflections on Article 60 of the Vienna Convention', p. 32.

[15] Oppenheim, vol. ii, 7th edn. by Lauterpacht, 1952, p. 141.

[16] Commentary on Draft Art. 18, Fitzmaurice, *Fourth Report on the Law of Treaties*, Doc. A/CN.4/120, 17 Mar. 1959, *YILC*, vol. ii, 1959, p. 37, at p. 67, para. 85.

[17] See Art. 30 and Commentary, *The Harvard Draft Convention on the Law of Treaties*, pp. 1134–44, 1203; McNair, 1961, pp. 474–84, 571; Sinha, pp. 88–90, 207–8; Simma, 'Reflections on Article 60 of the Vienna Convention', p. 31.

involve non-performance of a provision in the treaty other than that which has been violated.[18] It has been explained in the literature that the need for securing an adequate remedy for the breach of one treaty may justify retaliatory action against another treaty.[19] McNair accepts this position provided that it could be shówn that of the two treaties 'each was the consideration for the other and that they were intended to be interdependent'.[20]

The fourth limitation concerns the requirement of making a prior demand for reparation. Oppenheim, for example, instanced a refusal to perform a treaty obligation as a mode of negative reprisal.[21] He further added that resort to reprisals would be lawful only if preceded by an unsuccessful demand for reparation.[22]

The fifth limitation concerns the termination or suspension of multilateral treaties on the grounds of breach. The views of the publicists may be placed in four categories. Publicists who fall within the first category take the view that the non-fulfilment of a treaty provision by one party does not justify the unilateral termination of that treaty by another.[23] In their view, however, the contracting parties other than the defaulting one may withhold performance of their obligations under the treaty in relation to that party.[24] Some of the publicists who belong to this category maintain that a party which is particularly injured by the breach may lawfully suspend its obligation in relation to the defaulting party.[25]

The publicists who fall within the second category appear to affirm the right of reprisals according to the type of the multilateral agreement that has been violated. In distinguishing between law-making treaties and contractual treaties, they concede that only with respect to the latter may the right be exercised.[26] Fitzmaurice, for example, takes the view that 'a fundamental breach by one party of a treaty on human rights could neither justify termination of the treaty, nor corresponding breaches of the treaty even in respect of nationals of the offending party'.[27] The third group of publicists

---

[18] See Draft Art. 18(2), Fitzmaurice, *Second Report on the Law of Treaties*, Doc. A/CN.4/107, 15 Mar. 1957, *YILC*, vol. ii, 1957, p. 16, at p. 30; also Commentary on Draft Art. 20(3), Waldock, *Second Report on the Law of Treaties*, Doc. A/CN.4/156 and Add. 1–3, 20 Mar., 10 Apr., 30 Apr., and 5 June 1963, *YILC*, vol. ii, 1963, p. 36, at p. 76, para. 14; Sinha, p. 215, para 2.

[19] See Draft Art. 18(1), 37 (F), Fitzmaurice, *Fourth Report on the Law of Treaties*, Doc. A/CN.4/120, 17 Mar. 1959, *YILC*, vol. ii, 1959, p. 37, at pp. 45 and 50.

[20] McNair, 1961, p. 571 n. (*e*).

[21] Oppenheim, vol. ii, 7th edn. by Lauterpacht, 1952, p. 140.

[22] Ibid., p. 143; see also Simma, 'Reflections on Article 60 of the Vienna Convention', p. 13.

[23] See Kelsen, *Principles of International Law*, 1952, p. 358; McNair, 1961, p. 580.

[24] Kelsen, *Principles of International Law*; McNair, 1961, p. 583.

[25] See Dahm, *Völkerrecht*, vol. iii, 1961, p. 137; Verdross, *Völkerrecht*, 1964, p. 178.

[26] See Art. 20, Fitzmaurice, *Fourth Report on the Law of Treaties*, Doc. A/CN.4/120, 17 Mar. 1959, *YILC*, vol. ii, 1959, p. 37, at p. 46; for similar views see Simma and other references cited by him, Simma, 'Reflections on Article 60 of the Vienna Convention', p. 46.

[27] Commentary on Art. 19.1(iv), Fitzmaurice, *Second Report on the Law of Treaties*, Doc. A/CN.4/107, 15 Mar. 1957, *YILC*, vol. ii, 1957, p. 16, at p. 54, para. 125. For text of Art. 19 see

simply maintain that an aggrieved State may withdraw from the treaty on grounds of breach only in the cases where all the other parties are responsible for that breach.[28]

Finally, the fourth category may be illustrated by Draft Article 11 as proposed by Riphagen in the *Sixth Report on State Responsibility*:

1. The injured State is not entitled to suspend the performance of its obligations towards the State which has committed the internationally wrongful act to the extent that such obligations are stipulated in a multilateral treaty to which both States are parties and it is established that:

   (a) The failure to perform such obligations by one State party necessarily affects the exercise of the rights or the performance of obligations of all other States parties to the treaty; or
   (b) Such obligations are stipulated for the protection of collective interests of the States parties to the multilateral treaty; or
   (c) Such obligations are stipulated for the protection of individual persons irrespective of their nationality.

2. The injured State is not entitled to suspend the performance of its obligations towards the State which has committed the internationally wrongful act if the multilateral treaty imposing the obligations provides for a procedure of collective decisions for the purpose of enforcement of the obligations imposed by it, unless and until such collective decision, including the suspension of obligations towards the State which has committed the internationally wrongful act, has been taken; in such case, subparagraphs 1(*a*) and 1(*b*) do not apply to the extent that such decision so determines.[29]

Furthermore, Riphagen stated in Draft Article 13 that if the breach committed 'constitutes a manifest violation of obligations arising from a multilateral treaty, which destroys the object and purpose of that treaty as a whole', the injured State is entitled to suspend her obligations towards the defaulting State.[30]

B.2. JURISPRUDENCE

B.2.1. The Tacna–Arica Arbitration, *1925*[31]

Paragraph 1 of Article 3 of the Treaty of Ancon of 1883 between Chile and Peru stipulated that the provinces of Tacna and Arica should remain 'subject to Chilean laws and authority during a period of ten years.'[32] Paragraph 2 of

---

ibid., p.31; see also Fitzmaurice, 'The General Principles of International Law Considered from the Standpoint of the Rule of Law', *R.d.C.*, vol. 92(2), 1957, at p. 120, s.70.

[28] See Guggenheim, *Lehrbuch des Völkerrechts*, vol. i, 1948, p. 109; Delbez, *Les Principes généraux du droit international public*, 1964, p. 339.

[29] Riphagen, *Sixth Report on (1) The Content, Forms and Degrees of State Responsibility and (2) The 'Implementation' (Mise en Œuvre) of International Responsibility and the Settlement of Disputes*, Doc. A/CN.4/389, 2 Apr. 1985, pp. 21–2.

[30] Ibid., p. 23.

[31] *RIAA*, vol. ii, p. 923.

[32] Ibid., p. 926.

the same Article provided that a plebiscite should be held at the end of that period to determine whether sovereignty over the two provinces was to remain with Chile or to revert to Peru.[33]

Peru alleged that Chile had been pursuing a policy which she described as 'Chilenization' of the aforementioned provinces.[34] Further, she concluded that such conduct on the part of the Chilean Government prevented the execution of the plebiscite in accordance with Article 3 of the Treaty.[35] Consequently, Peru held herself to be discharged from her obligation under that Article.[36]

This dispute was submitted by special agreement to the President of the United States for arbitral settlement.[37] President Coolidge, who acted as sole arbitrator, concluded that although he did not condone the 'Chilenization' process, he nevertheless was unable to uphold Peru's contention.[38] He added that

It is manifest that if abuses of administration could have the effect of terminating such an agreement, it would be necessary to establish such serious conditions as the consequence of administrative wrongs as would operate to frustrate the purpose of the agreement, and, in the opinion of the Arbitrator, a situation of such gravity has not been shown.[39]

The above remarks clearly indicate that only a very serious breach of Article 3 could have justified the release of Peru from her obligation under that Article. However, although the Arbitrator disapproved of the 'Chilenization' process, he made no allusion as to whether such a process entitled Peru to take retaliatory measures short of terminating the Treaty.

B.2.2. The Diversion of Water from the River Meuse, 1937[40]

In this dispute the Netherlands as the Applicant State requested the Court to adjudge and declare that certain works constructed by Belgium were in violation of the Treaty of 1863.[41] Belgium, for her part, contended that, 'by constructing certain works contrary to the terms of the Treaty, the Applicant has forfeited the right to invoke the treaty against the Respondent'.[42] Thus, without holding the Treaty to have been terminated, Belgium claimed the right to suspend one of its provisions in response to a breach of that same provision by the Netherlands.

---

[33] Ibid.
[34] Ibid., p. 935.
[35] Ibid., p. 929.
[36] Ibid.
[37] See Art. 2 of the Protocol of Arbitration between Chile and Peru, 20 July 1922, ibid., p. 923.
[38] Ibid., p. 943.
[39] Ibid., pp. 943–4.
[40] *PCIJ*, 1937, ser. A/B, no. 70, p. 4.
[41] Ibid., pp. 5–6.
[42] Ibid., p. 8.

The Court held that the Netherlands had not acted in breach of her Treaty obligation.[43] In similar vein, the Court ruled that the conduct complained of by the Netherlands did not violate the terms of the Treaty.[44] Consequently, the Court was not disposed to adopt a position with respect to the Belgian contention.[45] However, Judge Anzilotti stated that the principle of *inadimplenti non est adimplendum* underlying the Belgian contention 'is so just, so equitable, so universally recognized that it must be applied in international relations also'.[46] In his view, therefore, the Netherlands was precluded from invoking the Treaty as a basis for her claim against Belgium.[47] This approach found support from Judge Hudson, who indicated that the principle of *exceptio non adimpleti contractus* should apply to treaty relations.[48] He maintained that 'where two parties have assumed an identical or a reciprocal obligation, one party which is engaged in a continuing non-performance of that obligation should not be permitted to take advantage of a similar non-performance of that obligation by the other party'.[49] In conclusion, although the Court declined to pronounce on the Belgian contention, significant weight has been attached to the views expressed by Judge Anzilotti.[50]

B.2.3. The Namibia (South West Africa) Advisory Opinion, *1971*[51]

The Security Council recognized the validity of the termination by the United Nations General Assembly[52] of South Africa's Mandate over South West Africa.[53] It further declared that the continued presence of South Africa in Namibia was illegal, and called upon States to act in accordance with that declaration. Thereafter, the Security Council requested the Court for an Advisory Opinion on the following question: 'What are the legal consequences for States of the continued presence of South Africa in Namibia, notwithstanding Security Council Resolution 276(1970)?'.[54]

In examining the legality of the termination of the Mandate by the General Assembly on account of the breach of its terms by South Africa, the Court

---

[43] Ibid., pp. 29–30.

[44] Ibid., pp. 20, 25–7.

[45] Ibid., p. 30.

[46] Diss. Op., ibid., p. 45, at p. 50.

[47] Ibid.

[48] Ibid., Sep. Op., p. 73, at p. 77.

[49] Ibid., p. 77.

[50] See Commentary on Draft Art. 57 concerning 'Termination or Suspension of the operation of a treaty as a consequence of its breach', *YILC*, vol. II, 1966, p. 254, para. 4; Jiménez de Aréchaga, 'International Law in the Past Third of a Century', *R.d.C.*, vol. 159(1), 1978, p. 1, at p. 81; Sinclair, *The Vienna Convention on the Law of Treaties*, 2nd edn., 1984, p. 201 n. 128; Zoller, pp. 16–17.

[51] *ICJ Reports*, 1971, p. 16.

[52] General Assembly Resolution 2145 (XXI) (1966), *UNGAOR*, 21st Sess., suppl. 16(A/6316), 1966, pp. 2–3.

[53] Security Council Resolution 276 (1970), *Yearbook of the United Nations*, 1970, p. 752.

[54] Security Council Resolution 284 (1970), ibid., p. 754.

stated that 'a relationship was established between all Members of the United Nations […] and each mandatory Power'.[55] It further observed that '[o]ne of the fundamental principles governing the international relationship thus established is that a party which disowns or does not fulfil its obligations cannot be recognized as retaining the rights which it claims to derive from the relationship'.[56] The Court recognized that the Mandate was an international agreement which had the character of a treaty.[57] It further accepted that General Assembly Resolution 2145(XXI) determined that South Africa, by committing a material breach, had repudiated that treaty.[58] Hence in the opinion of the Court, '[t]he resolution in question is […] to be viewed as the exercise of the right to terminate a relationship in case of a deliberate and persistent violation of obligations which destroys the very object and purpose of that relationship'.[59]

Having reached these conclusions, the Court recognized the existence of the following general principle of law:

[T]hat a right of termination on account of breach must be presumed to exist in respect of all treaties […]. The silence of a treaty as to the existence of such a right cannot be interpreted as implying the exclusion of a right which has its source outside of the treaty, in general international law.[60]

Professor Briggs argued that the Court did not produce any evidence in support of its assertion that there existed a general principle of law providing for 'a right of termination on account of breach'.[61] The implication of these remarks is that Briggs himself was in effect denying the existence of such a principle. With all due respect, the present writer takes the view that the 'implied right' affirmed by the Court is derived from an established principle of international law. It is conceded none the less that the right in question must not be exercised in an arbitrary manner. To borrow the phrase adopted by the International Law Commission, its invocation 'does not *ipso facto* put an end to the treaty'.[62]

B.2.4. Appeal Relating to the Jurisdiction of the ICAO Council, *1972*[63]

The justification offered by India for the suspension in 1971 of her aviation

---

[55] *ICJ Reports*, 1971, p. 16, at p. 45, para. 90.
[56] Ibid., para. 91.
[57] Ibid., p. 47, para. 94.
[58] Ibid., para. 95.
[59] Ibid.
[60] Ibid., para. 96.
[61] Briggs, 'Unilateral Denunciation of Treaties: The Vienna Convention and the International Court of Justice', *AJIL*, vol. 68, 1974, p. 51, at p. 55.
[62] Report of the Commission on the work of its eighteenth session, Doc. A/6309/Rev. 1, 4 May–19 July 1966, *YILC*, vol. ii, 1966, p. 172, at p. 254, para. 5.
[63] *ICJ Reports*, 1972, p. 46.

treaties[64] with Pakistan was not said to rest on the treaties themselves.[65] Rather, it lay on 'a principle of general international law, or of international treaty law, allowing of suspension or termination on this ground'.[66] The Court held that this contention could not have the effect of nullifying jurisdictional clauses.[67] At the same time, however, it added that such a contention was not 'necessarily wrong but that [its] validity has not yet been determined'.[68] These remarks clearly do not pursue very far the question of the legality under customary international law of terminating or suspending a violated treaty.

Pakistan claimed that the Court had no jurisdiction since one of India's contentions was that the treaties were not in force.[69] The Court did not uphold this contention for, *inter alia*, the reason that

What India has affirmed is that the Treaties [...] are suspended (or that their operation is suspended) as between herself and Pakistan. This is not the same thing as saying that they are not in force in the definitive sense, or even that they have wholly ceased to be in force as between the two Parties concerned.[70]

The above remarks make it clear that the Court did not view the suspension by India of the treaties as tantamount to a termination of their legal existence. The conclusion to be drawn is that where counter-measures take the form of a temporary non-performance of a treaty obligation, the legal existence of that treaty is not thereby placed in question. Thus, the jurisdictional clauses of such a treaty may be invoked to test the legality of its suspension by the aggrieved party. Moreover, since the treaty in question is not definitively terminated, it will become operative again once the breach that caused the suspension has been rectified.

B.2.5. The US–France Air Services Award, *1978*[71]

As has been noted elsewhere,[72] this Award dealt with the dispute concerning the Air Services Agreement of 27 March 1946 between France and the United States. The Tribunal was asked to determine whether the United States had the right to take counter-measures notwithstanding her commitment to peaceful settlement under the aforesaid Agreement.[73] The Tribunal, however, far from confining its attention to the specific question before it, pronounced on the legality of counter-measures in general. It stated as follows:

---

[64] The 1944 Chicago International Civil Aviation Convention, and International Air Services Transit Agreement, texts: Hudson, *International Legislation*, vol. ix, pp. 204 and 228.
[65] *ICJ Reports*, 1972, p. 63, para. 30(*c*).
[66] Ibid.
[67] Ibid., pp. 53–4, para. 16(*b*); p. 64, para. 31.
[68] Ibid., p. 64, para. 31.
[69] Ibid., p. 52, para. 14.
[70] Ibid., p. 53, para. 16(*a*).
[71] *ILR*, vol. 54, 1979, p. 304.
[72] Cf. *supra*, ch. 4 s. D.
[73] *ILR*, vol. 54, 1979, p. 312, para. 2 (B); cf. *infra*, ch. 9.

If a situation arises which, in one State's view, results in the violation of an international obligation by another State, the first State is entitled, within the limits set
by the general rules of international law pertaining to the use of armed force, to
affirm its right through 'counter-measures'.[74]

Thus, according to the Tribunal, only an underlying breach can justify
resort to counter-measures.[75] Furthermore, such measures should be preceded
by a demand for redress,[76] and conform with the principle of proportionality.[77] Having decided that the United States had not infringed any of these
conditions, the Tribunal concluded that she had the right to impose certain
counter-measures against France.[78]

This decision has a direct bearing on the legality of counter-measures
within the context of the law of treaties. It affirms the right of an aggrieved
State to resort to counter-measures in response to a treaty violation. Such
measures, furthermore, may involve the temporary suspension of certain
rights accruing to the offending State under that treaty. This implies that the
status quo will be maintained between the contending parties without the
treaty being irrevocably terminated.

B.3. STATE PRACTICE

B.3.1. The Franco-American Treaties, 1778–90[79]

The United States and France concluded several treaties concerning commercial, political, and consular relations between 1778 and 1790.[80] When the
United States signed the Jay Treaty with Great Britain in 1794, the French
Government considered its provisions to be inconsistent with the aforementioned treaties.[81] Not only did the United States reject that allegation,
but she asserted that France had herself repeatedly violated the Franco-
American Treaties. Consequently, the United States passed an Act on 7 July
1798 terminating these treaties.[82] She justified such a step by claiming that
her attempts to negotiate an amicable settlement with France had been
repelled.[83] The abrogating Act provided that

[74] *ILR*, vol. 54, 1979, p. 337, para. 81.
[75] Ibid., p. 338, para. 84.
[76] Ibid., p. 337, para. 81.
[77] Ibid., pp. 338–9, paras. 83 and 90.
[78] Ibid., p. 341, para. 99.
[79] Moore, *Digest*, vol. v, p. 356.
[80] Treaty of Amity and Commerce, 1778, Treaty of Alliance, 1778, Separate and Secret
Reserving Right of King of Spain to Agree to the Foregoing Treaties, 1778, and Convention
Defining and Establishing the Functions and Privileges of Consuls and Vice Consuls, 1788.
Text: Malloy, vol. i, pp. 468, 479, 482, 490.
[81] See extract from letter of the French Foreign Minister to the US Ambassador in France
cited in *Hooper* v *The United States*, 22 *The United States Court of Claims Report*, 1887, pp. 414–
415.
[82] See Moore, *Digest*, vol. v, p. 356.
[83] Ibid.

[T]he United States are of right freed and exonerated from the stipulations of the treaties and of the consular convention, heretofore concluded between the United States and France; and that the same shall not henceforth be regarded as legally obligatory on the Government or citizens of the United States.[84]

The French Government did not accept the above provision as constituting a valid termination of the Treaties concerned.[85]

In 1779 the United States sent plenipotentiaries to Paris in order to negotiate a new treaty for the settlement of the claims relevant to the dispute. They were instructed to take into consideration the fact that the Franco-American Treaties had been abrogated by the Act of 1798. Once more the French Government asserted that the treaties had not been annulled.[86] In view of the disagreement on this point, Article 11 of the Convention of 1800 stipulated that the question of claims should form the subject of future negotiations.[87] Significantly, the Article further provided that until the parties had agreed upon that question, 'the said treaties and convention shall have no operation'.[88] This Article, however, was deleted by the Senate of the United States.[89] Upon exchanging the ratification, Napoleon declared that the Senate's amendment meant that 'the two states renounce their respective pretensions, which are the object of the said article'.[90] The senate of the United States approved the French Declaration, and ratified the treaty accordingly.[91]

The above facts evoked responses from several publicists to the effect that the United States did not unilaterally terminate the Franco-American Treaties by the Act of 7 July 1798.[92] In the opinion of these publicists, the United States purchased a release from her obligations under the treaties by waiving her spoliation claims against France. Sinha, on the other hand, suggested that policy considerations prompted the United States to abandon her strict legal rights.[93] The present writer inclines to the view held by Sinha. The reason for this preference is that the United States had consistently maintained that she had the right to terminate the treaties unilaterally on account of their breach by France.

---

[84] Ibid.

[85] Ibid, p. 357.

[86] Ibid.

[87] Text: Malloy, vol. i, p. 496, at p. 497.

[88] Ibid.

[89] Moore, *Digest*, vol. v, p. 357.

[90] Ibid.

[91] Ibid.

[92] See ibid., pp. 357–8; Hyde, vol. ii, 1922, p. 89, n. 1; Garner and Jobst, 'The Unilateral Denunciation of Treaties by One Party Because of Alleged Non-Performance by Another Party or Parties', *AJIL*, vol. 29, 1939, p. 569, at pp. 582–83; commentary on Art. 27 of *The Harvard Draft Convention on the Law of Treaties*, p. 1086.

[93] Sinha, p. 109.

B.3.2. The Ancient Treaties between Great Britain and Spain[94]

The Spanish authorities denied British subjects the enjoyment of certain commercial benefits to which they were entitled under several treaties. The British Foreign Office sought the opinion of the Law Officers of the Crown as to whether such breach constituted ground for reprisals.[95] It is noteworthy that this request was made only after repeated attempts at amicable settlement proved to be unsuccessful.[96] The following views were expressed in the Report submitted by Mr Robinson, one of the Law Officers:

The refusal to execute particular articles of Treaty is universally held to be an abrogation of the whole Treaty, at the discretion of the injured Party. But the effect of such abrogation may be different, as to ulterior measures, according to the amount of the injury sustained—as they may affect territorial rights, or essential interests of commerce, or matters of lighter import. Considerations of Policy therefore in such questions form a material feature in the question of right, & of these I cannot presume to judge.[97]

Mr Robinson then concluded that Spain's refusal to carry out her obligations under the treaties amounted to 'an abrogation of a positive interest, which may justify measures of forcible reparation'.[98] Further, he considered that the British Government would 'be justified in adopting measures, that may be deemed necessary, and expedient, to enforce the due execution of the Treaty'.[99]

McNair casts doubt on the continuing validity of the view that the breach of a particular article of a treaty affects the legal status of the whole treaty.[100] The stance adopted by him in this respect is not inconsistent with the provisions of Articles 44 and 60 of the Vienna Convention on the Law of Treaties.

B.3.3. Convention between Great Britain and Russia, relative to the Russian Dutch Loan, 1831[101]

By virtue of Article 1 of the 1815 Convention between Great Britain, Russia, and the Netherlands, Great Britain agreed to bear half of the Dutch debt owed to Russia as a quid pro quo for the retention of four Dutch Colonies. Article 5 of the same Convention provided that the said payment 'shall cease and determine, should the Possession and Sovereignty [...] of the Belgic

---

[94] Parry (ed.), *Law Officers' Opinions to the Foreign Office 1793–1860*, 1970 (hereinafter cited as Parry), vol. 80, p. 248.

[95] Ibid., p. 249.

[96] Ibid.

[97] Report dated 6 Apr. 1825, ibid., p. 250.

[98] Ibid., p. 251.

[99] Ibid.

[100] McNair, 1961, p. 484, and p. 557, n. 1.

[101] *BFSP*, vol. 19, 1830–1, p. 1226.

Provinces at any time pass or be severed from the Dominion of His Majesty the King of the Netherlands'.[102]

In 1830 a rebellion against the Dutch Government led to the creation of the separate State of Belgium. This new situation rendered it necessary for Great Britain and Russia to examine afresh the stipulations of the 1815 Convention. A Convention was accordingly signed between the two States in 1831.[103] It was stipulated in its first Article that the British Sovereign should recommend to his Parliament to continue payments concerning the Dutch debt to Russia. In Article 2, the Russian Emperor agreed not to compromise the neutrality of Belgium without the prior consent of Great Britain.[104]

In 1846 Russia concluded a Treaty with Austria and Prussia whereby the Free State of Cracow was annexed to Austria.[105] Mr Hume, a Member of the British Parliament, expressed his opinion that Russia, by so doing, acted in breach of the Treaty of Vienna of 1815. Accordingly, he put forward the resolution that the payments to Russia of the Dutch debt reaffirmed in the 1831 Treaty 'should be henceforth suspended'.[106] Speaking on behalf of the Government, Viscount Palmerston agreed with Mr Hume on the principle that breach of a treaty would entitle the aggrieved party to terminate it.[107] He added, however, that the annexation of Cracow would not justify Great Britain in 'suspending or discontinuing the payment of the Russian-Dutch Loan'.[108] He also pointed out that Britain's obligation to pay part of that Loan was in consideration for her retention of the four Dutch Colonies.[109] It is noteworthy that the views expressed by Palmerston were based on a Report submitted by the Queen's Advocate.[110]

Finally, it is possible to conclude from the foregoing narrative that only a breach which affects the objects of a treaty can justify its termination by the aggrieved party.

B.3.4. *The Declaration of Paris respecting Maritime Law, 1856* [111]

The Prussian Government stated that it would consider itself released from further obligations towards Denmark under the Declaration of Paris, if the Danish blockade of certain German ports continued to be insufficient. It also threatened to commission privateers to harass Danish trade. The British

---

[102] Ibid., vol. 2, 1814–15, p. 378, at pp. 379–80.
[103] Ibid., vol. 19, 1830–31, p. 1226.
[104] Ibid., p. 930.
[105] Ibid., vol. 35, 1846–7, p. 1088.
[106] *Hansard HC Debs.*, vol. 90, 4 Mar. 1847, col. 879.
[107] Ibid., vol. 91, 16 Mar. 1847, col. 92.
[108] Ibid., col. 97.
[109] Ibid., cols. 97–8.
[110] Dated 27 Jan. 1847, FO 83.2333, Parry, vol. 62, p. 508, at p. 511.
[111] Signed by Great Britain, Austria, France, Prussia, Russia, Sardinia, and Turkey, on 16 Apr. 1856. Text: *BFSP*, vol. 46, 1855–6, pp. 26–7.

Government asked Lord Phillimore, the Queen's Advocate, to submit a Report on the legal issues involved.

Lord Phillimore held that, prior to taking such actions, Prussia should seek a ruling from the Prize Court in Denmark on her alleged grievance. He elaborated on this view as follows:

Prussia is not entitled [...] to maintain that she is released from the obligation to observe every provision contained in that Declaration, on the ground that one of them has been suffered by other States to be in fact, not in terms, abrogated; while those other States absolutely deny this fact, and point to the proper tribunal appointed by the law of Nations for deciding the controversy, by which they are willing that the fact should be investigated.[112]

As regards the commissioning of the privateers by Prussia, he stated that such a step 'would amount to a cancellation on her part of the Declaration of Paris'.[113] From this he envisaged two consequences: first, 'Prussia would certainly have no right to demand from other States who subscribed the declaration, the observance of any part of its provisions'.[114] Secondly, she would incur responsibility for violating the treaty towards the other contracting parties.[115]

B.3.5. *The withdrawal of Germany from the Locarno Treaty of 1925*[116]

The Treaty of Mutual Guarantee, known as the Locarno Treaty, was concluded in 1925 between Germany, Belgium, France, Great Britain, and Italy.[117] One of its principal objects was to guarantee the maintenance of peace between Germany on the one side, and Belgium and France on the other; another was to secure the boundaries between these three States.[118] Article 3 of the treaty expressly provided that disputes between the parties should be settled by peaceful means including, for instance, resort to adjudication.

The Treaty of Mutual Assistance between France and the Soviet Union was signed on 2 May 1935, but its instruments of ratification were not exchanged until 27 March 1936.[119] Article 1 of the Protocol annexed thereto effectively bound France to render military assistance to the Soviet Union in the event of an attack on her territory by Germany.[120] Towards the end of May 1935, Germany declared that by concluding this treaty with the Soviet

---

[112] Report dated 21 June 1864, FO 83.2330, McNair, 1961, p. 851, at p. 582; see also the two further Reports by the Law Officers dated 23 Dec. 1868, and 18 Jan. 1871, ibid., pp. 583–6.

[113] Ibid.

[114] Ibid., pp. 582–3.

[115] Ibid., p. 583.

[116] Text: *AJIL*, vol. 20, suppl., 1926, pp. 22–5.

[117] Cf. *supra*, ch. 2 s. F.

[118] Arts. 1 and 2 of the Locarno Treaty.

[119] Text: *AJIL*, vol. 30, suppl., 1936, p. 177.

[120] Ibid., p. 179.

Union, France had acted in breach of the Locarno Treaty.[121] Subsequent to this, Germany announced her withdrawal from that treaty.[122] She took that step notwithstanding the several offers that were made to her by France to have the dispute settled by amicable means.[123] The German Government rejected these offers on the ground that the dispute was not justifiable since it was not exclusively of a legal character.[124]

Although Germany considered the conclusion of the Franco-Soviet Pact as a justification for her withdrawal from the Locarno Treaty on 7 March 1936 it is significant that the Pact did not come into force until 27 March 1936.[125] This raises the question of whether a treaty may be abrogated on the basis of an anticipated breach.[126] Finally, however, it must be borne in mind that Germany engineered her withdrawal from the Locarno Treaty as a pretext for her intended militarization of the Rhineland.[127] This factor is largely responsible for the obscurity surrounding her legal approach to the dispute.

B.3.6. The Treaties of Alliance and Mutual Assistance between the Soviet Union and the United Kingdom, 1942,[128] and the Soviet Union and France, 1944[129]

One of the main objects of each of these treaties was the prevention of renewed aggression by Germany in the post-war period.[130] In both cases each Contracting Party undertook 'not to conclude any alliance and not to take part in any coalition directed against [the other contracting Party]'.[131]

The United Kingdom and France became Parties to the 1954 Paris Treaties.[132] According to the terms of these treaties, Germany was to be admitted as a Member of the North Atlantic Treaty of 1949. This development was viewed by the Soviet Union as being in breach of the aforementioned two Treaties of Alliance and Mutual Assistance. Accordingly, the Soviet Government warned that if either the United Kingdom or France should ratify the Paris Agreements, it would terminate its Treaty of Alliance and Mutual Assistance with the State responsible.[133] Thus, following the rati-

---

[121] *RIIA, Documents*, 1935, vol. i, p. 169.
[122] Memorandum addressed by Germany on 7 Mar. 1936 to the Locarno Powers. Text: ibid., 1936, p. 41.
[123] *RIIA, Documents*, ibid., p. 114.
[124] Ibid.
[125] *RIIA, Documents, Survey of International Affairs*, 1936, p. 256.
[126] Cf. *supra*, ch. 4 s. F.
[127] See generally Sinha, p. 151.
[128] Text: *BFSP*, vol. 144, 1940–2, p. 1038.
[129] Text: *AJIL*, vols. 39–40, suppl. 1945–6, p. 83.
[130] See Art. 4 of the 1942 Treaty, and Art. 3 of the 1944 Treaty.
[131] Art. 7 of the 1942 Treaty, and Art. 5 of the 1944 Treaty.
[132] Texts: *RIIA, Documents*, 1954, pp. 102–7.
[133] See Note dated 20 Dec. 1954 to the UK Government, ibid., 1955, pp. 213–15, and Note dated 20 Dec. 1954 to the French Government, *KCA*, 1955, p. 14239.

fication of the Paris Agreements by the United Kingdom and France, the Soviet Union formally terminated her Treaties of Alliance and Mutual Assistance with these two States.[134]

It is noteworthy that both the British Government and the French Government denied the allegation of breach of the treaties made against them by the Soviet Union. In addition to this, they also maintained that the unilateral termination of the treaties by the Soviet Union was unlawful since the breach alleged by that country had not occurred.[135] The significance of this instance of State practice is that all the parties concerned recognized the occurrence of prior breach to be a prerequisite for unilateral termination of treaties.

B.3.7. The Agreement between the United Kingdom and Egypt regarding the Suez Canal Base, 1954.[136]

Article 12 of the Anglo-Egyptian Treaty of 1954 stipulated that it should remain in force for a period of seven years from the date of its signature.[137] On 29 October 1956 Israel launched an attack on Egyptian territory.[138] The British and French Governments reacted to this crisis by sending an ultimatum to Egypt and Israel.[139] When the Egyptian Government paid no heed to the terms of the ultimatum, Anglo-French forces immediately began to attack Egyptian territory. This conduct was viewed by Egypt as a violation of the United Kingdom's obligations under the Agreement. Accordingly, the Agreement was terminated by a Presidential Decree on 1 January 1957.[140] The British Government thereupon announced that it 'did not recognize the Egyptian Government's right to abrogate the treaty by unilateral action'.[141]

The aforementioned events call for a brief comment. The stance taken by Egypt indicates that a treaty which has been in some respect seriously violated by one party, may be terminated by the other. As regards the position adopted by the British Government, it is not certain whether this was based on principle, or on the facts of the particular dispute.

B.3.8. The views of the parties in the Case Concerning the Air Services Agreement of 27 March 1946, *1978*[142]

Although the views of the United States and France were primarily expressed in relation to a violation of a commitment to peaceful settlement,[143] it is

---

[134] Ibid.
[135] For the views expressed by the British Government see *RIIA, Documents*, 1955, p. 216. For the views expressed by the French Government see *KCA*, 1955, p. 14027.
[136] *BFSP*, vol. 161, 1954, p. 75.
[137] Ibid., p. 77.
[138] *RIIA, Documents*, 1956, p. 242.
[139] Ibid., p. 261.
[140] *KCA*, 1957, p. 15300.
[141] Ibid.
[142] *ILR*, vol. 54, 1979, p. 304.
[143] *Cf. infra*, ch. 9.

reasonable to suppose that they are of general application. To begin with, despite the differences between the parties in their interpretation of the conditions for resort to counter-measures, they both clearly agreed on the following principle: that breach of a treaty justifies the application of counter-measures.[144] For France, only a material breach could justify the termination, or the suspension of the violated treaty.[145] While the United States did not contradict the tenor of this view, nevertheless she allowed scope for 'proportional counter-measures short of termination or suspension'.[146] It is noteworthy that France upheld the principle of proportionality, and even invoked it to establish that the United States' action was incommensurate with the alleged breach on her part.[147] France also maintained that resort to counter-measures should be preceded by a formal demand.[148] Although the United States addressed several demands to France, none the less it is not clear whether she regarded the making of such demands as a prerequisite of counter-measures.

B.4. CONCLUSIONS AS TO THE POSITION IN CUSTOMARY LAW

After an examination of the pertinent doctrinal views, jurisprudence, and State practice, the following conclusions are offered on the question of the right to terminate or suspend a treaty by way of reprisal.

  1. The preponderant view is that a material breach entitles an aggrieved party to terminate or suspend its obligations under the treaty as against the defaulting party.

  2. In the case of a minor breach, the aggrieved party may withhold performance of its obligation under the treaty without affecting the legal validity of the treaty in a definitive sense.

  3. The injured party must exercise its right of reprisal within reasonable time.

  4. The aggrieved party must make a demand for redress before it can resort to retaliatory measures.

  5. A measure taken by way of reprisal must be proportionate to the breach. None the less, there is no definite legal requirement that such a measure should be restricted to the violated provision, or indeed to the violated treaty.

  6. Where there is a machinery for the settlement of disputes, the aggrieved party is precluded from taking retaliatory measures pending the outcome of the proceedings within that machinery.

---

[144] *USPIL*, 1978, p. 771.
[145] Ibid., p. 772.
[146] Ibid.
[147] Ibid., p. 775.
[148] Ibid., p. 773.

7. The non-performance of treaty obligations as a reprisal should not extend to humanitarian conventions.

8. Where a party to a multilateral treaty violates it to the extent that only one contracting party is injured, the latter is not entitled to withhold performance of its obligations in relation to the other parties who are not guilty of the breach. However, the injured party may withhold performance of its obligations towards the defaulting party.

C. THE VIENNA CONVENTION ON THE LAW OF TREATIES, 1969

C.1. INTRODUCTION

The International Law Commission had from its inception given special attention to the codification and progressive development of the law of treaties. The United Nations Conference on the Law of Treaties was convened in Vienna, from 26 March to 28 May 1968, and from 9 April to 23 May 1969.[149] The Conference had, as the basis for concluding the Convention, the Draft Articles on the law of treaties prepared by the International Law Commission (the Commission).[150] At its close the Conference decided to adopt the Vienna Convention on the Law of Treaties (the Convention).[151] This Convention entered into force on 27 January 1980.

The Convention is not in its entirety declaratory of positive international law,[152] nor does it purport to be so. Thus, the eighth preambular *considerandum* of the Convention affirms that 'the rules of customary international law will continue to govern questions not regulated by the provisions of the present Convention'. Moreover, Article 43 provides that the termination of the suspension of a treaty under the terms of the Convention would not invalidate obligations embodied in that treaty to which the parties were also bound by other norms of international law. A further illustration to show the relation between the Convention and customary law is Article 73. This Article stipulates that the provisions of the Convention 'shall not prejudge any question that may arise in regard to a treaty from [...] the international responsibility of a State'.

Article 60 of the Vienna Convention is of particular significance for the present work as it lays down the rules which regulate the termination or suspension of a treaty as a consequence of its breach. In the *Namibia Advisory*

---

[149] *UNCLT Doc.*

[150] See *Report of the International Law Commission on the work of its eighteenth session*, Doc. A/6309/Rev.1, 3–28 Jan. 1966, *YILC*, vol. ii, pp. 172–274.

[151] *UNCLT Doc.*, pp. 289–301.

[152] See e.g. Arts. 9(2), 15(*a*), 19–23, 40(5), and 41; see also *YILC*, vol. ii, 1966, p. 177, para. 15; Sinclair, *The Vienna Convention on the Law of Treaties*, 2nd edn., 1984, pp. 10–21. For a discussion on how customary law may be generated by treaty see the *North Sea Continental Shelf Case, ICJ Reports*, 1969, pp. 41–5, paras. 70–80.

Opinion the Court had an occasion to consider the rules concerning termination of a treaty on the ground of material breach. It stated: 'The rules laid down by the Vienna Convention on the Law of Treaties concerning termination of a treaty relationship on account of breach (adopted without a dissenting vote) may in many respects be considered as a codification of existing customary law on the subject.'[153]

In the *ICAO Council Case*, the Court indicated that there was a need to see whether 'according to the definition of a material breach of a treaty contained in Article 60 of the 1969 Vienna Convention on the Law of Treaties, there has been a violation by Pakistan of a provision essential to the accomplishment of the object or purpose of a treaty'.[154] The remarks made by the Court in these two excerpts have some bearing on the relation between Article 60 and the customary law rules governing the termination and suspension of treaties. However, the use of the phrase 'may in many respects', in the first excerpt implies that the Court did not regard Article 60 as a complete codification of the pertinent customary law rules. The reference made in the second excerpt to Article 60 does not clearly indicate whether that Article is a complete embodiment of the same customary law rules. Be that as it may, the present writer sees a need at this point for a further analysis of the provisions of Article 60 and its legislative history.

C.2. THE CONCEPT OF MATERIAL BREACH

Article 60 of the Vienna Convention stipulates the existence of material breach as a ground for the termination or suspension of either bilateral or multilateral treaties. In paragraph 3 of that Article the concept of material breach is defined as follows:

A material breach of a treaty, for the purposes of this Article, consists in:

> (*a*) a repudiation of the treaty not sanctioned by the present Convention, or
> (*b*) the violation of a provision essential to the accomplishment of the object or purpose of the treaty.

The use of the term 'material breach' in this provision merits a consideration of the antecedents which led to its eventual adoption by the Commission. It was first proposed by Sir Humphrey Waldock,[155] the Special Rapporteur, in preference to the term 'fundamental breach' suggested by his predecessor, Sir Gerald Fitzmaurice.[156] In the draft proposed by the latter, fundamental breach was defined as

---

[153] *ICJ Reports*, 1971, p. 16, at p. 47, para. 94.

[154] Ibid., 1972, p. 46, at p. 67, para. 38.

[155] See Draft Art. 20 ('Termination or suspension of a treaty following upon its breach'), Waldock, *Second Report on the Law of Treaties*, Doc. A/CN.4/156 and Add. 1–3, 20 Mar., 10 Apr., 30 Apr., and 5 June 1963, *YILC*, vol. ii, 1963, p. 36, at pp. 72–3, paras. 1–5.

[156] See Draft Art. 19(2), Fitzmaurice, *Second Report on the Law of Treaties*, Doc. A/CN.4/107, 15 Mar. 1957, *YILC*, vol. ii, 1957, p. 16, at p. 31.

a breach of the treaty in an essential respect, going to the root or foundation of the treaty relationship between the two parties, and calling in question the continued value or possibility of that relationship in the particular field covered by the treaty.[157]

It was further provided in the draft that the breach

must be tantamount to a denial or repudiation of the treaty obligation, and such as either to (a) destroy the value of the treaty for the other party; (b) justify the conclusion that no further confidence can be placed in the due execution of the treaty by the party committing the breach; or (c) render abortive the purpose of the treaty.[158]

The strict criteria set by Sir Gerald for determining what constituted a 'fundamental breach' are an indication of his concern to safeguard against abuse of fundamental breach as grounds for the termination of treaties. While prescribing such strict standards for the invocation of that type of breach, he nevertheless recognized the need to cater for breaches of a less serious character. Thus, he explicitly distinguished fundamental breach from 'cases where a breach by one party of some obligation of a treaty may justify an exactly corresponding non-observance by the other, or as a retaliatory measure, non-performance of some other provision of the treaty'.[159] In his opinion there was no question, in such cases, of the treaty itself being terminated, 'but merely of particular breaches and counter-breaches, or non-observances, that may or may not be justified according to circumstances'.[160]

As has been noted, Waldock employed in his draft the term 'material breach' in preference to that of 'fundamental breach'.[161] His reason for this preference was that the definition of 'fundamental breach' as given by Fitzmaurice appeared 'to put the concept of a "fundamental" breach rather high'.[162] The word "fundamental", he explained, might bear the implication that only the breach of a provision relevant to one of the central purposes of a treaty could justify termination of that treaty.[163] As an illustration, he pointed out that a compromissory clause in a treaty which had a character subordinate to its central purposes might induce some parties to be bound by that treaty.[164]

Waldock, for his part, set three criteria for determining the occurrence of material breach as grounds for the termination or suspension of a treaty. These were: (a) a repudiation of a treaty; (b) a breach so substantial that it effectively set aside any provision (i) concerning which no reservation was permitted, or (ii) the failure to comply with which would be incompatible

---

[157] Ibid., Art. 19(2) (i).
[158] Ibid., Art. 19(2) (ii) and (iii).
[159] Art. 18(2), ibid., p. 30.
[160] Ibid., p. 39.
[161] See *supra*, nn. 155-7.
[162] Waldock, *Second Report on the Law of Treaties*, Doc. A/CN.4/156 and Add. 1–3, 20 Mar., 30 Apr., and 5 June 1963, *YILC*, vol. ii, 1963, p. 36, at p. 76, para. 12.
[163] Ibid., p. 75, para. 11.
[164] Ibid.

with the object and purpose of the treaty; or (*c*) a refusal to implement a provision for judicial settlement procedure, or to comply with any judgment handed down under such a procedure.[165] Professor Tunkin, with some justification, remarked that these criteria 'seemed to have been somewhat arbitrarily chosen'.[166] The second criterion was criticized by both Mr Tsuruoka and Mr Rosenne for the reason that reservations would virtually be impossible in the case of bilateral treaties.[167] Mr Verdross went further by casting doubt on the very existence of any objective criterion for differentiating between material and non-material breach. Consequently, he proposed that either the word 'material' should be expunged, or that the Commission should permit the right of suspension only.[168] A revised text of Draft Article 20 followed the line suggested by Tsuruoka and Rosenne, though it ignored the proposal made by Verdross.[169]

Having thus far cited the views expressed by some members of the Commission with respect to the materiality of breach, it is pertinent at this point to refer to the stance finally taken by the Commission. In its Commentary on Draft Article 57, the Commission declared that it was unanimous in recognizing 'that the right to terminate or suspend must be limited to cases where the breach is of a serious character'.[170] By way of amplification the Commission stated that

It preferred the term 'material' to 'fundamental' to express the kind of breach which is required. The word 'fundamental' might be understood as meaning that only the violation of a provision directly touching the *central* purposes of the treaty can ever justify the other party in terminating the treaty. But other provisions considered by a party to be essential to the effective execution of the treaty may have been very material in inducing it to enter into the treaty at all, even although these provisions may be of an ancillary character. Clearly, an unjustified repudiation of the treaty—a repudiation not sanctioned by any of the provisions of the present articles—would automatically constitute a material breach of the treaty; and this is provided for in sub-paragraph (*a*) of the definition. The other and more general form of material breach is that in sub-paragraph (*b*), and is there defined as a violation of a provision essential to the accomplishment of any object or purpose of the treaty.[171]

---

[165] Draft Art. 20(2) ('Termination or suspension of a treaty following upon its breach'), ibid., p. 73, para. 2.

[166] Ibid., vol. i, p. 122, para. 9.

[167] Ibid., p. 126, paras. 50 and 56.

[168] Ibid., p. 125, para. 48.

[169] Ibid., p. 245, para. 92. The new version, with minor amendments, became part of Draft Art. 57 which was proposed by the Commission, and which was adopted at Vienna as Art. 60. See the Commission's *Report on the work of its eighteenth session*, 4 May–19 July 1966, Doc. A/6309/Rev. 1, *YILC*, vol. ii, 1966, p. 172, at p. 253.

[170] commentary on Draft Art. 57, ibid., at p. 225, para. 9.

[171] Ibid.

It should be noted at this point that the Commission omitted all reference to breach of a treaty which does not fall within the category of material breach as defined in paragraph 3 of Article 60. This implies that redress for non-material breach may be obtained by exercising the right of non-forcible counter-measures. The question to be asked, however, is whether material violation of a treaty may be responded to by counter-measures. The present writer submits that the answer should be in the affirmative, for the reason that the Vienna Convention provisions have not superseded the customary law right of reprisals.

Paragraph 3 of Article 60 provides that a material breach of a treaty, for the purposes of this article, consists in:

(*a*) a repudiation of the treaty not sanctioned by the present Convention; or
(*b*) the violation of a provision essential to the accomplishment of the object or purpose of the treaty.

As regards the first criterion listed in paragraph 3(*a*) above, it must be interpreted in such a way as would conform with the general limitation imposed by Article 73 of the Convention. According to this interpretation, the non-performance of a treaty obligation as a lawful counter-measure can never constitute a material breach for the purposes of Article 60.

As to the second criterion, paragraph 3(*b*) above is merely concerned with the character of the treaty provision that has been violated. Thus, it takes no account of the seriousness of the breach that has occurred. Consequently, an insignificant breach can be regarded as 'material' even where it affects an ancillary provision. Such a situation, however, arises only where that provision is deemed by the aggrieved party to be central to the purpose and object of the treaty. *A fortiori*, a remedy for breach of an ancillary provision not so deemed can only be found through the customary law of reprisals.

C.3. MATERIAL BREACH OF A BILATERAL TREATY

Paragraph 1 of Article 60 of the Vienna Convention provides: 'A material breach of a bilateral treaty by one of the parties entitles the other to invoke the breach as a ground for terminating the treaty or suspending its operation in whole or in part.' What immediately draws the attention in this provision is the adoption of the formula 'to invoke as a ground'. The Commission explained that in employing this formula it intended to emphasize that 'the right arising under the article is not a right arbitrarily to pronounce the treaty terminated'.[172] In consequence, such a right can only be exercised in accordance with the procedure prescribed in the Convention.[173] This feature marks a distinction between the right accruing to an aggrieved party under

---

[172] Ibid., p. 254, para. 6.
[173] See Art. 65–8, and the Annex of the Convention.

the Convention, and that which accrues to it under the customary law of reprisals. It should, however, be stated that in the case of the latter, the only procedural requirement is the making of an unfulfilled demand for redress.[174]

It is now proposed to examine the kind of remedy envisaged in paragraph 1 of Article 60. As regards the option of termination, it is clear beyond doubt that such a course produces a definitive result. In this respect Article 70(1) (*a*) of the Convention provides that the termination of a treaty 'releases the parties from any obligation further to perform the treaty'. Although such a remedy is related to the general principle of non-forcible counter-measures, it is not identical to it. The difference between the two lies in the fact that non-forcible counter-measures do not necessarily have irreversible consequences. As concerns the option of suspension, Article 72(1) (*a*) of the Convention stipulates that such conduct releases the parties from mutual obligations during the period of the suspension. Subparagraph 1(*b*) of the same Article provides that the suspension 'does not otherwise affect the legal relations between the parties established by the treaty'. The Commission emphasized that 'the legal nexus between the parties established by the treaty remains intact and that it is only the operation of its provisions which is suspended'.[175] This limitation brings the remedy of suspension under the Convention approximately into line with the non-performance of obligation by way of counter-measure.

As regards the concept of proportionality, it has been shown that proportionality is one of the conditions of resort to counter-measures.[176] By contrast, neither the text of Article 60 nor its *travaux préparatoires* make any reference to proportionality. However, the application of such a condition to Article 60 may be implied on the basis of customary law[177] as well as on logic.

A further ground for differentiating between counter-measures and the remedies envisaged in Article 60(1) concerns what constitutes the objects in each case. In the case of the former, the range of such objects is very wide since it can extend to treaties other than the one that has been violated. With respect to the latter, only the violated treaty may be terminated or suspended. One could envisage, however, situations in which termination or suspension under Article 60(1) would have no effect on the defaulting State. The present writer subscribes to the view expressed by Mr de Luna that in such situations 'the injured State could then, as a reprisal, suspend the application of another treaty'.[178]

---

[174] Cf. *supra*, Ch. 5.

[175] See Commentary on Draft Art. 68 concerning 'Consequences of the suspension of the operation of a treaty', *YILC*, vol. ii, 1966, p. 267, para. 3.

[176] Cf. *supra*, Ch. 6.

[177] See the eighth preambular *considerandum* of the Convention, cited in *supra*, Ch. 8 s. C.1.

[178] Commenting on Draft Art. 20 ('Termination or Suspension of a Treaty Following Upon its Breach').

A final ground for distinction between the two types of remedies concerns the performance of obligations imposed by general international law. It is noteworthy that Article 43 expressly provides that termination or suspension under the Convention 'shall not in any way impair the duty of any State to fulfil any obligation embodied in the treaty to which it would be subject under international law, independently of the treaty'. Such restriction set on the options open to an aggrieved State does not appear entirely incompatible with the restriction imposed by customary law on the right of resort to counter-measures. In the latter case, however, provided that there are no collateral constraints,[179] an aggrieved State may suspend a treaty provision even if it contains some obligation under general international law.

Finally, it is noteworthy that in the course of a debate on an earlier draft of the present Article 60(1), some members of the Commission, including the Special Rapporteur, ventured into the realms of the law of reprisals.[180] Eventually, however, Waldock considered that it was better 'not to introduce the law of reprisals as such'[181] into that Article. Commenting on Draft Article 57, the Commission declared its position as follows:

The right to take this action arises under the law of treaties independently of any right of reprisal, the principle being that a party cannot be called upon to fulfil its obligations under a treaty when the other party fails to fulfil those which it undertook under the same treaty.[182]

C.4. MATERIAL BREACH OF A MULTILATERAL TREATY

A distinction is made in Article 60 of the Convention between action which may be taken by all the other parties, and that which may be taken by an individual party acting alone. Each category of action will accordingly be examined separately.

C.4.1 Action taken in concert by the other parties

In the case of a material breach of a multilateral treaty, Article 60(2) (*a*) provides:

A material breach of a multilateral treaty by one of the parties entitles:

    (*a*) the other parties by unanimous agreement to suspend the operation of the treaty in whole or in part or to terminate it either:

---

[179] *YILC*, vol. i, 1963, p. 121, para. 79. See *supra*, ch. 7.

[180] See Waldock's *Second Report on the Law of Treaties*, Doc. A/CN.4/156 and Add. 1–3, 20 Mar., 10 Apr., 30 Apr., and 5 June 1963, *YILC*, vol. ii, 1963, p. 36, at p. 73, para. 1; for remarks by Mr de Luna see *YILC*, vol. i, 1963, p. 121, para. 79; for remarks by Mr Verdross, see ibid., p. 125, para. 48; for further remarks by Waldock, see ibid., p. 245, para. 94.

[181] *YILC*, vol. i, 1963, p. 132, para. 41.

[182] Commentary on Draft Art. 57, *Report of the International Law Commission on the work of its eighteenth session*, 4 May–19 July 1966, Doc. A/6309/Rev. 1, *YILC*, vol. ii, 1966, p. 172, at p. 255, para. 6.

  (i) in the relation between themselves and the defaulting State, or
  (ii) as between all the parties.

It should be observed first that the text of this provision, in contrast to that of Article 60(1), makes no reference to the formula 'to invoke as a ground'.[183] This implies that the breach of a treaty *ipso facto* entitles all the parties other than the wrongdoer to terminate or suspend that treaty without having to comply with the procedures prescribed by Section IV of the Convention. It must, however, be emphasized that this freedom of action is more apparent than real due to the requirement of unanimity. Needless to say, such a requirement is in practice difficult to fulfil. It remains to be said that in the case of counter-measures there is no hard and fast rule respecting unanimity.

To turn now to the objects against which action may be taken. According to subparagraph (i), above, only the defaulting State is designated as a target. Such a designation indicates a relationship between the action specified in subparagraph (i), and an action which fell within the category of counter-measures. This is not to say, however, that the two are identical. The reason for this conclusion is that the differences already noted[184] between the remedy envisaged in Article 60(1), and counter-measures would *mutatis mutandis* apply also to subparagraph (i). As regards the objects specified in subparagraph (ii), the fact of unanimity between the parties implies that they cannot be viewed as victims of the action involved. In such a case, therefore, no relationship can be said to exist between the action permissible under subparagraph (ii), and that which may be taken by way of counter-measures.

C.4.2. *Action by a party specially affected by the breach*

Article 60(2) of the Vienna Convention deals with the position of a party specially affected by a material breach of a multilateral treaty. Subparagraph (*b*) of that provision provides that such a party may invoke the breach in question 'as a ground for suspending the operation of the treaty in whole or in part in the relations between itself and the defaulting State'. The Commission took the position that when an individual party reacts alone, its position is 'similar to that in the case of a bilateral treaty, but that its right should be limited to suspending the operation of the treaty in whole or in part as between itself and the defaulting State'.[185] Accordingly, it is submitted that the analysis already undertaken concerning the relation between Article 60(1) and counter-measures[186] would *mutatis mutandis* apply to any possible relation between counter-measures and Article 60(2) (*b*). However, since

---

[183] A British proposal to insert the formula 'to invoke as a ground' in the text of paras. 2(*a*) and 2(*b*) was rejected. See A/CONF.39/L.29, *UNCLT Doc.*, pp. 111–12, paras. 14–16.

[184] Cf. *supra*, s. C.3.

[185] Commentary on Draft Art. 57, *Report of the International Law Commission on the work of its eighteenth session*, 4 May–19 July 1966, Doc. A/6309/Rev. 1, *YILC*, vol. ii, 1966, p. 172, at p. 255, para. 7.

[186] See *supra*, s. C.3.

Article 60(2) (*b*) differs from Article 60(1) in so far as it deals with bilateral relationships in the context of multilateral treaties, a further analysis is called for.

What should immediately be noted is that Article 60(2) does not take as its basis the division between the categories of obligations which may be found in multilateral treaties.[187] Support for such an interpretation might mistakenly be derived from these remarks of the Commission: '[I]t would be inequitable to allow a defaulting State to continue to enforce the treaty against the injured party, whilst itself violating its obligations towards that State under the treaty'.[188] A possible inference to be drawn from this is that even a law-making treaty could be suspended by an aggrieved party *vis-à-vis* the defaulting party. In other words, an aggrieved party could go so far as to suspend obligations incorporated in a treaty to which it would be bound under customary law.

Clearly this cannot be the case, otherwise it would be difficult to reconcile the right set out in subparagraph (*b*) with the limitation specified by Article 43. It is therefore submitted that only obligations which lie outside the scope of customary law may be suspended on the basis of subparagraph (*b*). It is relevant at this juncture to refer to the views expressed by the present writer on the question of collateral constraints on the legality of counter-measures.[189] The position has been taken that counter-measures which, for example, violate human rights or diplomatic immunities cannot be lawfully invoked as justification for wrongful conduct. The fact that violations of that nature are evidently impermissible both under subparagraph (*b*), and under the principle of counter-measures, indicates that a relationship exists between these two means of redress.

C.4.3. *Action by any other party*

Article 60 paragraph 2(*c*) deals with a special class of treaties such as disarmament treaties where breach by one party radically affects the substratum of the treaty as between all the parties. The Commission observed that in such cases the remedies specified in paragraphs 2(*a*) and (*b*) of Article 60 might not provide sufficient protection to the interests of an individual

---

[187] Fitzmaurice drew such distinctions in his Draft Arts. 18(1) and 19(1); see Fitzmaurice, *Second Report on the Law of Treaties*, 15 Mar. 1957, Doc. A/CN.4/107, *YILC*, vol. ii, p. 16, text at pp. 30–1, and Commentary at p. 53, para. 115: compare with Waldock's Commentary on Draft Art. 20, see Waldock, *Second Report on the Law of Treaties*, 20 Mar., 10 Apr., 30 Apr., and 5 June 1963, Doc. A/CN.4/156 and Add. 1–3, *YILC*, vol. ii, 1963, p. 36, at pp. 76–7, para. 15.

[188] Commentary on Draft Art. 57, *Report of the International Law Commission on the work of its eighteenth session*, 4 May–9 July 1966, Doc. A/6309/Rev. 1, *YILC*, vol. ii, 1966, p. 172, at p. 255, para. 7.

[189] Cf. *supra*, ch. 7.

party.[190] It further noted that such a party would probably not be able to suspend the treaty as against the defaulting State without at the same time undermining its own commitments to the other parties.[191] Thus, according to the provisions of subparagraph (*c*), when such circumstances are present, the party concerned will be entitled 'to invoke the breach as a ground for suspending the operation of the treaty in whole or in part with respect to itself'. It is noteworthy that the substance of this provision is more or less consistent with the stance taken by the United States[192] regarding her right to withdraw from the Nuclear Test Ban Treaty.[193]

To revert to the question of whether a relationship exists between Article 60 and counter-measures, the use of the phrase 'with respect to itself' in paragraph 2(*c*) excludes the possibility of such a relationship existing. The reason being that, unlike the case of counter-measures, the provision under review permits the suspension of obligations under the treaty *vis-à-vis* all the parties, though they are innocent of breach.

C.5. PROVISIONS IN A TREATY APPLICABLE IN THE EVENT OF BREACH

Article 60(4) provides that the rules contained in paragraphs 1 to 3 of that Article 'are without prejudice to any provision in the treaty applicable in the event of a breach'. Commenting on this paragraph, the Commission stated that the rule embodied therein 'merely reserves the rights of the parties under any specific provisions of the treaty applicable in the event of breach'.[194] Thus, in the event of a breach of treaty according to the terms of which the parties are committed to amicable settlement, the aggrieved party is generally precluded from taking action under Article 60. It is submitted, therefore, that the stipulation made in paragraph 4 of Article 60 is identical to the principle of counter-measures.[195]

C.6. PROVISIONS WHICH MAY NOT BE SUSPENDED OR TERMINATED

Paragraph 5 of Article 60 provides that '[p]aragraphs 1 to 3 do not apply to provisions relating to the protection of the human person contained in treaties of a humanitarian character, in particular to provisions prohibiting any

---

[190] Commentary on Draft Art. 57, *Report of the International Law Commission on the work of its eighteenth session*, 4 May–19 July 1966, Doc. A/6309/Rev. 1, *YILC*, vol. ii, 1966, p. 172, at p. 255, para. 8.

[191] Ibid.

[192] See the remarks made by the Secretary of State before the Senate Committee on Foreign Relations on 12 Aug. 1963, and also the 'legal brief' of the Legal Adviser of the Department of State, entitled 'Right of the United States to withdraw from the Nuclear Test Ban Treaty in the event of violation by another party', Whiteman, *Digest of International Law*, vol. 14, 1970, pp. 473–4.

[193] 5 Aug. 1963, text: *BFSP*, vol. 167, 1963–4, p. 178.

[194] *Report of the International Law Commission on the work of its eighteenth session*, 4 May–19 July 1966, Doc. A/6309/Rev. 1, *YILC*, vol. ii, 1966, p. 172, at p. 255, para 10.

[195] Cf. *infra*, ch. 9.

form of reprisals against persons protected by such treaties.' This provision effectively provides that a material breach of a treaty does not constitute a ground for termination or suspension where the breach affects provisions concerning humanitarian treatment. Moreover, it applies specifically to provisions prohibiting reprisals against individuals protected by humanitarian treaties.

It is noteworthy that the rule contained in paragraph 5 is reminiscent of the principle advocated by Fitzmaurice according to which humanitarian treaties could not be abrogated.[196] It should also be noted that the court stated in the *Namibia Case* as follows:

> The general principle of law [is] that a right of termination on account of breach must be presumed to exist in respect of all treaties, except as regards provisions relating to the protection of the human person contained in treaties of humanitarian character (as indicated in Art. 60, para. 5, of the Vienna Convention).[197]

In sum, it is indisputably affirmed that treaty provisions of a humanitarian character cannot be violated under Article 60. A similar stance has been taken by the present writer as regards the constraints on the use of counter-measures.[198] However, in the case of Article 60 other provisions in the same treaty which have no humanitarian character may be terminated or suspended. The same is also true in the case of counter-measures, with the added possibility that the action taken may be directed against a treaty other than that which has been violated.

D. CONCLUSIONS

Under customary international law a breach of treaty may be responded to by taking counter-measures after an unsuccessful demand for reparation. By contrast, the right of termination or suspension under Article 60 of the Vienna Convention has been made subject to very stringent conditions. Most importantly, the Article deals fairly strictly with the concept of material breach, and makes no reference to minor breaches. This may be interpreted as an implicit recognition of the right to resort to counter-measures for less serious breaches. The second major condition for invoking Article 60 is that an aggrieved party must follow a very lengthy procedure before it can terminate or suspend.

There can be no doubt that proportionality, which is a condition of counter-measures, applies to action taken under Article 60 of the Vienna Convention. This conclusion is based on ordinary legal logic, which implies that the Convention should be understood in the context of other rules of international

---

[196] Fitzmaurice, 'The General Principles of International Law Considered from the Standpoint of the Rule of law', *R.d.C.*, vol. 92(2), 1957, p. 6, at p. 120. Cf. *supra*, ch. 7 s. C.1.

[197] *ICJ Reports*, 1971, p. 16, at p. 47, para. 96.

[198] Cf. *supra*, ch. 7 s. C.1.

law. However, it may be stated that, unlike the case of counter-measures, action taken under Article 60 must be restricted to the treaty that has been violated.

Counter-measures may, subject to certain exceptions, be taken against a treaty provision which embodies obligations imposed by international law independently of that treaty. In contrast, Article 43 of the Vienna Convention excludes such a possibility under the regime established by the Convention.

A final distinction between the category of counter-measures and Article 60 concerns the effects of the action taken. In the case of counter-measures, it is only in exceptional circumstances that the effects are irreversible. Conversely, under Article 60 (multilateral treaties excepted) an aggrieved party always has the option to put an end to the treaty.

It is is noteworthy that under Article 60 and according to the principle of counter-measures an aggrieved party is precluded from resort to action if the treaty stipulates peaceful settlement.[199] Furthermore, provisions concerning humanitarian treatment cannot be violated.

To conclude, although the regime established by Article 60 represents a very specific form of counter-measures which deals only with the issue of material breach, it can to a certain extent be compared with the principle of non-forcible counter-measures. This is because they both reflect the same doctrine, notwithstanding that the rationale for the former appears to be based exclusively on reciprocity.[200]

---

[199] For some suggested distinctions regarding the relation between a commitment to peaceful settlement and counter-measures see *infra*, ch. 9 s. E.

[200] For the various motivations for counter-measures see *supra*, ch. 4 s. C.

9

The Legality of Non-forcible Counter-measures in the Context of Obligations in Respect of Peaceful Settlement of Disputes

A. INTRODUCTION

There is a general principle of international law which provides that States should settle their disputes by amicable means. This principle is now enshrined in paragraph 3 of Article 2 of the Charter of the United Nations. The tenor of this provision clearly suggests that international disputes should be settled by peaceful methods rather than coercive means. In this chapter, however, it is not intended to address the general question of peaceful settlement of disputes. The specific issue to be considered concerns the legality of counter-measures in the presence of a commitment to peaceful settlement. Naturally, the extent to which a given commitment may be held to be binding should in the first place be ascertained by applying the normal tools of treaty interpretation.[1] Thus, where the nature of the commitment is found to be categorical, resort to counter-measures will prima facie be unlawful. By implication, therefore, the commitment to peaceful settlement of disputes will be deemed to prevail over the right to take reprisals under customary law. This position is clearly in accord with this statement by the International Court: 'Without attempting to enter into, still less pronounce upon any question of *jus cogens*, it is well understood that, in practice, rules of international law can, by agreement be derogated from in particular cases, or as

---

[1] See *The Wimbledon Case, PCIJ*, Ser. A, no. 1, 1923, p. 7, at pp. 22ff.; *The Acquisition of Polish Nationality Case, PCIJ*, Ser. B, no. 7, 1923, p. 6, at pp. 16ff.; *The Treatment of Polish Nationals, PCIJ*, Ser. A/B, no. 44, 1932, p. 4, at pp. 23–4; *The Legal Status of Eastern Greenland, PCIJ*, Ser. A/B, no. 53, 1933, p. 22, at pp. 68–9 and p. 71; Judge Anzilotti, Diss. Op., ibid., p. 76, at p. 94; *The Lighthouses Case, PCIJ*, Ser. A/B, no. 62, 1934, p. 4, at p. 25; *The Reparation for Injuries Case, ICJ Reports*, 1949, p. 174, at p. 185; Fitzmaurice, *Fifth Report on the Law of Treaties*, Doc. A/CN.4/130, *YILC*, vol. ii, 1960, p. 69, at pp. 72–107; Waldock, *Third Report on the Law of Treaties*, Doc. A/CN.4/167, *YILC*, vol. ii, 1964, p. 5, at pp. 52–62; *ILC Report on the Law of Treaties to the General Assembly*, Doc. A/6309/Rev. I, *YILC*, vol. ii, 1966, p. 169, at pp. 217–22; E. Lauterpacht, ed., *International Law: Being the Collected Papers of Hersch Lauterpacht*, vol. i, *General Works*, 1970, p. 87; Tunkin, *Theory of International Law*, 1974, p. 142; Akehurst, 'The Hierarchy of the Sources of International Law', *BYIL*, vol. 47, 1974–5, p. 273.

between the parties.'[2] However, the lack of compulsory adjudication and the difficulties which may arise in implementing decisions rendered by international tribunals will inevitably affect the attitude of States towards commitments to peaceful settlement. In some situations, therefore, policy considerations may justify resort to counter-measures notwithstanding the existence of such commitments.

The remaining sections of this chapter will embark upon an examination of the jurisprudence, State practice, and the views of the publicists pertaining to the question under review. In addition, it will be shown how far the legality of counter-measures in the presence of a commitment to peaceful settlement is influenced by the various motivations underlying the measures taken.

B. JURISPRUDENCE

A search in the standard international law materials published prior to 1979 reveals a lack of judicial decisions concerning the legality of counter-measures in the context of a commitment to peaceful settlement. There is, however, a growing body of decisions by the European Court of Justice which has dealt with the legality of reprisals within the framework of the European communities. The first of these decisions will be discussed, while the others will merely be cited. Attention will then turn to two important international decisions, namely, *The Air Services Agreement Dispute* and the *Hostages Case*.

B.1. *THE COMMISSION OF THE EEC* V *LUXEMBOURG AND BELGIUM*, 1964[3]

This case is the first of several decisions of the Court of Justice of the European Communities on the legality of counter-measures in matters concerning community law. The defendant States, contrary to Article 12 of the Treaty of Rome,[4] imposed special customs duties on licences for skimmed milk powder imported from other Member States. They then claimed the following two justifications for their conduct: (*a*) the failure by the Community to establish a common organization of the Market in milk; and (*b*) the right of a contracting party injured by the breach of another to withhold performance of treaty obligations *vis-à-vis* that defaulting State.[5]

The Court rejected the aforementioned submissions, holding that the Treaty of Rome had established a new legal order which possessed the necessary procedure to deal with breach. The Court explained that 'except where otherwise expressly provided, the basic concept of the Treaty requires

---

[2] *The North Sea Continental Shelf Cases, ICJ Reports*, 1969, p. 4, at p. 42, para. 72.
[3] Cases No. 90 and 91/63, 1964, *European Court Reports* (hereinafter cited as *ECR*), p. 625.
[4] For text of the Treaty of Rome see 298 *UNTS*, 4300.
[5] *ECR*, 1964, p. 625.

that the Member States shall not take the law into their own hands. Therefore the fact that the Council failed to carry out its obligations cannot relieve the defendants from carrying out theirs.'[6] It should be remembered that the alleged breach in this case was attributed to the organs of the Communities rather than to the Member states against which the restrictions had been imposed. This fact is sufficient to cast doubt on the legality of the defendants' conduct as a counter-measure. More pertinent to the subject-matter of this chapter is the clear indication in the judgment that resort to counter-measures under customary law is precluded by the possibility of recourse to Community Law.[7]

B.2. *CASE CONCERNING THE AIR SERVICES AGREEMENT OF 27 MARCH 1946*, 1978[8]

This is the first case in which an international tribunal has pronounced expressly on the legality of non-forcible counter-measures in the presence of a commitment to peaceful settlement. Of the two questions put to the Tribunal, the first was concerned with issues of potential interest mainly to aviation circles. Underlying the second question were many legal issues, including particularly the conditions of the legality of counter-measures in the context of a commitment to amicable settlement.[9]

In the course of its answer to the second question, the Tribunal posed a further question which ran thus:

Can it be said that resort to such counter-measures, which are contrary to international law but justified by a violation of international law allegedly committed by the State against which they are directed, is restricted if it is found that the Parties previously accepted a duty to negotiate or an obligation to have their dispute settled through a procedure of arbitration or of judicial settlement?[10]

In attempting to settle this point the Tribunal did not reject the assertion that when the parties commenced negotiations, the principle of good faith required that they should refrain from taking any action that might escalate the dispute.[11] Nevertheless, the Tribunal stressed the necessity for examining the text of the provision in which the commitment was embodied in order to

---

[6] Ibid., see also the opinion delivered by the Advocate-General, ibid., p. 635, at pp. 644–5, para. 3.

[7] For affirmation of this principle *obiter dictum*, see *Defrenne* v. *Sabena*, Case 43/75, *ECR*, 1976, p. 455, at p. 475, para. 33; *Commission of the European Communities* v. *France*, Case No. 232/78, *ECR*, p. 2729, at p. 2739, para. 9; see Editorial Comment, 'The Mutton and Lamb Story: Isolated Incident or the Beginning of a New Era?', *Common Market Law Review*, vol. 17, 1980, p. 311, at p. 313; *R*. v. *Kirk*, Case 63/83; *The Times*, 11 July 1984, p. 7.

[8] *ILR*, vol. 54, 1979, p. 304; for the text of the Agreement see 139 *UNTS*, 1879.

[9] *ILR*, vol. 54, 1979, p. 312, para. 2.

[10] Ibid., p. 338, para. 84.

[11] Ibid., pp. 338–9, paras. 85–6.

establish whether it was of a kind which precluded counter-measures.[12] It then applied this rule to the pertinent provisions of the Air Services Agreement between the United States and France.[13] The Tribunal held that neither these provisions, nor general international law, prohibited resort to counter-measures in the present case.[14]

By way of elaboration, the Tribunal made the following statement:

[T]he Tribunal does not believe that it is to lay down a rule prohibiting the use of counter-measures during negotiations, especially where such counter-measures are accompanied by an offer for a procedure affording the possibility of accelerating the solution of the dispute.[15]

The Tribunal further emphasized that counter-measures would be allowed in the period preceding the commencement of judicial proceedings. This position would particularly apply to disputes in which the conclusion of a *compromis* was still pending. In support of its position, the Tribunal stated that 'States have not renounced their right to take counter-measures in such situations.'[16] Moreover, in the view of the Tribunal, this solution would be preferable 'as it facilitates States' acceptance of arbitration or judicial settlement procedure'.[17]

The Tribunal also examined the question of whether counter-measures should be permitted 'where there is arbitral or judicial machinery which can settle the dispute'.[18] Despite its sympathy with the frequent assertions of writers that counter-measures would be precluded in such circumstances, it nevertheless concluded:

If the proceedings form part of an institutional framework ensuring some degree of enforcement of obligations, the justification of counter-measures will undoubtedly disappear, but owing to the existence of that framework rather than solely on account of the existence of arbitral or judicial proceedings as such.[19]

The view was then taken that the scope of a Tribunal's powers to indicate interim measures of protection would determine whether the parties involved still retained the right to impose counter-measures.[20] In other words, the less power a tribunal possesses, the more freedom of action the parties enjoy.

Finally, the following extract from the Award summarizes the conclusion reached by the Tribunal with respect to the legality of counter-measures in the context of a commitment to peaceful settlement:

[12] Ibid., p. 339, para. 87.
[13] Ibid., para. 88.
[14] Ibid., para. 89.
[15] Ibid., p. 340, para. 91.
[16] Ibid., para. 95.
[17] Ibid.
[18] Ibid., p. 340, para. 94.
[19] Ibid.
[20] Ibid., p. 341, para. 96.

Under the rules of present-day international law, and unless the contrary results from special obligations arising under particular treaties, notably from mechanisms created within the framework of international organizations, each State establishes for itself its legal situation vis-à-vis other States. If a situation arises which, in one State's view results in the violation of an international obligation by another State, the first State is entitled, within the limits set by the general rules of international law pertaining to the use of armed force, to affirm its rights through 'counter-measures'.[21]

B.3. THE RELEVANCE OF THE *CASE CONCERNING UNITED STATES DIPLOMATIC AND CONSULAR STAFF IN TEHRAN*, 1980[22]

B.3.1. Background

On 29 November 1979 the United States instituted proceedings against Iran for the purpose, *inter alia*, of securing the release of her nationals who were being detained in the premises of the American Embassy in Tehran.[23] Both States were parties to one or more of several Conventions and Protocols.[24] On 15 December 1979 the Court indicated provisional measures of protection.[25] Part A of the Order was addressed to Iran asking her to release the hostages and restore to the United States full possession of her occupied premises. As well as being rejected publicly by the Iranian Minister for Foreign Affairs, this Order was not acted upon by other Iranian officials.[26] Part B of the Order required that '[t]he Government of the United States of America and the Government of the Islamic Republic of Iran should not take any action and should ensure that no action is taken which may aggravate the tension between the two countries or render the existing dispute more difficult of solution'.[27]

In disregard of the above Order, the United States launched operation 'Rice Bowl' in Iranian territory in the hope of rescuing the hostages. Owing to technical ineptitude the operation failed, and the rescue attempt had to be abandoned. This episode brings into focus the question how far an aggrieved party has freedom of action to attain by other means an objective which is currently being sought by judicial process. The remaining parts of this section

---

[21] Ibid., p. 337, para. 81.

[22] *ICJ Reports*, 1980, p. 3.

[23] *ICJ Pleadings*, 1982, pp. 7–8.

[24] The Vienna Convention on Diplomatic Relations, 1961, 500 *UNTS*, 7310; text of its Optional Protocol concerning the Compulsory Settlement of Disputes, 500 *UNTS*, 7312; The Vienna Convention on Consular Relations, 1963, 596 *UNTS*, 8638; text of its Optional Protocol concerning the Compulsory Settlement of Disputes, 596 *UNTS*, 8640; The Convention on the Prevention and Punishment of Crimes against Internationally Protected Persons, Including Diplomatic Agents, 1973, text: *UNGAOR*, 28th Sess., suppl. 30(A/9030), 1973, pp. 147–8; the Treaty of Amity, Economic Relations, and Consular Rights, 1955, between USA and Iran, 284 *UNTS* 4132.

[25] *ICJ Reports*, 1979, p. 7, at pp. 20–1, para. 47.

[26] Ibid., 1980, p. 35, para. 75.

[27] Ibid., 1979, p. 21, para. 47.I.B.

will examine the manner in which the Court approached the aforesaid question.

B.3.2. The reaction of the Court to the rescue mission

The Court recognized the 'understandable feelings of frustration'[28] brought on the United States by the continued detention of the hostages despite previous calls for their release that were echoed by the Security Council and by the Court itself.[29] It also noted that although the case was ready for hearing, it had to be postponed at the request of the Agent of the United States who indicated that some delicate negotiations were in progress. Subsequent to this, the same Agent further asked for an expedited hearing. Notwithstanding the Court's accession to all the requests made on behalf of the United States Government, it came to learn of the rescue mission at the very time when the text of the judgment was being prepared. As an expression of its displeasure at such action, the Court emphasized that

> an operation undertaken in those circumstances, from whatever motive, is of a kind calculated to undermine respect for the judicial process of international relations; and to recall that in paragraph 47, I. B. of its Order of 15 December 1979 the Court had indicated that no action was to be taken by either party which might aggravate the tension between the two Countries.[30]

The remarks in the above passage might on first impression suggest that they were exclusively concerned with the use of force, and hence would be of no relevance to non-forcible counter-measures. A closer examination of the judgment reveals this impression to be unfounded. By stating that the rescue operation was '*of a kind* calculated to undermine respect for judicial process',[31] the Court was probably extending its stricture to a wide range of actions including non-forcible counter-measures. Moreover, the Court stated explicitly that it was not required to make any pronouncement on the legality of the rescue operation, or on any possible question of responsibility flowing from it.[32] From this it may reasonably be deduced that the remarks of the Court could apply without distinction to each and every measure taken that is likely to impede the judicial process while a case is *sub judice*. According to this interpretation, resort to non-forcible counter-measures would be objectionable in situations where their imposition might impair the judicial functioning. Such a conclusion is compatible with the dissenting opinion of Judge Morozov, who stated that 'some indication should have been included in the judgment that the Court considers that settlement of the dispute

---

[28] Ibid., p. 43, para. 93.
[29] Security Council Resolutions 457 (1979) and 461 (1979); Provisional Order of 15 Dec. 1979, *ICJ Reports*, 1979, p. 7.
[30] Ibid., 1980, p. 43, para. 93.
[31] Ibid., emphasis added.
[32] Ibid., p. 44, para. 94.

between the United States and the Islamic Republic of Iran should be reached exclusively by peaceful means'.[33] It is also in line with the remarks made by Judge Lachs in his separate opinion: 'the Applicant having instituted proceedings, is precluded from taking unilateral action, *military or otherwise*, as if no case is pending'.[34]

B.3.3. The reaction of the Court to the non-forcible counter-measures adopted by the United States Government

The Court took cognizance of all the various measures adopted by the United States in response to the actions for which she held the Government of Iran responsible.[35] It should, however, be noted that no examination of the legality of these measures was ever undertaken. Nevertheless, in the process of establishing its own jurisdiction by the provisions of the 1955 Treaty of Amity between the United States and Iran, the Court indicated in a somewhat cursory manner that

They were measures taken in response to what the United States believed to be grave and manifest violations of international law by Iran, including violations of the 1955 Treaty itself. In any event any alleged violation of the Treaty by either party could not have the effect of precluding that party from invoking the provisions of the Treaty concerning pacific settlement of disputes.[36]

The second sentence in the above passage unequivocally denotes that counter-measures could never have the effect of nullifying jurisdictional clauses. This is a mere affirmation of the view of the Court on the same question in the *ICAO Case*.[37]

Judge Morozov asserted in his dissenting opinion that the United States, in taking action against Iran during the period of judicial deliberation, had thereby forfeited any legal right for reparation.[38] With due respect, such a radical slant, depriving as it did the applicant State of the right to seek reparation, hardly stands up to legal scrutiny. The process by which a claim for reparation could be barred entails the making of either a defence or a counter-claim by the respondent State. In the *Hostages Case*, as is well known, Iran did not avail herself of such opportunities.[39]

Judge Tarazi, commenting on the right of resort to counter-measures during the period of adjudication, remarked that '[t]he Applicant State must refrain from taking any decisions on the planes of either domestic or inter-

---

[33] Ibid., p. 57, para. 8; see also Judge Tarazi, Diss. Op., ibid., p. 58, at p. 64, para. 3.

[34] Ibid., p. 47, at p. 48, emphasis added.

[35] Ibid., pp. 16–17, paras. 30–1.

[36] Ibid., p. 28, para. 53.

[37] *ICJ Reports*, 1972, p. 46, at p. 53, para. 16(*b*); cf. *supra*, ch. 8 s. B.2.4.

[38] See Judge Morozov, Diss. Op., *The Hostages Case*, *ICJ Reports*, 1980, p. 53, para. 4.

[39] Ibid., p. 41, para. 88.

national law which could have the effect of impeding the proper administration of justice'.[40]

Commenting on the views expressed by Morozov and Tarazi to the effect
that the counter-measures taken by the United States were incompatible with
submission to the judicial process, Professor Schachter stated that

The fact that the two dissenting judges raised this point lends significance to the
silence of the majority. One might reasonably infer from that silence that the Court's
judgment impliedly constituted a rejection of the position of the two dissenting judges
on the illegality of the economic counter-measures during the pendency of the
litigation.[41]

With deference, the present writer finds the inference drawn by Schachter to
be totally misconceived. The point is that, since Iran had not taken part in
the proceedings, the Court did not have to address the particular question of
whether counter-measures could be enforced both before and during the
adjudication period. Be that as it may, the fact remains that Iran continued
to ignore the Court's Provisional Order according to which she was required
to release the hostages and to desist from other unlawful acts. The implication
of this was that the Court was rendered incapable of offering any effective
remedy during the adjudication period. Such a situation, in the opinion of
the present writer, was of a kind that could justify the continued imposition
of counter-measures by the United States while the dispute was *sub judice*.

C. STATE PRACTICE

The position adopted by States as regards counter-measures in the context
of obligations in respect of amicable settlement of disputes is particularly
enlightening. Although there is no unanimity, it is quite clear that the preponderant view held by States considers the exhaustion of third party settlement procedures as a prerequisite of counter-measures.

C.I. THE OPINION OF THE SWISS MINISTER OF THE DEPARTMENT OF POLICY, 1928[42]

Since the factual background of this Opinion has already been narrated, it
need not be repeated here.[43] Initially, the Opinion set forth the notion of
necessity as a starting-point for assessing the grounds for resort to non-
forcible reprisals. It then stressed that such a criterion would remain unful-

---

[40] Diss. Op., ibid., p. 63, para. 3(*b*).
[41] Schachter, 'International Law in Theory and Practice: General Course in Public International Law', *R.d.C.*, vol. 178(5), 1982, p. 167, at p. 174.
[42] *Répertoire Suisse*, vol. iii, pp. 1785–96.
[43] Cf. *supra*, ch. 2 s. G.2.

filled where the aggrieved party had resorted to acts of reprisal prior to the invocation of third party proceedings to which it was previously committed.[44]

C.2. ACTS OF THE CONFERENCE FOR THE CODIFICATION OF INTERNATIONAL LAW, 1930[45]

On this occasion, a number of States expressed opinions pertinent to the question under review in their replies to point X(*b*) of the request for information.[46] Belgium, for example, indicated that a State should not incur liability with respect to reprisals where such a State could show that she was unable to 'obtain satisfaction by pacific means'.[47] Denmark similarly affirmed that 'reprisals should be entirely excluded'[48] where the parties were bound by treaty not to exacerbate their disputes. Great Britain, on the other hand, merely observed that '[w]ith the improved machinery now provided by international agreements for the investigation and pacific solution of disputes, the cases where resort to acts of reprisals would be legitimate must be very few'.[49]

The views uttered by Switzerland were largely consistent with those she had expressed in 1928, except for a few noticeable discrepancies. These are evident in the following excerpt from her reply:

[N]o State should resort to reprisals, *i.e.* replying to an illegal act committed against it with another illegal act, if there is any possibility, when diplomatic protests fail, of submitting the dispute to a Court of arbitration or to the Permanent Court of International Justice under a treaty of compulsory arbitral or judicial settlement. Naturally, however, it would be entitled to apply reprisals pending the judicial or arbitral settlement of the dispute, unless the competent tribunal decrees that the *status quo* shall be maintained.[50]

It will be recalled that the opinion expressed by Switzerland in 1928 recognized the discharge of a treaty obligation in respect of peaceful settlement as a prerequisite of legitimate reprisals.[51] This stance was subsequently reaffirmed in the first sentence of the above excerpt. It is difficult to reconcile such a stance with the position of principle expressed in the second sentence. This apparent contradiction, however, is slightly mitigated by the proviso that reprisals should be vacated where a Court ordered the maintenance of the status quo.

---

[44] *Répertoire Suisse*, vol. iii, p. 1788, para. II(*b*).
[45] *Conference for the Codification*, p. 5, at p. 128.
[46] Ibid.
[47] Ibid.
[48] Ibid., pp. 128–9.
[49] Ibid., p. 129; similar views were expressed by India and New Zealand.
[50] Ibid., p. 130.
[51] Cf. *supra* ch. 2 s. G.2.

C.3. THE VIEWS EXPRESSED BY THE NETHERLANDS GOVERNMENT, 1970[52]

During the deliberation of the Sixth Committee of the General Assembly on the Principles of International Law concerning Friendly Relations, the Netherlands Government made certain observations on the question of the legality of non-forcible counter-measures.[53] The following two conditions of legitimacy figured among those mentioned: (*a*) '[counter-measures are] admissible only if negotiations for the purpose of obtaining reparation had been conducted in vain'; and (*b*) that the 'obligations arising from treaties must also be taken into account, especially those establishing international organisations with regard to settlement of disputes'.[54]

The first of these conditions appears to apply generally to all types of counter-measures. Thus, disputes between parties bound by obligations in respect of peaceful settlement would *a fortiori* be subject to that condition. That being the case, recourse to counter-measures should be conditional on the negotiations for reparation reaching an impasse.

As regards the second condition, the use of the term 'must be taken into account' is susceptible of two interpretations. In one sense, it could mean that a treaty obligation in respect of peaceful settlement should be strictly upheld. In another sense, it could imply that the aforesaid obligation would have to be fulfilled in the light of policy considerations.

C.4. PLEADINGS IN THE *CASE CONCERNING THE APPEAL RELATING TO THE JURISDICTION OF THE ICAO COUNCIL*, 1972[55]

C.4.1. Introduction

India and Pakistan are parties to the Convention on International Civil Aviation, 1944 (the Convention), and the International Air Services Transit Agreement, 1944 (the Transit Agreement). A dispute arose between the two states following an incident in which an Indian aircraft was hijacked and diverted to Pakistan.

It is proposed here to deal only with the views of the contending parties on the compatibility of obligations in respect of peaceful settlement with the right to take unilateral counter-measures.[56] This necessitates a return to the provisions underlying those obligations. Thus, the pertinent parts of Article 84 of the Convention and of Article 2 of the Transit Agreement respectively read:

---

[52] *NLYIL*, vol. i, 1970, p. 171, para. 13.12; cf. ch. 3 s. B.
[53] *UNGAOR*, 23rd Sess., 6th Com., 1095th mtg., 13 Dec. 1968, p. 3.
[54] Ibid.
[55] *ICJ Pleadings*, 1973, pp. 3 ff. For the Court's decision see *ICJ Reports*, 1972, p. 46. For a discussion of that decision see *supra*, ch. 8 s. B.2.4.
[56] For a brief background of this dispute see *supra*, ch. 5 s. D.3.

If any disagreement between two or more contracting States relating to the interpretation or application of this Convention and its Annexes cannot be settled by negotiation, it shall on the application of any State concerned in the disagreement, be decided by the Council [...].[57]

If any disagreement between two or more contracting States relating to the interpretation or application of this Agreement cannot be settled by negotiation, the provisions of Chapter XVIII of the above-mentioned Convention shall be applicable.[58]

C.4.2. *The views expressed by India*

Two grounds of objection had been raised by India with respect to the jurisdiction of the ICAO Council: (*a*) The involvement of Pakistan in the hijacking of an Indian aircraft constituted material breach of the Convention and of the Transit Agreement which entitled India to suspend the two instruments *vis-à-vis* Pakistan. Thus, since the Council's jurisdiction was confined to 'interpretation or application' of the treaties, the Council could not examine matters relating to the 'termination or suspension' of these treaties.[59] (*b*) The action taken by India was based on general international law, and not on the treaties.

The assertion made by India that the jurisdiction of the Council had not encompassed the 'termination or suspension' of the treaties cannot be supported. One can only be guided by the following remarks made by the Court in the Advisory Opinion on *Interpretation of Peace Treaties*: 'In as much as the disputes relate to the question of performance or non-performance of the obligations provided for in the [treaties], they are clearly disputes concerning the interpretation or execution of the [treaties in question].'[60] The inference to be drawn from this passage is that a jurisdictional clause governing resort to third party settlement cannot be nullified on the basis of such distinctions as were made by India.

As to the second ground, India argued that she was exercising her right of termination under customary international law and not under the treaties. Furthermore, she stated that even if she had complained, she would have obtained no effective remedy. She claimed, accordingly, that the only course open to her was to apply reciprocal measures.[61] It is submitted by the present writer that since the ICAO Council was not in a position to impose an effective sanction, the unilateral action taken by India could be justified despite her commitment to peaceful settlement under the treaties. At the same

---

[57] Text of the Convention is reprinted in Hudson, *International Legislation*, vol. ix 1942–5, no. 640, 1950, p. 168, at p. 204.
[58] Text of the Agreement, ibid., no. 641, p. 228, at p. 230.
[59] *ICJ Pleadings*, 1973, p. 53, para. 85.
[60] *ICJ Reports*, 1950, p. 65, at p. 75; see also Sep. Op. of Judge Jiménez de Aréchaga, *ICAO Case*, ibid., 1972, p. 140, at p. 147, para. 20.
[61] Ibid., p. 223, para. 53.

time, however, it must be stated that such unilateral action should not have the effect of nullifying the jurisdictional clause applying to that dispute.

C.4.3. *The views expressed by Pakistan*

Pakistan argued that any question relating to a breach of the agreements or their suspension would concern their interpretation and application. In view of this, it would fall within the jurisdiction of the Council.[62] As regards the significance of the existence of a dispute settlement procedure under the treaties, she made the following submission: 'when Pakistan denied that any breach of the agreements had taken place, India could not unilaterally suspend the agreements since a remedy under Article II, Section 2, of the Transit Agreement, and Article 84 of the Convention, is available'.[63] This succinct passage shows that, where an allegation of breach is denied, recourse to counter-measures will be precluded if a remedy is available under an existing agreement between the parties for the peaceful settlement of disputes.

C.5. THE VIEWS OF THE PARTIES IN THE *CASE CONCERNING THE AIR SERVICES AGREEMENT OF 27 MARCH 1946*, 1978[64]

C.5.1. *The argument of the French Government*

The French Government asserted pointedly that, according to both the theory of reprisals and the law of treaties, 'suspension could have taken place only if the injured State had had no other means to ensure respect of the treaty; Article X of the 1946 Agreement shows that this was not the case here'.[65] By way of amplification, France argued that counter-measures should not be applied where other modes of redress were available. In this particular dispute the modes instanced by her were as follows: the process of negotiations and consultations, the making of a formal demand, and resort to arbitral settlement.

As regards the first mode mentioned, France alleged that the United States had failed to discharge her obligation to negotiate disputes in good faith, as was required of her under general international law, and under Articles VIII, X, and XIII of the Agreement.[66] As concerns consultations, it was the view of the French Government that the United States should have agreed in the course of that process to 'negotiate' a new deal independently of what was

---

[62] Ibid., p. 384, para. 42.

[63] Ibid.

[64] *ILR*, vol. 54, 1979, pp. 304ff.

[65] Ibid., p. 320, para. 17; the text of Article X reads: 'Except as otherwise provided in this agreement or its Annex, any dispute between the Contracting Parties relating to the interpretation or application of this Agreement or its Annex which cannot be settled through consultation, shall be referred for an advisory report to the [ICAO Council]'; text of the Agreement, 139. *UNTS*, 1879.

[66] *Digest USPIL*, 1978, pp. 773–4.

provided in the Agreement.[67] With respect to the second mode indicated, France insisted on the submission of a formal demand as a condition of resort to counter-measures.[68] Finally, she contended that the United States Government was precluded from using counter-measures since arbitral procedure could have provided redress.

C.5.2. *The argument of the United States Government*

The United States rejected the position taken by France with respect to the legality of counter-measures in situations where other means of redress were available. Thus, in her view, the theory of reprisals upon which France placed so much reliance was relevant only to armed reprisals.[69] Accordingly, different considerations would apply to questions involving a temporary withdrawal of rights under a treaty. Without further elaboration the United States asserted that

the French position of total abstention pending dispute settlement would represent a drastic change from the existing state of customary international law and could hardly be accepted until institutions of international adjudication have evolved to the point that there are tribunals in place with the authority to indicate interim measures of protection on an immediate basis.[70]

She then proceeded to explain that the position assumed by France could work to the advantage of a treaty violator, and therefore such a party would have no incentive for reaching an expediated settlement.

As regards the initiatives taken in order to achieve an amicable settlement, the United States pleaded that she had made several demands, all of which remained unfulfilled. Hence, she could see no merit in the view expressed by France that, had the action ordered by the CAB been preceded by a renewed demand, satisfaction would have been forthcoming.[71] Furthermore, the United States contended that, by taking part in consultations and by submitting written observations, she had fulfilled her obligation to negotiate as was required by both general international law and the Agreement.[72] She added by way of amplification that the duty to consult did not mean 'to renegotiate a *quid pro quo* for a right which already exists'.[73]

Finally, with reference to the question of abstention from resort to counter-measures prior to reaching an arbitral settlement, the United States observed: 'we do not accept the proposition that an injured party must defer all action until after the outcome of an arbitration. This proposition finds no support

---

[67] Ibid., p. 774.
[68] Ibid., p. 773.
[69] Ibid.
[70] Ibid.
[71] Ibid.
[72] Ibid., p. 774.
[73] Ibid.

in the theory of nonforcible reprisals [...] and is likewise unsupported by treaty law doctrine.'[74]

D. THE LITERATURE

The legality of non-forcible counter-measures in the context of a commitment to peaceful settlement of disputes has never hitherto received any substantial treatment from publicists. Such limited views as have been expressed in the literature will be analysed in this section. First to be discussed are the views of the majority which hold that an obligation in respect of peaceful settlement excludes the right of resort to counter-measures. This will be followed by an examination of the material in which the opposite standpoint is demonstrated.

D.1. THE VIEWS OF THE PUBLICISTS WHO MAINTAIN THAT A COMMITMENT TO PEACEFUL SETTLEMENT PRECLUDES RECOURSE TO COUNTER-MEASURES

According to Dumbauld, an agreement to have recourse to adjudication entails in itself an implied 'obligation to refrain from all acts tending to stultify the arbitration and render the decision nugatory'.[75] He elaborated further that

Any conduct unreconcilable with the arbitration agreement is forbidden. Self-help, destruction of the subject-matter of the controversy, and any action anticipating the decision are among the measures banned. In general, all acts are ruled out which tend to stultify the pacific procedure involved.[76]

The same question has been touched on by Jessup in the course of discussing the denunciation of treaties in the event of breach. He states that '[in] such cases it is highly suitable for an international tribunal to pass judgment on the merits of the claim of the state which seeks to free itself from its obligation'.[77]

The position taken by the American Law Institute is that, in the event of a breach of an agreement, the aggrieved party may take certain retaliatory measures 'except as otherwise provided in the agreement'.[78] It is submitted that this expression precludes retaliatory denunciation of treaties that contain a provision stipulating peaceful settlement. In similar vein Oppenheim writes that if the offending State refuses reparation, the aggrieved State can, '*consistently with any existing obligation of pacific settlement*, exercise such means

---

[74] Ibid.
[75] Dumbauld, *Interim Measures of Protection in International Controversies*, 1932, p. 182.
[76] Ibid., pp. 183–4.
[77] Jessup, *A Modern Law of Nations*, 1948, p. 152.
[78] American Law Institute, *Restatement of the Law: Second, Foreign Relations Law of the United States*, 1965, s. 158(1), p. 484.

as are necessary to enforce adequate reparation'.[79] The inference to be drawn here is that counter-measures will be prima facie unlawful if they are applied in a manner inconsistent with an existing obligation towards peaceful settlement.

The restraint imposed by a commitment to peaceful settlement on the use of counter-measures is given its strongest emphasis by Professor Bowett in the following elucidation:

Where an economic dispute arises within the context of a treaty providing specific procedure for the settlement of disputes, no unilateral resort to reprisals is permissible prior to the use of the pacific procedures. Thus, whether it be an arbitration clause in a commercial treaty or the procedures before Commissions established under treaties regulating fisheries or rivers, or the disputes clauses under the ICAO, ITU, UPU Conventions, or the Complaints procedures under GATT or EFTA or the various Commodity Agreements, or the judicial proceedings before the Court of the European Communities, the prior exhaustion of these procedures must be regarded as a condition precedent to any right of reprisals.[80]

Bowett adds that economic reprisals are subject to the traditional pre-conditions of the customary law of reprisals, one of which is that redress 'by other means must be either exhausted or unavailable'.[81] This position, which had first been taken by Bowett in 1972, was subsequently reaffirmed by him in 1976: 'where a treaty also provides a specific machinery for dealing with disputes, a complaining State will be bound to use that machinery and cannot, for example, resort to unilateral self-help'.[82] These remarks, it should be observed, were directed at the specific question of the legality of economic coercion. In Chapter 10 of the present work it will be demonstrated that counter-measures assume, in the majority of cases, the character of economic coercion.[83] Accordingly, the remarks made by Professor Bowett could generally apply *mutatis mutandis* to the category of counter-measures. This said, the view that observance of a commitment to peaceful settlement should in all circumstances be maintained cannot be attributed to Bowett.

D.2. THE VIEWS OF THE INTERNATIONAL LAW COMMISSION

In its report on Article 30 concerning counter-measures, the Commission made only passing reference to the conditions of resort to counter-measures. One such condition that featured in a footnote required the observance of 'any procedures for peaceful settlement previously agreed upon by the

---

[79] Oppenheim, vol. i, 8th edn. by Lauterpacht, 1955, p. 254, emphasis added.

[80] Bowett, 'Economic Coercion and Reprisals by States', *Virginia Journal of International Law*, vol. 13(1), 1972, p. 1, at p. 11.

[81] Ibid., p. 10.

[82] Bowett, 'Economic Coercion: Past and Present. International Law and Economic Coercion', *Virginia Journal of International Law*, vol. 16(2), 1976 at p. 248; see also p. 252.

[83] Cf. *infra*, ch. 10.

parties'.[84] This conspicuous neglect of any detailed analysis is equally apparent in the Special Rapporteur's Eighth Report on State responsibility.[85] He
did, however, indicate that there existed several categories of breach in
relation to which international law had merely created a right in the wronged
State to seek reparation. In such instances, therefore, recourse to counter-
measures would not be permissible unless the aggrieved party had 'first tried
to obtain adequate reparation'.[86]

In the course of the Commission's deliberations on Article 30 concerning
counter-measures, Professor Yankov stated unequivocally that 'the concept
of a "prior claim" should be taken to signify that the application procedure
had been exhausted, particularly in the case of coercive action'.[87] On the other
hand, Judge Schwebel adopted a generalized position, as this passage would
indicate: 'In the current state of international law and international life, it
was regrettable, but none the less inevitable, that States must retain a right
to take reprisals in response to acts committed in violation of their legal
rights.'[88] Schwebel's remarks indicate that an aggrieved State is entitled to
preserve her rights by taking counter-measures. Nevertheless, they beg the
question as to whether counter-measures may be taken notwithstanding the
existence of a commitment to peaceful settlement.

Professor Riphagen, the Special Rapporteur for Part Two of the Draft
Articles, has examined the question of the inadmissibility of reprisals where
alternative means of peaceful settlement are available.[89] Although he recognizes the merit of restraint in such circumstances, he is none the less able to
appreciate the plight of an aggrieved State. As a middle course between such
conflicting considerations, he suggests that international tribunals should be
empowered to order interim measures of protection which bear the character
of reciprocity as opposed to reprisals.[90]

The Special Rapporteur has proposed, as a further step, that reprisals
should be precluded as soon as a dispute becomes *sub judice*.[91] To this he
appends three conditions, namely: (*a*) the *compromis* should not rule out
interim measures at the instance of either of the contending parties; (*b*) where
interim measures have been ordered, they should be complied with; and (*c*)
the *compromis* should stipulate that the parties will accept as binding the
judgment of the tribunal.

Finally, Riphagen has envisaged that a situation could arise whereby the

---

[84] Doc. A/34/10, *YILC*, vol. ii, part 2, 1979, p. 87, at p. 118 n. 595.

[85] Ago, Doc. A/CN. 4/318 and Add. 1–4, *YILC*, vol. ii, part 1, 1979, p. 3, at p. 43 n. 191.

[86] Ibid., p. 39, para. 80; this view was adopted in the *ILC Report on State Responsibility*, Doc.
A/34/10, *YILC*, vol. ii, part 2, 1979, p. 87, at p. 116, para. 4.

[87] *YILC*, vol. i, 1979, p. 58, para. 31.

[88] Ibid., p. 56, para. 25.

[89] Riphagen, *Fourth Report on the Content, Forms and Degrees of State Responsibility* (Part 2
of the Draft Articles), UN Doc. A/CN. 4/366/Add. 1, 15 Apr. 1983, p. 21, para. 58.

[90] Ibid., p.20, para. 54; p. 23, para. 61.

[91] Ibid., p. 23, para. 61.

matter would be 'beyond reprisals and dispute settlement as a means to obtain a return to legitimacy'.[92] He illustrated this by the occurrence of 'an internationally wrongful act [which] is in fact so manifest *and* at the same time in law so serious as to destroy the object and purpose of the whole body of rules to which the obligation breached by that wrongful act belongs'.[93]

D.3. THE VIEWS OF THE INSTITUTE OF INTERNATIONAL LAW

In its 39th Session, held in Paris in 1934, the Institute of International Law adopted a resolution concerning the regime of reprisals in time of peace. Article 5 of that resolution provides that reprisals are illegal where parties to a dispute had committed themselves previously to peaceful settlement. This Article also precludes resort to reprisals where a dispute has been submitted to a tribunal which possesses the power to make provisional orders, provided that the Respondent State does not pursue evasive or delaying tactics with regard to the tribunal's jurisdiction. The text of Article 5, adopted unanimously by the Institute, reads as follows:

Les représailles même non armées sont interdites quand le respect du droit peut être effectivement assuré par des procédures de règlement pacifique. En conséquence, elles doivent être considérées comme interdites notamment:

1. Lorsqu'en vertu du droit en vigueur entre les parties, l'acte dénoncé comme illicite est de la compétence obligatoire de juges ou d'arbitres ayant compétence aussi pour ordonner, avec la diligence voulue, des mesures provisoires ou conservatoires et que l'État défendeur ne cherche pas à éluder cette juridiction ou à en retarder le fonctionnement:

2. Lorsqu'une procédure de règlement pacifique est en cours, dans les conditions envisagées au 1°, à moins que les représailles n'aient été légitimement prises auparavant, réserve faite de leur cessation décidée par l'autorité saisie.[94]

D.4. THE VIEWS OF THE PUBLICISTS WHO MAINTAIN THAT AN OBLIGATION TO PEACEFUL SETTLEMENT DOES NOT PRECLUDE COUNTER-MEASURES

The first example concerns the position taken by the Harvard Research Group on the question of violation of treaty obligations.[95] Article 27(*a*) of the Harvard Draft Convention stipulates that an aggrieved party should seek a declaration from a competent tribunal to release it from the further performance of obligations owed to the defaulting party. Article 27(*b*), which is of a particular significance to the present enquiry, states: 'Pending agreement by the parties upon and decision by a competent international tribunal

---

[92] Ibid., para. 64.
[93] Ibid.
[94] *Annuaire*, 1934, p. 709.
[95] *The Harvard Draft Convention*, *AJIL*, supplement, vol. 29, 1935, p. 1077.

or authority, the party which seeks such a declaration may provisionally suspend performance of its obligations under the treaty vis-à-vis the State charged with the failure.'[96] It is to be noted that neither this paragraph, nor the comment accompanying it, makes any explicit reference to the question of whether a commitment to peaceful settlement may simply be overlooked. Nevertheless, there is an indication to the effect that an aggrieved party would be entitled to suspend its obligations even during the adjudication period.

Professor Cheng, writing in 1962, specifically affirmed the right of resort to counter-measures in the context of bilateral international aviation treaties. He stated: 'The position is different, however, when in the opinion of one of the parties, the other contracting party has committed a breach of the agreement. Then the principle *inadimplenti non est adimplendum* applies and the party aggrieved is entitled to take proportionate retaliatory measures.'[97] The view expressed by Cheng in this passage is best understood in the light of the nature of the commitment to peaceful settlement under a Bermuda-type Agreement. It is noteworthy that the wording of Article IX of the Bermuda Agreement[98] is comparable to that of Article X of the Air Services Agreement of 1946 between the United States and France. In the *Air Services Agreement Arbitration*, the Tribunal held that the commitment to peaceful settlement mentioned in Article X did not preclude the right of recourse to counter-measures.[99] At the same time, however, the Tribunal envisaged the possibility of a commitment to peaceful settlement being expressed in such trenchant terms as would rule out any resort to counter-measures.[100] On the assumption that such a distinction was recognized by Cheng, it might be inferred that his aforementioned remarks were not intended to apply to all types of peaceful settlement provisions irrespective of the manner in which they are expressed.

The relation between counter-measures and the submission of disputes to arbitration was examined more recently in an article by Mrs Lori Damrosch.[101] What lends more importance to her views is her previous position as Deputy Agent for the United States in the *Air Services Agreement Arbitration*. The main question to occupy the attention of Mrs Damrosch was 'whether customary international law does or should constrain [States'] flexibility to act when they have entered into a prior agreement to submit disputes to third-party resolution'.[102] She admitted at the outset that the

---

[96] Ibid., pp. 1094–5.

[97] Cheng, *The Law of International Air Transport*, 1962, p. 482.

[98] For the text of the Bermuda Agreement of 1946, see *United Kingdom Treaty Series*, no. 3, 1946.

[99] *ILR*, vol. 54, 1979, p. 339, paras. 88–9.

[100] Ibid., pp. 338–9, paras. 84–6.

[101] Damrosch, 'Retaliation or Arbitration—or Both? The 1978 United States–France Aviation Dispute', p. 785.

[102] Ibid., p. 805.

preponderant view of the authorities was in support of the position taken by France regarding abstention from retaliation prior to an arbitral decision.[103] Subsequently, however, she illustrated the inherent flaw in that position by reference to the *Hostages Case*, remarking that '[t]he Iran example also makes clear that a dispute settlement clause in a treaty that codifies obligations under customary international law should not be regarded as depriving an aggrieved party of its customary international law remedy, retaliatory sanctions'.[104] To this Damrosch added the proviso that the right to initiate counter-measures would terminate in situations where a tribunal possessed the means to attain the objectives which might otherwise necessitate the exercise of that right.[105]

E. SOME SUGGESTED DISTINCTIONS

E.1. GENERAL

The question of how far an obligation in respect of peaceful settlement is binding must first be assessed by reference to the general rules of treaty interpretation. Thus, if it transpires that there is in reality a definite commitment to peaceful settlement between the parties concerned, resort to counter-measures by either party must be considered as prima facie unlawful. This general rule applies particularly where the treaty containing that rule establishes mechanisms for ensuring its implementation. There may, however, be situations in which the desired mechanisms prove inadequate. It is here that an aggrieved State could justifiably resort to counter-measures on the basis of customary law. Such a course is made possible because the principle of counter-measures retains, from the standpoint of applicability, a separate existence from the rule concerning peaceful settlement on the level of treaty law.[106] Hence, in order to determine whether counter-measures may be applied in a given case notwithstanding a commitment to peaceful settlement, account must be taken of the different motivations behind the measures taken. This will be examined next.

E.2. THE SIGNIFICANCE OF THE AVAILABILITY OF THIRD PARTY SETTLEMENT PROCEDURE WHERE THE MOTIVE FOR COUNTER-MEASURES IS TO INDUCE PEACEFUL SETTLEMENT

Where the *raison d'être* of counter-measures is shown to be an inducement to settle a dispute, the availability of third party settlement procedure obliges

---

[103] Ibid., p.806.

[104] Ibid., pp. 805–6.

[105] Ibid., p. 806.

[106] On the point of principle see: *Case Concerning Military and Paramilitary Activities in and Against Nicaragua, ICJ Reports*, 1986, p. 14, at p. 95, para. 178.

the parties concerned to refrain from counter-measures. This view is based on the common-sense notion which provides that a State should not demonstrate conduct that is prima facie inconsistent with a commitment to peaceful settlement. However, where it appears that counter-measures will facilitate acceptance of third party settlement procedure, the aggrieved party may justifiably initiate such measures during the period before the case becomes *sub judice*. It stands to reason that the party which resorts to counter-measures in these circumstances must clearly indicate its willingness to submit the dispute to adjudication. Furthermore, once the defaulting party has agreed to resort to peaceful settlement, the counter-measures taken against it must be terminated forthwith.

E.3. THE SIGNIFICANCE OF THE AVAILABILITY OF THIRD PARTY SETTLEMENT PROCEDURE WHERE THE MOTIVE FOR COUNTER-MEASURES IS SELF-PROTECTION

Although the contending parties may have entered into a commitment to settle disputes amicably, one could envisage a number of situations in which the motive of self-protection could justify resort to counter-measures. First, at the pre-adjudication stage it may happen that the alleged wrongdoer resorts to prevarication and unnecessary protraction with a view to causing a breakdown in the negotiations. Secondly, the parties to a dispute may have concluded a *compromis* for third party settlement procedure without, however, agreeing to abide by the judgment of that third party. Thirdly, the latter may not have been empowered to order measures of interim protection; or else, in the event of its being so empowered, its orders may be flouted by a party that has been given a reasonable period to comply with such orders. Fourthly, it is possible that a party against which a decision is taken refuses to implement it without any justification. Indeed, the rightfulness of counter-measures taken under any of these circumstances ought not to be questioned notwithstanding the existence of a commitment to peaceful settlement, and notwithstanding the fact that a tribunal has been seized of the dispute. Moreover, although counter-measures are not normally permitted when interim measures of protection have been ordered by a tribunal, they may nevertheless be taken where such interim measures are not carried out.

As has been mentioned elsewhere,[107] when the rationale for counter-measures is self-protection, a wide scope for action is permissible. This does not, however, mean that the measures taken are not subject to the rule of proportionality. It follows, therefore, that where counter-measures are imposed in order to enforce a judgment, they must be' proportionate to

---

[107] Cf. *supra*, ch. 6 s. C.2.2.

the damages awarded and, where damages are not quantified, should be limited to the degree of injury recogized in the judgment.[108]

E.4 THE SIGNIFICANCE OF THE AVAILABILITY OF THIRD PARTY SETTLEMENT PROCEDURE WHERE THE MOTIVE FOR COUNTER-MEASURES IS RECIPROCITY

Where situations such as those envisaged in the preceding subsection involve less serious implications, reciprocity rather than self-protection will be the underlying motivation for taking counter-measures. Thus, parallel to the reasoning pursued in the preceding subsection, a wronged party may, arguably, have recourse to counter-measures in order to preserve its rights and to restore a level of equity. Although counter-measures based on reciprocity may be initiated before the process of arbitration has commenced, they must be terminated as soon as a tribunal is in a position to act. This stricture, however, is subject to the proviso that the alleged wrongdoer will carry out whatever interim measures of protection have been ordered by the tribunal.

E.5. THE SIGNIFICANCE OF THE AVAILABILITY OF THIRD PARTY SETTLEMENT PROCEDURE WHERE THE MOTIVE FOR COUNTER-MEASURES IS PARTLY AN INDUCEMENT TO SETTLE, AND PARTLY EITHER SELF-PROTECTION OR RECIPROCITY

Despite our attempt to compartmentalize the effects of the various motives for counter-measures, such distinctions may not be possible in every instance. One could take as an example the case in which negotiations for concluding a *compromis* are long drawn out. The consequence of such a protraction may be to compound further the injury sustained by the aggrieved party and at the same time to remove from the offending party any incentive for peaceful settlement. In such a case resort to counter-measures may conceivably be motivated partly by an inducement to settle, and partly by either self-protection or by reciprocity. It is submitted that the principles governing a case in which self-protection figures as one of the underlying motivations should be the same as those which apply when self-protection is the exclusive objective. As to the case in which reciprocity is allied to a desire to achieve a speedy settlement, the rules governing the situation will be the same as those when a speedy settlement is the exclusive motivation.[109]

---

[108] See generally Kelsen, *Principles of International Law*, 1952, p. 395; Rosenne, *The Law and Practice of the International Court*, vol. i, 1965, pp. 127, 136–7; Nantwi, *The Enforcement of International Judicial Decisions and Arbitral Awards in Public International Law*, 1966, pp. 142–3.

[109] Cf. *supra*, ch. 4 s. C.3.

E.6. THE SIGNIFICANCE OF THE EXISTENCE OF AN INSTITUTIONAL
FRAMEWORK FOR PEACEFUL SETTLEMENT

The purpose of this subsection is to examine whether resort to counter-measures is permissible where there is a mechanism established within the framework of an international institution. Such a mechanism may be illustrated by reference to the complaint system under the GATT, the IMF, or the European communities. As a general proposition, compliance with the mechanism established by any of these institutions is considered to be a prerequisite of lawful counter-measures.

With regard to the GATT,[110] Article 1 of that Agreement provides for most-favoured-nation treatment in order to eliminate discriminatory measures among the parties. Article 11 makes restrictions or prohibitions on export unlawful, and Article 13 prohibits discriminatory quantitative restrictions. Article 23 provides that the contracting parties may authorize a contracting party to suspend the application to any other party of any obligations under the agreement. Thus, a unilateral action which violates, for example, either Article 11 or Article 13 is prima facie unlawful, for the reason that such action has not been authorized under Article 23. It is noteworthy, however, that the Agreement does not exclude policy considerations; Articles 20 and 21 state that an action taken in breach of the Agreement may nevertheless be held lawful where the motivation is to protect the essential security of the sanctioning State.

As concerns the IMF,[111] the Fund's Rules and Regulations provide procedures which enable an aggrieved member to complain against another member for non-fulfilment of its obligations.[112] Further, the Agreement authorizes the Fund to impose sanctions in appropriate cases. Thus, it may make a declaration of ineligibility to use the Fund's resources either because a member 'is using the general resources of the Fund in a manner contrary to the purposes of the Fund',[113] or because a member 'fails to fulfill any of its obligations' under the Agreement.[114]

From the above, it is clear that the Fund's Agreement not only prescribes specific procedures for the settlement of disputes, but also ensures the enforcement of obligations by means other than unilateral action. Pertinent to this, Sir Joseph Gold states that 'even if a member introduces discriminatory or other restrictions without the approval of the Fund, other members are not

---

[110] Dated 30 Oct. 1947, 55 *UNTS*, 814.I.(*b*).
[111] For the text of the IMF Agreement as amended see: International Monetary Fund, *Articles of Agreement*, 1978.
[112] *Rules and Regulations*, Rules H-2, H-3, K-4, M-4, M-5, *The International Monetary Fund, 1945–1965*, vol. iii: Analysis, ed. Horsefield, 1969, pp. 293–4, 299, and 301.
[113] Art. V s. 5, International Monetary Fund, *Articles of Agreement*, 1978, pp. 13–14.
[114] Art. XXVI s. 2(*a*), ibid., p. 72.

entitled to adopt counter-measures without the Fund's approval if they are measures that require the Fund's approval'.[115]

The inhibition placed on the freedom to take unilateral action by an aggrieved party is not categorical. This view is supported by the Executive Board's Decision No. 144 (52/51).[116] This Decision provides for a special procedure for the approval of restrictions imposed by members for the preservation of national or international security. Thus, it stipulates that when a member intends to impose such a restriction it should notify the Fund either in advance, or within thirty days of the imposition of that restriction. Such flexibility clearly favours a State contemplating counter-measures.

For an illustration from recent State practice, the restrictions that had been imposed by the United States against Iran were stated to be in response to 'an unusual and extraordinary threat to the national security, foreign policy and economy of the United States'.[117] Although the United States had not immediately invoked Decision No. 144 (52/51), it did so within the thirty-day limit prescribed in that Decision. It is to be noted that the Fund raised no objection to the claim made by the United States Government that the restrictions imposed by it were motivated by national security considerations.[118]

As regards the Iranian stance, Mr Rashdzadeh[119] remarked that the measures taken by the United States 'provided an illegal precedent for any country issuing an international reserve currency to deny the holder at any time the right of usage of such currencies'.[120] As concerns the particular question of whether the aforementioned restrictions had been imposed in accordance with the terms of Decision No. 144 (52/51), he stated that '[o]ne fails to see how such measures [...] could possibly enhance security. [...] such actions were not designed to preserve the financial and monetary security of the United States, which was in no way endangered. Rather, it was merely an excuse to put pressure on a nation.'[121]

It emerges from the substance of the two preceding paragraphs that the concept of 'national security' is susceptible to diametrically opposed interpretations. However, the ultimate decision rests with the 'Fund' since it has the power to object to measures purportedly taken on the basis of national security. To relate this to the Carter Freeze Order, had the Fund objected to

[115] Gold, 'Some Characteristics of Operation', *The International Monetary Fund, 1945–1965*, vol. ii: Analysis, ed. Horsefield, 1969, p. 582, at p. 592.

[116] Dated 14 Aug. 1958, *IMF Selected Decisions of the Executive Directors and Selected Documents*, 3rd issue, 1965, pp. 75–6, 82.

[117] Executive Order No. 12170, 44 *Fed. Reg.*, 65729, 1979.

[118] See letter from Director of the IMF Legal Department to Professor Edwards. Text: *AJIL*, vol. 75, 1981, pp. 900–1.

[119] The temporary alternate Governor of the Fund.

[120] International Monetary Fund, *Summary Proceedings of the Thirty-fifth Annual Meeting of the Board of Governors*, 1980, p. 179, at p. 181.

[121] Ibid., p. 182.

the steps taken by the United States, the lawfulness of that Order as a counter-measure could have been called in question.

Attention may now be turned to the framework established by the European Communities. Although the Treaty of Rome[122] does not provide for sanctions against failure to comply with judicial decisions, the jurisprudence of the European Court categorically rules out any possibility of recourse to counter-measures.[123] This preclusion is commonly held to be based on 'the new legal order' which transcends the pertinent rules of customary international law.[124] The question is thus begged as to whether an aggrieved party can take counter-measures at all to thrust a recalcitrant party into prompt execution of a judicial decision.

The present writer recognizes that the European Communities have established a framework which obliges an aggrieved Member State to exhaust all available legal and political means towards achieving an amicable settlement. However, once such means have been exhausted to no avail, an aggrieved Member State would in practice be left without any effective remedy under that framework. It is submitted therefore that in such circumstances an aggrieved party may exercise the right of reprisals under customary law in order to obtain redress.[125] Thus, it may impose a reciprocal levy which is inconsistent with its obligations under the Treaty, or else it may suspend the performance of some obligation owed to the defaulting Member State under another treaty. Such counter-measures cannot be regarded as incompatible with the mechanism established by the European Communities since the wrongfulness of the conduct which provoked their imposition will already have been established by the Court of Justice of the European Communities. Finally, it must be stressed that such fierce retaliation should be resorted to only in cases of exceptional hardship.

F. CONCLUSIONS

The foregoing review of the jurisprudence, State practice, and the literature has brought to light the existence of divergent views as to whether counter-measures may be taken when there is a prior commitment between the parties for peaceful settlement. The proponents of the view that the existence of third party settlement procedure should not obviate the right of resort to counter-measures justify their position by two main arguments. First, that the pro-

---

[122] 298 *UNTS*, 4300.

[123] Cf. *supra*, ch. 8 s. B.1.

[124] See Audretsch, *Supervision in European Community Law*, 1978, p. 85; for a general discussion see Panhuys, 'Conflict between The European Communities and other rules of international law', *Common Market Law Review*, vol. 3, 1966, p. 420, at p. 448; Wyatt, 'New Legal Order, or Old?', *European Law Review*, vol. 7, 1982, p. 147, at pp. 159–60.

[125] See Kapteyn and Verloren van Themaat, *Introduction to the Law of the European Communities after the accession of new Member States*, 1973, p. 27; Audretsch, *Supervision in European Community Law*, p. 82; Wyatt, 'New Legal Order, or Old?', pp. 165–6.

hibition of counter-measures in the context of a commitment to peaceful settlement is not supported by State practice, and hence forms no part of customary international law. Such an assertion, in the opinion of the present writer, receives scant approbation from the majority of the instances of State practice examined in this chapter. At the same time, however, it needs to be recognized that nearly half these instances represented views of states that were expressed in the abstract and without relation to concrete cases.

The second argument relates to the damage that may be caused to an aggrieved party by the lack of effective international procedures for peaceful settlement. In view of such a possibility it is maintained that States have the right to preserve their interests by taking unilateral counter-measures. The present writer submits that this line of argument was more persuasive during the period in which the process of arbitration was at an experimental stage. Today, however, the availability of third party settlement procedures must put some degree of constraint on the right to take counter-measures. None the less, it is conceivable that in certain circumstances resort to unilateral counter-measures could be justified, notwithstanding a prior commitment to amicable settlement. Thus, for example, where recourse to such actions is the only feasible method for inducing the defaulting party to accept arbitration, the commitment can be ignored. It should be emphasized, however, that regardless of the motivation behind resort to counter-measures, jurisdictional clauses must not be nullified.

As regards the period in which a dispute is *sub judice*, the right to impose counter-measures must be assessed from a somewhat different angle. In addition to the attitude of the offending State, consideration should also be given to the issue of whether the tribunal is able to provide the protection sought. Where it is evident that such protection is not forthcoming, the motive of self-protection or that of reciprocity may justify the imposition of counter-measures. This argument brings to mind the circumstances which motivated the United States to continue her counter-measures against Iran even though the case was *sub judice*. By contrast, in the United States–France Air Services Case, the fact that the parties agreed on interim arrangements which maintained equality between them removed all justification for the continuance of counter-measures.

Where the parties belong to an institutional framework which prescribes peaceful settlement procedures, the exhaustion of those procedures will be regarded as a prerequisite for taking counter-measures. This view is based on the assumption that since the framework concerned contains within itself the means to remedy the grievance, the need to resort to counter-measures is obviated. It should be emphasized at the same time that the right to resort to counter-measures is merely held in abeyance. The implication, therefore, is that the right in question can be revived where the institutional framework proves to be ineffective.

The Legality of Economic Coercion in General International Law

A. THE PURPOSE

THE purpose of this chapter is to examine the legality of economic coercion in general international law.[1] Consideration will initially be given to the methodological problems to be faced, and the criteria to be adopted, in attempting to define economic coercion. An examination will then be made of the hypothesis according to which economic coercion is prima facie lawful, subject to certain exceptions. This will immediately be followed by an assessment of the hypothesis which provides that economic coercion is prima facie unlawful, subject to certain exceptions. Some conclusions will be offered regarding the extent to which each alternative hypothesis, if established, might affect the legality of counter-measures. In the absence of any clear principle reflecting either of the above alternatives, it will be shown that the legality of counter-measures in any given occasion may be determined without reference to the category of economic coercion.

B. IS ECONOMIC COERCION A DEFINABLE CONCEPT?

B.I. THE SCOPE OF THE ENQUIRY

The complexity and the peculiar characteristics of economic behaviour render any definition of the concept of economic coercion uniquely difficult to attain. In view of this, it is important as a matter of methodology to treat separately two distinct questions: first, the general approach to, and the problems commonly associated with, the defining of any given concept; and secondly, the special problem of defining economic coercion. This will be followed by an evaluation of the criteria which have been suggested by some writers for characterizing economic coercion as unlawful. The object of this exercise is to see whether they may be used for defining economic coercion.

---

[1] Although it is not proposed to undertake a specific study of the legality of economic coercion under the Law of Treaties, cursory reference will be made to this problem within the context of other issues discussed.

B.2. THE GENERAL APPROACH TO DEFINITIONS

The categories to be utilized in examining the general approach are threefold: the general definition, the enumerative definition, and the mixed definition.

The general definition method has the advantage of stating the intended result of any given rule. Its main defect, however, lies in its importation of terms that are themselves in need of a further definition. This inevitably results in an imprecision which renders any attempted definition wide of the mark. This said, such a method must not be completely discarded seeing that it can be utilized to compose a relatively functional definition.

The general definition method may be illustrated by reference to the definition of economic coercion embodied in the draft definition of aggression proposed by Bolivia.[2] It is a well-known fact that the Bolivian proposal was in response to the glutting by the Soviet Union in 1953 of the world market with cheap tin. With that in mind, Bolivia defined economic coercion as follows:

unilateral action whereby a State is deprived of economic resources derived from the proper conduct of international trade or its basic economy is endangered so that its security is affected and it is rendered unable to act in its own defence or to co-operate in the collective defence of peace shall likewise be deemed to constitute an act of aggression.[3]

The above text brings into focus the difficulties surrounding any attempt at employing the general definition method. To begin with, the opening two words of that text, referring as they do to unilateral action only, implicitly exclude action taken in concert by a group of States. Furthermore, the use of the term 'economic resources' is inappropriate since this term lacks precision. Finally, ambiguities can attend the respective meanings of the expressions 'the proper conduct of international trade', and 'the basic economy'.

As regards the usefulness of the enumerative method, its apparent lack of flexibility may give rise to undesirable results. An unscrupulous government might, for example, be encouraged to evade responsibility for reprehensible conduct by taking shelter behind a legal text. To borrow the words of Sir Austen Chamberlain, such a method would constitute 'a trap for the innocent and a signpost for the guilty'.[4] The point may be illustrated by reference to the definition of aggression proposed by the Soviet Union which ran thus:

---

[2] Submitted to the Special Committee on the Question of Defining Aggression, UN Doc. AC.66/L.9, 15 Sept. 1953.

[3] Ibid., para 3.

[4] *Hansard, HC Debs.*, vol. 210, col. 2105, 24 Nov. 1927, quoted by Eagleton, 'The Attempt to Define Aggression', *International Conciliation*, no. 263, 1930, p. 583, at p. 613.

3. That a State shall be declared to have committed an act of economic aggression which first commits one of the following acts:

    (a) Takes against another State measures of economic pressure violating its sovereignty and economic independence and threatening the basis of its economic life;

    (b) Takes against another State measures preventing it from exploiting or nationalising its own natural rights;

    (c) Subjects another State to an economic blockade.[5]

Aware of the dangers of too rigid an interpretation, the sponsor further proposed that acts not falling within these three classes might still be categorized by the Security Council as acts of aggression. The open-ended nature of the proposed definition exemplifies the inherent difficulty to be met in coining a definition on the basis of enumeration.

Turning to the mixed definition method, the definition of aggression[6] adopted by the General Assembly may pertinently be cited to highlight some of the difficulties to be encountered when this method is used. As can be seen, the definition of aggression is couched in Article 1 in broad terms:

Aggression is the use of armed force by a State against the sovereignty, territorial integrity or political independence of another State, or in any other manner inconsistent with the Charter of the United Nations, as set out in this Definition.[7]

Without attempting any analysis of this provision, it may be stated that the limitations inherent in the general definition method will also apply here. However, Article 2 of the same definition of aggression provides that the first resort to armed force which violates the Charter

shall constitute *prima facie* evidence of an act of aggression although the Security Council may, in conformity with the Charter, conclude that a determination that an act of aggression has been committed would not be justified in the light of other relevant circumstances including the fact that the acts concerned or their consequences are not of sufficient gravity.[8]

This Article is clearly dealing with the 'standard of proof' as well as with the Security Council's discretion in determining the fact of aggression. Further, there is an indication that neither the notion of 'priority',[9] nor that of *animus aggressionis* is to be taken as the sole criterion for defining aggression.

Article 3 states at the outset that any one of a certain range of acts shall qualify as aggression subject to, and in accordance with, Article 2. The explicit

---

[5] Text annexed to *Report of the Special Committee on the Question of Defining Aggression*, UN Doc. A/AC.66/L.11, 14 Oct. 1953, p. 1, at p. 2.

[6] Annexed to General Assembly Resolution 3314(XXIX), 14 Dec. 1974, *UNGAOR*, 29th Sess., suppl. 31 (A/9631), 1974, pp. 142–4, reprinted in *AJIL*, vol. 69, 1975, p. 480.

[7] Ibid.

[8] Resolution 3314(XXIX), p. 142.

[9] See Convention for the Definition of Aggression, between Romania, Union of Soviet Socialist Republics, Czechoslovakia, Turkey, and Yugoslavia, 1933, 140–8 *LNTS*, 3414.

reference to Article 2 is extremely important since any of the acts enumerated in Article 3 taken by itself would hardly constitute aggression. That said, Article 4 expressly stipulates that the list of acts classifiable as aggression is not exhaustive for the reason that the Security Council may determine what other acts constitute such conduct under the Charter.

In summary, the foregoing analyses have focused on some of the major problems confronting attempts to define any general concept. Since a perfect definition would clearly be unattainable, the aim should be simply to frame a wording that had reasonable utility. The ensuing subsection will in turn deal with the difficulties surrounding the particular question of defining economic coercion.

B.3. THE PARTICULAR QUESTION OF DEFINING ECONOMIC COERCION

Economic behaviour may take various forms and shades. Although it would be impossible to list every kind of economic activity, 'coercive' or otherwise, some instances may be cited so as to illustrate the complexity involved. While it is conceded that some economic activities, such as the suspension of a bilateral treaty or the freezing of assets belonging to another State, constitute economic coercion, measures of that nature are by no means coercive in all circumstances. For example, the action taken in a given case may well be looked upon as a legitimate counter-measure. Furthermore, there are some economic activities which, though generally of a non-coercive character, can in most cases be transformed into expressions of coercive behaviour. Thus price manipulation, which is commonly practised by States solely to maintain a healthy balance of payments, may equally be adapted to bring about coercive effects: for example, a particular commodity might be offered to different States at widely varying prices without there being any treaty to justify such disparity. Here the question must be raised whether a State selling a commodity is under any legal obligation to abandon her bargaining powers and conduct business with all States on equal terms.

To break fresh ground, the tendency in legal thinking should be to isolate cases of economic coercion of particular severity. In this respect one may cite as an example the expulsion of aliens. Although a State is entitled as a general rule to expel aliens, deliberate attempts to engender a refugee crisis through such action could be regarded as a typical instance of coercive economic conduct. To quote the words of Professor Parry: '[a] state need not admit [aliens], but once they are admitted they may not be arbitrarily expelled'.[10] For an illustration from State practice, in the early months of 1983 the Nigerian Government carried out a mass expulsion of foreign workers who came to Nigeria during the oil boom period. The declared motive for that

[10] Parry, 'Defining Economic Coercion in International Law', *Texas International Law Journal*, vol. 12, 1977, p. 1, at p. 4.

expulsion was the growing demand for jobs by Nigerians during the recession which was caused by a fall in oil prices.[11] As a direct consequence, an instant refugee problem was brought into being for the five States which received the deportees.[12] It is submitted that, although the right of the Nigerian Government to make that order would be justified on the grounds of self-protection, the manner in which it was carried out could not be supported.

It has been shown in Chapter 6 that counter-measures may be considered as disproportionate, and hence unlawful, where the concept of dependence or reliance has not been observed.[13] It is submitted that the same concept may also be used as a criterion for identifying the cases in which economic coercion appears to be particularly severe. Thus, an abrupt discontinuance of trade could be identified as one such case and be regarded as prima facie evidence of economic coercion. In this respect Professor Parry remarks:

> It would be difficult to maintain that state *A* must buy state *B*'s sugar crop (or permits its nationals to do so), or that state *A* must sell state *B* as much oil as it wants (or permits its nationals to do so). But it is not necessarily unreasonable to suggest that the abrupt termination or interference with an established trade pattern may approach the impermissible and may be capable of adequate enough definition.[14]

By way of amplification, the present writer takes the view that an abrupt discontinuance of trade may nevertheless be justified by the rationale underlying it. Accordingly, self-protection, for example, on a purely commercial basis may occasionally oblige a State to terminate supplies of a particular commodity abruptly. Thus Nigeria in 1982 suspended oil shipments to Ghana, stating that supplies would not be resumed until one-fifth of an oil debt totalling $150,000,000 had been paid.[15] Although this decision might be viewed by Ghana as a form of economic coercion, it could only appear to Nigeria as a way of protecting her trading interests.

The difficulty associated with defining economic coercion is seen further in the sphere of economic aid.[16] Although it is obvious that no Government is under any obligation either to offer or to accept economic aid, it is arguable nevertheless that a donor State is not at liberty to stipulate unreasonable terms. It is difficult, however, to discern clearly the point at which any given stipulation may be considered as unreasonable. A possible touchstone could be the invocation of the concept of proportionality in the broadest sense.

Presupposing that a donor–recipient relationship has been forged between two States, a reliance situation may be said to have arisen; hence, as a matter

---

[11] *KCA*, vol. 30, 1984, p. 32609.
[12] Benin, Ghana, Niger, Togo, and Upper Volta.
[13] Cf. *supra*, ch. 6 s. C.2.5.
[14] Parry, 'Defining Economic Coercion', 1977, p. 4.
[15] *KCA*, vol. 28, 1982, p. 31386.
[16] See McDougal and Feliciano, 'International Coercion and World Public Order: The General Principles of the Law of War', *Yale Law Journal*, vol. 67, 1958, p. 770, at pp. 794–5.

of proportionality, the donor State should in such a case be precluded from applying the aid as a leverage against the recipient State. For an illustration, a substantial quantity of aid, payable monthly by the United States Government to Laos, was withheld in January 1962 pending the fulfilment of certain demands. As soon as these demands were met the funds were released forthwith. A month later the United States Government was to exert similar pressure by suspending her monthly payment to Laos. The American behaviour was castigated in an official statement from Vientiane as an 'intolerable pressure',[17] and was held directly responsible for the steep rise in food prices in Laos.[18]

While conduct of that nature may be regarded as coercive, it should not be assumed that once economic aid has commenced, it cannot be suspended under any circumstances. Thus, it would be quite in order to withhold aid to dissuade a recipient State from engaging in wrongful conduct. It was with this intention that the Netherlands Government suspended payments forming part of a lucrative aid programme to Surinam until a clear indication of respect for human rights was forthcoming from that State.[19]

Attention will now focus on the criterion of 'intention' as used by Bowett for characterizing economic coercion as unlawful. Our purpose is to ascertain whether it can be employed for defining economic coercion. Bowett argues that 'measures not illegal per se may become illegal only upon proof of an improper motive or purpose'.[20] By way of elaboration he points out that, though the proposed criterion permits th protection of *economic* interests, it does not legitimize economic coercion injurious to another State 'when the motive is to further or protect the State's political interests'.[21] Bowett concedes, however, that in the absence of any clear demarcation between political and economic motives the yardstick would have to be 'the predominance of one over the other'.[22] Such an approach, with justification, finds little favour with Parry who, quoting Judge Hudson, remarked that 'if, as the old judge said, the thought of man is not triable, for the Devil himself knoweth not the thought of man, how much more difficult is it to ascertain with certainty the thought or motive and intent of a state'.[23] Be that as it may, the present writer takes the view that 'intention' may be gainfully used as a criterion for defining economic coercion but only with respect to cases in which States make revealing admissions.

Muir, on the other hand, suggests that the element of intention and of effect may jointly be used in characterizing unlawful economic coercion. In

---

[17] *KCA*, vol. 13, 1961–2, p. 18567.
[18] Ibid., p. 18915.
[19] *The Times*, 18 Dec. 1982, p. 5.
[20] Bowett, 'Economic Coercion and Reprisals by States', 1972, p. 5.
[21] Bowett, 'Economic Coercion: Past and Present', 1976, p. 249.
[22] Ibid.
[23] Parry, 'Defining Economic Coercion', 1977, p. 4.

his opinion, economic coercion would be illegal '[o]nly if the purpose is one of total annihilation of the target state, combined with the power seriously to compromise its security'.[24] The present writer would argue that, in principle, the elements of intention and effect could both be utilized in formulating a definition of economic coercion. This, however, is not to say that only the most extreme effects such as those evisaged by Muir could signify coercion.

B.4. AN OPINION

It is obvious that economic coercion is practised by virtually all States, powerful or weak. Yet economic coercion as a concept does not lend itself to a definition that is both exact and comprehensive. This difficulty was alluded to by Professor Riphagen: 'Besides the threat or use of force, there were of course other forms of pressure which were in certain circumstances illegal and reprehensible. But it seemed virtually impossible within the scope of a simple statement of principles to anticipate all the possible forces of pressure and counter-pressure.'[25] Given the array of obstacles which impede the attainment of a satisfactory definition of economic coercion in the abstract, perhaps the very foundation of such a question is placed in doubt. A more plausible approach would be to attempt an identification of the particular occasions in which economic coercion is reprehensible. According to this, the legality of any pressure, notwithstanding the tag attached to it, may be tested by its compatibility with the established rules of international law.

C. IS ECONOMIC COERCION PRIMA FACIE LAWFUL, SUBJECT TO CERTAIN EXCEPTIONS?

C.1. THE PURPOSE

The purpose of this section is to analyse the hypothesis that economic coercion is prima facie lawful, subject to certain exceptions. This entails an analysis of the position in customary law, the United Nations Charter, Resolutions of the General Assembly, and the subsequent practice of the parties to the Charter. Finally, it will be shown how far a principle that *permits* economic coercion can in fact affect the question of the legality of counter-measures.

---

[24] Muir, 'The Boycott in International Law', *Journal of International Law and Economics*, vol. 9, 1974, p. 186, at p. 203.
[25] *Summary Records of the 7th Meeting of the Special Committee on Principles of Friendly Relations*, UN Doc. A/AC.119/SR.7, 16 Oct. 1964, p. 9.

C.2. THE POSITION ACCORDING TO CUSTOMARY LAW

Customary international law presupposes the right of States to adopt their respective economic strategies. Hence, barring any conflicting treaty obligations, and subject to the rules of international law concerning the protection of aliens, a State may sever at will trade relations with any other.[26] This may be effected by a variety of subtle methods such as the levying of a high protective tariff or the imposition of excessively strict standards of sanitation. On the occurrence of breach, on the other hand, an aggrieved party is entitled by way of reprisals to suspend or relinquish trade obligations with the wrongdoer.[27] The latter, however, though free to protest or even retort against such reprisals, is not permitted to react as if they were violations of international law.

C.3. THE CHARTER OF THE UNITED NATIONS

The Charter of the United Nations does not explicitly deal with the legality of economic coercion.[28] In order to clarify the position categorically it is intended to examine those provisions of the Charter which are likely to contain implicit restrictions on the use of economic coercion.

c.3.1. Article 2(3) of the United Nations Charter

The text of Article 2 paragraph 3 of the Charter of the United Nations provides that '[a]ll Members shall settle their international disputes by peaceful means in such a manner that international peace and security, and justice, are not endangered'. It can hardly be inferred from this provision that it seeks to restrict the use of economic coercion as a means of settling disputes. An examination of the *travaux préparatoires* of the San Francisco Conference fails to resolve this obscurity. The Rapporteur of Committee I, for example, visualized its scope thus: 'A State would not be permitted to settle its dispute by force or to exert coercion and fight in order to impose its own solution to a controversy. The paragraph thus established clearly the principle of peaceful solution versus coercive solution.'[29] These remarks indicate that the principle of peaceful settlement laid down in Article 2(3) is a corollary to the principle

[26] Hyde and Wehle, 'Boycott in Foreign Affairs', *AJIL*, vol. 27, 1933, p. 1, at p. 3: Lauterpacht, 'Boycott in International Relations', *BYIL*, vol. 14, 1933, p. 123, at p. 130; Eagleton, *International Government*, 1957, p. 87; Muir, 'The Boycott in International Law', 1974, p. 192; see the 'Explanatory Memorandum to the Bill on reporting of foreign boycott measures, Netherlands State practice', *NLYIL*, vol. 13, 1982, pp. 237–8.

[27] Oppenheim, vol. ii, 7th edn. by Lauterpacht, 1952, p. 561; Stone, *Legal Controls of International Conflict*, 1954, p. 291.

[28] For the views of publicists who maintain that Art. 2(4) includes economic coercion see *infra* s. C.3.2.(iii).

[29] Report to Committee I, Doc. 944/1/1/34(1), 13 June 1945, United Nations Information Organizations, *Documents of the United Nations Conference on International Organization*, San Francisco, 1945 (hereinafter cited as *UNCIO Doc.*) vol. vi, p. 446, at p. 458, para. 3.

prohibiting threats or use of force as stated in paragraph 4 of the same Article. The reference in the former paragraph to 'peaceful means' is intended to exclude the use of force as an instrument for settling disputes. Accordingly, Article 2(3) cannot be interpreted as permitting or precluding the use of economic coercion.

C.3.2. Article 2(4) of the United Nations Charter

(i) *The text*
The text of Article 2 paragraph 4 of the Charter provides that

All Members shall refrain in their international relations from the threat or use of force against the territorial integrity or political independence of any State, or in any other manner inconsistent with the purpose of the United Nations.

As with the previous paragraph in the same Article, there is no clear prohibition on the use of economic coercion to be adduced from this text. However, there is some controversy over whether Article 2(4) in fact prohibits economic coercion.[30] Accordingly, an examination of the *travaux préparatoires*, the views of the two schools of thought, and the subsequent practice of the parties to the Charter is called for.

(ii) *The* travaux préparatoires
Brazil proposed an amendment to the original Dumbarton Oaks Draft Article 2(4) as follows: 'All Members of the Organisation shall refrain in their international relations from the threat or use of force and from the threat or use of *economic measures* in any manner inconsistent with the purposes of the Organisation.'[31] Although this amendment was rejected by Committee 1/1 with a vote of 26 to 2, the reports of the session do not, however, disclose the grounds on which the rejection was based.[32]

With reference to the Brazilian amendment, the delegate of the United States expressed the view that 'the intention of the authors of the original text was to state in the broadest terms an absolute all-inclusive prohibition; the phrase "or in any other manner" was designed to ensure that there should be no loopholes'.[33] This statement, begging the question as it does, appears to add little further enlightenment to the application of Article 2(4) to economic coercion. It is noteworthy that the Belgian delegate stated that 'the subcommittee had given the point about "economic measures" careful consideration and for good reasons decided against it'.[34]

---

[30] Cf. *infra*, s. c.3.2(iii).
[31] Doc. 2, G/7(4), 6 May 1945, *UNCIO Doc.*, vol. iii, 1945, p. 251, at pp. 253–4, no. 15, emphasis added; for text of the original Dumbarton Oaks Draft Art. 2(4) see Doc. 1, G.1, ibid., p. 3, line 16.
[32] Summary Report of the 11th Meeting of the Committee 1/1, Doc. 784 1/1/27, 5 June 1945, ibid., vol. vi, p. 331, at p. 334.
[33] Ibid., p. 335.
[34] Ibid., p. 334.

(iii) *The two main schools of thought*

A controversy has arisen concerning the full implication of the word 'force' in Article 2(4). One school of thought advocates a broad interpretation whereby the word 'force' is taken to embrace economic coercion. For Kelsen, it includes 'any action of a member State illegal under general international law which is directed against another State'.[35] Support for such wide interpretations was particularly in evidence in connection with the oil crisis during the Middle East war of 1973.[36] It is noteworthy that Professor Sir James Fawcett, in examining the scope of Article 2(4) in the context of General Assembly Resolutions 2131(XX)[37] and 2625(XXV),[38] has concluded that '[i]t is possible then that Article 2(4) could be extended to prohibit economic coercion which infringes or threatens the political independence of a State. But this is speculation and only broader conclusions can be drawn from this review of the principle of non-intervention.'[39]

A second school of thought contends that the word 'force' has a limited application, and therefore could not embrace economic coercion. Professor Goodrich and Mr Hambro, who were both engaged in the work of the San Francisco Conference, conclude that '[w]hile it is not explicitly stated, it can be presumed that the word "force" as used in this paragraph means only "armed force". The Charter does not specifically forbid the use of economic force, although it tries to create such conditions in the world that even economic warfare will be rendered superfluous.'[40]

(iv) *Interpretation of Article 2(4) by the Special Committee on Principles of International Law concerning Friendly Relations and Co-operation among States as evidence of the subsequent practice of the parties to the Charter*

The question whether the word 'force' should include economic coercion was examined by the Special Committee on Friendly Relations in the course of discussing the principle 'that States shall refrain in their international relations

---

[35] Kelsen, *International Law Studies: Collective Security under International Law*, vol. 49, 1957, p. 57, n. 5.

[36] Paust and Blaustein, 'The Arab Oil Weapon—A Threat to International Peace', *AJIL*, vol. 68(2), 1974, p. 410, at p. 417; Brosche, 'The Arab Oil Embargo and United States Pressure against Chile: Economic and Political Coercion and the Charter of the United Nations', *Case Western Reserve Journal of International Law*, vol. 7(1), 1974, p. 3, at p. 23; *University of Pennsylvania Law Review (Comment)*, 'The Use of Nonviolent Coercion: A Study in Legality under Article 2(4) of the Charter of the United Nations', *University of Pennsylvania Law Review*, vol. 122, 1974, p. 983, at p. 1010.

[37] *UNGAOR*, 20th Sess., suppl. 14 (A/6220), 1965, pp. 11–12.

[38] Ibid., 25th Sess., suppl. 28 (A/8028), 1970, p. 121.

[39] Fawcett, *Law and Power in International Relations*, 1982, p. 115.

[40] Goodrich and Hambro, *Charter of the United Nations, Commentary and Documents*, 1st edn., 1946, p. 70; see also Goodrich and Hambro with Simons, 3rd edn., 1969, p. 49; Bowett, *Self-defence in International Law*, 1958, p. 148, Brownlie, 1963, p. 362; Lillich, 'Economic Coercion and the "New International Economic Order": A Second Look at Some First Impressions', *Virginia Journal of International Law*, vol. 16(2), 1976, p. 233, at p. 236.

from the threat or use of force'.[41] In this respect the delegate of Czecho-slovakia proposed the following draft:

> 5. Every State has the duty to refrain from economic, political or any other form of pressure aimed against the political independence or territorial integrity of any State, and from undertaking acts of reprisals.[42]

A comparable proposal, submitted by Yugoslavia in concert with eight African States, ran thus:

> 2. The term 'force' shall include:
> (b) All forms of pressure including those of a political or economic character, which have the effect of threatening the territorial integrity or political independence of any State.[43]

The sponsors of these two proposals had argued that such a broad interpretation of the word 'force' was compatible with the provisions of Article 2(4) of the Charter where the generic term 'force' was used without any qualification. As part of the evidence the above-mentioned sponsors argued that the phrase 'armed force' was overtly adopted in Articles 41, 42, 43, and 46 of the Charter to denote a specific reference to armed force only.[44]

　The representatives of the Western Powers supported a restrictive interpretation of the word 'force' on the grounds that the *travaux préparatoires* of the Charter could not be read otherwise.[45] A fair summary of the views of this group is to be seen in this excerpt from a statement by Mr Sinclair, representing the United Kingdom: 'Certain forms of economic pressure were either undesirable in themselves or violated the principles of international law. But, however reprehensible they might be [. . .] they could hardly be brought within the ambit of the prohibition on the threat or use of force.'[46]

　The consensus of the Special Committee[47] was that the word 'force' as used in Article 2(4) of the Charter connoted armed force, and hence could not be stretched to include economic pressure. Accordingly, economic coercion was left to be regulated by the duty of non-intervention.

---

[41] General Assembly Resolution 2625(XXV), 24 Dec. 1970, *UNGAOR*, 25th Sess., Suppl. 28 (A/8028), 1970, p. 121.

[42] UN Doc. A/AC.125/L.16.

[43] UN Doc. A/AC.125/L.21, 22 Mar. 1966.

[44] *Report of the Special Committee on Friendly Relations*, UN Doc. A/6230, 1966. For the remarks made by Judge Elias see UN Doc. A/AC.119/SR.7, 16 Oct. 1964, p. 22. For the remarks made by the Yugoslav representative see UN Doc. A/AC.119/SR.17, 21 Oct. 1964, p. 7. For the remarks of the Egyptian representative see UN Doc. A/AC.125/SR.25, 1966, p. 12.

[45] e.g. USA Rep., UN Doc. A/AC.119/SR.3, 16 Oct. 1964, p. 12; French Rep., UN Doc. A/AC.119/SR.6, 18 Oct. 1964, pp. 5–6; Australia, UN Doc. A/AC.119/SR.10, 16 Oct. 1964, p. 7.

[46] UN Doc. A/AC.119/SR.16, 9 Sept. 1964, p. 12.

[47] UN Doc. A/AC.125, 1970, p. 34.

(v) *Conclusion on Article 2(4)*

On the basis of the evidence that has been analysed, it must be concluded that the word 'force' in Article 2(4) should be given a restricted interpretation. Consequently, Article 2(4) does not impose any constraint on economic coercion.

C.4. EXAMINATION OF THE PERTINENT RESOLUTIONS OF THE GENERAL ASSEMBLY

It is proposed to refer to some of the General Assembly Resolutions as evidence of the views of States on the legitimacy of economic coercion. The intention here is to examine only those parts of the Resolutions which appear to support the hypothesis that economic coercion is prima facie lawful. These Resolutions, mainly adopted on the initiative of Third World countries, have consistently recognized the freedom of States to conduct their own economic affairs.

This element of economic independence has been essentially linked with issues of human rights and self-determination. For example, the fourth pre-ambular *considerandum* of the 1962 Resolution on Permanent Sovereignty over Natural Resources provides that any measure dealing with the disposition of natural resources 'must be based on the recognition of the inalienable right of all States to freely dispose of their natural wealth and resources in accordance with their national interest and on respect for the economic independence of States'.[48] This clearly shows a tendency towards emphasizing control by developing countries over their natural resources. Indeed, the concept of economic self-determination has been steadily gaining recognition in a number of General Assembly Resolutions. Suffice it to quote here the pertinent paragraphs of Article 1 of the 1966 International Covenant on Economic, Social, and Cultural Rights which read:

1. All peoples have the right of self-determination. By virtue of that right they may freely determine their political status and freely pursue their economic, social and cultural development.

2. All peoples may, for their own ends, freely dispose of their natural wealth and resources without prejudice to any obligations arising out of international economic co-operation, based upon the principles of mutual benefit and international law. In no case may a people be deprived of its own means of subsistence.[49]

---

[48] General Assembly Resolution 1803(XVII), 14 Dec. 1962, *UNGAOR*, 17th Sess., suppl. 17(A/5217), 1962, pp. 15–16.

[49] General Assembly Resolution 2200(XXI), Annex., 16 Dec. 1966, *UNGAOR*, 21st Sess., suppl. 16(A/6316), 1966, p. 49; see also Art. 1(1) and (2) of International Covenant on Civil and Political Rights, 1966, *UNGAOR*, 21st Sess., suppl. 16(A/6316), 1966, p. 53.

The right of Third World countries to control their own natural resources has been amplified, in the *Declaration on the Establishment of a New International Economic Order*, to embrace the whole sphere of economic domain. The relevant parts of Article 4 of this Declaration provide:

> (*d*) Every country has the right to adopt the economic and social system that it deems to be the most appropriate for its own development and not to be subjected to discrimination of any kind as a result;
>
> (*e*) Full permanent sovereignty of every State over its natural resources and all economic activities. [. . .] No State may be subjected to economic, political or any other type of coercion to prevent the free and full exercise of this inalienable right.[50]

The last sentence in paragraph (*e*) above should not, however, be interpreted as precluding economic coercion *per se*; it merely seeks to safeguard the liberty to exercise the rights mentioned therein. Persistent demands by developing countries for improved trade relations with industrialized nations led to the adoption of the *Charter of Economic Rights and Duties of States* by the General Assembly in 1974.[51] In this connection Article 1 affirms that '[e]very State has the sovereign and inalienable right to choose its economic system [. . .] in accordance with the will of its people, without outside interference, coercion or threat in any form whatsoever'.[52] Although Article 1 provides that every State is free to choose her economic system without coercion from other States, it does not set any limit on the exercise of that freedom. A similar conclusion also applies to Article 4. It pertinently provides that 'in the pursuit of international trade and other forms of economic cooperation, every State is free to choose the forms of organization of its foreign economic relations'.

C.5. THE VIEW EXPRESSED BY A SENIOR OFFICIAL OF THE UNITED STATES DEPARTMENT OF STATE ON THE LEGALITY OF ECONOMIC COERCION AS EVIDENCE OF STATE PRACTICE

On 12 November 1976 Mr David Small[53] delivered an opinion expressly on the status of economic coercion in international law. In view of the direct relevance of this opinion to the question under review, it will be quoted *in extenso*:

---

[50] General Assembly Resolution 3201 (S-VII), 1 May 1974, adopted without vote, *UNGAOR*, 6th Special Sess. suppl. 1(A/9559), 1974, p. 3, at p. 4.

[51] General Assembly Resolution 3281(XXIX), 12 Dec. 1974, *UNGAOR*, 29th Sess., suppl. 31(A/9631), 1974, pp. 50–55.

[52] Ibid., p. 52.

[53] Assistant Legal Adviser for the Near Eastern and South Asian Affairs, Department of State.

Traditional international law adopted a *laissez-faire* approach toward the economic rights and duties of States, and it has long been considered an inherent right of an independent, sovereign state to exercise full control over its trade relations, including the withholding of exports and prohibition of imports with respect to any other state or states, absent treaty commitments to the contrary . . .

The Charter of the United Nations contains a number of very important and far-reaching restrictions on the use of armed force, but it says nothing at all about restrictions on the use of economic measures of coercion by individual states or groups of states. Conceivably, economic measures could give rise to a dispute, 'the continuance of which is likely to endanger the maintenance of international peace and security' within the meaning of article 33 of the Charter, but even that is nowhere made clear. Economic pressure may be unfriendly and even unfair, but economic coercion, *per se*, cannot generally be said to be prohibited by the U.N. Charter.[54]

C.6. SOME QUESTIONS OF PRINCIPLE

The empirical evidence examined above does not support the existence of a principle which *permits* economic coercion subject to certain exceptions. This is hardly surprising, as one could scarcely expect to find evidence of such a principle since the rules are generally *prohibitive*. However, if such a principle does exist, it would be much easier to justify the use of counter-measures since many of such measures involve economic coercion. In this sense it may be said that the prima facie legality of economic coercion merely affects the standard of proof, when counter-measures are invoked. In other words, it does not tell us about lawful counter-measures *as such*, particularly those which do not involve any application of economic coercion. In conclusion, it may be stated that the legality of counter-measures on a given occasion depends on whether certain conditions have been complied with.[55]

D. IS ECONOMIC COERCION PRIMA FACIE UNLAWFUL, SUBJECT TO CERTAIN EXCEPTIONS?

D.1. THE PURPOSE

In contrast to the preceding section, the intention here is to test the hypothesis that economic coercion is prima facie unlawful. The material that will be analysed consists mainly of General Assembly Resolutions. It must be stated at the outset that although these Resolutions are not binding in themselves, they provide evidence of the view of States on questions of international law. However, an attempt will be made to ascertain whether the prohibition of

---

[54] *Digest USPIL*, 1976, p. 577.
[55] Cf. *supra*, chs. 4, 5, and 6.

economic coercion envisaged in these Resolutions has evolved into specific rules of general international law. Also will be shown the extent to which the prima facie illegality of economic coercion can affect the legality of counter-measures.

D.2. THE DECLARATION ON THE INADMISSIBILITY OF INTERVENTION IN THE DOMESTIC AFFAIRS OF STATES AND THE PROTECTION OF THEIR INDEPENDENCE AND SOVEREIGNTY, 1965

The concept of non-intervention has been expressed in the Declaration on the Inadmissibility of Intervention in the Domestic Affairs of States and the Protection of Their Independence and Sovereignty.[56] The third preambular *considerandum* provides:

[A]ll peoples have an inalienable right to complete freedom, the exercise of their sovereignty and the integrity of their national territory, and that, by virtue of that right, they freely determine their political status and freely pursue their *economic*, social, and cultural development.[57]

In addition, the main text of the Declaration reads thus:

1. [A]rmed intervention and all other forms of interference or attempted threats against the personality of the State or against its political, economic and cultural elements, are condemned.
2. No State may use or encourage the use of economic, political or any other type of measures to coerce another State in order to obtain from it the subordination of the exercise of its sovereign rights or to secure from it advantages of any kind.
3. Every State has an inalienable right to choose its political, economic, social and cultural systems, without interference in any form by another State.

As regards the third preambular *considerandum*, it is clear that it addresses self-determination issues. Furthermore, the principles which it enunciates are by no means exclusively legal but have political undertones. These remarks could also be made with respect to paragraph 1 of the text. Although it has been indicated already[58] that not all forms of economic pressure necessarily constitute unlawful coercion, yet paragraph 1 above explicitly condemns any kind of interference in the economic affairs of another State.[59] The prohibition of economic coercion contained in paragraph 2 above is expressed in very vague terms. It simply refers to 'the subordination of the exercise of [the State's] sovereign rights' or the securing from that State of 'advantages of any kind'. It is evident from these words that the two forms of prohibited conduct vary a great deal in dimension. Suffice it to say that whereas 'the

[56] General Assembly Resolution 2131(XX), *UNGAOR*, 20th Sess., suppl. 14(A/6220), 1965, pp. 11–12.
[57] Ibid., p. 11, emphasis added.
[58] Cf. *supra*, s. B.3.
[59] Similar considerations apply to paragraph 5 of the Declaration.

subordination of the exercise of sovereign rights' will undoubtedly involve a serious violation of international law rules, the mere securing of 'advantages of any kind' will not necessarily involve any breach. In view of this variation it is thought that neither of them can be an appropriate criterion for determining unlawful economic coercion.

Notwithstanding all these difficulties, the texts of paragraphs 1 and 2 of the Declaration continued to be incorporated in subsequent General Assembly Resolutions. The fact of such repetitions, however, does not in itself establish the illegality of economic coercion; at best it can enhance the value of the Declaration as evidence of the views of States on the question considered.

Finally, a statement made by the Netherlands Government may be cited as evidence of State practice. It provides: 'The Declaration does not derogate from existing rules of international law. This means [...] that the prohibition on intervention in a State's affairs laid down in the Declaration does not affect the institutions of retorsion and reprisals, which are recognised by international law, albeit subject to certain rules.'[60] The view expressed in this statement has a special significance for the legality of counter-measures. There appears to be no doubt in the mind of the Dutch Government that the Declaration does not affect the right to resort to counter-measures, nor for that matter the conditions under which that right may be exercised.

D.3. THE DECLARATION ON PRINCIPLES OF INTERNATIONAL LAW CONCERNING FRIENDLY RELATIONS AND CO-OPERATION AMONG STATES IN ACCORDANCE WITH THE CHARTER OF THE UNITED NATIONS, 1970

D.3.1. The travaux préparatoires

The Special Committee on Friendly Relations was asked by the General Assembly to undertake a study of the principles of friendly relations 'in accordance with the Charter'.[61] The aim of this study was the progressive development and codification of these principles, so as to secure their more effective application. In effect, all such principles are already embodied in the text of the Charter. In recognition of this fact several statements were made in the Sixth Committee of the General Assembly. For example, in the words of Mr Yaseen: 'the content of the draft Declaration derived its value from its very source. Since its formulations constituted an attempt to clarify and interpret the fundamental principles of the Charter, they should be regarded as having binding force, to the same extent as the latter, and as forming part

---

[60] *Report of the Advisory Committee on Questions of International Law on measures against South Africa and the non-intervention duty to Parliament*, on 27 May 1982, *NLYIL*, 1983, p. 246, at p. 248.
[61] General Assembly Resolution 1966(XVIII), 16 Dec. 1963, *UNGAOR*, 18th Sess., suppl. 15(A/5515), 1963, p. 70.

of positive international law.'[62] To Mr Maiga of Mali, the Declaration was an interpretation of the Charter and 'consequently no State which adopted it could evade its responsibilities'.[63]

It is noteworthy that the Declaration under review was adopted unanimously by the General Assembly.[64] This fact by itself, however, is not sufficient to impel general acceptance that this instrument is declaratory of existing principles. By the same token, it can safely be assumed that it is not indicative of emergent rules unless it is clearly supported by State practice.[65] For the moment, if one accepts that the Declaration is an authoritative interpretation of the Charter there will be no justification for claiming that it precludes economic coercion. This conclusion is derived from the assumption that neither the text of the Charter nor its legislative history reveals sufficient evidence to support such a claim.[66]

D.3.2. Analysis of the pertinent provisions

The ninth preambular *considerandum* of the Declaration expresses 'the duty of States to refrain in their international relations from military, political, economic or any other form of coercion aimed against the political independence or territorial integrity of any State'. This may be understood as a prohibition of such forms of economic pressure as may result in serious damage to the sovereignty of a State. The third principle in the text of the Declaration deals with 'the duty not to intervene in matters within the domestic jurisdiction of any State, in accordance with the Charter'.[67] The substance of that duty has been elaborated as follows:

[A]ll [. . .] forms of interference or attempted threats against the personality of the State or against its political, economic and cultural elements, are in violation of international law.[68]

No State may use or encourage the use of economic [. . .] measures to coerce another State in order to obtain from it the subordination of the exercise of its sovereign rights *and* to secure from it advantages of any kind.[69]

The first paragraph above invites several criticisms. To begin with, the choice of the word 'interference' appears inappropriate for the reason that it does not permit of any possible distinction between trivial and serious forms

---

[62] Summary Records of Meetings of Sixth Committee (A/C.6/SR1180), *UNGAOR*, 25th Sess., 1180th mtg., agenda item 85, 24 Sept. 1970, p. 17, at p. 18, para 8.

[63] Ibid., 1181st mtg., p. 25, para 38; similar views by the delegate of Kenya, 1182nd mtg., p. 32, para. 60.

[64] This Declaration is annexed to General Assembly Resolution, 2625(XXV), adopted without a vote on 24 Oct. 1970, *UNGAOR*, 25th Sess., suppl. 28(A/8028), 1970, p. 122.

[65] Cf. *infra*, s. D.3.3.

[66] Cf. *supra*, s. C.3.

[67] *UNLAOR*, 25th Sess., suppl. 28(A/8028), 1970, p. 123.

[68] Ibid.

[69] Ibid., emphasis added.

of pressure. Objections, similarly, could be raised with respect to the term 'attempted threats'. Furthermore, with reference to threats 'against the personality of the State or against its political, economic and cultural elements', it would seem difficult enough to visualize interference with a State's personality, let alone her political, economic, and cultural elements. The strongest criticism, however, centres on the implication that economic coercion would be unlawful only where interference was injurious to all three elements (political, economic, and cultural) taken together.

As regards the second paragraph, a difference of a single word is to be noted between the text of the 1965 non-intervention Declaration and that of the Declaration currently reviewed. In the former, the concluding words of the sentence read 'to obtain from it the subordination of the exercise of its sovereign rights or to secure from it advantages of any kind', whereas in the latter the word 'and' has replaced the original 'or'. According to the Special Committee, this substitution was intended to bring the text into line with the corresponding provision of the Charter of the Organization of American States,[70] and therefore should not be taken as a restriction on the scope of the 1965 Declaration.[71] As a matter of interpretation, the present writer contends that it was in fact the 1970 Declaration which was subjected to the aforesaid restriction. This is evidenced by the juxtaposition of the two quite separate alternative conditions in the 1965 text, whereas the use of the word 'and' in the 1970 Declaration introduces a double condition for the manifestation of economic coercion.

D.3.3. *The subsequent practice of the parties*

There remains the possibility of taking subsequent practice of the parties as evidence of an emergent rule of customary law concerning prohibition of economic coercion on the basis of the Declaration. On this question State practice, as will be shown, sheds little light.

When entering reservations against the Declaration on the Establishment of a New International Economic Order,[72] the United States had indirectly referred to the normative significance of the provisions in the Friendly Relations Declaration which deal with economic coercion. Mr Scali, the United States representative, stated thus:

The United States does not support the provisions of the Declaration which refer only to the exertion of economic pressure for some ends, but which do not condemn generally the exercise of economic pressure. In this respect, the Declaration contrasts

[70] Dated 30 April 1948, 199 *UNTS*, 1609, Art. 16.
[71] *Report of the Special Committee on Principles of Friendly Relations, UNGAOR*, 25th Sess., suppl. 18(A/8018), 1970, p. 14.
[72] Adopted by the General Assembly Resolution 3201 (S-VI), *UNGAOR*, 6th Special Sess., suppl. 1(A/955), 1974, pp. 3–5.

unfavourably with that of [the] Principles of International Law concerning Friendly Relations and Co-operation among States.[73]

Whatever the comparative merits of the two instruments concerned, one may deduce from the above text that the United States gave implicit countenance to the prohibition on economic coercion as envisaged in the 1970 Declaration.

The views of the United States on economic coercion were amplified in a purposive statement by a senior official of the Department of State.[74] The statement also touches on the legal significance of the 1970 Friendly Relations Declaration. Thus, in reference to its ninth preambular *considerandum*, it was stated that '[t]his seems to acknowledge the existence of a duty not to use economic coercion for the purpose of destroying or dismembering a state. This is scarcely a radical rule. While the passage could imply more, its possible further implications are not widely agreed.'[75] As regards the reference to economic coercion in the third principle of the Declaration, the view taken by the author of the purposive statement was that

[The] provision is far from clear, but it seems to mean that two types of economic coercion are prohibited: that which attempts to coerce a state not to exercise its legal rights and that which attempts to extort advantages. [...] The broad acceptability of this formulation results from its ambiguity. Under it ... the United States can defend suspension of economic assistance [...] on the grounds that the other state has no legal right to expropriate property without paying just compensation—and, on the contrary, that the other state has a duty to pay such compensation. [...]

In view of the extensive use of economic coercion by one state against another throughout the twentieth century, and in view of these rather modest legal efforts to restrict it, existing international law can probably best be described as narrowing only slightly the permissive legal regime of the past. The direction of development of the law is toward greater restriction on the use of economic coercion, but it has been a slow movement with, thus far, limited effects.

D.3.4. Conclusions

The prevailing impression after a review of the material presented in this section is that the principle of non-intervention has not crystallized into a clear rule prohibiting economic coercion. Moreover, the application of such a principle in the future will undoubtedly be affected by the inherent imprecision in the text of the Declaration. This should come as no surprise; the Declaration was a product of several compromises, with the provisions relating to economic coercion purposely couched in broad terms as a price for unanimity.[76] In the words of the Portuguese representative: 'Such a lack

[73] UN Doc. A/PV/229, 1 May 1974; reproduced in *ILM*, vol. 13, 1974, p. 774, at p. 747.

[74] Statement by Mr David Small, Assistant Legal Adviser for Near Eastern and South Asian Affairs, *Digest US PIL*, 1976, p. 576, at pp. 577–8.

[75] Ibid.

[76] *Report of the Special Committee on Principles of Friendly Relations, UNGAOR*, 25th Sess., suppl. 18(A/8018), 1970, p. 14.

of precision was dangerous and not only precluded real application of the principles involved but permitted all sorts of abuse.'[77]

D.4. THE CHARTER OF ECONOMIC RIGHTS AND DUTIES OF STATES, 1974[78]

D.4.1. Prohibition of economic coercion

Article 1 of the Economic Charter deals in broad terms with freedom from economic coercion: 'Every State has the sovereign and inalienable right to choose its economic system as well as its political, social and cultural systems in accordance with the will of its people, without outside interference, coercion or threat in any form whatsoever.'[79] The apparent economic freedom envisaged in this text has been qualified in some of the ensuing Articles of the Economic Charter. Thus, Article 5 emphasizes the duty of States to refrain from applying economic and political measures which would limit the right to form 'organizations of primary commodity producers'.[80] Similarly Article 7, which secures the right of a State to choose her own means and goals of development, to mobilize her resources, and to implement economic reforms, requires as a duty the co-operation of other States in removing obstacles that may hinder the full exercise of that right.[81] Article 16, for its part, declares that States practising certain coercive policies are to be held responsible for the payment of compensation to the aggrieved parties.[82] Following this, Article 17 lays down that economic assistance to developing countries should be 'consistent with their development needs and objectives, with strict respect for the sovereign equality of States and *free of any conditions derogating* from their sovereignty'.[83] Finally, on the specific question of economic coercion, Article 32 provides that 'No State may use or encourage the use of economic, political or any other type of measures to coerce another State in order to obtain from it the subordination of the exercise of its sovereign rights.'[84]

[77] Summary Record of Meetings of Sixth Committee (A/C.6/SR and Corr. 1), *UNGAOR*, Agenda item 85, 1182nd mtg., 25 Sept. 1970, p. 27, para. 3.
[78] Adopted by a vote of 120 in favour, 6 against, and 10 abstentions as part of the General Assembly Resolution 3281(XXIX), 12 Dec. 1974, *UNGAOR*; those against were: Belgium, Denmark, German Federal Republic, Luxemburg, United Kingdom, and the United States, 29th Sess., suppl. 31 (A/9631), 1974, pp. 50–5.
[79] Ibid., p. 52, without a negative vote or abstention, see *ILM*, vol. 14, 1975, p. 264.
[80] Ibid., no vote was taken.
[81] Ibid., without a negative vote or abstention.
[82] Ibid., p. 53, no vote was taken.
[83] Ibid., p. 54, without a negative vote or abstention, ibid., p. 265, emphasis added.
[84] Ibid., p. 55, without a negative vote but with 8 abstentions.

D.4.2. The legal significance of the Economic Charter

It has been noted that the Economic Charter was approved by the General Assembly as part of Resolution 3281 (XXIX). It is proposed to examine whether the Economic Charter as a whole is perceived as a binding instrument. The evidence, as we shall see, reveals that it is not. Thus, notwithstanding the adoption of this instrument by the majority of States, several of its more important Articles received negative votes from capital-exporting countries. Further, so far from being a declaration of pre-existing principles, the Charter (Article 2 excepted) is generally programmatic with strong political undertones. As an illustration, the preamble of the Charter embraces a wide range of programmatic economic and social purposes, but omitting any reference to international law standards.[85] It should be recalled here that a proposal was made by the Group 77 inviting the General Assembly to adopt the Charter as 'a first measure of codification and progressive development'.[86] After pressure, however, from several States that description was removed from the final draft. A similar wording intended for the last preambular *considerandum* was likewise deleted.[87] Such excision would suggest that the Economic Charter was not necessarily intended as a legally binding instrument.

The records of the working group on the Economic Charter disclose the existence of two distinct views regarding its legal nature. One view held that it should be made into a legally binding instrument, while the other rejected such an endeavour as being unrealistic.[88]

Professor Dupuy has indicated in the Award of the *Texaco Arbitration*[89] that the Economic Charter provided evidence of the legal position pertaining to the concept of good faith. Brower and Tepe conclude that '[t]here is not sufficient reciprocity of interest to persuade the developed States to be legally bound by all the terms of the Charter'.[90] Going still further, Professor Seidl-Hohenveldern has described the Charter as merely 'a non-binding recommendation of the General Assembly'.[91] From a different perspective, Professor Brownlie argues that '[i]n technical terms there is no evidence

---

[85] e.g. the 4th *considerandum* declares that it is a fundamental purpose of the Economic Charter '*to promote* the establishment of the new international economic order', emphasis added.

[86] UN Doc. A/C.2/L.1386, 1974, p. 2.

[87] *Second Report of the Working Group on the Charter*, UN Doc. TD/B/AC.12/2/Add. 1, 1973, p. 20.

[88] See *First Report of the Working Group on the Charter*, UN Doc. TD/B/AC.12/L. 1973, p. 6; see *Second Report*, generally pp. 3, 5, 7, 8, 15, 16, 17, 19 and 27.

[89] *ILM*, vol. 17, 1978, p. 1, at p. 31, paras. 90–1.

[90] Brower and Tepe, 'The Charter of Economic Rights and Duties of States: A Reflection or Rejection of International Law?' *International Lawyer*, vol. 9, 1975, p. 295, p. 318.

[91] Seidl-Hohenveldern, 'International Economic Soft Law', *R.d.C.*, vol. 163(2) 1979, p. 169, at p. 188.

of an *opinio juris*, but of a set of general social and economic directive principles'.[92]

The conclusion to be drawn from the foregoing review is that the Economic Charter as a whole was not conceived as a legally binding instrument at the time of its adoption. Furthermore, there is no evidence of an *opinio juris* in the subsequent practice of the parties.

D.4.3. The legal significance of Articles 1 and 32 of the Economic Charter

The crucial question is whether the prohibition on economic coercion formulated in Articles 1 and 32 may be regarded as a statement of the existing law. Article 1 sets the theme within broad limits, dealing with the sovereign right of every State to choose, *inter alia*, her economic system freely, and without outside interference or coercion. The Charter of the United Nations cannot, however, be assumed as a basis for supporting the ideal envisaged in Article 1 of the Economic Charter. Although this Article was unanimously adopted, subsequent State practice nowhere points to its having emerged as a new development in international law.

As regards Article 32, despite its being adopted *nemine contradicente*, the fact that there were eight abstentions ruled out unanimity. Moreover, the text of this Article is strongly reminiscent of the language used in General Assembly Resolution 2131(XX).[93] The view held by the present writer is that the pertinent parts of Resolution 2131(XX) do not categorically prohibit economic coercion.[94] Finally, there is no evidence to suggest that Article 32 merits a conclusion different from that reached in connection with the normative value of Article 1.

D.5. AN OPINION

The Resolutions that have been reviewed bear witness to the endeavours by the General Assembly to place restrictions on economic coercion. It has been argued, however, in some quarters that the Resolutions 'cannot have legal pretensions'.[95] Professor Lillich, on the other hand, considers such an attitude 'unnecessarily dogmatic'.[96] The better view is succinctly expressed by Professor Bowett who recognizes these Resolutions as 'indicative of the gradual acceptance of a concept whose influence cannot be ignored'.[97] The present

---

[92] Brownlie, 'Legal Status of Natural Resources', *R.d.C.*, vol. 162, 1979, p. 245, at p. 266; see generally Brownlie, 1979, pp. 542–3.

[93] Resolution 2131(XX), *UNGAOR*, 20th Sess., suppl. 14(A/6220), 1965, pp. 11–12.

[94] See *supra*, D.2.

[95] Haight, 'The New International Economic Order and the Charter of Economic Rights and Duties of States', *International Lawyer*, vol. 9(4), 1975, p. 591, at p. 597.

[96] Lillich, 'Economic Coercion', 1976, p. 237.

[97] Bowett, 'Economic Coercion', 1976, p. 246; see also Shihata, 'Arab Oil Policies and the New International Economic Order', *Virginia Journal of International Law*, vol. 16(2), 1976, p. 261, at p. 268.

writer takes the position that, although these Resolutions have not as yet evolved into clearly defined rules proscribing economic coercion, there are signs that they are gradually narrowing down the permissible character of that concept.

It is now proposed to see how this affects the legality of counter-measures. As has been pointed out, the majority of counter-measures involve some element of economic coercion. It follows, therefore, if economic coercion is regarded as prima facie unlawful, it would be more difficult in evidential terms to establish the legality of counter-measures. However, even if the hypothesis which provides that economic coercion is prima facie unlawful is proved as correct, it will have no effect on counter-measures that do not involve any economic coercion. Finally, leaving evidential questions aside, the prima-facie illegality of economic coercion will not in any event throw light on how lawful counter-measures may be determined.

E. ECONOMIC COERCION: CERTAIN OTHER RAMIFICATIONS

B.I. THE PURPOSE

This brief section aims at filling the gaps in legal reasoning that remained from the previous testing of the hypotheses as to whether economic coercion is prima facie lawful or unlawful. Thus, a more realistic approach to the problem would be to test the compatibility of a particular economic conduct with those rules of international law which apply in the particular circumstances. Such a course is tantamount to an admission that a certain degree of coercion is inevitable, and hence only the severest cases which give rise to breach of the established rules of international law should be isolated. The usefulness of this approach for determining the legality of counter-measures will be demonstrated in the ensuing subsection.

B.2. SOME QUESTIONS OF PRINCIPLE

The material examined in sections C and D basically provides that there are no rules of international law which categorically pronounce either on the prima-facie legality or prima-facie illegality of economic coercion. What is more, some of that material lends itself to contrasting interpretations. Nevertheless, it should not thereby be assumed that the tenor of international law is to leave the category of economic coercion *as such* unregulated, even in cases of clear violation of established principles. Individual rules of international law may be applied to determine the legality of economic conduct on a given occasion. Thus, the issue of the legality will depend on the operation of particular rules of international law in particular contexts. For instance, in their protests against the sanctions imposed by the United

States in connection with the Siberian gas pipeline, none of the aggrieved European Governments referred to these sanctions as 'economic coercion'. Instead, they were challenged for being inconsistent with the principle of jurisdiction.[98]

Whereas the above illustration was exclusively concerned with the violation of the principle of jurisdiction, situations might arise in which different sets of rules could be violated. Thus, suppose that Ruritania and Utopia have concluded an agreement concerning the employment of Ruritanian nationals in Utopia. Then suppose that Utopia has suspended that agreement alleging that Ruritania has defaulted on settling an insubstantial debt. Imagine further that this suspension has entailed the personal hardship of thousands of Ruritanian workers. In such a case the Utopian conduct would have to be justified in its particular context. Thus, the question may well be asked whether the 'international minimum standard' or human rights standards have been violated. Furthermore, recourse may be had not only to the terms of the agreement between the parties but also to any pertinent international instruments such as the General Agreement on Tariffs and Trade.[99]

It may be gleaned from the above account that cases involving serious economic coercion may be identified by their lack of compatibility with the rules of international law. As regards counter-measures, it would be incorrect to suggest that their implementation would be wrongful merely because they are inconsistent with any particular rule of international law. It is submitted that the lawfulness of counter-measures on any given occasion may be determined by applying the conditions of the legality of counter-measures to the particular circumstances of that occasion. This may be done without any reference to the category of economic coercion.

---

[98] Cf. *supra*, ch. 7, s. c.7.
[99] Dated 30 Oct. 1947, 55 *UNTS*, 814.1(*b*).

Conclusion

An attempt will now be made to summarize the major characteristics of the existing legal regime as it has been analysed in the preceding chapters. The purpose of this book has been fourfold: (*a*) to determine whether non-forcible counter-measures constitute an autonomous category of justification for wrongful conduct; (*b*) to identify precisely the conditions for lawful resort to counter-measures; (*c*) to examine some of the more significant collateral constraints on the legality of counter-measures; and (*d*) to indicate the manner in which the *raison d'être* of counter-measures may contribute towards the determination of their legality.

As regards the first main line of enquiry indicated above, it seems indisputable that non-forcible counter-measures form a recognized category of justification for internationally wrongful conduct. In other words, when a State displays conduct which is in breach of her international obligations towards another State, such conduct will not be regarded as wrongful if it can be justified as a lawful counter-measure. The measures which an aggrieved State may impose could take a positive or a negative form. The freezing of assets belonging to the defaulting State would be an example of the former, while the non-performance of treaty obligations towards such a State would be an illustration of the latter.

There are several factors which explain the necessity for retaining non-forcible counter-measures as a means of enforcing international legal order. First, the constraint on the right to use force is not paralleled by the imposition of any obligation regarding resort to third party settlement procedure. In view of this fact, the taking of counter-measures may in some cases prove to be necessary as a means of stimulating the offending party to agree to a settlement. Secondly, even where the offending party agrees to a settlement, in some circumstances there might be inadequate international machinery for enforcing compliance with the terms of that settlement. Not surprisingly, therefore, an aggrieved State may in some cases feel compelled to resort to self-help measures. Thirdly, recourse to counter-measures may serve to restore an equitable balance between the disputing parties until a solution is found. Fourthly, the symbolic effect of counter-measures is as important as their instrumental effect. Obviously, no State will want to be portrayed as a delinquent State which does not perform her international obligations until she is pressurized to do so by means of self-help measures. Fifthly, although counter-measures may sometimes assume a persistent character, for the most part they merely involve temporary measures. This inherent flexibility enhances the value of counter-measures as an instrument of redress.

The second principal focus of the present study is concerned with the conditions of the legality of counter-measures. These are: (*a*) the occurrence of breach; (*b*) the making of an unsuccessful demand to obtain reparation; and (*c*) compliance with the principle of proportionality.

As pertains to the occurrence of breach, it is quite clear that lawful counter-measures must be preceded by an internationally wrongful conduct. By implication, therefore, counter-measures cannot be taken on the basis of an anticipated breach. A related issue concerns the question of whether counter-measures may be taken by the aggrieved State on the basis of a bona fide belief as to the existence of breach. The present writer takes the view that an aggrieved State acting on such a basis must incur responsibility where the belief held by her is shown to be mistaken. He concedes, nevertheless, that a 'margin of appreciation' should be allowed when a State assesses breach as a precipitating factor for resorting to counter-measures.

A particular question is whether every type of breach of international law justifies resort to counter-measures. There is little doubt that the answer should be in the negative. In the first place, where the wrongfulness of conduct is precluded by an exonerating circumstance such as *force majeure,* resort to counter-measures is not permitted during the prevalence of such a circumstance. Secondly, where the wrongful conduct violates a self-contained regime, the aggrieved State is precluded from resort to counter-measures taken solely on that ground. Thirdly, where the breach involves a violation of fundamental human rights, the aggrieved State may not retaliate by imposing reciprocal measures. It needs to be emphasized, however, that several other illustrations could be cited to show that not every form of wrongful conduct can be responded to by counter-measures.

The question of determining which State has the right to apply counter-measures depends on whether the particular State claiming such a right can be regarded as an aggrieved party. In effect, therefore, the State in question assumes the burden of proof so as to establish that she has in fact suffered a direct or indirect injury. Pertinent to the issue under review, where a State rests her claim on injury to interests which she has 'through' another State, she cannot be looked upon as an aggrieved party by virtue of that fact alone. It is necessary for her to establish that that other State is no longer in a position to protect the interests in question. By the same token where the claim is grounded on the breach of a special interest provision in a multilateral treaty, a party making that claim must prove that it is entitled to invoke that provision. With equal weight the same reasoning applies, *mutatis mutandis,* to the case in which a claim is based on a breach of a treaty obligation in favour of a third party. As regards the breach of universally recognized rules of international law, any State is entitled, on the basis of the principle of *erga omnes* obligations, to claim that she is an aggrieved party.

As concerns the making of a demand for redress, it is submitted that in order for any counter-measure to be regarded as lawful it must be preceded by a request of that kind. It needs to be stated that an aggrieved party is not required in the course of presenting its demand to adhere to any specific procedure. None the less, the demand must be expressed in such decisive terms as would impress upon the defaulting State the seriousness of the legal implications involved. Furthermore, it has to be communicated by an accredited representative of the aggrieved State. There is probably a case for arguing that where a State adamantly adopts an ostrich-like attitude *vis-à-vis* the receiving of a demand, she must be deemed to have received that demand.

Proportionality is the third condition of the legality of counter-measures. It is indisputable that counter-measures must, in the first place, have some degree of proportionality with the alleged breach. However, the process of determining the exact criteria by which proportionality may be judged presents some difficulty. It is here that policy considerations assume a greater significance than they normally do. It is submitted, therefore, that the motivations for resorting to counter-measures, namely, self-protection, reciprocity, and a desire to achieve a speedy settlement, may be used as the main criteria for determining proportionality. Thus, in cases of unusual danger such as when the nationals of the aggrieved State are seized as hostages, that State will be entitled on the ground of self-protection to employ counter-measures of extreme severity in order to secure their release. As a further example of the wide scope of action permitted, a breach of an important treaty provision may be responded to by the non-performance of obligations arising from an altogether different treaty. Finally, counter-measures based on self-protection could in some cases assume an irreversible character. For instance, where a demilitarization treaty exists between two States, and one of them acts in a manner incompatible with that treaty, the other State may terminate it irrevocably.

As regards the proportionality of counter-measures when reciprocity is the underlying motivation, the steps taken must be equivalent to, or analogous with, the obligation breached. Unlike the case of self-protection, counter-measures based on reciprocity may only be resorted to as a temporary expedient. It should be recognized, however, that in some situations reciprocity is of no help in assessing proportionality. Suffice it to mention in this connection that general international law precluded the United States from seizing Iranian diplomats during the hostage crisis in Tehran, in spite of repeated public demands for such action.

As concerns the case in which the objective is a speedy settlement, the counter-measures taken may be maintained in an asymmetrical ratio to the breach. This imbalance against the interests of the defaulting party serves as a stimulus to that party to expedite the process of settlement. However, the party which imposes the counter-measures must at the same time make an offer for third party settlement as evidence of a readiness on its part to contain the dispute. Furthermore, the measures taken must be vacated as soon as the contending parties have agreed on interim arrangements such as would restore the status quo. Finally, it needs to be emphasized that when counter-measures are motivated exclusively by a desire for a speedy settlement, their scope can never be as extensive as when the motive for their imposition is self-protection.

A further question concerning the relationship between the various motivations underlying counter-measures and proportionality arises when there is a combination of motives. For instance, self-protection and a desire for a speedy settlement may together figure as motivations for taking a particular counter-measure. In such a case, proportionality should be assessed on the basis of self-protection in that it is the dominant motive. On the other hand, where the counter-measures are motivated both by a desire for a speedy settlement and reciprocity, proportionality should be judged on the basis of the former motive in view of the relatively wider scope of action which it permits.

The significance of policy considerations for assessing proportionality was touched on by the Tribunal in the *Air Services Award*, 1979. It was there that the Tribunal laid emphasis on the relationship between the effects of the breach and the effects of counter-measures. The keynote of this approach is that it permits an aggrieved State to take into consideration even the likely effects of a breach in determining the proportionality of her response. Such a licence, however, could raise some controversial questions. Be that as it may, the 'effects approach' can by no means dispense with the necessity of taking into account the purposes of counter-measures when establishing proportionality.

The search for the criteria by which proportionality may be measured has extended to the factor of 'dependence or reliance'. There is room for the view that a sudden disruption in the supply of a commodity vital to a regular customer is to be regarded as disproportionate to its intended purpose. Thus, it is arguable that where counter-measures involve conduct of that nature, they may be held to be inconsistent with the rule of proportionality. However, where an aggrieved party has no other avenue of redress, the factor under review should not be employed as a criterion for judging the proportionality of the measures taken.

Attention may now focus on the conclusions reached concerning the more significant of the collateral constraints. It must be stated at the outset that norms of *jus cogens* cannot be derogated from in the course of taking counter-measures. It is pertinent to add that counter-measures which entail, for instance, the incarceration or torture of aliens cannot be viewed as lawful since such conduct constitutes a breach of established human rights standards.

As regards the confiscation of alien property, it is clear that such conduct will be inconsistent with the international norm as to lawful expropriation, and no less with the international minimum standard doctrine. Nevertheless, the question still remains open as to whether an otherwise unlawful expropriation can be justifiable when it is carried out as a counter-measure. The answer will most probably be in the negative in cases where the expropriation has irreversible effects. As regards the legality of counter-measures which do not go beyond a mere temporary freezing of aliens' assets, there appears to be no firm guidance on this point in State practice. None the less, it is submitted that such temporary measures may be viewed as an appropriate expedient for limiting the effects of the breach. A related question is whether human rights standards preclude the seizing of alien property as a counter-measure. Although there appears to be no definite answer to this question, few would disagree that counter-measures which are racially motivated cannot be regarded as lawful.

A further issue to be raised concerns the effect of injury inflicted upon property belonging to a third State or her nationals on the legality of counter-measures. The general rule is that injury to a third party does not affect the legality of counter-measures imposed by an aggrieved State against a delinquent State. There are particular difficulties, however, inherent in the application of such a rule. For instance, a third State which suffers serious injury as a consequence of counter-measures aimed by State A at State B will undoubtedly be extremely agitated. In view of this, where there are various options open to the aggrieved party when contemplating counter-measures, it should adopt the course of action which is likely to cause least harm to the third State. At the same time it needs to be emphasized that any form of injury to a third State must be redressed, otherwise that State will be entitled to resort to counter-measures in her own right.

Respecting the breach of a self-contained regime, it is submitted that where such a regime possesses its own mechanism for redressing the wrongful conduct, counter-measures should not be imposed. As an illustration, the rules of diplomatic law specify the privileges and immunities to be accorded by the receiving State to diplomatic missions. These same rules also prescribe the sanctions to be imposed by the receiving State against members of such missions who abuse their privileged status. It is because of this self-contained nature of the rules of diplomatic law that resort to counter-measures is precluded.

A further observation on the sacrosanct nature of diplomatic law relates to the fear of reciprocal action. This fear is in itself a major deterrent on the use of counter-measures in response to breaches of diplomatic rules.

Nevertheless, where unlawful conduct violates rules of international law that are outside the particular self-contained regime, there seems no reason why counter-measures should not be applied. Examples of such violations would include breaches of established human rights standards, of treaty provisions, or of obligations to make reparation for injury.

By analogy with the self-contained nature of the rules of diplomatic law, it is probably the case that innocent passage through territorial sea may not be suspended as a counter-measure. This supposition is confirmed by the fact that State practice does not provide a single instance where such passage has been suspended as a counter-measure. The same argument would apply, *mutatis mutandis,* to the suspension of innocent passage through straits. In either case, however, the aggrieved State may apply counter-measures against the delinquent State in another sphere of relations not involving innocent passage.

The rule of exhaustion of local remedies has some bearing on the legality of counter-measures. Where injury to an alien entails a breach of an obligation of conduct, his State of nationality may resort to counter-measures without the need for him to exhaust local remedies. As regards a breach of an obligation of result, the crucial issue is whether the defaulting State merely has an initial choice as to the means to be employed, or whether she has an opportunity to rectify an incompatible situation produced by her initial conduct. In the former case, once the choice has been made without in fact achieving the required result, counter-measures may be taken to remedy any consequential injury. As to the latter case, only where an aggrieved alien seeks local remedies to no avail may counter-measures be taken. However, this condition will not apply where the subsequent conduct of the State of the forum constitutes a denial of justice.

On the question of whether the principles of jurisdiction constitute a constraint on the application of counter-measures, State practice provides no clear direction. It is submitted, none the less, that such measures should be enforced by the courts of third States if the State imposing them could establish their legality. In effect, therefore, the extraterritorial application of counter-measures depends on whether they are intrinsically lawful, rather than on whether they are consistent with the principles of jurisdiction. Finally, although there is no evidence in State practice, it may plausibly be argued that a breach of an *erga omnes* obligation should give an incentive to third States to support counter-measures intended to quell that breach.

The legality of counter-measures within the law of treaties may be assessed on the basis of the rules of customary law, and in the light of the 1969 Vienna Convention on the Law of Treaties. According to the former, a material breach of a treaty entitles an aggrieved party to terminate or suspend its obligations towards the defaulting party. Where the breach is of a minor nature, the aggrieved party may only withhold temporarily the performance of its obligation towards the offending party. In special circumstances, an aggrieved party may withhold performance of obligations arising from customary law, or from a treaty other than that which has been violated. In every case, however, the counter-measures taken must be preceded by an unsuccessful demand for reparation, and must also bear some degree of proportionality to the breach. Furthermore, the measures taken should not involve the suspension of provisions concerning humanitarian treatment.

The regime created by the Vienna Convention on the Law of Treaties has certain similarities with the category of counter-measures, chiefly in that they both essentially reflect the same doctrine. It must be pointed out, however, that the conventional regime deals exclusively with the concept of material breach, and is subject to an elaborate procedural system. Moreover, it permits retaliatory steps only against the treaty that has been violated. Consequently, the remedy envisaged in Article 60 is restricted mainly to steps based on the notion of reciprocity.

A particular question addressed in this book concerns the legality of counter-measures in the presence of a commitment to peaceful settlement of disputes. The general rule of customary law is that such a commitment precludes resort to counter-measures. None the less, in the present state of international relations, it would seem necessary that a certain flexibility should be allowed in the interpretation of that rule. Hence, it is arguable that the rationale behind counter-measures may be taken as the basis for determining whether they can in fact be imposed notwithstanding a commitment to peaceful settlement. Thus, where the objective is a speedy settlement, counter-measures may be resorted to if such steps are the sole means of inducing the defaulting party to achieve that settlement. As regards the motivations of self-protection and reciprocity, it is arguable that they may justify recourse to counter-measures even when the dispute is *sub judice*. As an illustration, where interim measures of protection ordered by a tribunal are flouted by one party, the other party may, after a reasonable period has elapsed, resort to counter-measures. In such a case, where the motivation is self-protection, a wide scope of action is permitted. By contrast, where reciprocity is the motive, the permissible range of action will naturally be restricted by the limits inherent in that notion.

An issue to be raised here is whether a party to a multilateral treaty providing for an autonomous legal regime may take counter-measures against another contracting party for breach of that treaty. It is submitted that such a treaty regime should be insulated from counter-measures for as long as it is capable of providing an effective remedy for wrongful conduct. By implication, therefore, where that regime fails to provide such a remedy, an aggrieved party may resort to counter-measures against a recalcitrant contracting State on the basis of reciprocity or self-protection.

The last topic to be examined in this book concerns the legality of economic coercion. There is no evidence of any clear principle which indicates whether economic coercion is prima facie lawful or prima facie unlawful. Furthermore, even if such a question could be determined, there would be little to be gleaned therefrom as concerns the legality of counter-measures. However, if economic coercion is looked upon as prima facie unlawful, it would be difficult in evidential terms to establish the legality of counter-measures. This view is based on the fact that counter-measures invariably entail a degree of economic coercion.

Appendix

List of Documents of the International Law Commission

DIPLOMATIC IMMUNITIES AND PRIVILEGES

Secretariat of the International Law Commission Memorandum, *Diplomatic Intercourse and Immunities*, Doc. A/CN.4/98, 21 February 1956, *Yearbook of the International Law Commission*, ii, 1956, pp. 129–72.

Summary records of the meetings of the ninth session .(23 April–28 June 1957) *concerning Diplomatic Intercourse and Immunities*, *Yearbook of the International Law Commission*, i, 1957, pp. 2–231.

SANDSTRÖM, A., *Proposed Draft Articles concerning Diplomatic Intercourse and Immunities*, Doc. A/CN.4/116/Add. 1 and 2, 2 May 1958, *Yearbook of the International Law Commission*, ii, 1958, pp. 16–19.

Diplomatic intercourse and immunities. Report to the General Assembly on the work of the ninth session, 28 April–4 July 1957, Doc. A/3859, Chapter 3, 'Diplomatic Intercourse and Immunities', *Yearbook of the International Law Commission*, ii, 1958, pp. 89–105.

Summary records of the meetings of the tenth session (28 April–4 July 1958) *concerning Diplomat Intercourse and Immunities*, *Yearbook of the International Law Commission*, i, 1958, pp. 90–200.

Report to the General Assembly on the work of the tenth session, 28 April–4 July 1958, *General Assembly Official Records*, Thirteenth Session, suppl. 9(A/3859), Chapter 3, 'Diplomatic Intercourse and Immunities', pp. 11–27.

LAW OF TREATIES

LAUTERPACHT, SIR HERSCH, *First Report on the Law of Treaties*, Doc. A/CN.4/63, 24 March 1953, *Yearbook of the International Law Commission*, ii, 1953, pp. 90–162.

—— *Second Report on the Law of Treaties*, Doc. A/CN.4/87, 8 July 1954, *Yearbook of the International Law Commission*, ii, 1954, pp. 123–39.

FITZMAURICE, SIR GERALD, *Second Report on the Law of Treaties*, Doc. A/CN.4/107, 15 March 1957, *Yearbook of the International Law Commission*, ii, 1957, pp. 16–70.

—— *Third Report on the Law of Treaties*, Doc. A/CN.4/115, 18 March 1958, *Yearbook of the International Law Commision*, ii, 1958, pp. 20–46.

—— *Fourth Report on the Law of Treaties*, Doc. A/CN.4/120, 17 March 1959, *Yearbook of the International Law Commission*, ii, 1959, pp. 36–81.

—— *Fifth Report on the Law of Treaties*, Doc. A/CN.4/130, 21 March 1960, *Yearbook of the International Law Commission*, ii, 1960, pp. 69–107.

WALDOCK, SIR HUMPHREY, *First Report on the Law of Treaties*, Doc. A/CN.4/144, 26 March 1962, *Yearbook of the International Law Commission*, ii, 1962, pp. 27–80.

—— *Addendum to the First Report on the Law of Treaties*, Doc. A/CN.4/144/Add.1 *Yearbook of the International Law Commission*, ii, 1962, pp. 80–3.

—— *Second Report on the Law of Treaties*, Doc. A/CN.4/156 and Add. 1–3, 20 March, 10 April, 30 April, and 5 June 1963, *Yearbook of the International Law Commission*, ii, 1963, pp. 36–94.

Report to the General Assembly on the Work of the fifteenth session, 6 May–12 July 1963, *General Assembly Official Records*, Eighteenth Session, suppl. 9(A/5509), Chapter 2, pp. 2–29.

WALDOCK, SIR HUMPHREY, *Third Report on the Law of Treaties*, Doc, A/CN.4/167 and Add. 1–3, 3 March, 9 June, 12 June, and 7 July 1964, *Yearbook of the International Law Commission*, ii, 1964, pp. 5–65.

Report to the General Assembly on the work of the sixteenth session, 11 May–24 July 1964, *General Assembly Official Records*, Nineteenth Session, suppl. 9(A/5809), Chapter 2, pp. 3–34.

WALDOCK, SIR HUMPHREY, *Fourth Report on the Law of Treaties*, Doc. A/CN.4/177 and Add. 1 and 2, 19 March, 25 March, and 17 June 1965, *Yearbook of the International Law Commission*, ii, 1965, pp. 3–72.

—— *Fifth Report on the Law of Treaties*, Doc. A/CN.4/183 and Add. 1–4, 15 November 1965, 4 December 1965, 20 December 1965, 3 January 1966, and 18 January 1966, *Yearbook of the International Law Commission*, ii, 1966, pp. 1–50.

—— *Sixth Report on the Law of Treaties*, Doc. A/CN.4/186 and Add. 1–7, 11 March, 25 March, 12 April, 11 May, 17 May, 24 May, 1 June and 14 June 1966, *Yearbook of the International Law Commission*, ii, 1966, pp. 51–103.

Report to the General Assembly of the work of the eighteenth session, 4 May–19 July 1966, *General Assembly Official Records*, Twenty-first Session, suppl. 9(A-/6309/Rev.1), Chapter 2, pp. 7–100.

OTHER RELEVANT DOCUMENTS

United Nations Conference on the Law of Treaties, First Session, *Official Records*, A/CONF. 39/11.

United Nations Conference on the Law of Treaties, Second Session, A/CONF. 39/11, Add. 1.

STATE RESPONSIBILITY

GARCIA-AMADOR, F., *Second Report on International Responsibility*, Doc. A/CN.4/106, 15 February 1957, *Yearbook of the International Law Commission*, ii, 1957, pp. 104–30.

AGO, R., *First Report on State Responsibility*, Doc. A/CN. 4/217 and Add. 1, 7 May 1969 and 20 January 1970, 'Review of the Previous Work on the Codification of the Topic of the International Responsibility of States', *Yearbook of the International Law Commission*, ii, 1969, pp. 125–56.

——*First Report on State Responsibility,*/ Doc. A/CN.4/217/Add. 2, 5 April 1971, 'Review of the Previous Work on the Codification of the Topic of the International Responsibility of States, Addendum, *Yearbook of the International Law Commission,* 1971, pp. 193–8.

——*Second Report on State Responsibility,* Doc. A/CN.4/233, 20 April 1970, Chapter 1, 'The Internationally Wrongful Act as a Source of Responsibility, *Yearbook of the International Law Commission,* ii, 1970, pp. 177–97.

——*Third Report on State Responsibility,* Doc. A CN.4/217/Add. 2, 'The Internationally Wrongful Act of the State, Source of International Wrongful Act of the State, Source of International Responsibility', 5 March, 7 April, 28 April, and 18 May 1971, Chapter 2 'The "Act of the State" According to International law', *Yearbook of the International Law Commission,* ii (1), 1971, pp. 233–74.

——*Fourth Report on State Responsibility,* Doc. A/CN.4/264 and Add. 1, 30 June 1972 and 9 April 1973, 'The Internationally Wrongful Act of the State, Source of International Responsibility', Chapter 2, 'The "Act of the State" According to International Law (cont.), *Yearbook of the International Law Commission,* 1972, ii, pp. 72–152.

——*Fifth Report on State Responsibility,* Doc. A/CN.4/29/and Add. 1–2, 22 March, 14 April, and 4 May 1976, 'The Internationally Wrongful Act of the State, Source of International Responsibility (cont.),' Chapter 3 'Breach of an International Obligation', *Yearbook of the International Law Commission,* ii(1), 1971, pp. 4–54.

——*Sixth Report on State Responsibility,* Doc. A/CN.4/302 and Add. 1–3, 15 April, 7 June, 5, and 14 July 1977, 'The Internationally Wrongful Act of the State, Source of International Responsibility (cont.),' Chapter 3, 'Breach of an International Obligation (cont.)', *Yearbook of the International Law Commission,* ii(1), 1977, pp. 4–43.

Report to the General Assembly on the twenty-ninth session (9 May–29 July 1977), Doc. A/32/10; Chapter 2, 'State Responsibility, Article 20: Breach of an international obligation requiring the adoption of a particular course of conduct; Article 21: Breach of an international obligation requiring the achievement of a specified result; Article 22: Exhaustion of local remedies', *Yearbook of the International Law Commission,* ii(2), 1977, pp. 9–50.

AGO, R., *Seventh Report on State Responsibility,* Doc. A/CN.4/307 and Add. 1–2, 29 March, 17 April, and 4 July 1978, 'The Internationally Wrongful Act of the State, Source of International Responsibility (cont.), Chapter 3, 'Breach of an International Obligation (cont.)', *Yearbook of the International Law Commission,* ii(1), 1978, pp. 32–60.

——*Eighth Report on State Responsibility,* Doc. A/CN.4/318 and Add. 1–4, 24 January, 5 February, and 15 June 1979, 'the Internationally Wrongful Act of the State, Source of International Responsibility (cont.)', Chapter 5 'Circumstances Precluding Wrongfulness. Legitimate application of a Sanction', *Yearbook of the International Law Commission,* ii(1), pp. 39–47.

Summary records of the meetings of the thirty-first session (14 May–3 August 1979), 'Concerning Legitimate Application of a Sanction, *Yearbook of the International Law Commission,* i, 1979, pp. 55–63.

Report to the General Assembly on the work of the thirty-first session (14 May–3 August 1979), Doc. A/34/10, Chapter 3, 'State Responsibility', Chapter 5, 'Circumstances

Precluding Wrongfulness, Article 30 Counter-Measures in Respect of an Internationally Wrongful Act, *Yearbook of the International Law Commission,* ii(2), 1979, pp. 115–22.

Report to the General Assembly on the thirty-second session (5 May–25 July 1980), *General Assembly Official Records,* Thirty-fifth Session, suppl. 10(A/35/10), Chapter 5, 'Circumstances Precluding Wrongfulness', pp. 69–111.

RIPHAGEN, W., *Preliminary Report on the Content, Forms and Degrees of State Responsibility* (Part 2 of the Draft Articles), UN Doc. A/CN.4/330, 1 April 1980.

—— *Second Report on the Content, Forms and Degrees of State Responsibility* (Part 2 of the Draft Articles), UN Doc. A/CN.4/344, 1 May 1981.

—— *Third Report on the Content, Forms and Degrees of State Responsibility* (Part 2 of the Draft Articles), UN Doc. A/CN.4/354/Add. 1, 12 March 1982.

—— *Third Report on the Content, Forms and Degrees of State Responsibility* (Part 2 of the Draft Articles), UN Doc. A/CN.4/354, 30 March 1982.

—— *Third Report on the Content, Forms and Degrees of State Responsibility* (Part 2 of the Draft Articles), UN Doc. A/CN.4/354 and Add. 2, 5 May 1982.

—— *Fourth Report on the Content, Forms and Degrees of State Responsibility* (Part 2 of the Draft Articles), UN Doc. A/CN.4/366/Add. 1, 15 April 1983.

—— *Fifth Report on the Content, Forms and Degrees of State Responsibility* (Part 2 of the Draft Articles), UN Doc. A/CN.4/380, 4 April 1984.

Summary records of the meetings of the thirty-sixth session concerning State Responsibility (7 May–27 July), *Yearbook of the International Law Commission,* i, 1984, records of the 1858th meeting to the 1867th meeting, pp. 259–320.

Report of the International Law Commission on the work of its thirty-sixth session (7 May–27 July 1984), Doc. A/39/10, *Yearbook of the International Law Commission,* ii(2), 1984, Chapter 7, 'State Responsibility', pp. 99–104.

RIPHAGEN, W., *Sixth Report on (1) The Content, Forms and Degrees of State Responsibility, and (2) The 'Implementation' (Mise en Œuvre) of International Responsibility and the Settlement of Disputes* (Parts 2 and 3 of the Draft Articles), UN Doc. A/CN.4/389, 2 April 1985.

THE LAW OF THE SEA

Report to the General Assembly on the Work of its Eighth Session (23 April–4 July 1956), Doc. A/3159, Chapter 2, 'Law of the Sea', *Yearbook of the International Law Commission,* ii, 1956, pp. 254–300.

Succession of States in Respect of Matters Other Than Treaties, Report to the General Assembly on the work of its thirty-first session (14 May–3 August 1979), Doc. A/34/10, Chapter 2, 'Succession of States in Respect of Matters Other Than Treaties', *Yearbook of the International Law Commission,* ii(2), 1979, pp. 10–82.

Bibliography

ACEVEDO, D., 'The US Measures against Argentina resulting from the Malvinas Conflict', *American Journal of International Law*, 78, 1984, pp. 323–44.

Bibliography

AKEHURST, M., 'Reprisals by Third States', *British Yearbook of International Law*, 44, 1970, pp. 1–18.

—— 'Jurisdiction in International Law', *British Yearbook of International Law*, 46, 1972–3, pp. 145–257.

—— 'Custom as a Source of International Law', *British Yearbook of International Law*, 47, 1974–5, pp. 1–53.

—— 'The Hierarchy of the Sources of International Law', *British Yearbook of International Law*, 47, 1974–5, pp. 273–85.

—— *A Modern Introduction to International Law*, 4th ed., London: George Allen and Unwin, 1984.

AMERASINGHE, C., *State Responsibility for Injuries to Aliens*, Oxford: Clarendon Press, 1967.

AMERICAN LAW INSTITUTE, *Restatement of the Law: Second, Foreign Relations Law of the United States*, St Paul: American Law Institute, 1965.

—— *Restatement of the Law: Foreign Relations Law of the United States (Revised)*, Tentative Draft 2, Philadelphia: American Law Institute, 1981.

—— *Restatement of the Law: Foreign Relations Law of the United States (Revised)*, Tentative Draft 3, Philadelphia: American Law Institute, 1982.

—— *Restatement of the Law: Foreign Relations Law of the United States (Revised)*, Tentative Draft 5, Philadelphia: American Law Institute, 1984.

ARANGIO-RUIZ, G., 'The Normative Role of the General Assembly of the United Nations and the Declaration of Principles of Friendly Relations', *Recueil des Cours de l'Académie de Droit International de La Haye*, 137(3), 1972, pp. 419–628. and Oxford: North-Holland Publishing Company, 1978.

AUFRICHT, H. 'Extrinsic Evidence in International Law', *Cornell Law Quarterly*, 35, 1949–50, pp. 327–48.

BAXTER, R., 'Multilateral Treaties as Evidence of Customary International Law', *British Yearbook of International Law*, 41, 1965–6, pp. 275–300.

BIRCH, T., *A Collection of the State Papers of John Thurloe*, vi, London: Executor of the late Mr Fletcher Gyles, 1742.

BOCKSLAFF, K., 'The Pipeline Affair of 1981/82: A Case History', *German Yearbook of International Law*, 27, 1984, pp. 28–37.

BOORMAN III, J., 'Economic Coercion in International Law: The Arab Oil Weapon and Its Ensuing Juridical Issues', *Journal of International Law and Economics*, 9, 1974, pp. 205–31.

BORCHARD, E., 'Reprisals on Private Property', *American Journal of International Law*, 30, 1926, pp. 108–13.
—— *The Diplomatic Protection of Citizens Abroad or The Law of International Claims*, New York: The Bank Law Publishing Co., 1928.
BOWETT, D., *Self-defence in International Law*, Manchester: Manchester University Press, 1958.
—— 'Reprisals Involving Recourse to Armed Force', *American Journal of International Law*, 66(1), 1972, pp. 1–36.
—— 'Economic Coercion and Reprisals by States', *Virginia Journal of International Law*, 13(1), 1972, pp. 1–12.
—— 'Economic Coercion: Past and Present. International Law and Economic Coercion', *Virginia Journal of International Law*, 16(2), 1976, 245–59.
—— 'Jurisdiction: Changing Patterns of Authority Over Activities and Resources', *British Yearbook of International Law*, 53, 1982, pp. 1–26.
BRIDGE, J., 'The Law and Politics of United States Foreign Policy Exports Controls', *Legal Studies*, 4(1), March 1984, pp. 2–29.
BRIERLY, J., 'Sanctions', *Transactions of the Grotius Society*, 17, 1932, pp. 67–84.
—— *The Law of Nations, An Introduction to the International Law of Peace*, 6th edn. by Sir Humphrey Waldock, New York and Oxford: Oxford University Press, 1963.
BRIGGS, H., *The Law of Nations, Cases, Documents and Notes*, New York: Appleton-Century-Crafts, 1953.
—— *Law of Nations*, 2nd edn., London: Stevens & Sons, 153.
—— 'Codification Treaties and Provisions on Reciprocity, Non-Discrimination or Retaliation', *American Journal of International Law*, 56, 1962, pp. 475–82.
—— 'Reflections on the Codification of International Law by the International Law Commission and by other Agencies', *Recueil des Cours de l'Académie de Droit International de La Haye*, 126(1), 1969, pp. 233–316.
—— 'Unilateral Denunciation of Treaties: The Vienna Convention and the International Court of Justice', *American Journal of International Law*, 68, 1974, pp. 51–68.
BROMS, B., 'The Definition of Aggression', *Recueil des Cours de l'Académie de Droit International de La Haye*, 154(1), 1977, pp. 301–99.
BROSCHE, H., 'The Arab Oil Embargo and United States Pressure against Chile: Economic and Political Coercion and the Charter of the United Nations', *Case Western Reserve Journal of International Law*, 7(1), 1974, pp. 3–35.
BROWER, C., AND TEPE, J., 'The Charter of Economic Rights and Duties of States: A Reflection or Rejection of International Law?', *International Lawyers*, 9, 1975, pp. 295–318.
BROWNLIE, I., *International Law and the Use of Force by States*, Oxford: Oxford University Press, 1963.
—— *Loaves and Fishes: Access to Natural Resources and International Law*, An Inaugural Lecture, London: London School of Economics and Political Science, 1978.
—— *Principles of Public International Law*, 3rd edn., Oxford: Oxford University Press, 1979.
—— 'Legal Status of Natural Resources, *Recueil de Cours de l'Académie de Droit International de La Haye*, 162(1), 1979, pp. 245–317.
—— *Basic Documents on Human Rights*, 2nd edn., Oxford: Clarendon Press, 1981.

—— *System of the Law of Nations, State Responsibility*, Part I, Oxford: Clarendon Press, 1983.

—— *Basic Documentary in International Law*, 3rd edn., Oxford: Clarendon Press, 1983.

BRUNSVOLD, B., AND BAGARAZZI, J., 'Licensing Impact of Foreign Policy Motivated Retroactive Re-export Regulations', *Case Western Reserve Journal of International Law*, 15, 1983, pp. 289–328.

BUTLER, SIR GEOFFREY, AND MACCOBY, S., *The Development of International Law*, London, New York, and Toronto: Longmans, Green, 1928.

BYNKERSHOEK, C. VAN, *Quaestionum Juris Publici Libri Duo*, 1737, a translation of the text by T. Frank, ed. J. B. Scott (The Classics of International Law, 2), Washington: Carnegie Endowment for International Peace, Division of International Law, 1930.

CHANCE, J., ed., *British Diplomatic Instructions 1689–1789*, i, *Sweden, 1689–1727*, London: The Royal Historical Society, 1922.

CHENG, B., *General Principles of Law as Applied by International Courts and Tribunals*, London: Stevens & Sons, 1953.

—— *The Law of International Air Transport*, London and New York: Stevens & Sons and Oceana Publications, 1962.

COLBERT, E., *Retaliation in International Law*, New York: Columbia University, King's Crown Press, 1948.

COLOMBOS, C., *The International Law of the Sea*, 6th edn., London: Longmans, Green, 1967.

Common Market Law Review (Editorial Comment), 'The Mutton and Lamb Story: Isolated Incident or the Beginning of a New Era?', *Common Market Law Review*, 17, 1980, pp. 311–14.

COUNCIL OF EUROPE, *European Conventions and Agreements*, i, *1949–1961*, Strasbourg: Council of Europe, 1971.

CRANDALL, S., *Treaties, Their Making and Enforcement*, Washington: John Byrne, 1916.

CRAWFORD, J., *The Creation of States in International Law*, Oxford: Clarendon Press, 1979.

DAHM, G., *Völkerrecht*, iii, Stuttgart: W. Kohlhammer Verlag, 1961.

D'AMATO, A., 'The Concept of Human Rights in International Law', *Columbia Law Review*, 82, 1982, pp. 1110–59.

DAMROSCH, L., 'Retaliation or Arbitration—or Both? The 1978 United States–France Aviation Dispute', *American Journal of International Law*, 74, 1980, pp. 785–807.

DAVID, A., *The Strategy of Treaty Termination, Lawful Breaches and Retaliations*, New Haven and London: Yale University Press, 1975.

DE BERNHARDT, G,. ed., *Handbook of Commercial Treaties, &c., Between Great Britain and Foreign Powers*, London: HMSO, 1912.

DEFIEFFER, D., 'Extraterritorial Applications of US Export Controls—The Siberian Pipeline', *Proceedings of American Society of International Law*, 1983, pp. 242–3.

DELBEZ, L., *Les Principes généraux du droit international public*, Paris: R. Pichon and R. Durand-Auzias, 1964.

DE MARTENS, C., *Nouvelles causes célèbres du droit des gens*, ii, Paris: Brockhaus & Avenarius, 1843.

DEMPSEY, P., 'Economic Aggression and Self-Defence in International Law: The Arab

Oil Weapon and Alternative American Response Thereto', *Case Western Reserve Journal of International Law*, 9, 1977, pp. 253–321.

DENZA, E., *Diplomatic Law, Commentary on the Vienna Convention on Diplomatic Relations*, Dobbs Ferry, NY: Oceana Publications, 1976.

DOLZER, R., 'New Foundation of the Law of Expropriation of Alien Property', *American Journal of International Law*, 75, 1981, pp. 553–89.

DOMKE, M., 'Foreign Nationalizations', *American Journal of Law*, 55, 1961, pp. 585–616.

DOXEY, M., *Economic Sanctions and International Enforcement*, London: Macmillan, 1980.

—— 'International Sanctions in Theory and Practice', *Case Western Reserve Journal of International Law*, 15, 1983, pp. 273–88.

DRAPER, G., 'Diplomatic Immunities and Privileges', *House of Commons, First Report from the Foreign Affairs Committee, Session 1984–85. The Abuse of Diplomatic Immunities and Privileges*, London: HMSO, 1984, pp. 68–76.

DUMBAULD, E, *Interim Measures of Protection in International Controversies*, The Hague: Martinus Nijhoff, 1932.

EAGLETON, C., 'The Attempt to Define Aggression', *International Conciliation*, 263, 1930, pp. 583–652.

—— *International Government*, New York: The Ronald Press Company, 1957.

EDWARDS, R., 'Extraterritorial Application of the US Iranian Assets Control Regulations', *American Journal of International Law*, 75, 1981, pp. 870–902.

ELIAS, T., *The Modern Law of Treaties*, Dobbs Ferry, NY and Leiden: Oceana Publications and A. W. Sijthoff, 1974.

ELLICOTT, J., 'Extraterritorial Application of US Export Controls—The Siberian Pipeline', *Proceedings of American Journal of International Law*, 1983, pp. 262–7.

EUROPEAN COMMUNITIES, 'Comments on the U.S. Regulations Concerning Trade with U.S.S.R.', *International Legal Materials*, 21, 1982, pp. 891–904.

EVENSEN, J., 'Evidence Before International Courts', *Nordisk Tidsskrift For International Ret Og Jus Gentium: Acta Scandinavica Juris Gentium*, 25, 1955, pp. 44–62.

FALK R., 'The Iran Hostage Crisis: Easy Answers and Hard Questions', *American Journal of International Law*, 74, 1980, pp. 411–17.

FANSHAWE, R., *Original Letters of his Excellency Sir Richard Fanshawe During his Embassies in Spain and Portugal: Which, together with divers Letters and Answers From the Chief Ministers of State of England, Spain and Portugal, contain the whole Negotiations of the Treaty of Peace between those Three Crowns*, London: Abel Roper, 1701.

FAWCETT, SIR JAMES, 'The Exhaustion of Local Remedies: Substance or Procedure?', *British Yearbook of International Law*, 30, pp. 452–8.

—— 'Intervention in International Law', *Receuil des Cours de l'Académie de Droit International de La Haye*, 103(2), 1961, pp. 347–421.

—— *Law and Power in International Relations*, London: Faber and Faber, 1982.

FELDMAN, M., 'Extraterritoriality: Conflict and Overlap in National and International Regulations', *Proceedings of American Society of International Law*, 1981, pp. 30–42.

FENWICK, C., *International Law*, 4th edn., New York: Appleton-Century-Crofts, 1965.

FITZMAURICE, SIR GERALD, 'The General Principles of International Law Considered from the Standpoint of the Rule of Law', *Recueil des Cours de l'Académie de Droit International de La Haye*, 92(2), 1957, pp. 5–227.

FREEMAN, A., *The International Responsibility of States for Denial of Justice*, London, New York, and Toronto: Longmans, Green, 1938.

GARNER, J., AND JOBST III, V., 'The Unilateral Denunciation of Treaties by One Party Because of Alleged Non-Performance by Another Party or Parties', *American Journal of International Law*, 29, 1935, pp. 569–85.

GEBREHANA, T., *Duty to Negotiate, an Element of International Law*, Uppsala: Svenska Institut för Internationell Rätt, 1978.

GENTILI, A., *De Jure Belli Libri Tres*, 1612, a translation of the text by J. C. Rolfe, ed. J. B. Scott (The Classics of International Law, 2), Washington: Carnegie Endowment for International Peace, 1933.

GOLD, SIR JOSEPH, 'Some Characteristics of Operation', *The International Monetary Fund, 1945–1965*, ii, *Analysis*, ed. M. de Vries, J. Horsefield, J. Gold, M. Gumbart, G. Lovasy, and E. Spitzer, Washington, DC: International Monetary Fund, 1969, pp. 582–91.

—— 'Reciprocity and Legal Order', *The International Monetary Fund, 1945–1965*, ii, *Analysis*, Washington, DC: International Monetary Fund, 1969, pp. 591–4.

—— *The Fund Agreement in the Courts*, ii, *Further Jurisprudence Involving the Articles of Agreement of the International Monetary Fund*, Washington, DC: International Monetary Fund, 1982.

—— ' "Exchange Contracts", Exchange Control, and the IMF Articles of Agreement: Some Animadversions on *Wilson, Smithett & Cope Ltd.* v *Teruzzi*', *International and Comparative Law Quarterly*, 33(4), 1984, pp. 777–810.

GOLDIE, L., 'Liability for Damage and the Progressive Development of International Law', *International and Comparative Law Quarterly*, 14, 1965, pp. 1189–264.

GOODRICH, L., HAMBRO, L., AND SIMONS, A., *Charter of the United Nations Commentary and Documents*, 3rd edn., New York and London: Columbia University Press, 1969.

GOODWIN-GILL, G., 'The Limits of the Power of Expulsion in Public International Law', *British Yearbook of International Law*, 47, 1974–5, pp. 55–156.

GORE-BOOTH, LORD, ed., *Satow's Guide to Diplomatic Practice*, 5th edn., London and New York: Longmans, 1974.

GOULD, W., *An Introduction to International Law*, New York: Harper & Brothers Publishers, 1957.

GRAEFRATH, B., AND STEINIGER, P., 'Kodifikation der völkerrechtlichen Verantwortlichkeit', *Neue Justiz: Zeitschrift für Recht und Rechtswissenschaft*, 8, 1973, pp. 227–8.

GREEN, C., 'The US–French Air Services Arbitration', *Cambridge Law Journal*, 38, 1979, pp. 233–8.

GREEN, N., *International Law (Law of Peace)*, 2nd edn., Estover, Plymouth: Macdonald & Evans, 1982.

GREENE, P., 'The Arab Economic Boycott of Israel: The International Law Perspective', *Vanderbilt Journal of Transnational Law*, 2(77), 1978, pp. 77–94.

GREENWOOD, C., 'The US–French Air Services Arbitration', *The Cambridge Law Journal*, 38, 1979, pp. 233–80.

GROSS, L., 'The Case Concerning United States Diplomatic and Consular Staff in Tehran, Phase of Provisional Measures', *American Journal of International Law*, 74, 1980, pp. 395–410.

GROTIUS, H., *De Jure Belli Ac Pacis Libri Tres*, Book III, 1646, a translation of the text by F. Kelsey and others, ed. J. B. Scott (The Classics of International Law, 2), Washington: Carnegie Endowment for International Peace, Division of International Law, 1925.

GUGGENHEIM, P., *Lehrbuch des Völkerrechts*, i, Basle: Verlag für Recht und Gesellschaft, 1948.

—— *Répertoire suisse de droit international public: Documentation concernant la pratique de la Confédération en matière de droit international public 1914–1939*, iii, Berne: Département Politique Fédéral, 1975.

HAIGHT, J., 'The New International Economic Order and the Charter of Economic Rights and Duties of States', *International Lawyer*, 9(4), 1975, pp. 591–604.

HALL, W., *A Treatise on International Law*, 2nd edn., Oxford: Clarendon Press, 1884; 8th edn. by P. Higgins, Oxford: Clarendon Press, 1924.

HALLECK, H., *International Law; Or, Rules Regulating the Intercourse of States in Peace and War*, San Francisco: H. H. Bancroft, 1861.

HARASZTI, G., *Some Fundamental Problems of the Law of Treaties*, Budapest: Akadémiai Kiadó, 1973.

HARVARD LAW SCHOOL, *The Harvard Draft Convention on the Law of Treaties*, supplement to the *American Journal of International Law*, 29, 1935, pp. 655–1125.

HATSCHEK, J., *An Outline of International Law*, trans. C. Manning, London: G. Bell and Sons, 1930.

HEFFTER, A., *Le Droit international public de l'Europe*, Paris: Cotillon, éditeur, Libraire du Conseil d'état, 1857.

HEIN, W., 'Remarks Concerning Extraterritorial Application of US Export Controls—The Siberian Pipeline', *Proceedings of the American Society of International Law*, 1983, pp. 243–50.

HERTSLET, L., ed., *A Complete Collection of the Treaties and Conventions and Reciprocal Regulations at Present subsisting Between Great Britain and Foreign Powers and of the Laws, Decrees, and Orders in Council concerning the same; So Far as they Relate to Commerce and Navigation, to the Repression of the Slave Trade; And to the Privileges and Interests of the Subjects of the High Contracting Parties*, vol. ii, London: T. Egerton, 1820.

HIGGINS, R., 'Derogations under Human Rights Treaties', *British Yearbook of International Law*, 48, 1976–7, pp. 281–320.

—— 'Legal Responses to the Afghan–Iranian Crisis', *Proceedings of American Society of International Law*, 74, 1980, pp. 250–5.

—— 'The taking of Property by the State: Recent Developments in International Law', *Recueil des Cours de l'Académie de Droit International de La Haye*, 176(2), 1982, pp. 263–391.

HINDMARSH, A., 'Self-Help in Time of Peace', *American Journal of International Law*, 26, 1932, pp. 315–26.

HINTON, A., 'Legal Responses to the Afghan/Iranian Crisis', *Proceedings of American Society of International Law*, 74, 1980, pp. 248–50.

HOLLAND, T., *Studies in International Law*, London and New York: Henry Frowde and Stevens & Sons, 1898.

HOUSE OF COMMONS, First Report from the Foreign Affairs Committee, Session 1984–5, *The Abuse of Diplomatic Immunities and Privileges*, London: HMSO, 1985.

HUDSON, M., ed., *International Legislation*, i, *1919–21*, Washington, DC; Carnegie Endowment for International Peace, 1931.

—— *International Legislation*, ix, *1942–5*, New York: Carnegie Endowment for International Law, 1950.

HURST, SIR CECIL, *The Collected Papers of Sir Cecil Hurst*, London: Stevens & Sons, 1950.

HYDE, C., *International Law Chiefly as Interpreted and Applied by the United States*, ii, Boston: Little, Brown, 1947.

—— AND WEHLE, L., 'Boycott in Foreign Affairs', *American Journal of International Law*, 27, 1933, pp. 1–10.

INSTITUT DE DROIT INTERNATIONAL, 'Le Régime de représailles en temps de paix', *Annuaire de l'Institut de Droit International*, 38, 1934, pp. 1–161, 623–94, 708–11.

INTERNATIONAL MONETARY FUND, *Articles of Agreement*, Washington, DC: International Monetary Fund, 1978.

—— *Summary Proceedings of the Thirty-fifth Annual Meeting of the Board of Governors*, Washington, DC: International Monetary Fund, 1980.

JACKSON, J., *World Trade and the Law of GATT*, New York: Bobbs-Merrill, 1969.

JANKOVIC, B., *Public International Law*, Epping, Essex: Bowker Publishing Company, 1983.

JENKS, C., *International Immunity*, London and New York: Stevens & Sons and Oceana Publications, 1961.

—— *The Prospects of International Adjudication*, London and Dobbs Ferry, NY: Stevens & Sons and Oceana Publications, 1964.

JENNINGS, SIR ROBERT, 'The Limits of State Jurisdiction', *Nordisk Tidsskrift For International Ret Og Jus Gentium: Acta Scandinavica Juris Gentium*, 32, 1962, pp. 209–29.

JESSUP, P., *A Modern Law of Nations*, New York: The Macmillan Company, 1948.

JIMÉNEZ DE ARÉCHAGA, E., 'International Law in the Past Third of a Century', *Recueil des Cours de l'Académie de Droit International de La Haye*, 159(1), 1978, pp. 1–344.

JOHNSON, D., 'The Effects of Resolutions of the General Assembly of the United Nations', *British Yearbook of International Law*, 32, 1955–6, pp. 97–129.

KALSHOVEN, F., *Belligerent Reprisals*, Leiden: A. W. Sijthoff, 1971.

KAPTEYN, P., AND VERLOREN VAN THEMAAT, P., *Introduction to the Law of the European Communities after the accession of new Member States*, London, Deventer, and Alphen aan den Rijn: Sweet & Maxwell, Kluwer, and Samson, 1973.

KELSEN, H., *Principles of International Law*, New York: Rinehart, 1952.

—— *International Law Studies: Collective Security Under International Law*, 49, Part III.2.C., Washington, DC: United States Government Printing Office, 1954, pp. 101–10.

KNIGHT, W., ' "Failsafe" Legal Structures to Protect US Assets of Foreign Investors', *International Business Lawyer*, 9(3), 1981, pp. 109–14.

KUYPER, P., 'The European Community and the US Pipeline Embargo: Comments on Comments', *German Yearbook of International Law*, 27, 1984, pp. 72–96.

LAUTERPACHT, E., ed., *International Law: Being the Collected Papers of Hersch Lauterpacht*, i, *The General Works*, Cambridge: Cambridge University Press, 1970.

LAUTERPACHT, SIR HERSCH, 'The So-called Anglo-American and Continental Schools of Thought in International Law', *British Yearbook of International Law*, 12, 1931, pp. 31–62.

—— 'Boycott in International Relations', *British Yearbook of International Law*, 14, 1933, pp. 125–40.

—— ed., *International Law: A Treatise*, by C. Oppenheim, ii, *Disputes, War and Neutrality*, 6th edn., London, New York, and Toronto: Longmans, Green, 1940.

—— *International Law and Human Rights*, London: Stevens & Sons, 1950.

—— 'Sovereignty over Submarine Areas', *British Yearbook of International Law*, 27, 1950, pp. 376–433.

—— ed., *International Law: A Treatise* by L. Oppenheim, ii, *Disputes, War and Neutrality*, 7th edn., London: Longmans, Green, 1952.

—— ed., *International Law: A Treatise* by L. Oppenheim, i, *Peace*, 8th edn., London, New York, and Toronto: Longmans, Green, 1955.

—— *The Development of International Law by the International Court*, London: Stevens & Sons, 1958.

LAWRENCE, T., *The Principles of International Law*, London and New York: Macmillan, 1895.

LEAGUE OF NATIONS, *Conference for the Codification of International Law. Responsibility of States for Damage caused in their Territory to the Person or Property of Foreigners*, iii, C.75.M.69.1929.V, Bases of Discussion, Geneva, 1929.

LILLICH, R., 'Economic Coercion and the "New International Economic Order": A Second Look at Some First Impressions', *Virginia Journal of International Law*, 16(2), 1976, pp. 233–44.

—— *The Human Rights of Aliens in Contemporary International Law*, Manchester: Manchester University Press, 1984.

LOWE, A., *Extraterritorial Jurisdiction*, Cambridge: Grotius Publications, 1983.

—— 'Public International Law and the Conflict of Laws: The European Response to the United States Export Administration Regulations', *International and Comparative Law Quarterly*, 33(3), 1984, pp. 515–30.

—— 'International Law Issues Arising in the "Pipeline" Dispute: The British Position', *German Yearbook of International Law*, 27, 1984, pp. 54–71.

MACCOBY, S., 'Reprisals as a Measure of Redress short of War', *The Cambridge Law Journal*, 2, 1924–6, pp. 60–73.

MACDONALD, R., 'Economic Sanctions in the International System', *Canadian Yearbook of International Law*, 7, 1969, pp. 61–91.

MCDOUGAL, M., AND FELICIANO, F., 'The Initiation of Coercion: A Multi-Temporal analysis', *American Journal of International Law*, 52, 1958, pp. 241–59.

—— 'International Coercion and World Public Order: The General Principles of the Law of War', *Yale Law Journal*, 67, 1958, pp. 771–845.

—— 'Legal Regulations of Resort to International Coercion: Aggression and Self-defence in Policy Perspective', *Yale Law Journal*, 68, 1959, pp. 1057–165.

—— *Law and Minimum World Public Order, The Legal Regulation of International Coercion,* New Haven and London: Yale University Press, 1961.

MCNAIR, LORD, 'The Legal Meaning of War, and Relation of War to Reprisals', *Transactions of the Grotius Society,* 1926, pp. 29–51.

—— *International Law Opinions, Selected and Annotated,* ii, *Peace,* Cambridge: The Syndics of the Cambridge University Press, 1956.

—— 'The Seizure of Property and Enterprises in Indonesia: Opinion', *Nederlands Tijdschrift voor Internationaal Recht,* 6, 1959, pp. 218–56.

—— *Law of Treaties,* Oxford: Clarendon Press, 1961.

—— *Selected Papers and Bibliography.* Leiden and Dobbs Ferry, NY: A. W. Sijthoff and Oceana Publications, 1974.

—— and WATTS, A., *The Legal Effects of War,* Cambridge: Cambridge University Press, 1966.

MAHAN, A., *The Influence of Sea Power Upon History, 1660–1783,* London: Sampson Low, Marston, Searle, & Rivington, 1889.

MALANCZUK, P., 'Counter-measures and Self-defence as Circumstances Precluding Wrongfulness in the ILC's Draft Articles on State Responsibility', *Zeitschrift Für ausländisches öffentliches Recht und Völkerrecht,* 1983, pp. 705–812.

MALLOY, W., ed., *Treaties, Conventions, International Acts, Protocol and Agreements Between the United States of America and Other Powers, 1776–1901,* i and ii, Washington, DC: Government Printing Office, 1910.

MANN, F., 'The Doctrine of Jurisdiction in International Law', *Recueil des Cours de l'Académie de Droit International de La Haye,* iii(1), 1964, pp. 9–162.

—— 'The State Immunity Act 1978', *British Yearbook of International Law,* 50, 1980, pp. 43–62.

—— *The Legal Aspects of Money,* Oxford: Clarendon Press, 1982.

MANNING, W., *Commentaries on the Law of Nations,* London, Dublin, and Edinburgh: Sweet, Milliken and Son, and Clark, 1839.

MARSDEN, R., ed., *Documents Relating to Law and Custom of the Sea,* i, AD *1205–1648,* Publication of the Navy Records Society, 49, 1915.

—— *Documents Relating to Law and Custom of the Sea,* ii, AD *1649–1767,* Publications of the Navy Record Society, 50, 1916.

MARSTON, G., 'United Kingdom Protection of Trading Interests Act 1980', *Journal of World Trade Law,* 14, 1980, pp. 461–5.

MARTENS, DE, *Nouvelles causes célèbres du droit des gens,* ii, Leipzig, and Paris: F. A. Brockaus and Avenarius, 1843.

MATHIAS, C., 'Extraterritorial Application of US Export Controls—The Siberian Pipeline', *Proceedings of American Journal of International Law,* 1983, pp. 256–9.

MEESSEN, K., 'Extraterritoriality of Export Control: A German Lawyer's Analysis of the Pipeline Case', *German Yearbook of International Law,* 27, 1984, pp. 97–108.

MENDELSON, M., 'Interim Measures of Protection in Cases of Contested Jurisdiction', *British Yearbook of International Law,* 46, 1972–3, pp. 259–322.

—— 'The Legal Character of General Assembly Resolutions: Some Considerations of Principle', in K. Hossain, ed., *Legal Aspects of the New International Economic Order,* London and New York: Francis Pinter and Nichols Publishing Company, 1980, pp. 95–107.

MERON, T., 'The Incidence of the Rule of Exhaustion of Local Remedies', *British Yearbook of International Law*, 35, 1959, pp. 83–101.

MOORE, J., ed., *History and Digest of the International Arbitrations to which the United States has been a Party*, i, Washington, DC: Government Printing Office, 1898.

—— *A Digest of International Law*, v, vi, and vii, Washington, DC: Government Printing Office, 1906.

MOYER, H., AND MABRY, L., 'Export Controls as Instruments of Foreign Policy: The History, Legal Issues, and Policy Lessons of the Recent Cases', *Law and Policy in International Business*, 15, 1983, pp. 1–171.

MUIR, J., 'The Boycott in International Law', *Journal of International Law and Economics*, 9, 1974, pp. 187–204.

NAFZIGER, J., 'Nonaggressive Sanctions in the International Sports Arena', *Case Western Reserve Journal of International Law*, 15, 1983, pp. 329–42.

NAHLIK, S., 'The Grounds of Invalidity and Termination of Treaties', *American Journal of International Law*, 65, 1971, pp. 736–56.

NANTWI, E., *The Enforcement of International Judicial Decisions and Arbitral Awards in Public International Law*, Leiden: A. W. Sijthoff, 1966.

O'CONNELL, D., *The International Law of the Sea*, ed. I. Shearer, Oxford: Clarendon Press, 1982.

OPPENHEIM, L., *International Law: A Treatise*, i, *Peace*, London, New York, and Bombay: Longmans, Green, 1905.

—— *International Law: A Treatise*, ii, *War and Neutrality*, London, New York, and Bombay: Longmans, Green, 1906.

—— *International Incidents for Discussion in Conversation Classes*, Cambridge: Cambridge University Press, 1909.

—— ed., *The Collected Papers of John Westlake on Public International Law*, Cambridge: Cambridge University Press, 1914.

OSAKWE, C., 'Contemporary Soviet Doctrine of Sources of International Law', *Proceedings of American Society of International Law*, 1979, pp. 310–24.

OWEN, R., AND DAMROSCH, L., 'The International Legal Status of Foreign Government Deposits in Overseas Branches of U.S. Banks', *University of Illinois Law Review*, 1982, pp. 305–18.

PANHUYS, H., 'Conflict between the European Communities and other Rules of International Law', *Common Market Law Review*, 3, 1966, pp. 420–49.

PARDIEU, C., 'The Carter Freeze Order: Specific Problems Relating to the International Monetary Fund', *International Business Lawyer*, 9(3), 1981, pp. 97–101.

PARRY, C., ed., *Law Officers' Opinions to the Foreign Office 1793–1860*, 80, 1970, Westmead: Gregg International Publishers.

—— 'Defining Economic Coercion in International Law', *Texas International Law Journal*, 12, 1977, pp. 1–4.

PARTRIDGE, C., 'Political and Economic Coercion: Within the Ambit of Article 52 of the Vienna Convention on the Law of Treaties', *International Lawyer*, 5(4), 1971, pp. 755–69.

PAUST, J., AND BLAUSTEIN, A., 'The Arab Oil Weapon—A Threat to International Peace', *American Journal of International Law*, 68(2), 1974, pp. 410–39.

PERLOW, G., 'Taking Peacetime Trade Sanctions to the Limit: The Soviet Pipeline

Embargo', *Case Western Reserve Journal of International Law*, 15, 1983, pp. 253–72.

PHILLIMORE, SIR ROBERT, *Commentaries upon International Law*, London: Butterworths, 1885.

PHILLIPSON, C., *The International Law and Custom of Ancient Greece and Rome*, ii, London: Macmillan, 1911.

POLLOCK, SIR FREDERICK, *The League of Nations*, London: Stevens and Sons, 1922.

REISMAN, W., 'The Enforcement of International Judgements', *American Journal of International Law*, 63, 1969, pp. 1–27.

REPORT OF A STUDY GROUP OF THE DAVID DAVIES MEMORIAL INSTITUTE OF INTERNATIONAL STUDIES, *International Disputes, The Legal Aspects*, London: Europa Publications, 1972.

RIESENFIELD, S., 'Jus Dispositivum and Jus Cogens in International Law in the light of a recent decision of the German Supreme Constitutional Court', *American Journal of International Law*, 60, 1966, pp. 511–15.

ROOT, E., 'The Outlook for International Law', *Proceedings of American Society of International Law*, Ninth Annual Meeting, 1915, pp. 2–11.

ROSENNE, S., The International Court of Justice, Leiden: A. W. Sijthoff, 1957.

—— *The Law and Practice of the International Court*, i and ii, Leiden: A. W. Sijthoff, 1965.

—— *The Law of Treaties, A Guide to the Legislative History of the Vienna Convention*, Leiden and Dobbs Ferry, NY: A. W. Sijthoff and Oceana Publications, 1970.

ROSENTHAL, D., AND KNIGHTON, W., *National Laws and International Commerce: The Problem of Extraterritoriality*, London, Boston, and Henley: Routledge & Kegan Paul, 1982.

ROSS, A., *A Textbook of International Law*, London, New York, and Toronto: Longmans, Green, 1947.

ROUSSEAU, C., *Principes généraux du droit international public*, i, Paris: Édition A. Pedonc, 1944.

ROZENTHAL, A., 'The Charter of Economic Rights and Duties of States and the New International Economic Order', *Virginia Journal of International Law*, 16(2), 1976, pp. 309–22.

RUBIN, A., 'The Hostages Incident: The United States and Iran', *Yearbook of World Affairs*, 36, 1982, pp. 213–40.

RUSSELL, R., AND MUTHER, J., *A History of the United Nations Charter, The Role of the United States 1940–1945*, Washington, DC: The Brookings Institution, 1958.

SANDIFER, D., *Evidence before International Tribunals*, rev. edn., Charlottesville: University Press of Virginia, 1975.

SATOW, SIR ERNEST, *The Silesian Loan and Frederick The Great*, Oxford: Clarendon Press, 1915.

SCHACHTER, O., 'Enforcement of International Judicial and Arbitral Decisions', *American Journal of International Law*, 54, 1960, pp. 1–24.

—— 'International Law in Theory and Practice: General Course in Public International Law', *Recueil des Cours de l'Académie de Droit International de La Haye*, 178(5), 1982, pp. 9–395.

SCHNEEBERGER, E., 'Reciprocity as a Maxim of International Law', *The Georgetown Law Journal*, 37, 1948, pp. 29–41.

SCHNEIDER, H., 'Problems of Recognition of the Carter Freeze Order by the German Courts', *International Business Lawyer*, 9(3), 1981, pp. 103–4.

SCHREIBER, O., 'Economic Coercion as an Instrument of Foreign Policy: U.S. Economic Measures Against Cuba and the Dominican Republic', *World Politics*, 25(3), April 1973, pp. 387–413.

SCHWARZENBERGER, G., 'International Jus Cogens', *Texas Law Review*, 43, 1965, pp. 455–78.

——'The Fundamental Principles of International Law', *Recueil des Cours de l'Académie de Droit International de La Haye*, 87(1), 1955, pp. 195–385.

——AND BROWN, E., *A Manual of International Law*, 6th edn., Milton: Professional Books, 1976.

SCHWEBEL, S., 'Aggression, Intervention and Self-Defence in Modern International Law', *Recueil des Cours de l'Académie de Droit International de La Haye*, 136(1), 1972, pp. 411–45.

SCHWELB, E., 'Some Aspects of International Jus Cogens as formulated by the International Law Commission', *American Journal of International Law*, 61(2), 1967, pp. 946–75.

SCOTT, J., ed., *The Hague Conventions and Declarations of 1899 and 1907*, 2nd edn., New York: Oxford University Press, 1915.

——*The Reports to the Hague Conferences of 1899 and 1907*, Oxford: Clarendon Press, 1917.

——ed., *The Hague Court Reports*, 2nd ser., New York: Oxford University Press, 1932.

SEIDL-HOHENVELDERN, I., 'Title to Confiscated Foreign Property and Public International Law', *American Journal of International Law*, 56, 1962, pp. 507–10.

——'International Economic "Soft Law"', *Recueil des Cours de l'Acdémie de Droit International de La Haye*, 163(2), 1979, pp. 169–246.

SEN, B., *A Diplomat's Handbook of International Law and Practice*, The Hague: Martinus Nijhoff, 1965.

SHIHATA, I., 'Destination Embargo of Arab Oil: Its Legality under International Law', *American Journal of International Law*, 68(2), 1974, pp. 591–627.

——'Arab Oil Policies and the New International Economic Order', *Virginia Journal of International Law*, 16(2), 1976, pp. 261–88.

SIEGHART, P., *The International Law of Human Rights*, Oxford: Clarendon Press, 1983.

SIMMA, B., 'Reflections on Article 60 of the Vienna Convention on the Law of Treaties and its Background in General International Law', *Österreichische Zeitschrift für öffentliches Recht*, 20, 1970, pp. 5–83.

SIMSON, J., AND FOX, H., *International Arbitration Law and Practice*, London: Stevens & Sons, 1959.

SINCLAIR, SIR IAN, *The Vienna Convention on the Law of Treaties*, Manchester and Dobbs Ferry, NY: Manchester University Press and Oceana Publications, 1973.

——'Responses to Extraterritorial Exercise of Jurisdiction: The Diplomatic Response', a paper read to the International Law Association Conference on Extraterritorial Application of Laws and Response Thereto held in London on 11 and 12 May 1983. Copy provided by courtesy of the author.

——*The Vienna Convention on the Law of Treaties*, 2nd edn., Manchester: Manchester University Press, 1984.

——'A Memorandum concerning the Status of the Diplomatic Courier and the unaccompanied Diplomatic Bag', *House of Commons, First Report from the Foreign Affairs Committee, Session 1984–85. The Abuse of Diplomatic Immunities and Privileges*, London: HMSO, 1984, pp. 78–81.

SINHA, B., *Unilateral Denunciation of Treaty Because of Prior Violation of Obligations by the Other Party*, The Hague: Martinus Nijhoff, 1966.

SKUBISZEWSKI, K., 'Use of Force by States. Collective Security. Law of War and Neutrality, Sørensen, 1968, pp. 753–843.

SLOAN, B., 'The Binding Force of a "Recommendation" of the General Assembly of the United Nations', *British Yearbook of International Law*, 25, 1948, pp. 1–33.

SMALL, D., 'Foreign Boycotts', *Digest of United States Practice in International Law*, Washington, DC: Department of State, 1976, pp. 576–84.

SØRENSEN, M., ed., *Manual of Public International Law*, London: Macmillan, 1968.

STEELE, R., ed., *The Iran Crisis and International Law*, Charlottesville: The John Bassett Moore Society of International Law, University of Virginia Law School, 1981.

STEIN, T., 'Contempt, Crisis, and the Court: The World Court and the Hostages Rescue Attempt', *American Journal of International Law*, 76, 1982, pp. 499–531.

STONE, J., *Legal Controls of International Conflict: A Treatise on the Dynamics of Disputes and War-Law*. London: Stevens & Sons, 1959.

——'Hopes and Loopholes in the 1974 Definition of Aggression', *American Journal of International Law*, 71, 1977, pp. 224–46.

STOWELL, E., *Intervention in International Law*, Washington, DC: John Byrne, 1921.

——*International Law: A Restatement of Principles in Conformity with Actual Practice*, London: Pitman, 1931.

STRUPP, K., *Éléments du droit international public*, i, Paris: Les Éditions internationales, 1930.

TAMMES, A., 'Means of Redress in the General International Law of Peace', *Essay in Memory of H. F. van Panhuys*, Alphen aan den Rijn and Rockville, Md.: Van Panhuys, Sijthoff and Noordhoff, 1980.

THOMAS, A., AND THOMAS, A., *Non-Intervention, the Law and its Import in the Americas*, Dallas: Southern Methodist University Press, 1956.

TRIGGS, G., 'Extraterritorial Reach of United States Legislation: The International Law Implications of the Westinghouse Allegations of a Uranium Producer's Cartel', *Melbourne University Law Review*, 12, 1979, pp. 250–83.

TRINDADE, A., *The Application of the Rule of Exhaustion of Local Remedies in International Law*, Cambridge: Cambridge University Press, 1983.

TUNKIN, G., *Theory of International Law*, London: George Allen and Unwin, 1974.

TWISS, T., *The Law of Nations considered as Independent Political Communities. On the Rights and Duties of Nations in Time of War*, London: Longmans, Green and Roberts, 1863.

UNGER, S., 'Extraterritorial Application of US Export Controls—The Siberian Pipeline', *Proceedings of the American Society of International Law*, 1983, pp. 250–6.

UNITED NATIONS, *Systematic Survey of Treaties for the Pacific Settlement of International Disputes, 1928–1948*, Lake Success, NY: United Nations, 1948.

UNITED NATIONS INFORMATION ORGANIZATIONS, *Documents of the United Nations Conference on International Organization, San Francisco*, London and New York: United Nations Information Organizations, vols. 3 and 6, 1945.

University of Pennsylvania Law Review (Comment), 'The Use of Nonviolent Coercion: A Study in Legality under Article 2(4) of the Charter of the United Nations', *University of Pennsylvania Law Review*, 122, 1974, pp. 983–1011.

VAGTS, D., 'The Pipeline Controversy: An American Viewpoint', *German Yearbook of International Law*, 27, 1984, pp. 38–53.

VALLAT, SIR FRANCIS, 'Declaratory Judgments', *Current Legal Problems*, 17, 1964, pp. 1–6.

VANCE, D., 'Recent Developments: Export Controls', *Texas International Law Journal*, 18, 1983, pp. 203–19.

VATTEL, E., *The Law of Nations: or, Principles of the Law of Nature, Applied to the Conduct of Nations and Sovereigns*, 1797, edn. by J. Chitty, London: Sweet, Stevens & Sons, and Maxwell, 1834.

VERDROSS, A., *Völkerrecht*, ed. S. Verosta and K. Zemanek, Vienna: Springer-Verlag, 1964.

VERZIJL, L., *International Law in an Historical Perspective*, iii, Leiden: A. J. Sijthoff, 1976.

VIERDAG, E., 'The Law Governing Treaty Relations between Parties to the Vienna Convention on the Law of Treaties and States not Party to the Convention', *American Journal of International Law*, 76, 1982, pp. 779–801.

VISSCHER, C. de, 'L'Interprétation du pacte au lendemain du différend italo-grec', *Revue de droit international et de législation comparée*, 5, 1924, pp. 213–30, 377–96.

WALDOCK, SIR HUMPHREY, 'The Regulation of the Use of Force by Individual States in International Law', *Recueil des Cours de l'Académie de Droit International de La Haye*, 81(2), 1952, pp. 455–516.

——'The Plea of Domestic Jurisdiction Before International Legal Tribunals', *British Yearbook of International Law*, 31, 1954, pp. 96–142.

——'General Course on Public International Law', *Recueil des Cours de l'Académie de Droit International de La Haye*, 106(2), 1962, pp. 5–250.

WENGLER, W., 'Public International Law. Paradoxes of a Legal Order', *Recueil des Cours de l'Académie de Droit International de La Haye*, 158(5), 1977, pp. 16–85.

WESTLAKE, J., *International Law*, ii, *War*, 2nd edn., Cambridge: Cambridge University Press, 1913.

WESTRICK, K., 'The Legality of Freeze Orders and the Extra-Territorial Effect of Foreign Freeze Orders in Germany in the Light of the Iranian Events', *International Business Lawyer*, 9(3), 1981, pp. 105–8.

WHARTON, F., *A Digest of the International Law of the United States taken from Documents issued by Presidents and Secretaries of State and from Decisions of Federal Courts and Opinions of Attorneys-General*, iii, Washington, DC: Government Printing Office, 1887.

WHEATON, H., *Elements of International Law*, 8th edn. by R. Dana, London: Sampson Low, 1866.

——*Elements of International Law*, i, 6th edn. by A. Berriedale Keith, London: Stevens & Sons, 1929.

WHITE, G., *Nationalization of Foreign Property*, London: Stevens & Sons, 1961.

——'A New International Economic Order?', *Virginia Journal of International Law*, 16(2), 1976, pp. 323–45.

WHITEMAN, M., *Digest of International Law*, 12, Washington, DC: Department of State, 1971.

—— *Digest of International Law*, 14, Washington, DC: Department of State, 1970.

—— *Some Aspects of the Covenant of the League of Nations*, Oxford and London: Oxford University Press and Humphrey Milford, 1934.

WOOLSEY, T., *Introduction to the Study of International Law*, 5th edn., London: Sampson Low, Marston, Searle & Rivington, 1879.

WRIGHT, Q., 'Opinion of Commission of Jurists on Janina–Corfu Affair', *American Journal of International Law*, 18, 1924, pp. 536–44.

—— 'The Strengthening of International Law', *Recueil des Cours de l'Académie de Droit International de La Haye*, 98(3), 1959, pp. 5–289.

—— 'The Termination and Suspension of Treaties', *American Jounral of International Law*, 61, 1967, pp. 1000–5.

WYATT, D., 'New Legal Order, or Old?', *European Law Review*, 7, 1982, pp. 147–66.

YATES III, G., 'The Rhodesian Chrome Statute: The Congressional Response to United Nations Economic Sanctions Against Southern Rhodesia', *Virginia Law Review*, 58(1), 1972, pp. 511–51.

ZANDER, M., 'Diplomatic Immunity. Libyan Embassy Affair: Should the Vienna Convention be amended?' *The Lawyer*, May/June 1984, pp. 5–6.

ZOLLER, E., *Peacetime Unilateral Remedies: An Analysis of Countermeasures*, Dobbs Ferry, NY: Transnational Publishers, 1984.

Index

Note: *Entries including reprisals should be taken to mean reprisals by and/or against*